Library of
Davidson College

The Song in the Story

THE *Song* IN THE STORY

Lyric Insertions in French

Narrative Fiction, 1200–1400

MAUREEN BARRY McCANN BOULTON

University of Pennsylvania Press
Philadelphia

University of Pennsylvania Press
MIDDLE AGES SERIES
Edward Peters, Series Editor

A complete listing of the books in this series
appears at the back of this volume

Frontispiece: Paris, Bibliothèque Nationale, français 1586, f. 51: Guillaume de Machaut's *Remede de Fortune*; an arrangement of narrative verse, lyric verse, music, and miniature on the page. (Photograph: Bibliothèque Nationale, Paris)

Copyright © 1993 by the University of Pennsylvania Press
All rights reserved
Printed in the United States of America
Library of Congress Cataloging-in-Publication Data
Boulton, Maureen Barry McCann, 1948–
    The song in the story: lyric insertions in French narrative fiction, 1200–1400 / Maureen Barry McCann Boulton.
    p. cm. — (Middle Ages series)
    Includes bibliographical references (p.) and index.
    ISBN 0-8122-3199-6
    1. French literature—To 1500—History and criticism. 2. Songs, French—History and criticism. 3. Lyric poetry—History and criticism. 4. Narration (Rhetoric) 5. Rhetoric, Medieval. 6. Fiction—Technique. 7. Intertextuality. I. Title. II. Series.
PQ151.B65 1993
841'.040901—dc20   93-22097
                                                               CIP

To my Father
Wallace Andrew McCann

Contents

List of Abbreviations	xi
Preface	xiii
1. Introduction	1
Lyrics and Narratives: Genres and Origins	2
Lyric and Narrative: Relationships Possible and Actual	3
Words and Music	5
Lyric Insertions and Medieval Poetic Theory	9
Lyric Insertions and Modern Critics	15
The Song in the Story	18
2. Songs as Monologues: The Hero as Singer	24
Roman de la Rose or *Guillaume de Dole*	26
Roman de la Violette	35
Roman de Tristan en Prose	42
La Chastelaine de Vergi	51
Conte du Cheval de Fust or *Meliacin*	54
Roman du Castelain de Couci et de la Dame de Fayel	61
Meliador	66
Ysaÿe le Triste	72
3. Songs as Description	80
The Music of the Court	83
The Music of the Anti-Court	103

The Song of the Shepherdess	111
Songs as Characterization; The Allegorical Singers	114

4. Songs as Plot — 120

Song as Action	120
Song as Narration	132

5. The Song as Message — 143

Song as Declaration	144
Song as Letter	152
Song as Amorous Dialogue	170

6. The Song and the *Dit*: The Poet as Hero — 181

Nicole de Margival	183
Guillaume de Machaut	188
Jean Froissart	202
Oton de Grandson	223
Christine de Pizan	228

7. The Song as Refrain: Lyrics as Elements of Form — 243

Stanzaic Works	245
Non-Stanzaic Works	254

8. Conclusion — 272

Lyric and Narrative	273
Formal Experimentation	281
Coherence from Disruption: The Poetics of Contrast	287
The Poetics of Allusion	289

Appendices	295
1. List of Narrative Works Containing Lyric Insertions	295
2. Music in the Manuscripts	298
Bibliography	301
Index	323

Abbreviations

CFMA	Classiques français du moyen âge
GRLMA	*Grundriss der romanischen Literaturen des Mittelalters*. I, *Généralités*. Ed. Maurice Delbouille. Heidelberg: Winter, 1972. IV, *Le Roman à la fin du XIIIe siècle*. Ed. Jean Frappier. Heidelberg: Winter, 1978–84. VI, *La littérature didactique, allégorique, et satirique*. 2 parts. Ed. Jürgen Beyer. Heidelberg: Winter, 1968.
HLF	*Histoire littéraire de la France, ouvrage commencé par les religieux bénédictins de la congrégation de Saint-Maur, continué par les membres de l'Institut*. 40 vols. Paris: Imprimerie Nationale, 1733–1974.
SATF	Société des anciens textes français
TLF	Textes littéraires français
TLL	*Travaux de linguistique et de littérature*
ZRP	*Zeitschrift für romanische Philologie*

Preface

> Are quotations anything more than simply raisins in the cake, and can their aesthetic effect go beyond the momentary delight that raisins offer the palate?
>
> H. Meyer, *The Poetics of Quotation in the European Novel*

As the intertextual character of medieval literature is increasingly recognized by modern critics, the incorporation of songs into other works emerges as a central problem of medieval poetics. Many types of songs, with or without musical accompaniment, became "lyric insertions" in lyric, dramatic, and narrative works, and inevitably altered the containing text. Understanding the nature of the relationship between the text and its insertions is essential to a grasp of medieval intertextuality.

The term "lyric insertion" identifies a technique present in a substantial corpus of medieval French texts produced between the early thirteenth century and the beginning of the fifteenth. Aside from the inclusion of lyric poems or songs, the nearly one hundred texts produced containing inserted lyrics have little in common: they include both poetic and prose works, romances, *fabliaux*, narrative *lais, dits,* chronicles, and didactic works, as well as lyric poetry (motets and *chansons avec des refrains*) and drama (both *jeux* and *moralités*). Of the songs interpolated in them, some were borrowed from the contemporary repertoire, while others were composed for a specific narrative or dramatic setting, and given the incomplete state of the evidence it is not always possible to distinguish the borrowed songs from the others. Some inserted songs were quoted in their entirety, while others were inserted as fragments, and they also represent the principal lyric genres: *rondeau, chanson d'amour, ballade, complainte, lai,* motet.

This variety indicates quite clearly that the phenomenon of the lyric insertion is a general literary technique rather than a characteristic of a specific genre or subgenre. Nevertheless, some patterns do emerge from the diversity. First of all, the vast majority of incorporating texts are narrative in nature, although they vary greatly in genre as well as in length. Secondly, the lyric character of the insertions is acknowledged almost without exception in the incorporating narrative. Thirdly, there is no significant difference in the treatment of songs that are composed for a specific context and those that are borrowed from another source. Indeed, some authors, such as Machaut, borrow their own compositions.

These facts have determined the scope of my study. I have concentrated on narrative forms because these preponderate, and I have excluded the lyric and dramatic appearances of insertions as extraneous to the main development of the technique. The fact that borrowing songs does not seem to change the technique suggests strongly that the device is essentially inter-generic. Even when lyric fragments are interpolated into new songs generic boundaries are crossed—*chansons* and motets incorporate refrains from *rondeaux*. Accordingly, I have concentrated on the relationship between two disparate elements in a single work, on the interruption of the narrative movement by a lyric "pause." This study is thus an attempt to answer the general question "Why were *songs* inserted into *stories* in the thirteenth and fourteenth centuries?" and its more specific corollary "Why were *these* songs inserted into *this* story?"

Given the scope of the book—the number of narratives under discussion and the even greater number of lyrics they contain—it was not possible to treat every work with absolute thoroughness. I have not, for example, examined all the manuscripts of these works, but have usually relied on modern editions. Nor have I examined all variant readings. I have, however, tried to take account of them when it seemed appropriate. The translations of the numerous quotations from Old and Middle French are my own: their aim is rather to convey accurately the sense of the original than to give an impression of its style.

I would like to express my thanks to Dr. Elspeth M. Kennedy, who supervised an earlier form of this book as an M.Litt. thesis at Oxford, for her invaluable advice and continuing encouragement over the years. The severe criticisms of Nicholas Mann and A. H. Diverres, the examiners of my thesis, are responsible for many improvements in this study. The anonymous readers of the University of Pennsylvania Press have greatly improved this book through their careful reading and generous criticism, and I am enormously grateful for their help, although they bear no responsibility for such errors as remain. I am also indebted to the Institute for Scholarship in the Liberal Arts of the University of Notre Dame for its generous support of research publication.

My debt to my husband, without whose support and criticism this book would never have seen the light of day, cannot be expressed, and this acknowledgment must suffice.

M.B.M.B.
South Bend, Indiana
St. George's Day 1992

1. Introduction

The practice of quoting songs or song fragments in narrative texts arose first in northern France in the early thirteenth century and remained popular there for another two hundred years. For reasons that are yet obscure the device in question—which eventually came to involve lyrics that were not meant to be sung at all—remained primarily a French phenomenon. While it occurs in more than seventy works in French, examples from other literatures of the period are rare.[1]

What I shall call "lyric insertions" are found in works of a variety of different genres: dramatic and lyric, as well as narrative, but the last are by far the most numerous. A narrative in which lyric poems or songs are inserted is essentially a hybrid creation, combining two disparate forms. Such mixed compositions raise a whole series of literary questions about poetic form, and about the relationships between song and speech and between lyric and narrative genres. They thus illustrate most vividly the intertextual character of medieval literature. An examination of the whole corpus of such narratives ought to illustrate how medieval poets working within a tradition responded to and modified the conventions of that tradition. That has been my goal in the present study of a subject neglected by scholarship until recently, and still inadequately addressed.[2] The terms

---

1. In both Italian and German literature, the phenomenon is represented by a single narrative text: Dante's *Vita Nuova* and Ulrich von Lichtenstein's *Frauendienst*. It is more common in Spanish; lyrics occur in San Pedro's *Arnalte et Lucenda*, Flores's *Grimalte y Gradissa*, the *Libro de Alexandre*, the *Libro del cavallero Zifar*, *Amadis de Gaula*, the *Historia troyana polimétrica*, Hita's *Libro del Buen Amor*, and the *Celestina*. See Alan Deyermond, "Lyric Traditions in Non-Lyrical Genres," in *Studies in Honor of Lloyd A. Kasten*, ed. Theodore S. Beardsley et al., Hispanic Seminary of Medieval Studies (Madison: University of Wisconsin Press, 1975) pp. 39–52.

2. The topic of "lyric insertions in medieval French narratives" has received increasing attention since I first embarked on it more than fifteen years ago: many of the works exhibiting the device have recently been studied for the first time in a century, and others have just appeared in critical editions. Nevertheless, despite three dissertations on the subject besides my own, no systematic study has yet appeared in print: Anne Preston Ladd, "Lyric Insertions in Thirteenth Century French Narrative" (Ph.D. Diss., Yale University, 1977); Maria Veder Fowler, "Musical Interpolations in 13th- and 14th-Century French Narratives" (Ph.D. Diss., Yale University, 1979); M. B. M. Boulton, "Lyric Insertions in French Narrative Fiction in the

in which I plan to discuss this question are set forth in the remainder of this introductory chapter.

Lyrics and Narratives: Genres and Origins

What, exactly, is a "lyric insertion"? I have used the term to refer to songs or lyric poems of any origin that were quoted either fully or in part in a larger literary (usually narrative) context. The insertions themselves are exceedingly diverse in form and origin and represent virtually all the principal lyric genres of the period—*rondeau, chanson courtoise, ballade, virelai, complainte, lai,* motet. While many complete songs were quoted, a similar number of quotations were partial, consisting of a single stanza of a *chanson courtoise,* for instance, or only the refrain of a *rondeau.* Likewise, some songs were certainly borrowed from the contemporary repertoire, just as many were apparently composed by the authors of the incorporating narrative texts. Indeed, in the absence of other attestations, it is often impossible to know whether a song was borrowed. It was once assumed that if most of the songs in a romance were borrowed from the repertoire, then all of the fragments must represent complete songs now lost to us. In two romances, however—*Meliacin* and the *Roman du Castelain de Couci*—we find both insertions borrowed from other authors and songs attributable to the author of the romance. The authorship of many of the *refrains*[3] which suit their narrative context so aptly is much harder to prove, but when they are attested nowhere else, it seems likely that they may have been created by the narrative authors. Borrowed songs do not seem to have functioned differently from those deliberately composed for insertion. Authors such as Guillaume de Machaut, who are known to have written both parts of interpolated texts, sometimes pillaged their own repertoire rather than writing new songs for a specific setting. The heart of the device thus seems to lie less in quotation or in borrowing than in combining genres.

If the insertions are diverse in nature, so too are the narratives that contain them. One finds lyric insertions in romances, both prose and verse,

---

Thirteenth and Fourteenth Centuries" (M.Litt. Thesis, University of Oxford, 1980); and Helen Solterer, "'Acorder li chans au dit': The Lyric Voice in French Medieval Narrative, 1220–1320" (Ph.D. Diss., University of Toronto, 1986).

3. I use the italicized form to represent the French word, which denotes short refrain-like fragments which may or may not have been repeated at the end of stanzas in an original context.

in *fabliaux*, in narrative *lais*, in *dits*, in didactic works, and in memoires. Strangely, the work that comes most readily to mind when one first thinks of lyric insertions—*Aucassin et Nicolette*—does not in fact fit our definition. Its sung portions are not independent songs, but *laisses*. The prose and verse passages occur in regular alternation, but neither could stand alone.[4]

Lyric and Narrative: Relationships Possible and Actual

As an element of narrative technique, the lyric insertion device introduces an element of disruption into the narrative work. Whereas a narrative is an account of a series of past events usually, but not always, told in the third person, the lyric poet speaks directly and in the present tense. The author of a narrative may arrange the events artistically rather than chronologically, but there is always movement toward a conclusion. A lyric like a *chanson courtoise*, in contrast, concentrates on a single moment; it is atemporal and static. Its individual stanzas are juxtaposed, and their order may even vary in different manuscript copies.

The combination of these two distinct and often opposed literary types into a single work was a challenge that received many different solutions from French writers of the thirteenth and fourteenth centuries—solutions that reflect changing attitudes toward literature and the relationship among genres. Consequently the shifting configurations of lyric and narrative elements will be one of the major themes of this study. The two most straightforward methods of combining lyric and narrative—singing a narrative (e.g., the *chanson de geste*) or recounting in song (e.g., the *pastourelle* or *chanson d'histoire*)—involve no combination of genres or insertions, and so are not directly relevant here, but they represent ends of the spectrum of possibilities open to the authors of our period.[5]

Perhaps the most acute problem confronting an author who used lyric insertions was the need to account for the song, since it was an extraneous element that would inevitably interrupt, if not break, the narrative line of the plot. The task of making a quotation plausible in its context was often accomplished by creating a setting in which singing was appropriate. Social occasions that normally included musical entertainment were an obvious choice. More interesting was the attribution of love songs to a single

---

4. See below Chapter 8, under "Formal Experimentation."
5. See John Stevens, *Words and Music in the Middle Ages: Song, Narrative, Dance and Drama, 1050–1350* (Cambridge: Cambridge University Press, 1986), pp. 199–267, 471–76.

character as expressions of emotions, usually his own. In a set of such works it is possible to trace the evolution of the hero from a mere singer of borrowed songs to the poet-lover-narrator of the fourteenth century. As we shall see below, these songs not only interrupted the sequence of events, but actually determined the narrative content of the containing work.

Despite the apparent necessity for a logical context in which songs might be introduced, several authors of the fourteenth century renounced any attempt to blend the disparate elements of their works. In Jean Acart's *Amoureuse Prise*, for example, the lack of narrative setting for the lyrics emphasizes the rupture of the narrative and creates a tension between the continuity of the plot and the discrete completeness of the songs. The songs punctuate the narrative, dividing it into sections in a manner reminiscent of the *chanson avec des refrains*.[6]

Fitting the quotation into its new setting was particularly difficult when the insertions were borrowed, because the author had to reconcile contradictions between two independent texts. He might iron out inconsistencies by altering the song, or by quoting only a portion of it, but there often remained some uneasiness in the juxtaposition. In the most successful works, such as *Guillaume de Dole*, this tension was exploited deliberately. One might not expect any discord at all between parts of a work composed by a single author, but even here lyric insertions introduce temporal disparities. The *Amoureuse Prise*, where the *rondeaux* and *ballades* anticipate later developments in the story, comes again to mind as an example of a work in which the contrast between the combined forms remained sharp.

Whatever measures were taken to reconcile the songs to a narrative setting, however, they always remained essentially extraneous and intrusive. Because they could circulate independently, they raised the possibility of other performances, other audiences, other contexts. They continued to direct the reader/listener's attention beyond the narrative itself, forcing an intertexual interpretation of the work.

This dual character of lyric insertions—independent compositions, though part of a larger whole—is inherent in the device, and it will be useful to consider how their separateness was maintained. Through meter, rhyme, register, and music, inserted songs always stand apart from their contexts. Were they not so distinguished, they would disappear into the narrative and cease to exist.

The most obvious metrical contrasts between song and story occur in the prose romances, where the flow of long and complex sentences is

---

6. This is a *chanson* with a different *refrain* at the end of each stanza; for example, Thibaut de Champagne's "Chançon ferai, que talenz m'en est pris."

emphatically interrupted by stanzas of octosyllabic or alexandrine verse. The inserted *lais* could, even if they did not in fact, circulate independently, and some of the narratives (*Perceforest*, for example) were recopied without their lyric passages. More subtle, but nonetheless perceptible, are the contrasts between lyric and narrative meter in the verse romances, where the insertions frequently cut the succession of octosyllabic lines with verses of five, six, seven, nine, or ten syllables. In a similar fashion, the rhyme scheme of an insertion normally disrupts the sequence of rhyming couplets of the narrative. Occasionally, however—as in *Guillaume de Dole* and the *Roman de la Violette*—insertions may be preceded by an unpaired line, whose rhyme is completed by the first line of the following song. This technique has the effect of binding text and insertion through the identity of sound, while at the same time heightening the metrical contrast of the paired lines.

Lyric and narrative might also differ significantly on the basis of what Paul Zumthor has called "register." Zumthor developed the idea of register while studying the *chanson courtoise*, and defined it as an ensemble of communicative conventions, a complex of motivations, of lexical, rhetorical, and syntactic probabilities, which constitute a distinctive poetic language.[7] Alongside what he called the "requête amoureuse," the register of the courtly *chanson*, he identified a second register of "la bonne vie," distinguished by phonetic, syntactic, semantic, and figurative features.[8] Both lyrics and narratives may belong to either register. Although a lyric insertion may function simply as an extension of the register of the narrative text, examples of registral contrast abound. As these contrasts were both deliberate and significant, the evolution of a poetics of contrast will be one of the preoccupations of this study.

Words and Music

Lyric insertions are set off from their narrative settings by meter, rhyme, and register, but most dramatically by their musical quality. Medieval lyric

---

7. Paul Zumthor, *Langue et techniques poétiques à l'époque romane (XIe–XIIIe siècles)*, Bibliothèque française et romane, C, Etudes littéraires, 4 (Paris: Klincksieck, 1963), pp. 141–52; *Essai de poétique médiévale* (Paris: Seuil, 1972), pp. 231–32, 239–40.

8. Pierre Bec, *La lyrique française au moyen âge (XIIe–XIIIe siècles)*, 2 vols. (Paris: Picard, 1977–78), I, pp. 28, 30, 33, has proposed the terms "registres aristocratisant" and "popularisant" to express this distinction. Christopher Page (*Voices and Instruments of the Middle Ages: Instrumental Practice and Songs in France, 1100–1300* [Berkeley: University of California Press, 1986], p. 38) proposed the terms "High Style" and "Lower Style," both of which may be courtly.

poetry, at least until the second half of the fourteenth century, was sung poetry. But were the songs actually meant to be sung in these new contexts? An affirmative answer is indicated by much of the textual and manuscript evidence. Characters are described as singing quoted songs in a variety of narrative settings: in groups as accompaniment for their dances; in solitude as expressions of amorous meditation; in a lady's presence as a plea for her favor.[9] Furthermore, several manuscripts contain musical notation set on staves below the lyric text. On the other hand, there are cases where lyric insertions were apparently *not* sung: the stanza by the Châtelain de Couci quoted in the *Chastelaine de Vergi*, for example, serves to explain the hero's emotions but is not sung, or even spoken, in the narrative. The author cited the stanza as a point of comparison, and its significance for the text is verbal and semiotic, rather than musical. Reading the printed edition of Baudoin de Condé's *Prison d'Amours* creates a similar impression. Its *refrains* seem to be invoked as if they were proverbs: the fact that they *are* songs appears more significant than any actual music, for it is their content that matters. Nevertheless, in one manuscript of the text (Vienna, Ö.N.B., Ms. 2621) staves appear under all of the *refrains*, and three of them have musical notation. Clearly, the manuscript evidence on this point is by no means unambiguous.[10] Although most lyric insertions were transcribed without musical notation, a significant number of them were provided with it, and still more were meant to be since staves were drawn or spaces were left for them in the manuscript. If the absence of notation can be used to argue a lack of interest in music,[11] the presence of blank staves might just as easily indicate nothing more than a shortage of music-scribes.[12] The manuscripts of the *Panthere d'Amors* and the Oxford manuscript (Bodleian Library, Douce 308) of the *Tournoi de Chauvenci* are more difficult to explain. Despite the fact that there is music in other manuscripts for the songs of Adam de la Halle quoted by Nicole de Margival, none was included in any of the manuscripts of his *Panthere*. Nor is there any music in the Douce

---

9. For a discussion of the performance of medieval French songs, see Nigel Wilkins, *The Lyric Art of Medieval France*, 2nd revised edition. (Fulbourn, Cambs.: New Press, 1989), pp. 24–57.

10. See Appendix 2 for a summary of the musical evidence. See also Isidore Silver, "The Marriage of Poetry and Music in France: Ronsard's Predecessors and Contemporaries," in *Poetry and Poetics from Ancient Greece to the Renaissance: Studies in Honor of James Hutton*, ed. G. M. Kirkwood, Cornell Studies in Classical Philology, 38 (Ithaca, N.Y.: Cornell University Press, 1975), pp. 152–84.

11. As for instance, Michel Zink, *Roman rose et rose rouge: Le roman de la rose ou de Guillaume de Dole de Jean Renart* (Paris: Nizet, 1979), p. 27.

12. Stevens, *Words and Music*, p. 41.

manuscript of the *Tournoi*, even though another section of the book contains a *chansonnier* with notation.[13]

How are we to interpret the musical evidence of the manuscripts? To what extent should it inform our analysis of lyric insertions? On the one hand, the musical quality of the insertions is of prime importance: since medieval lyric poetry was sung, its music had a great role in its affective impact. This impact, and the relationship between the words and the melody of medieval songs, are subjects of considerable controversy.[14] In a stimulating study, John Stevens argues that the relationship between words and music varied with the type of song.[15] In the *chanson courtoise*, for example, the two parts were parallel in form, but each was a self-sufficient, beautiful object in its own right.[16] For dance-songs, by contrast, the relationship was much simpler, with a virtual note-to-syllable correspondence and a clear underlying rhythm.

Stevens has also shown that, while the music plays an important role in establishing the rhyme of a song, there is no inherent bond between the melody and particular words, for the same music accompanies different words in successive stanzas.[17] Nevertheless, the relationship between verbal accent and melody remains an important factor in a song's impact, as J. A. van Os has argued.[18] The fact that the words and music can be

---

13. Douglas Kelly, noting the separability of the words and the music, gave primacy to the text: *Medieval Imagination: Rhetoric and the Poetry of Courtly Love* (Madison, Wis.: University of Wisconsin Press, 1978), "Appendix: Music and Poetry," pp. 239–56, especially. p. 256. In contrast, Paul Zumthor, *Essai de poétique médiévale*, (p. 369), assumed that the inserted songs were indeed sung by the reader.

14. Hendrik van der Werf, *The Chansons of the Troubadours and Trouvères: A Study of the Melodies and Their Relation to the Poems* (Utrecht: A. Oosthoek's Uitgeversmaatschappij, 1972), pp. 35–45, has surveyed the main points of the dispute.

15. See also the essay by Ewald Jammers, "Die Rolle der Musik im Rahmen der romanischen Dichtung des XII. und XIII. Jahrhunderts," in *GRLMA*, I *Généralités*, ed. Maurice Delbouille (Heidelberg: Winter, 1972), pp. 483–537. Useful analyses of specific examples may be found in *The Medieval Lyric: A Project Supported by the National Endowment for the Humanities and Mount Holyoke College*, ed. Howell Chickering and Margaret Switten, 3 vols. (South Hadley, Mass.: Mount Holyoke College, 1987–88).

16. Stevens, *Words and Music*, p. 38. Van der Werf observes that in some *chansons* word accents coincide with prominent places in the melody, but that such accord is not the rule.

17. Cf. Stevens, *Words and Music*, especially "Music and Meaning: The Problem of Expressiveness," pp. 372–409. See also Théodore Gerold, *La Musique au moyen âge*, CFMA 73 (Paris: Champion, 1932), pp. 161–215.

18. J. A. van Os, "Structures mélodiques et rythme déclamatoire dans la chanson de trouvère," in *Langue et littérature françaises du moyen âge*, ed. R. E. V. Stuip (Amsterdam: Van Gorcum, 1978), pp. 51–62. See also the articles in *The Medieval Lyric: Commentary Volume*, ed. Chickering and Switten: Leo Treitler, "Music and Language in Medieval Songs," pp. 12–17; and Margaret Switten, "Remarks on Versification with Some Definitions of Poetic Styles and Forms," pp. 59–75.

considered separately does not mean that either is dispensable. Nicolas Ruwet, reflecting on the nature of song, proposed (in another context) a dialectical relationship between music and words, with possible variants ranging from contradiction to agreement.[19]

The importance of music for inserted lyrics varies considerably with the type of song, the type of narrative, the function of the lyric within the narrative, and the manuscript evidence. Possibilities range from songs with notation in the manuscript attributed to a singer, through lyrics which might or might not have been sung, to *refrains* used out of context as proverbs, which were almost certainly not sung. During the course of the fourteenth century, music and poetry became increasingly separate. Guillaume de Machaut, for example, wrote many poems for which he composed no music, and Froissart, Oton de Grandson, and Christine de Pizan clearly intended their poetry to be read, although they knew that some of it might well be set to music.[20] When singing was intended, however, the affective importance of the music was undoubtedly great. Unfortunately, for medieval songs of any type this is extremely difficult to analyze without examining actual performance and audience perception.[21] In any case, the music used with inserted songs is susceptible to analysis only intermittently, for the melodies of most insertions have not been transmitted.

Even without notation (which would in fact be meaningful to few modern readers), lyric insertions differ from the surrounding narrative in that they imply performance, even in the absence of performers. In examining the performative aspect of poetry, James A. Winn referred to Dante's observation that we recognize a "song" even when we see only the written, unrecited script. In such circumstances, we either "read it aloud or hear its sounds in our minds."[22] However, since most medieval narrative in our

---

19. Nicolas Ruwet, "Fonction de la parole de la musique vocale," *Revue belge de musicologie*, 15 (1961): 8–28; reprinted in *Langage, musique, poésie* (Paris: Seuil, 1972), pp. 41–67.

20. See Daniel Poirion, *Le poète et le prince: L'évolution du lyrisme courtois de Guillaume de Machaut à Charles d'Orléans*, Université de Grenoble Publications de la Faculté des Lettres et Sciences Humaines, 35 (Paris: Presses Universitaires de France, 1965; repr. Geneva: Slatkine, 1978), pp. 146–67, 202, 216, 313–14; and Nigel Wilkins, "The Post-Machaut Generation of Poet-Musicians," *Nottingham Medieval Studies*, 12 (1968): 40–84.

21. Some work has been done on the music of inserted lyrics. In addition to the dissertation by Fowler cited in note 2, see Maria Veder Coldwell, "*Guillaume de Dole* and Medieval Romances with Musical Interpolations," *Musica Disciplina*, 35 (1981): 55–86; there is also a thesis in progress on *Le rondeau* by Marie-Henriette Fernandez at the Université de Toulouse/Le Mirail.

22. James A. Winn, *Unsuspected Eloquence: A History of the Relations between Poetry and Music* (New Haven: Yale University Press, 1981), p. 86.

period was read aloud,[23] the social circumstances of its presentation added an element of performance even to the narrative, and moved it closer to drama than contemporary reading habits allow. It is useful in this context to recall Edmond Faral's observation: "Même les oeuvres destinées à être lues sont écrites en fonction d'une mise en scène rudimentaire."[24] It would be interesting to know to what extent those who read aloud narratives with lyric insertions differentiated their rendering of narrative and lyric elements, but I have found no evidence to answer this question.

Lyric Insertions and Medieval Poetic Theory

The essence of the lyric insertion device is the mixture of separate literary elements. Such hybridization was already well established in Latin literature, and the *prosi-metrum* of late-classical origin is usually mentioned as a possible ancestor of the insertion device. E. R. Curtius surveyed the various combined forms in medieval Latin literature, but judged their effectiveness harshly: "All these minglings and transitional forms testify to the same taste. They betray a childish delight in play and variegated color."[25] Despite the severity of this judgment, I hope to demonstrate that Jean Renart and his successors were guided less by "childish delight" than by principles fundamental to the rhetorical tradition of the *artes poeticae*.

In the prologue to his *Roman de la Rose*, now commonly called *Guillaume de Dole* to distinguish it from its more celebrated namesake, Jean Renart gave clear indications of his poetic practice.[26] Although it has been

---

23. Erich Auerbach, *Literary Language and Its Public*, trans. Ralph Manheim (New York: Pantheon Books, 1965), p. 204; H. J. Chaytor, *From Script to Print: An Introduction to Medieval Vernacular Literature* (Cambridge, Mass.: Harvard University Press, 1945; repr. Cambridge: W. Heffer, 1950), p. 10; Ruth Crosby, "Oral Delivery in the Middle Ages," *Speculum*, 11 (1936): 88–110; Pierre Gallais, "Recherches sur la mentalité des romanciers français du moyen âge," *Cahiers de Civilisation Médiévale*, 7 (1964): 479–93, esp. pp. 483 ff.; and Paul Zumthor, *La poésie et la voix dans la civilisation médiévale* (Paris: Presses Universitaires de France, 1984), esp. pp. 37–66.
24. Edmond Faral, *Les Jongleurs en France au moyen âge* (Paris: Champion, 1910), p. 234.
25. Ernst Robert Curtius, *European Literature and the Latin Middle Ages* (Bern, 1948; English trans. Willard R. Trask [New York: Bollingen Foundation, 1953]; repr. Harper and Row, 1963), p. 152.
26. The romance has been variously dated between ca. 1200 and 1228. According to G. Servois in his edition *Le roman de la rose ou de Guillaume de Dole*, SATF (Paris: Firmin Didot, 1893), p. lxxxvi, it was written between October 1199 and May 1202; Rita Lejeune-Dehousse in *L'oeuvre de Jean Renart* (Paris: Droz & Liège: Faculté de Philosophie et Lettres, 1935), pp. 73–130, gave the dates 1212–13; Félix Lecoy in his edition *Jean Renart: Le roman de la rose ou de*

studied more than once,[27] the passage is important enough to be examined again:

> Cil qui mist cest conte en romans,
> ou il a fet noter biaus chans
> por ramenbrance des chançons,
> veut que ses pris et ses renons
> voist en Raincïen en Champaigne
> et que li biaus Miles l'apregne
> de Nantuel, uns des preus del regne;
> car aussi com l'en met la graine
> es dras por avoir los et pris,
> einsi a il chans et sons mis
> en cestui *Romans de la Rose*,
> qui est une novele chose
> et s'est des autres si divers
> et brodez, par lieus, de biaus vers
> que vilains nel porroit savoir.
> Ce sachiez de fi et de voir,
> bien a cist les autres passez.
> Ja nuls n'iert de l'oïr lassez,
> car, s'en vieult, l'en i chante et lit,
> et s'est fez par si grant delit
> que tuit cil s'en esjoïront
> qui chanter et lire l'orront,
> qu'il lor sera nouviaus toz jors.
> Il conte d'armes et d'amors
> et chante d'ambedeus ensamble,

Guillaume de Dole, CFMA, 91 (Paris: Champion, 1970), pp. vi–viii, and "Sur la date du *Guillaume de Dole*," *Romania*, 82 (1961): 370–402, esp. p. 395, n.1, placed it later, ca. 1228. Since Lecoy, the question has been reopened by Carmela Mattioli, in "Sulla datazione del *Guillaume de Dole*," *Cultura Neolatina*, 25 (1965): 91–112, who has returned to an earlier date, 1200–1211, while Rita Lejeune, in "Le roman de *Guillaume de Dole* et la principauté de Liège," *Cahiers de Civilisation Médiévale*, 17 (1974): 1–24, modified her original estimate and proposed 1208–10. The precise date is not material to my discussion; there seems to be general agreement that it was written after *Galeran de Bretagne* and before the *Roman de la Violette*.

27. E.g., Stevens, *Words and Music*, pp. 168–69; David Hult, *Self-Fulfilling Prophecies: Readership and Authority in the First* Roman de la Rose (Cambridge: Cambridge University Press, 1986), pp. 202–3. Pierre-Yves Badel in "Rhétorique et polémique dans les prologues de romans au moyen âge," *Littérature*, 20 (1975): 81–94, esp. pp. 88–89, highlighted the atypical character of this prologue. The passage is quoted from Lecoy's edition.

s'est avis a chascun et samble
que cil qui a fet le romans
qu'il trovast toz les moz des chans,
si afierent a ceus del conte.
(vv. 1–29)

[He who cast this story as a romance, in which he has transcribed the music of beautiful songs in order to remember them, wishes that his reputation and renown may reach the district of Reims in Champagne, and that the fair Miles of Nanteuil, one of the noblemen of the kingdom, may learn of it; for just as one puts red dye into cloth to give it honor and worth, so has he put songs and music in this *Romance of the Rose*, which is a new thing; and it is different from others, and is decorated here and there with fine verses, so that a villein (or peasant) could not understand it. Know this truly, he has surpassed the others. Never will anyone tire of hearing it, for, if you wish, you sing and read in it, and it is made with such great delight that all who shall hear it sung and read will enjoy it, and it will always be new. It tells of arms and of love and sings of both together, so that everyone will think, and it will seem, that he who wrote the romance composed all the words of the songs, so well do they suit those of the story.]

"Ramenbrance" is the first justification adduced here for the quotation of songs, and indeed Jean Renart's *Rose* is the earliest "anthology" of old lyrics, a sort of *recueil commenté*.[28] But the desire to remember them suggests that the songs were in danger of being forgotten, and their inclusion bathes the romance in a nostalgic twilight. At the same time, the evocation of past literary pleasures sets the new work in a problematic relationship with the quoted songs, raising the question of their appeal for the audience of Jean Renart's contemporaries. One is obliged to ask if the values implied in the songs are still viable in their new setting.

In the next section of the prologue, these questions seem to receive affirmative answers: the insertion of the songs will delight the courtly audience (vv. 19–20), but will exclude the "vilains" who cannot appreciate such refinement. As *vilenie* is excluded, "traditional" *courtoisie* must by implication be affirmed, but as outlined below in my analysis of the ro-

---

28. On memory and remembrance, see Harry Caplan, "Memoria: Treasure-House of Eloquence," in *Of Eloquence: Studies in Ancient and Medieval Rhetoric*, ed. with an introduction by Anne King and Helen North (Ithaca, N.Y.: Cornell University Press, 1970), pp. 196–246.

mance, the old values and the old genres are in fact systematically modified in their new context.[29]

At three different points in the prologue (vv. 19, 22, 24–25), the author points out that this new technique combined not just lyric and narrative modes, but strongly contrasting forms of expression—song and speech.[30] In two other places he insists on the musical character of the songs: he has "fet noter biaus chans" (2), and he refers also to the "son" (10) of the songs—the melody, that is, as opposed to the words. In presenting this new mixture of forms, the author appeals to well-known principles of rhetoric: while his quotations are the ornaments of his narrative, standing out like embroidery on cloth, they also suit their environments so well that the whole is a seamless web. The passage (vv. 14, 27–29) alludes to the rhetorical principles of *ornatus* and *decorum*. The analogy between the inserted songs and the dye (vv. 8–9) used to color cloth is a clear reference to the principle of stylistic ornament or *ornatus*. The ideal of ornament, although alien to the modernist aesthetic that has prevailed for the last half-century, was widely appreciated in the Middle Ages.[31] Geoffroi de Vinsauf, for instance, devoted nearly two-thirds of his *Poetria Nova* (composed 1200–1212) to a discussion of rhetorical figures, which he referred to as "colors," and "garments."[32] In a similar fashion, Mathieu de Vendôme used the image of polychromed sculpture to describe the role of ornament in a text.[33] At the same time that Geoffroi expounded the devices of ornament,

---

29. See below Chapter 2, under "Guillaume de Dole."
30. On the two actions, see Gustav Thurau, *Singen und Sagen: Ein Beitrag zur Geschichte des dichterischen Ausdrucks* (Berlin: Weidmannische Buchhandlung, 1912) and Manfred Günter Scholz, *Hören und Lesen: Studien zur primären Rezeption der Literatur im 12. und 13. Jahrhundert* (Wiesbaden: R. Steiner, 1980). See also the review of Scholz's book by Franz Lebsanft, "Horen und Lesen im Mittelalter," *Zeitschrift für französische Sprache und Literatur*, 92 (1982): 52–64.
31. Curtius, *European Literature*, p. 71. Cf. Edgar de Bruyne, *Etudes d'esthétique médiévale*, 3 vols. (Bruges: De Tempel, 1946), II, p. 28; and Paul Zumthor, "Rhétorique et poétique latines et romanes," in *GRLMA*, I (1972): 57–91, especially p. 69.
32. Edmond Faral, ed., *Les arts poétiques du XIIe et du XIIIe siècle: Recherches et documents sur la technique littéraire du moyen âge* (Paris: Champion, 1924), pp. 194–262, vv. 737–39, 740–41, and 767, 769; but see Alice M. Colby, *The Portrait in Twelfth Century French Literature: An Example of the Stylistic Originality of Chrétien de Troyes* (Geneva: Droz, 1965), pp. 5–8 on the limitations of Faral's work, and pp. 91–103 on Geoffroi and Mathieu. The treatise has been translated by Margaret F. Nims, *The Poetria Nova of Geoffrey of Vinsauf* (Toronto: Pontifical Institute of Mediaeval Studies, 1967); and by Jane Baltzell Kapp in *Three Medieval Rhetorical Arts*, ed. James J. Murphy (Berkeley: University of California Press, 1971), pp. 27–108. See also the useful comments in *Medieval Literary Criticism: Translations and Interpretations*, ed. O. B. Hardison, Jr. et al. (New York: Frederick Ungar, 1974), pp. 29–36, 123–44; and James J. Murphy, *Rhetoric in the Middle Ages: A History of Rhetorical Theory from St. Augustine to the Renaissance* (Berkeley: University of California Press, 1974, pp. 168–73.
33. Faral, ed., *Les arts poétiques*, pp. 109–93; esp. Book III, 2, pp. 167–68; *Matthew of Vendôme, the Art of Versification*, translated with introduction by Aubrey E. Galyon (Ames: Iowa State University Press, 1980), p. 87.

however, he recommended discretion in their use (vv. 765, 780, 1850). This discretion is the principle of *decorum* (also called *congruentia*), which required appropriateness in the choice of style and the use of ornaments: the expression must be suited to the thought.[34]

When Jean Renart described his inserted songs as the "dye" in the fabric of his text, he put them in the same category as the figures of speech or colors of rhetoric listed by Geoffroi de Vinsauf and Mathieu de Vendôme, among others. His originality lay in the substitution of borrowed "colors" for the more usual forms of ornament. Placed in their new context, the borrowed songs became a new category of rhetorical figure. In terms of medieval literary theory, Jean Renart, by inventing the lyric insertion device, extended the contemporary rhetorical repertoire in a manner wholly compatible with the principles of traditional rhetoric.

Jean Renart himself claimed (vv. 24–29) that his innovation constituted a fitting ornament because the songs shared the subject of the narrative (*armes et amors*), and were so cleverly inserted that they suited their context perfectly—so perfectly, indeed, that they might have been composed by the author. No one has contested the first part of this claim, but the second part has attracted the scorn of critics: Félix Lecoy, for example, referred to Jean's "excès de complaisance, une satisfaction quelque peu outrecuidante."[35] Did Jean really hope to fool his audience? Hardly, it would seem, as he actually identified some of the real authors in the text. On the other hand, he made a strong claim to *decorum* or appropriateness. Jean stressed the suitability of the subject of the songs in the prologue, and an examination of the text itself reveals other areas of congruity. The songs suit the characters who sing them and the context of the performance: the nobles of the imperial court sing *rondeaux* to accompany their dances; the heroine and her mother sing *chansons de toile* as they embroider; and the emperor Conrad himself sings the most important group of songs, a series of *chansons d'amour* that express his love for the heroine. The principle of stylistic *decorum* is also relevant from another perspective, for as Edmond Faral observed, the three levels of style of classical rhetoric—the humble, the middle, and the sublime—were distinguished in the twelfth and thirteenth centuries not on the basis of subject matter, but on that of the social rank of the speaker. It is thus significant that almost all of the *chansons d'amour*, which were classified under the sublime style by Dante almost a century later, should be sung by the emperor.

---

34. The concept was derived from classical rhetoric and transmitted in the *ars dictaminis* of the twelfth century. See Edgar de Bruyne, *Etudes d'esthétique médiévale*, I, pp. 53–54; II, p. 11.

35. *Guillaume de Dole*, p. XXII.

The *chansons* Jean quoted conformed by definition to the highest aesthetic standards of his day and were thus most suitable for use as ornament. It is significant that his position was later supported by Dante in his *De Vulgari Eloquentia* (1304–6). Although composed about a century after the first use of lyric insertions, Dante's essay is useful because it is the first medieval treatise to deal with the practice of vernacular poets while remaining informed by the Latin rhetorical tradition.[36] Book II of this work deals with the *canzone* or song, and a good number of its examples are taken from the work of Occitan and French poets. The highest literary art, Dante asserted, should deal with the most noble subjects, and included among these were arms and love. Such lofty subjects should be presented in the highest style, and cast in the most perfect form, the *canzone* or *chanson*.[37] Many though not all lyric insertions actually conform to these rhetorical standards. Of the forty-seven lyric pieces Jean Renart inserted in his *Roman de la Rose*, sixteen are *chansons courtoises*, including three in Occitan, all of which sing of love. The remaining songs, however, belong to a variety of different genres and conform to aesthetic standards rather different from those outlined by Dante.

In asserting that the quotations so suited their new contexts that they might have been written by the author, Jean directed our attention to a second crucial issue raised by the technique, that of the tension between quotations and the surrounding narrative. How does an author fit independent compositions into his own work without sacrificing coherence? This tension is a problem in the use of any quotation,[38] but it is intensified by the musical character of quoted songs. These two concerns—the aesthetic effect of the insertions, and their tendency to interrupt, logically and musically, the narrative thread—exercised all of Jean Renart's imitators in the succeeding century and a half, although none addressed the problems so

---

36. Dante Alighieri, *De Vulgari Eloquentia*, ed. Aristide Marigo, 3rd ed. (Florence: Felice le Monnier, 1957). It is translated in Hardison, *Medieval Literary Criticism*, pp. 152–86, with a useful introduction, pp. 143–52; and by Robert S. Haller, *Literary Criticism of Dante Alighieri* (Lincoln: University of Nebraska Press, 1973), pp. 3–60.

37. On Dante and the style of the *chanson courtoise*, see Roger Dragonetti, *Technique poétique des trouvères dans la chanson courtoise: Contribution à l'étude de la rhétorique médiévale* (Bruges: De Tempel, 1960; repr. Slatkine, 1979), pp. 18–20; on the use of ornament in the *chanson* see pp. 32–61.

38. On this problem in other contexts, see Herman Meyer, *The Poetics of Quotation in the European Novel*, trans. Theodore and Yetta Ziolkowski (Princeton, N.J.: Princeton University Press, 1968); Graciela Reyes, *Polifonía Textual: La Citación en el Relato Literario*, Bibliotheca románica hispánica, II, Estudios y ensayos, 340 (Madrid: Gredos, 1984), which has a good bibliography; and Antoine Compagnon, *La seconde main ou le travail de la citation* (Paris: Seuil, 1979).

forthrightly. Each author had to exploit the aesthetic possibilities of the insertions, while at the same time confronting the musical nature of the songs chosen, and resolving the almost inevitable inconsistencies between the borrowed elements and his own text.

Lyric Insertions and Modern Critics

For nearly a century, lyric insertions have attracted occasional attention from scholars, but most have studied them only as examples of lyric poetry and have not examined their narrative setting or the relationship between the lyric and narrative elements in hybrid compositions. Only now is the insertion technique recognized as a central issue in the literary history of medieval France. A century ago Alfred Jeanroy, the first scholar to investigate narrative works containing lyric insertions, did so in the context of his research on the origins of lyric poetry. It was he who began the compilation of a list of works employing the technique, a list which has been expanded by other scholars over the years.[39] The fullest list published to date, by the German scholar Friedrich Ludwig (1923),[40] went unnoticed by most scholars until recently. Thus D. L. Buffum's supplement to Jeanroy's list, published in his edition of the *Roman de la Violette* (1928),[41] and Nico van den Boogaard's more complete census of works containing lyric insertions (1969),[42] missed several works noted by Ludwig. Albert Henry, in the commentary to his edition of *Cleomadés*,[43] mentioned several works missed by Ludwig, and I myself have discovered a dozen more.[44]

Jeanroy, Boogaard, and Ludwig were primarily interested in the development of lyric poetry and compiled their lists in the search for documentary evidence for the history of specific genres. Many of their successors

---

39. Alfred Jeanroy, *Les origines de la poésie lyrique en France au moyen âge: Etude de littérature française et comparée* . . . (Paris: Hachette, 1889; 2nd ed. with additions and bibliographical appendix, Paris: Champion, 1904; 4th ed. Paris: Champion, 1969), pp. 116ff.
40. Friedrich Ludwig, "Die Quellen der Motetten 'ältesten Stils,'" *Archiv für Musikwissenschaft*, 5 (1923; repr. 1964): 185–222; esp. pp. 214–18.
41. D. L. Buffum, *Le roman de la violette ou de Gerart de Nevers par Gerbert de Montreuil*, SATF (Paris: Champion, 1928), pp. lxxxiii, n.1 and 363.
42. Nico H. J. van den Boogaard, *Rondeaux et refrains du XIIe siècle au début du XIVe: Collationnement, introduction et notes*, Bibliothèque française et romane, D: Initiation, textes et documents, 3 (Paris: Klincksieck, 1969), pp. 313–38.
43. Albert Henry, *Les oeuvres d'Adenet le Roi*, V *Cleomadés*, vol. 2: *Introduction, notes, tables*, Travaux de la Faculté de Philosophie et Lettres, 26 (Brussels, 1971), pp. 675–76 and 676 n.3.
44. See Appendix 1 for a chronological list of narrative works containing lyric insertions.

have shared this preoccupation.[45] Gaston Paris took a rather different approach to the songs used by Jean Renart, in an essay included in the introduction to Servois's edition of Jean Renart's *Roman de la Rose*.[46] He mined the romance for information about the social conditions surrounding the performance of songs, the genres in vogue, and the attribution and possible dating of individual poems. In a similar vein, Albert Henry compiled a sort of dictionary of musical instruments on the basis of references in *Cleomadés*,[47] and Jean Maillard has drawn attention to information on musical technique found in the *Tristan en Prose*.[48] These studies make important contributions to our understanding of medieval French poetry and social life, but do not explore the structure of the containing romances, or explain why particular songs were included in them.

To date, these questions have been addressed most directly by the editors of the individual texts, although their inquiry has usually focused on a single text set in a restricted context. Moreover, their primary goal has generally been to identify the songs themselves, and occasionally the author's source for the device. Jeanroy and Gennrich attempted generalizations on the development of the technique, but their primary interest in lyric poetry, rather than in the relationship of lyric to narrative, shaped their view of the device.[49] Albert Henry similarly contrasted Adenet's use of songs with earlier models, particularly *Guillaume de Dole* and the *Lai d'Aristote*.[50] His is one of the best attempts to situate an author's practice in a literary context, although the number of works chosen for the comparison

---

45. See, for example, the work of Ernst Hoepffner on the *chanson royale*, the *ballade*, and the *rondel*, pp. xlviii–lxii of his edition of *La prise amoureuse von Jehan Acart de Hesdin*, Gesellschaft für romanischen Literatur, 22 (Dresden, 1910), and "Les poésies lyriques du *Dit de la panthère* de Nicole de Margival," *Romania*, 46 (1920): 204–30; and Friedrich Gennrich on the *ballade* and the *rondel*, pp. 107–15 of his edition of the *Dame a la Lycorne*, Gesellschaft für romanischen Literatur, 18, (Dresden, 1908). Gennrich continued this work in *Rondeaux Virelais und Balladen*. 2 vols., Gesellschaft für romanische Literatur, 43, 47 (Dresden, Halle a.S.: 1921–27).
46. "Les Chansons," *Le roman de la rose ou de Guillaume de Dole*, pp. lxxxix–cxxi.
47. *Cleomadés*, II, pp. 693–726.
48. Jean Maillard, "Coutumes musicales au moyen âge d'après le *Tristan* en prose," *Cahiers de Civilisation Médiévale*, 2 (1959): 341–53; "Lais avec notation dans le *Tristan* en prose," *Mélanges offerts à Rita Lejeune, professeur à l'Université de Liège*, 2 vols. (Gembloux: J. Duculot, 1969), II, pp. 1347–64.
49. Jeanroy (*Origines*, pp. 116–17, n.3) implied that the *chanson d'amour* ceased to be used for insertions after the *Roman de la Violette*, but the *Conte du Cheval de Fust (Meliacin)*, written half a century later, contains stanzas from some twenty *chansons*. Gennrich (*Dame a la Lycorne*, pp. 122–23) contended that the insertions in *Guillaume de Dole*, the *Violette*, and the *Tournoi de Chauvenci* are largely "unmotivated," while those in the *Dame a la Lycorne* are meant to fulfill the author's artistic purpose.
50. *Cleomadés*, II, pp. 677–78.

is fairly small. Douglas Kelly made a considerably broader survey, and returned to the approach of Gaston Paris in seeking to define "the use made of short poems in contemporary society."[51] Unlike his predecessor, who was interested in the social circumstances surrounding the songs, Kelly concentrated on the emotional or psychological motivation for the performance of the songs. In the introduction to her edition of the *Roman de la Poire*, Christiane Marchello-Nizia reported briefly the results of examining twenty-five poetic works with lyric insertions.[52] Much more detailed than this summary is Sylvia Huot's perceptive analysis of a smaller number of texts.[53] In her study, Huot discussed *Guillaume de Dole*, the *Roman du Castelain de Couci*, the *Roman de la Poire*, the *Panthere d'Amors*, as well as the works of Machaut and Froissart, in terms of the transition from an oral to a written poetic.

In contrast to these studies rooted in textual analysis, three critics have proposed theoretical models to account for the phenomenon as a whole. Jacqueline Cerquiglini distinguished two categories of narratives containing lyric insertions.[54] The first group of narratives, which use a method of insertion she calls *collage*, comprises those works in which there is no identity between the *I* of the songs and the *I* of the narration. In the narratives of this group, she maintains, the lyrics are merely juxtaposed to the narrative; despite a thematic relationship, the two parts remain essentially independent. In the second group, where the lyric and the narrative *I* coincide, she calls the mode of insertion *montage*, which means that the songs are the source, both chronologically and ideologically, of the text. The two categories appear in practice to correspond to the works of the thirteenth and fourteenth centuries, respectively. Cerquiglini also invented a third classification, called *collage-montage*, to deal with Froissart's *Meliador*, which juxtaposes its songs to the narrative, but which was actually composed for the purpose of displaying those songs. This schema sketches the history of the device very vividly. Because it treats works only in aggregate, however, it understates the variety of purposes served by the lyrics in any given narrative.

---

51. Kelly, *Medieval Imagination*, p. 239.
52. Christiane Marchello-Nizia, *Le roman de la poire par Tibaut*, SATF (Paris: Picard, 1984), pp. xxi–xxiv.
53. Sylvia Huot, *From Song to Book: The Poetics of Writing in Old French Lyric and Lyrical Narrative Poetry* (Ithaca, N.Y.: Cornell University Press, 1987).
54. Jacqueline Cerquiglini, "Pour une typologie de l'insertion," *Perspectives médiévales*, 3 (1977): 9–14; and *"Un Engin si soutil": Guillaume de Machaut et l'écriture au XIVe siècle* (Paris: Champion, 1985), pp. 22–32.

18   Chapter 1

Two other scholars have based their analyses on the narrative function of the lyric insertion. M. Accarie, in distinguishing the different types of insertion used by Jean Renart, established rather different categories: *chansons descriptives* (or *décoratives*), used as elements of description in scenes of court life; *chansons sentimentales*, in which characters express their emotions; *chansons structurelles*, which contribute to the organization of the work; and *chansons-déplacement*, which cover a transition from one place to another.[55] He did not apply these categories to any other works, however, and his categories do not exhaust the possibilities.

In trying to account more fully for the particular problems posed by *Meliador*, Jane Taylor took a different approach and proposed a model calculated to deal with the individual insertion.[56] Using Roman Jakobson's distinction between "code" and "message" as the theoretical basis of her model, she tried to determine whether the function of a given lyric is poetic or communicative.[57] At one extreme of her schema, the lyric is treated as an element of communication; it is essentially referential, and so forms part of the plot or *diegesis*.[58] For insertions at the other end of the spectrum, their lyric form is the essential element, and thus the code is stressed. This model has the advantage of focusing attention on the individual lyric in its context, and is thus a marked improvement on all earlier approaches. It is also flexible enough to admit the distinction of different types of poetic or communicative functions.

The Song in the Story

This book attempts a comprehensive examination of the use of the lyric insertion device in medieval French narrative. My approach to the subject has a strong empirical basis. After compiling what I hope is a nearly

---

55. M. Accarie, "La fonction des chansons du Guillaume de Dole," in *Mélanges Jean Larmat. Regards sur le Moyen Age et la Renaissance (Histoire, langue, et littérature)*, Annales de la Faculté des Lettres et Sciences Humaines de Nice, 39 (Nice, 1982; Paris: Les Belles Lettres, 1983), pp. 13–29.

56. Jane H. M. Taylor, "The Lyric Insertion: Torwards a Functional Model," in *Courtly Literature: Culture and Context*, Selected Papers from the Fifth Triennial Congress of the International Courtly Literature Society, Dalfsen, The Netherlands, 9–16 August 1986 (Amsterdam and Philadelphia: John Benjamins, 1990), pp. 539–48.

57. Roman Jakobson, *Essais de linguistique générale*, 2 vols. (Paris: Editions de Minuit, 1963–73), I, pp. 209–48.

58. The term is taken from Gérard Genette, *Narrative Discourse: An Essay in Method*, trans. Jane E. Lewin (Ithaca, N.Y.: Cornell University Press, 1980; first published Paris: Seuil, 1982), p. 27 and n.2.

exhaustive list of narrative works that include inserted lyrics, I examined every lyric insertion in each of the seventy-two narratives composed between 1200 and 1405 that I found to contain such insertions (including several that have yet to be edited), and have attempted to determine the literary function or functions of that lyric within the work. On the basis of that general analysis (involving several hundred inserted lyrics), I distinguished six different functions, and I have devoted a chapter to each of them.

My analysis of the lyric insertions has been guided by Jakobson's insights, and I have treated the songs as linguistic events, each possessing what he terms a *destinateur*, a message, and a *destinataire*.[59] This is certainly true of inserted lyrics, the majority of which are performed by characters in the narrative, but the communicative situation is complicated by the fictional quality of the linguistic event. The episode containing the lyric, and in fact the work as a whole, is also a message from the author to the audience or reader, so that every inserted song has a double audience—one fictional and the other real. In the chapters that follow, the emphasis of the analysis falls on the scene, the particular context of the individual song. At the same time, I have tried to take account both of its relationship to the sequence of events in the plot, and of its double audience. In order to make clearer the historical development of the use of the device, the works within each section of the chapters are arranged chronologically, and there is a chronological list of works containing lyric insertions in Appendix 1.

Jakobson's terminology has been useful in distinguishing the different functions of songs in the text, and hence in organizing the material into chapters. The insertions can be roughly divided into those whose function is essentially communicative and those with a poetic function. "Communicative" describes the function of songs clearly embedded in the narrative and attributed to a character who sings them as a form of communication. In contrast, songs with a "poetic" function affect the formal structure of the work. These lyric insertions are generally not attributed to characters within the narrative, but divide that narrative into sections.

Within the group of "communicative" insertions, a distinction must

---

59. There is some controversy over the treatment of literary texts as linguistic events; the peculiarly social circumstances of medieval "reading" make such an assumption more appropriate than for a modern novel or lyric poem. Roger Fowler, *Literature as Social Discourse: The Practice of Linguistic Criticism* (Bloomington: University of Indiana Press, 1981), esp. pp. 80–85, criticizes the emphasis of Jakobson's analyses, but his argument that a literary text should be treated as a *"process*, the communicative interaction of implied speakers and thus of consciousnesses and communities" (p. 94) tends to support my use of Jakobson's terminology.

be drawn between the use of lyric insertions in passages which are essentially descriptive in nature and those which have a "dramatic" role in the text. The attribution of a song to a character for the purpose of expressing or analyzing his (or occasionally her) sentiments—what Jakobson calls the emotive function—eventually became the most successful application of the device. Although the number of lyrics used in this way by Jean Renart is relatively small—only one-quarter of the total number—most of these fragments are longer than those in the descriptive passages. Later authors followed his practice and eventually composed complete songs for the purpose. The evidence for this part of the topic is vast, and I have discussed it under two headings. The second chapter is concerned with the various ways songs are related to the interior monologue, hitherto the principal device for revealing the inner thoughts of a character, whereas Chapter 6 investigates the special problems presented by the insertion of songs into first-person narratives, in which the poet is also the hero, and thus both singer and narrator.

Descriptions of scenes of court life were a conventional part of medieval romance from its beginnings. Jean Renart's innovation was to make explicit a standard feature of the description of festive occasions: in describing scenes where singing was mentioned, he included the words of the songs. Chapter 3 is devoted to the technique of using insertions to enhance the liveliness of the descriptions of celebrations and its development by his imitators.

Jean Renart employed only one song in his romance for an essentially narrative purpose: to effect a major shift in the plot of his story. Examples of the narrative use of lyrics in the works of later authors are rare, partly no doubt because it is difficult to make the motivation convincing, but also because it is not often repeatable within a work. Nonetheless, several authors attempted in this way to bring the lyric insertions under stricter narrative control. Although not always successful, these instances merit consideration in a chapter of their own and accordingly are examined in Chapter 4.

When songs are sung to a listener, the situation is altered, for the singer is usually intent upon making an impression on the listener. Such lyrics, performed in the presence of both lady and lover, are more directly communicative than those discussed in Chapter 2, which (sung in solitude) are essentially introspective. These songs and their relationship to the dialogue are the subject of the fifth chapter.

The discussion so far has assumed that a lyric insertion dictates its narrative environment, at least to the extent of requiring a context to account for it. This is not always the case. In several works, songs punctuate the narrative at more or less regular intervals, with little or no motivating context. Chapter 7 focuses on those works which illustrate the poetic function of lyrics, and helps to prove my earlier point by contrast. When the rationalizing context is suppressed, the songs are not clearly subordinated to the story line. Their intrusiveness becomes a significant distraction from the narrative, and the linear movement is weakened. In the end, the structure of these works takes on a stanzaic quality, as the songs begin to overwhelm the story.

In the examination of individual works included in the chapters just outlined, it will become clear that the different functions of lyric insertions in a narrative context tended to be divided among the various genres and registers embraced by the body of medieval lyric poetry. Hence, passages describing the perfomance of the *carole* quote *rondets de carole*, while the *chanson courtoise* occurs in the context of a hero's monologue lamenting the rigors of love. This said, it must be borne in mind that this is a tendency only and not an invariable rule. Nevertheless, in a literature as sensitive to levels of style and register as that of the Middle Ages, it is clear that such choices were made with care. We notice in Jean Renart's *Rose*, to take the earliest example, that *rondets de carole* are the songs used to accompany dancing, while in a scene modeled on the setting of the *chanson de toile* the heroine and her mother sing such songs as they sew. Similarly, most of the *chanson* stanzas quoted in the romance are sung by its hero and are expressions, however ironic or unconscious, of his sentiments. Similar associations of genre and function are apparent in many of the works considered, but they are by no means inflexible. As the discussion in Chapter 2 will make clear, the hero's choice of a *rondet* for his final song is a shift of genre and register which implies an abandonment of the values embodied in the *chanson courtoise*.

Jean Renart asserted a desire to preserve the songs he quoted from oblivion, but his attitude (and that of his successors) toward the ideology of those songs was not unambiguous. On the one hand he incorporated icons of courtly ideology into his romance, including not only songs of French *trouvères* but even Provençal stanzas by Jaufré Rudel and Bernart de Ventadorn. On the other, he placed these songs in a setting characterized by the easy, pleasurable love of the *rondet de carole*. The difficult ethos of *fin' amors* was thus surrounded by the less demanding desire for the "good life," and the tension between the two modes of love is reflected in the action described in the narrative verse.

When all the songs in a work belong to a single register, or were composed by its author, the tension between the lyric ideology and the incorporating narrative takes other forms. Guillaume de Machaut, for example, used prose letters, as well as narrative verse to serve as foils for his songs in his *Voir Dit*. Froissart used a different strategy in his *Joli Buisson de Jonece*, where his inspiration is a ten-year-old portrait of his lady, that is, a lady who no longer exists in that form.[60]

In considering the tension between the two parts of the composite works, it is important to remember that we are dealing with various linguistic combinations of narrative verse and song, prose and song, and even, in the *Dame a la Lycorne*, Guillaume de Machaut's *Voir Dit*, and Froissart's *Prison Amoureuse*, all three forms. These forms correspond roughly to the three types of discourse recognized by medieval Latin theorists: prose, metrical verse, and rhythmical verse.[61] The three types of discourse are not to be confused with the three levels of style referred to above, of which only the humble was extensively used in Latin by this time.[62] The authors of secular narrative works in the vernacular, who were certainly familiar with classical rhetoric, generally chose the grace and elegance of the middle style, while the sublime found new application in the treatment of the love theme, particularly, but not exclusively, in lyric poetry.

Given these distinctions taken from medieval rhetorical theory, it is clear that works containing lyric insertions are combinations of types of discourse and styles as well as of genres. The term "combination" is misleading, however, for it suggests that the parts are merely juxtaposed and fails to imply the complex relationship (or relationships) between them.[63] In this context, Mikhail Bakhtin's term "dialogical" is a useful adjective for describing the connections among the different types of language combined in a single work. In an essay on the precursors of the novel,[64] Bakhtin

---

60. See the discussion in Chapter 6, below.
61. Murphy, *Rhetoric in the Middle Ages*, p. 157.
62. Curtius, *European Literature*, p. 149.
63. Cf. J. Cerquiglini's term "montage."
64. *The Dialogical Imagination: Four Essays by M.M. Bakhtin*, ed. Michael Holquist, trans. Caryl Emerson and Michael Holquist (Austin: University of Texas Press, 1981), pp. 41–83. See also *Problems of Dostoevsky's Poetics*, trans. R. W. Rotsel (Ann Arbor, Mich.: Ardis, 1973); repr. Minneapolis: University of Minnesota Press, 1984); the discussion by Julia Kristeva in *Semiotikè: Recherches pour une sémanalyse* (Paris: Seuil, 1969; Points, 96. Paris: Seuil, 1978), pp. 82–112; Tzvetan Todorov, *Mikhail Bakhtin: The Dialogical Principle*, trans. Wlad Godzich,

demonstrated that the juxtaposition of different images of language is an essential characteristic of the novel, though found also in earlier works. He then argued that the author's attitude toward these linguistic "images" is never neutral, but that he questions, contradicts, and exaggerates them. In other words, the author is in a "dialogical relationship" with the languages he presents. At the same time, the different images of language engage in similar sorts of dialogue with each other.

This concept of "dialogism" is illuminating in the context of lyric insertions, for it helps to explain the relationship among the various parts of a hybrid work. The different lyric registers, the sung and spoken modes of discourse, are not simply juxtaposed in Jean Renart's *Rose* and its successors. On the contrary, the different registers and images of language "converse" with each other: they enter into a dialogue and comment on each other; and an understanding of the resultant metadialogue of each work is of central importance to its interpretation.

In the chapters that follow, I shall consider these themes in the context of the individual work, and then in a concluding chapter examine them from a more general standpoint. I hope in this way to demonstrate that lyric insertions, far from being literary freaks, were in fact central to the poetic practice of medieval France.

Theory and History of Literature, 13 (Minneapolis: University of Minnesota Press, 1984); and Cesare Segre, "What Bakhtin Left Unsaid: The Case of the Medieval Romance," in *Romance: Generic Transformations from Chrétien de Troyes to Cervantes*, ed. Kevin Brownlee and Marina Scordilis Brownlee (Hanover, N.H.: University of New England Press for Dartmouth College, 1985), pp. 23–46. Segre points out that the mixing of styles and registers corresponds not to social but to literary variegation, i.e. the "intertextuality which is at the heart of the creative activity of medieval poets" (p. 31).

2. Songs as Monologues: The Hero as Singer

Most of the songs quoted in the narratives I shall examine are united in theme: however different they may be in tone and register, most lyric insertions are love songs. The relationship of these insertions to their enclosing narrative is, at first glance, perfectly straightforward. The words of a song are put into the mouth of a character, and the author makes the tacit claim that the song expresses the sentiments of that character. On closer examination, however, the situation is rather less transparent, for the quotation of a song inevitably sets up an implicit comparison between the present and original singers. Although a lyric insertion may fit easily into its new context, this is not always the case, and as we shall see, Jean Renart and his successors were quite clever at exploiting the resultant discordances.

The technique traditionally used by authors of romances for indicating the emotions of characters was the monologue, either spoken or interior. Although the earliest monologues were formally independent of songs, they derived much of their content from the rhetoric of the *chanson d'amour*. The similarity between the *chanson* and certain types of monologue has long been acknowledged, though infrequently treated.[1] Certainly both forms assume the same concept of love, and the monologue normally expresses this love by means of personifications and images borrowed from the courtly lyric. Paul Zumthor has pointed out that the "psychology" of romance characters is often no more than a rhetorical expansion of the central *formulae* of the *chanson* applied to either past or future action.[2]

Because of the relationship between monologues and *chansons*, it was

---

1. See Emil Walker, *Der Monolog im höfischen Epos: Stil und Literaturgeschichtliche Untersuchungen* (Stuttgart: W. Kohlhammer, 1928); Alfons Hilka, *Die direkte Rede als stilistisches Kunstmittel in den Romanen des Kristians von Troyes* (Halle: Niemeyer, 1903), pp. 71–108; Ilse Nolting-Hauff, *Die Stellung der Liebeskasuistik im höfischen Roman* (Heidelberg: C. Winter, 1959), pp. 30–66. On the monologue and its resemblance to the lyric, see Charles Muscatine, *Chaucer and the French Tradition* (Berkeley: University of California Press, 1957), pp. 12–23, 28–28.
2. Zumthor, *Essai de poétique médiévale*, pp. 341–42.

possible to associate the two forms in a narrative context and even to use a song to replace a monologue. However natural the procedure might initially appear, introducing a quotation from such a lyric into a monologue alters its nature and presents certain problems of composition. Although the authors who used this device did not always find it necessary to cast every singer as a poet, they had nevertheless to account for the performance of the song. A more serious problem arose from the relationship between the quoted song and the traditional monologue, whose function it tended to assume. Should the song stand alone, as the exclusive expression of the hero's emotions, or should it be combined with a monologue? If the latter arrangement were chosen, where should the song occur in relation to the monologue, and how should it be introduced? Yet another difficulty arose from the difference between the circumstances of the singer and those of the "je" of the song; the possibilities range along a continuum from close approximation to virtual contradiction, and illustrate Bakhtin's principle of "dialogism."[3] The seven romances I shall discuss in this chapter—*Guillaume de Dole*, the *Roman de la Violette*, the *Roman de Tristan en Prose*, *Meliacin*, the *Roman du Castelain de Couci*, *Meliador*, and *Ysaÿe le Triste*—illustrate most of the possible solutions to these problems. Each of the authors of these works attempted to create a setting for the lyric insertions—to provide a transition from linear narrative movement to "lyric pause." Sometimes the singer is portrayed in an attitude of meditation, where a recollection of the beloved is sufficient to inspire the song. On other occasions a typical theme of lyric poetry, particularly the "nature introduction," is incorporated into the narrative as the setting for the scene. How well these techniques succeeded we shall see as we examine them.

Although lyrics were normally placed in the mouths of the characters of narratives in the fashion just described, they could also be inserted into passages of the narrative that may best be described as analytical. Inserting a lyric into an analytical passage presented an altogether different problem for the author. Since the song is not ascribed to a character, there is no question of its performance, and hence its musical nature is of no interest. Because it is the author himself and not his character who asserts the appropriateness of the quotation, the possibilities for irony are reduced. These restrictions on the resonance of the device may account for its rarity: although it is theoretically useful as a device, I have found but a single example, in the *Chastelaine de Vergi*.

3. Cf. end of Chapter 1.

Roman de la Rose or *Guillaume de Dole*

Jean Renart's *Roman de la Rose*, commonly called *Guillaume de Dole*, established the practice of inserting lyrics. Twelve of the lyrics quoted in this romance are sung by the hero, or are performed at his request. Taken as a group, the songs mark the growth of the hero Conrad's love for the heroine, Liénor.[4] The insertion of these songs is comprehensible only in context, so the plot must be summarized in some detail.

The romance opens with a description of the emperor Conrad, a paragon of courtly and royal virtues. The effects of his largesse and wise government are manifested in the lavish court he keeps. In the midst of the facile diversions of his court, however, Conrad grows bored, for despite his skill in dalliance, he does not love, and he has no wife. One day, the minstrel Juglet begins a story about a valiant knight who "amoit une dame en France" (v. 665). When Conrad laments that there are no longer any such knights and ladies, Juglet describes Guillaume de Dole and his sister, Liénor, who live in his kingdom. Guillaume himself is outstanding for his prowess, generosity, and courtesy, while his sister is exquisitely beautiful. This introduction puts the other main characters in an explicitly literary context. The brother and sister are presented to the emperor as living embodiments of the virtues of fiction. His curiosity piqued by the descriptions, Conrad attaches Guillaume to his court, and diverts himself by thinking about the sister.

Juglet's description of Liénor de Dole intrigues Conrad. The difference in their rank rules out marriage, but her very ineligibility is an attraction, for Conrad may think about her without danger of involvement: "Mes por ce qu'el n'i porroit mie / avenir, i voel ge penser" (vv. 835–36; "But because it can never come about, I wish to think about it"). These lines indicate the emperor's emotional immaturity and prepare the listener (/reader) for the way he uses songs.

As they ride back to court, Conrad and Juglet sing part of a song by Gace Brulé. The stanza chosen describes the poet's faithful service to his

---

4. See Chapter 1, n. 26, for bibliography on editions and dating. Among recent studies, see especially Emmanuèle Baumgartner, "Les citations lyriques dans le *Roman de la Rose* de Jean Renart," *Romance Philology*, 35 (1981–82): 260–66; Marc-René Jung, "L'empereur Conrad, chanteur de poésies lyriques (Fiction et vérité dans le 'Roman de la Rose' de Jean Renart)," *Romania*, 101 (1980): 35–50; and Roger Dragonetti, *Le mirage des sources: L'art du faux dans le roman médiéval* (Paris: Seuil, 1987). The text is preserved in a single manuscript. Lecoy in his edition has restored lines to two songs on the basis of the versions found in the *chansonniers*; cf. pp. 175, n. 1460–66 and 176, n. 3756. I have not seen any evidence to suggest that the songs were otherwise altered by Renart to fit his romance.

lady, and begs her mercy. Its specific content is not at all relevant to Conrad's circumstances but it nevertheless reveals his ideal, and the role he will play at with increasing seriousness. This is the first *chanson* quoted in the romance, and the first intrusion of *fin' amors*. Conrad, too, enters the realm of literature, for he models himself on the courtly lover of the *chanson*. In the light of later developments in the plot, the last three lines of the stanza are suggestive. The poet says that he sings of the love which completely fills his thoughts:

> Et por ce chant, que nel puis oublier,
> la bon' amor dont Dex joie me doigne,
> car de li sont et vienent mi penser.
> (vv. 850–52)
>
> [And for this I sing, for I cannot forget it, the good love whose joy may God grant me, for my thoughts come from it.]

These lines anticipate what happens to Conrad: he begins by thinking of Liénor because she is ineligible, and therefore safe; but she comes to occupy his thoughts to such an extent that he falls in love with her. Thus, although Conrad's singing expresses nothing more than lightheartedness in this context, his song hints at the emotional development which follows. At the same time, the discrepancy between the emotion of the song and that of the singer is typical of Conrad's choices.

Conrad acts on his inclination and sends a messenger to summon Guillaume to court. The next morning, he sings a second song, introduced by a passage describing the beauty of the morning and the sun shining on an embroidered coverlet. In the context of the "displaced" nature introduction, the author says that his character sings: "Por l'amor bele Lïenor, / dont il avoit el cuer le non" (vv. 920–21; "for love of the beautiful Liénor, whose name he had in his heart"). The name that fills his heart belongs, of course, to a lady he has never seen. It seems therefore, that Conrad aspires not simply to *fin' amors*, but to an *amour lointain*. A stanza from Jaufré Rudel's famous song is quoted later in the romance, as part of the entertainment at a dinner given by Guillaume for his new friends. It is significant that, having chosen to dally with an *amour lointain*, it is not he but another character who invokes the song: the emblem of this type of *fin'amors* appears in the romance, but not in association with the hero who aspires to its ideal.

The beginning of the stanza that Conrad sings (by the Châtelain de

Couci) echoes the description of his surroundings with a typical evocation of spring. Thematically similar, the two passages point up the contrast between illusion and reality. Seen in one light, the Châtelain was moved by a real spring, while the emperor is inspired only by embroidery. From another point of view, the illusion of poetry is contrasted with the pedestrian reality of the context. The rest of the stanza does not suit the emperor's position at all: the poet sings of his desire to lie with his lady once more before leaving on crusade.

After the stanza, the author's only comment is: "Ensi se conforte en chantant" (v. 931; "thus he consoles himself by singing"). The juxtaposition of description and song is revealing. At the sight of a spring morning our hero's fancy turns at once to thoughts of love. The very day after he has first heard of Liénor, Conrad sings for love of her, to comfort himself. Clearly he is in love with love, if not yet with a particular lady. What is striking here is the lack of authorial commentary or meditative monologue. At points where one would expect some sort of description of the hero's state of mind, or an interior monologue that expresses his emotions, the author instead has his character sing stanzas of *chansons d'amour*.[5]

At this point, the scene shifts to Dole, where we see the reception of Conrad's messenger. Liénor is presented for the first time, carefully surrounded by her family, but in a perfectly literary context. She and her mother enact a *chanson de toile,* performing one of these songs as they embroider.[6]

After the messenger returns from Dole, Conrad sends Juglet to fetch Guillaume and eagerly awaits the knight's arrival. According to the passage which introduces his third song, much of his eagerness springs from the thought that Liénor may accompany her brother. The observations on the hero's frame of mind in this passage are rather vague: we are told that he is "mout hetiez" (v. 1443; "very joyous") and "liez d'estrange maniere" (v. 1449; "strangely happy"), and that he sings for joy. Yet the lines quoted from the song by Renaut de Beaujeu refer to the sorrows of love, and the last three lines mention death.[7] This is a clear instance of Conrad's tendency to associate himself with an attitude wholly foreign to him. The only "sorrow" he has yet suffered is eager anticipation of the arrival of his lady's brother, and considerable curiosity to see Liénor herself. The disparity

---

5. All but one (the last) of his twelve songs are *chansons d'amour*; although he is not the only character to sing them, no other character's sentiments are explored in this way.

6. See below, Chapter 3, under "The Music of the Court."

7. The manuscript contains only the first four lines of the first stanza and the last three of the second; Lecoy's edition supplies the intervening text.

between the song and the sentiments which provoke its performance is noticed by the author with characteristic irony: "Or sachiez de fi et de voir / qu'il prent toz les maus en bons grez" (vv. 1470–71; "Know truly and certainly that he accepted all this pain willingly"). Conrad enjoys imagining himself in the role of suffering lover and probably believes himself immune from any real pain.

The next two songs are performed by a minstrel, at Conrad's request, on two different occasions. The fourth—a stanza from an anonymous *chanson* —is only one of many songs said to be sung during the banquet held to welcome Guillaume to the court, but it is the only one actually quoted. The end of this insertion seems to predict the emperor's state of mind later in the romance:

> mes une amor me desvoie
> > et tient esgaré
> > ou j'ai mon pensé,
> en quel lieu que onques soie.
> (vv. 1773–76)

[But a love drives me mad and keeps me troubled, for I have my thoughts in a place where I have never been.]

Conrad will later find himself truly distracted by the thought of Liénor and unable to forget her even when forced to renounce her. A line (v. 2035) in the fifth song—a stanza by Gace Brulé—seems equally prophetic, for it refers to failing the lady, as Conrad will when he is taken in by the seneschal's ruse. In both cases, however, the context of the quotation is celebratory, and it is only the genre of the song that makes it suggestive.

Guillaume's exploits in tournaments bear out Juglet's claims for half of the pair, and Conrad begins to think quite seriously of Liénor (who did not, in fact, accompany her brother). In this section of the romance Guillaume's role as his sister's deputy becomes clear. As he wins Conrad's esteem, the emperor's attachment to Liénor grows proportionately. Eventually Conrad reveals to Guillaume his decision to marry her and to crush any opposition from his barons. He then turns to the young man and asks: "Savez vos cest vers?" (v. 3106; "Do you know this song?"). This bald question is the only introduction to the song, and we are left to puzzle out what it signifies, for the quotation is the only clue to Conrad's sentiments, as opposed to his intentions. He sings a stanza in which the poet prefers to remain loyal to his lady, even if rejected, rather than to be accepted by another:

> Mout est fouls, que que nus die,
> qui cuide que aillors bé,
> car miex aim son escondire
> q'autre m'eüst cuer doné.
> (vv. 3107–10)
>
> [He is most foolish, whatever he says, who thinks that I turn my expectations elsewhere, for I prefer her refusal to the heart that another would have given me.]

These sentiments seem strange in the context. Considering that Conrad has the enthusiastic consent of his beloved's brother, he is unlikely to encounter refusal from Liénor. Yet as Conrad clearly anticipates his vassals' opposition, the song may be interpreted as a declaration of his determination to pursue Liénor in the face of advice to seek a more eligible bride. The song, nevertheless, remains incongruous, for Conrad is proposing to marry the object of his *amour lointain*, a conclusion not included in the repertory of the *chanson*.

In the next scene, the opposition takes an unexpected form, for the seventh song, which concludes a conversation between Conrad and Guillaume, is overheard by the seneschal who is jealous of Conrad's esteem and envious of Guillaume's success. Once again the insertion—two stanzas of an otherwise unattested *chanson*—replaces any declaration by Conrad of his feelings. The quoted stanzas show Conrad's state of mind to be what one would expect. The first is a fairly typical combination of a nature introduction and an expression of devotion to love, and it reveals to the seneschal the secret of Conrad's partiality for Guillaume. As in the world of the *chanson*, so in that of the romance, love must be guarded as a secret. Once Conrad speaks openly of his love, he betrays himself to his enemy.

The interpretation of the second stanza, however, presents some difficulties. It opens with the line: "Ja fine amors ne sera sanz torment" (v. 3188; "Never will fine love be without torment"). The mention of *torment* at this point is puzzling, for Conrad now has every expectation of a happy ending to his suit. The future tense of the verb, however, is a hint that although Conrad is singing a conventional song which is not particularly applicable to himself, his words may be truer than he knows. Considered in the context of the seneschal's treacherous intentions, the foreshadowing in this line emerges clearly and is continued in the remainder of the stanza. The seneschal, like the *losengier* referred to in the song, is angered by *fin' amors,* and will do his best to torment the lovers and, if possible, destroy their affair. He decides to stop the match by seducing the girl. When he is unable even to see her, he uses the information, gleaned from her mother, that she has a birthmark (the *rose* of the title) on her thigh as evidence of an affair.

The seneschal's clever lie is effective—the proposed marriage is indeed broken off—but gains him little favor with the emperor. Conrad reacts to the slander against Liénor first in a monologue and then in a stanza quoted from another song by Gace Brulé. In the monologue he pours out his hatred of the seneschal. As for Liénor, he confines himself to ruing the day she was born. The song develops this theme, but its tone is considerably more bitter, and it ends with a cynical comment on the danger of jealousy and the fickleness of women:

ainz s'en doit on bien garder
d'encerchier par jalousie
ce qu'en n'i voudroit trover.
(vv. 3629–31)

[Thus should one refrain from seeking, out of jealousy, what one would rather not find.]

Although Conrad has in reality neither tested his lady's love nor been betrayed by Liénor, the stanza nevertheless gives vivid expression to his disappointment. At the same time, the audience, knowing more than the hero, perceives the irony of his behavior. He has been taken in by the slanderer and is guilty of misjudging his lady. He has, moreover, failed to recognize the *maus* of love which he had earlier professed himself willing to suffer.

His ninth song (vv. 3751–59), a stanza by the Châtelain de Couci, is similar in tone, and begins by reproaching Love for depriving him of solace and giving loyal service a poor reward. As before, however, Conrad's situation stands in ironic contrast to that of the poet he quotes. Whereas the poet complains of the cruelty of Love, and of his lady, who have so far denied him any reward, and hopes in this way to move his lady to pity,

Conrad's complaint has no purpose beyond the expression of his own pain. The song is followed by a passage of authorial commentary on Conrad's emotions:

> Or sachiez bien que cil haus hom,
> cil empereres, cil haus sire,
> pensis et dolanz s'en consire
> de l'amor a la damoisele,
> qu'encore l'en tient soz la mamele
> li maus qui nel let rehetier,
> et le doel dou bon chevalier
> qui se debat et fiert ses mains.
> (vv. 3760–67)

[Know well that this nobleman, this emperor, this lord, melancholy and sorrowful, does not console himself for the love of the lady, for the pain which does not let him rejoice he holds still beneath his breast, and the sorrow of the good knight, who argues with himself and strikes his fists.]

This is the sole explicit explanation of the hero's state of mind, and it occurs at a point which requires some comment. As Conrad had never met the girl he had chosen to marry, he might have been expected to forget her easily; the fact that he cannot requires a certain precision in the description of his sentiments and indicates the extent of his involvement with her.

Even after he has ruled out the possibility of marriage, Conrad continues to be haunted by the thought of Liénor and is reminded of a song by Renaut de Sabloeil, which he duly sings. The second stanza of this song in particular seems ill-suited to the present context:

> Las! j'ai dit par ma folie,
> ce sai de voir, grant outrage;
> mes a mon cuer prist envie
> d'estre legier et volage.
> A! Dame, si m'en repent.
> Mes cil a tart merci crie
> qui atent tant que il pent,
> por ce ai la mort deservie.
> (vv. 3891–98)

[Alas, I foolishly said a great outrage, this I know truly; but my heart wished to be frivolous and fickle. Ah! Lady, I repent of it. But he asks pardon late, who waits until he hangs; for this reason have I deserved death.]

The melancholy tone of the song suits the emperor's mood, but whereas the poet blames himself and seeks pardon, Conrad feels justified in his anger. Yet the song anticipates what is to come: in believing the seneschal's lies and repeating them to Liénor's brother, Conrad indeed utters *grant outrage*. Moreover, his repetition of the slander provokes an attempt on her life, when Guillaume's nephew tries to avenge the family honor by killing Liénor. In his song, Conrad unknowingly accepts responsibility for his blindness and asks pardon of his lady.

The scene returns to Dole, where Liénor discovers, in a most melodramatic way, her lost opportunity. As she evades the attempt upon her life, Liénor at last learns of the seneschal's slander against her, and how nearly she missed a throne. Determined to clear her name, she assumes a disguise and travels to the court.

Somewhat later, Conrad ruefully reflects upon his love affair in the words of the Vidame de Chartres which he has a minstrel perform. The quoted fragment opens with an evocation of spring and continues with the poet's reason for singing:

Chanter m'estuet, car plus ne m'en puis taire,
por conforter ma cruel aventure
qui m'est tornee a grant mesaventure.
(vv. 4131–33)

[I must sing, for I can no longer be silent, to solace my cruel adventure, which has turned out badly.]

This is exactly Conrad's reason for listening to the song. He regrets that he ever heard of Liénor, for she has caused him nothing but sorrow and pain. At the end of the performance, he exclaims at the aptness of the song to his own predicament: "a droiture / fu ciz vers fet por moi sanz doute" (vv. 4141–42; "truly, this song was made for me, without doubt").[8]

---

8. In the passage describing the May festival at Mainz (vv. 4646–63), Conrad and Liénor overhear the same song in different parts of the castle. The cheerful celebration of spring

When Liénor arrives at court she plants some jewelry in the seneschal's tent and then accuses him publicly of theft and desertion. The seneschal swears quite truthfully that he has never laid eyes on her and submits to an ordeal to prove it. He is acquitted, but when Liénor reveals her identity, his slander is exposed.

Conrad's last song in the romance, a *rondet de carole*, constitutes his proposal to Liénor: "Que demandez vos / quant vos m'avez?" (vv. 5106–7; "What do you ask for when you have me?"). This is the only *rondet* that he sings, and the change of genre is significant: it marks his abandonment of the *chanson* of sorrow and longing for the lighter register of the good life. The romance ends with a wedding, a public celebration of requited love. This final court scene is embellished with another series of songs, mainly *rondets*, and in this scene we see the emperor once again take his place at the head of his court, elegant and happy rather than pining and sorrowful.

Taken as a group, Conrad's songs mark a radical innovation in narrative technique. Systematically, throughout his romance, Jean Renart substituted lyric quotations for interior monologues as a means of exploring his hero's emotional life. Such a substitution was, of course, logically appropriate, because the nonlyrical interior monologue was not only a sort of "lyric pause" in the linear movement of the narrative,[9] but was profoundly influenced in its development by the lyric.

While the technical appropriateness of the songs is almost indisputable, most critics have been reluctant to admit the expressive aptness of Conrad's songs.[10] The mistake of these critics has been to treat the songs as literal expressions of the hero's emotions—an enterprise of dubious validity in any case, since the work of Guiette and Zumthor has demonstrated the general paucity of biographical reference in courtly poetry.[11] Such criticism

---

reveals their feelings indirectly as each reflects on how inappropriate the song is for the current situation. See below, Chapter 3, under "The Music of the Court."

9. Walker, *Der Monolog*, p. 4.

10. Cf. Lecoy, ed. cit., p. viii, and the remarks by A. P. Ladd, "Lyric Insertions," pp. 44–53. Rita Lejeune (*L'oeuvre de Jean Renart*, pp. 144–66) dissented from the common view; more recently Norris J. Lacy, in "'Amer par oïr dire': *Guillaume de Dole* and the Drama of Language," *The French Review*, 54 (1981): 779–87, has taken the romance and its technique seriously.

11. Robert Guiette, "D'une poésie formelle en France au moyen âge," *Revue des sciences humaines*, n.s. 54 (1949): 61–69 (repr. Paris: Nizet, 1972). Zumthor, *Essai de poétique médiévale*, pp. 206–8, 216–218. See also Leo Spitzer, "Note on the Poetic and the Empirical 'I' in Medieval Authors," *Traditio*, 4 (1946) 414–22; repr. *Romanische Literaturstudien 1936–1956* (Tübingen: Max Niemeyer, 1959), pp. 100–112. For a recent corrective to Zumthor's insistence on the circularity of medieval lyric, see Michel Zink, *Subjectivité littéraire autour du siècle de Saint Louis* (Paris: Presses Universitaires de France, 1985).

denies the author sufficient literary sensibility to perceive such discrepancies, and does him a signal injustice. Indeed, Jean Renart himself undermined the idea of direct expression, for a number of the songs are attributed to their poets, while others are performed by minstrels. The relationship between words and emotion is not in fact directly expressive, but rather semiotic. The songs mark, signal, or denote Conrad's feelings, rather than expressing them. As we have seen in the preceding analysis, the songs do indeed give a clear indication of the evolution of the hero's feelings, while the undeniable discrepancies are used to artistic effect. In several cases, the words appropriated by Conrad are more fitting than he realizes, because they anticipate future developments. In general, however, the distance between the hero and the songs he borrows is exploited to ironic effect, as Jean Renart portrays him striving (and failing) to live up to the ideal he sings. He thus sets the songs in a "dialogical" relationship with the narrative.

The analysis of Conrad's songs highlights the principal difficulty of Jean Renart's innovation: fitting borrowed songs into the emotional context created by the plot. Whereas he managed to exploit the ironic possibilities of his quotations, most of his successors sought to overcome this problem by a less radical use of the device, using either commentary or monologue as a transition from narrative to song.

Roman de la Violette

Although the *Roman de la Violette* was modeled fairly directly on the *Roman de la Rose*, its author, Gerbert de Montreuil, modified in important ways the technique he borrowed from Jean Renart.[12] While Conrad was the only character in the earlier romance to express his emotions in song, Gerbert

---

12. The romance has been edited by Douglas Labaree Buffum, *Le Roman de la Violette ou de Gerart de Nevers par Gerbert de Montreuil*, SATF (Paris: Champion, 1928), who also studied the insertions in "The Songs of the *Roman de la Violette*," in *Studies in Honor of A. Marshall Elliott*, 2 vols. (Baltimore: Johns Hopkins University Press, 1911), I, pp. 129–57. In the introduction to his edition, Buffum proposed the years 1227–29 for the date (pp. lv–lxxiii). The romance survives in four copies; where relevant, I have taken account of variants in discussing the text of the songs. There are instances, mentioned below, where Gerbert seems to have altered songs to suit his purposes.

Like Jean Renart, Gerbert used as insertions a great variety of genres: *refrains, pastourelles, chansons de mal-mariée*, an epic *laisse*, and *chansons d'amour*, including three in Occitan. On the language and meaning of the Occitan songs, see the forthcoming article by William D. Paden, "Old Occitan as a Lyric Language: The Insertions from Occitan in Three Thirteenth-Century French Romances," forthcoming in *Speculum* (1993).

allowed this means of expression to several characters and used *refrains* as well as stanzas of *chansons d'amour* for the purpose. Of the thirty-nine songs quoted in the *Violette*, thirteen are *chansons*, and nine of these are used expressively: five are sung by the hero, two by the heroine, and two others by secondary characters in love with the central couple. In contrast to Jean Renart's practice, Gerbert sometimes used song and monologue in conjunction. Gerbert's modifications of the insertion technique were in keeping with the more complex narrative situation of his work. The characters who sing their love are caught in situations more typical of the romance genre than is the courtly calm of *Guillaume de Dole*.

The *Violette* begins with a festive scene at the court of King Louis of France, where the participants amuse themselves by singing to accompany the *carole*. When the hero, Gerart, Count of Nevers, is asked to sing, he obliges, not with a *refrain* like the other singers, but with a stanza from a *chanson* by Gace Brulé in which he proclaims his defiance of envious rivals. He follows the song with a speech that opens and closes with *refrains* in which he brags of his happy love affair with the beautiful Euriaut. Like his predecessor Conrad, Gerart sings words whose ironic meaning becomes clear only as the plot develops.

Provoked by the boastful singing, an envious courtier named Lisiart challenges Gerart to a wager, claiming that he can win the lady.[13] Gerart accepts with well-founded confidence, for Euriaut will indeed spurn Lisiart's advances.

Euriaut, like Liénor, "enters singing," but in a more ominous context, for the malicious Lisiart eavesdrops on her. Her song is prompted by the thought of her absent lover, and replaces any other expression of her feelings:

Lors li souvint de son ami,
Dont souspire et plaint et gemi.
Apriés, quant elle a souspiré,
L'a un poi amours aspiré
A chanter, si com jou devin,
Un vier d'un boin son poitevin.
(vv. 317–22)

---

13. On the series of romances to exploit this theme, see Gaston Paris, "Le Cycle de la Gageure," *Romania*, 32 (1923): 481–551. Cf. the list of works mentioned by Félix Lecoy in his edition of *Guillaume de Dole*, p. XII, n. 1.

[Then she remembered her lover, for whom she sighs and laments and moans. Afterward, when she sighed, love inspired her a little to sing, as I guess, a stanza of a good song of Poitou.]

This stanza, from a *canso* by Bernart de Ventadorn,[14] is an emblem of *fin' amors*, and it is an original touch to have it sung by the lady. Euriaut's choice of a *son poitevin* proclaims her adherence to a particular ideal of love, while the words themselves stand as an unconscious defiance of Lisiart:

Non es enugs ni fallimens
Ni vilania, so m'es vis,
Mas d'ome can se fa devis
D'autrui amor, ni conoixens.
(vv. 324–27)

[There is no trouble, deception, treachery, so I think, unless someone makes himself clever at guessing the love of others, or knowing it.]

These lines, although composed by a man, are in perfect accord with the sentiments and circumstances of the woman who sings them. Furthermore, the narrative situation enacts the scene evoked in the quotation, which opens with a denunciation of envious spies, and continues by addressing such people.

Euriaut sings again in response to Lisiart's advances, and the fragment of a *chanson de mal mariée* constitutes the bulk of her reply. Declaring that his proposition is offensive to her, she goes on to sing her refusal in no uncertain terms: "Ains l'amerai, que j'en sui bien amee. / Laissié me ester, ne m'en proiés ja mais; / Sachiés de voir c'est parole gastee" (vv. 447–49; "So I shall love him by whom I am well loved. Leave me alone, do not ask me again; know truly that it is wasted breath"). The words of the song, which have been altered by Gerbert, suit their new context perfectly.[15] The choice of genre, on the other hand, is ironic, for where the original singer pro-

---

14. The language of the song obviously presented problems for the scribes. Ms. A contains a French translation of this song; B has a garbled provençal text of another song; D has a French version of the latter; and C has another variant of the same song. Cf. ed. cit., p. lxxxv and p. 16, note to vv. 324–31. Paden, "Old Occitan," argues that the ideal of *fin' amors* was as problematic for Gerbert as the language was for the scribes.

15. Cf. Boogaard, p. 198, No. 1186. Gerbert has substituted this refrain for "Quant plus me bat et destraint li jalous, tant ai je pluz en amours ma pensee" (Boogaard, p. 231, No. 1555). See Jeanroy, *Origines*, pp. 496–98 for the original text by Moniot d'Arras.

claimed her infidelity to her husband, Euriaut uses those same words to declare her loyalty to her first love.

The villain is not above treachery, however, and bribes a servant in order to spy upon the girl in her bath. When he returns to court, Lisiart uses his knowledge of the birthmark (the *violette*) on her breast to prove his conquest of Euriaut. He is declared the winner and is awarded the castle of Nevers, which was part of the wager. Enraged and humiliated, Gerart refuses to believe Euriaut's protestations of innocence; he threatens her, and finally abandons her in the forest. She is rescued by the Duke of Metz, who is instantly smitten. In an attempt to comfort her, he sings a stanza by Gace Brulé:

> Cil qui d'amours me conselle
> Que de li doie partir
> Ne set pas qui me resvelle
> Ne quel sont mi grief souspir.
> (vv. 1266–69)

[He who counsels me that I should leave love does not know what rouses me nor what are my grievous sighs.]

The song expresses his feelings and serves as a response before the fact to those who may advise him to shun "une esgaree fole" (v. 1243). If the duke is happy in thinking he has found a love that suits him, his choice of song is again ironic. The duke would be better advised to heed his own counsel: "Cil fait trop niche folie / Qui s'entremet del mestier / Dont il ne se set aidier" (1273–75; "He commits a stupid folly who undertakes a trade that he does not know how to ply"). The beleaguered Euriaut is obliged to feign madness in order to evade his attentions.

Once rid of Euriaut, Gerart recalls earlier victims of feminine treachery (Absalom and Solomon) and concludes, in terms virtually repeated in his next song, that the love of women must not be trusted: "Nus ne doit s'amie essaier; / Ki l'a, em pais le doit laissier / Sans esprouver de nule chose" (vv. 1308–10; "No one should test his beloved; whoever has her should leave her in peace without testing anything"). This song is interesting in its relationship to the monologue, which gives a pair of specific examples, while the stanza itself serves to clinch the argument. It is the first example in the romance of Gerbert's effort to integrate a quotation into the speech of his characters.

Meanwhile, wanting to know the worst, Gerart returns to Nevers, disguises himself as a minstrel, and offers to sing for the new master of the castle. In this guise, he overhears Lisiart and his accomplice discussing their conspiracy, and discovers Euriaut's innocence.

Although the lovers are separated for nearly four-fifths of the work, the lady Euriaut is kept present for the audience through Gerart's recollection of her. As soon as he discovers Lisiart's treachery, Gerart sets out in pursuit of Euriaut, encountering a variety of adventures on the way. He begins his search in Burgundy, where he rescues the beseiged lady of Vergy, but is wounded. He rides on to Châlons, where he is obliged to rest. The girl caring for him recalls him to his quest when she sings a *chanson de toile*: "Siet soi biele Eurïaus, seule est enclose" (v. 2303; "There sits the lovely Euriaut, enclosed, alone").[16] The sound of her name makes him *pensis* (v. 2315; "melancholy"), and he reproaches himself in a monologue:

"Las! fait il, cis maus m'a dechut,
Quant jou ai si longhement jut;
Assés puis jesir et chi estre;
Ja ne sarai ne liu ne l'estre,
Ou m'amie puisse trouver."
(vv. 2316–20)

["Alas!" he says, "this pain has betrayed me, for I have lain such a long time. I can lie enough and rest here; I will never know the place where I may find my beloved."]

He goes on to attribute his weakened state to his neglect of his lady, for his love was the source of his strength. He ends on a more vigorous note, determined to triumph over his *mal* and to find Euriaut. Then, to comfort himself, he sings a stanza of an otherwise unknown *chanson*: "Amors, quant m'iert ceste painne achievee / Qui si me fait a grant dolour languir?" (vv. 2339–40; "Love, when will this pain end, that has made me languish with such great sorrow?"). In the monologue, the pain of remorse intensifies the physical pain of his wound, and the dual sense of the word "pain" shapes the meaning of the stanza, which would in another context refer simply to the pain of love. This combination of monologue and song is not repeated

---

16. This is one of several songs used to advance the plot. Cf. below, Chapter 4, n. 9. This song is not attested elsewhere, and it is possible that it was written by Gerbert.

in the *Violette*. Although Gerart sings four more *chansons* in similar circumstances, they replace rather than complement any other expression of his emotions. Nevertheless, the relationship of the paired elements in this passage shows that the meaning of the songs is not obvious, but depends upon the context of insertion.

Gerart next stops at Cologne to aid the Duke Miles, besieged by the Saxons, and distinguishes himself in battle. Both the duke's daughter Aiglente and her servant Florentine fall in love with him. After the defeat of the Saxons, Gerart stays at the duke's castle. One evening, he is obliged to withdraw from the company when he is overwhelmed with sorrow for his lost Euriaut. While he is so preoccupied, he remembers a song that suits his mood:

> Destrois, pensis, en esmai,
> Cant de bonne amor souspris,
> Et faic semblant cointe et gai
> La ou sui plus d'ire espris.
> (vv. 3236–39)

> [Afflicted, melancholy, worried, I sing surprised by love and pretend to be gracious and gay where I am smitten with anger.]

Unfortunately, Aiglente overhears his song and assumes it is meant for her. When he rebuffs her advances, she resorts to a love potion, and the bespelled Gerart sings two songs inspired by his new lady.

The first of these follows a short speech in which he says he is afraid to address Aiglente because he is uncertain of her feelings. Though it fits the context well enough, the song (vv. 3641–47), an expression of his love and desire, is juxtaposed to the speech, rather than related to it. At the same time that his song reveals to the audience the strength of his infatuation with Aiglente, Gerart dashes the hopes of her servant girl, who also loves him. On hearing his song, the servant realizes that her mistress's schemes have succeeded, and that she has no chance.

Gerart's next song is likewise inspired by Aiglente. One day while riding in the forest he hears the song of a lark and is filled with joy; he thinks of his new lady and sings a *son poitevin*:

> Quant voi la loëte moder
> De joi ses eles contrel rai,

Qui s'oblide et laisse cader
Per la douçor qu'al cor li vai,
Diex! tant grant envide mi fai
De li quant vi la jausion!
(vv. 4187–92)

[When I see the lark, who forgets himself and lets himself fall, beat his wings against the sun for joy, for the sweetness that pierces his heart, God! how greatly I envy him when I see his rejoicing.]

The song, a version of a stanza by Bernart de Ventadorn, is dramatic evidence of Gerart's infidelity to Euriaut. There are only two Occitan songs in the romance, both by Bernart, and both sung by the principal characters of the romance: Euriaut's song symbolizes her loyalty, while Gerart's signals his lapse. Not only does he sing in circumstances identical to those that have earlier reminded him of Euriaut, but his quotation of a troubadour song invites judgment according to the rules of *fin'amors*. Text and song are further linked by the reference to the lark, who plays a decisive role in the plot. This is the bird that carried off Euriaut's ring, and now drops it in Gerart's hand. The ring, a symbol of his love for Euriaut, is sufficient to undo the spell of the potion and recall the hero to his quest.

Once he resumes his search, the thought of Euriaut moves Gerart to sing twice more, first a *refrain* that reflects his initial optimism: "Volentiers verroie / Cui sui amis; / Diex m'i maint a joie!" (vv. 4478–80; "Willingly would I see her whose lover I am; God grant me joy!"), and then a *chanson* by the Châtelain de Couci. The stanza quoted reflects the hero's discouragement at his continued failure to find a trace of Euriaut:

Et quant recort sa simple cortoisie
Et son douc vis et son vïaire cler,
Comment me puet li cuers el cors durer?
(vv. 4628–30)

[And when I recall her simple courtesy, her sweet face and her clear mien, how can my heart remain in my body?]

Whereas the poet wondered at his own ability to survive separation, his words, when sung by Gerart, take on a suggestion of guilt and anxiety—one that the audience knows to be well founded.

Gerart's travels finally take him to the vicinity of Metz, where he learns that a beautiful woman found by the duke in Burgundy is to be tried for murder. He arrives barely in time to offer himself as Euriaut's champion in a judicial combat. The pair exchange songs as they are reunited, and Gerart, after rescuing Euriaut, manages to expose Lisiart's earlier treachery and to regain his castle.[17]

As with his use of *refrains* in descriptive passages, Gerbert de Montreuil helped to establish as conventional the use of the hero's thought or memory of the heroine to prompt the singing of a *chanson*. Each of the four songs just discussed is introduced by a reference to remembering the lady (vv. 3227, 4621), her beauty (v. 3638, here Aiglente), or "fine amors" (v. 4184). As we have seen, three of these songs replace any other indication of the hero's sentiments, while one (beginning v. 3641) is juxtaposed to a speech made to another character.

The technique, applied to both hero and heroine, establishes a comparison between them, while the plot demonstrates Gerart's failure to live up to the ideal to which they both adhere. Although two other characters, the Duke of Metz and the daughter of the Lord of Bien Asis (or Illes Pertes, 5051–58), express themselves in this way, their songs are an immediate response to a situation, and are not therefore associated with memory. Their passion is thus shown to be of recent origin, and of less importance than the love of Gerart and Euriaut. We shall see how important this association between memory and song will become for the successors of Gerbert de Montreuil.

Roman de Tristan en Prose

The next major work in which inserted lyrics were employed for expressive purposes is different in both form and length from the first two. Although the *Roman de Tristan en Prose* may have been composed as early as 1225–30,[18] the extant versions seem to have been compiled no earlier than 1240.[19] The romance contains a substantial amount of lyric material, but the exact number of insertions cannot be established with any certainty until the edition undertaken by Renée L. Curtis and continued by Philippe Ménard

---

17. See below, Chapter 5, n. 37 on the songs in dialogue.
18. Eugène Vinaver, *Etudes sur le "Tristan" en prose: Les sources, les manuscrits, bibliographie critique* (Paris: Champion, 1925).
19. Emmanuèle Baumgartner, *Le "Tristan en prose": Essai d'interprétation d'un roman médiéval*, Publications romanes et françaises, 133 (Geneva: Droz, 1975), pp. 85–87.

is completed.[20] To the fifteen *lais* and six *lettres en forme de lai* listed by Emmanuèle Baumgartner in her study of the romance, I have added another from Paris, B.N. fr. 757.[21] The chronological relationship of the songs and the romance is a question that I have not tried to settle. Jean Maillard maintains that the lyrics are older than the text in which they survive,[22] and his opinion is accepted by Pierre Bec.[23] Jeanne Lods, on the other hand, suggested that some of the *lais* are due to later redactors,[24] a position supported by Renée Curtis, who has concluded that the idea of including lyric insertions is attributable to the second of the two authors of the romance, Hélie de Boron.[25]

After a lengthy treatment of Tristan's youthful adventures, the prose romance retells the principal incidents of the legend: the combat with the Morholt, the love potion, the discovery of the lovers, the sojourn in the forest, and Tristan's marriage to Iseut of the White Hands. These events, however, occupy only a small portion of the whole work, most of which is

20. *Le roman de Tristan en prose*, 3 vols., Arthurian Studies 12–14 (Cambridge: D.S. Brewer, 1985; vol. 1 first published Munich: Max Hueber Verlag, 1963; vol. 2 first published Leiden: Brill, 1976). The edition includes only the first two *lais*. The next section of the romance has been edited by Philippe Ménard, *Le Roman de Tristan en prose*, I. *Des aventures de Lancelot à la fin de la "Folie Tristan,"* II. *Du bannissement de Tristan du royaume de Cornouailles à la fin du tournoi du Château des Pucelles*, ed. Marie-Luce Chênerie and Thierry Delcourt, TLF 353, 387 (Geneva: Droz, 1987, 1990), using different principles; see pp. 9–32. These volumes include the next three *lais*. For the narrative context of the remaining songs, I have consulted Paris, B.N. fr. 335–36, which, as Baumgartner (p. 85) points out, represents a version familiar to most medieval readers. For a different opinion of this version, see Renée L. Curtis, "Pour une édition définitive du *Tristan* en prose," *Cahiers de Civilisation Médiévale*, 24 (1981): 91–99. For recent studies see Emmanuèle Baumgartner, *La Harpe et l'épée: Tradition et renouvellement dans le* Tristan *en Prose* (Paris: SEDES, 1990), and Jean Dufournet, ed., *Nouvelles Recherches sur le* Tristan *en prose: Etudes recueillies* (Paris: Champion, 1990).

21. Baumgartner, *Le "Tristan en prose,"* pp. 298–300, lists twenty-seven verse insertions, but I have not considered the riddles (*devinailles*) because they are not songs. Jeanne Lods in "Les parties lyriques du *Tristan* en prose," *Bulletin Bibliographique de la Société Internationale Arthurienne*, 7 (1955): 73–78, includes as lyrics only those letters that are described as sung in the text. Seventeen of the *lais* with musical notation have been edited by T. Fotitch and R. Steiner, *Les lais du roman de Tristan en prose d'après le manuscrit de Vienne 2542*, Münchener romanistische Arbeiten, 38 (Munich: Wilhelm Fink, 1974). See also Emmanuèle Baumgartner, "Sur les pièces lyriques du *Tristan* en prose," *Etudes de langue et de littérature du moyen âge offerts à Félix Lecoy* (Paris: Champion, 1973), pp. 19–25. The series of *lais* composed by members of the Arthurian court at Tristan's funeral found only in Paris, B.N., fr. 24400 seems not to be part of the main tradition.

22. Jean Maillard, *Evolution et esthétique du lai lyrique des origines à la fin du XIVe siècle* (Paris: Université de Paris, 1963), p. 85.

23. Bec, *La lyrique française*, I, pp. 208–9.

24. Lods, "Les parties lyriques," p. 78.

25. *Le roman de Tristan*, III, p. xxvii. On the authorship, see R. L. Curtis, "Who Wrote the *Prose Tristan*? A New Look at an Old Problem," *Neophilologus*, 67 (1983): 35–41; and "Les deux versions du *Tristan* en prose: examen de la théorie de Löseth," *Romania*, 84 (1963): 390–98; and "The Problems of the Authorship of the Prose Tristan," *Romania*, 79 (1958): 314–38. See also Baumgartner, *Le "Tristan en prose,"* pp. 88–98.

concerned with adventures of knights of the Round Table, based largely on material from the Vulgate Cycle.[26] The first part of the romance contains no insertions, although later in the text Tristan is said to have composed several *lais* during this period. Their insertion begins only after the major events of the love story have occurred.

Because this romance is less well-known and less easily accessible than most of the other works under consideration, it will be useful to list the *lais* together with an indication of who sings them and where they occur in the plot.

Some time after his marriage to Iseut of the White Hands, Tristan, accompanied by his brother-in-law Kaherdin, returns to Cornwall at the queen's request. Kaherdin falls in love with Iseut la Blonde, who attempts to spare the feelings of Tristan's friend. When Tristan finds a letter she had written to console Kaherdin, he thinks that she is in love with his friend, and mad with grief, he flees to the forest. It is here that he composes the first inserted *lai*. This *lai*, together with the next four, form a distinct group; they all arise from the misunderstanding between Tristan and Iseut caused by Kaherdin's passion for the queen. The first pair clearly echo each other, while the next three appear quite close to each other in the text. The group may be summarized briefly as follows:

1. *Lai Mortel of Tristan* (Löseth §80), "Ja fis chançonetes et lais";
2. *Lai Mortel of Iseut* (Löseth §91), "Li solex luist et clers et biaux," sung by Iseut as she prepares to kill herself after hearing a false report of Tristan's death;
3. First *Lai of Kaherdin* (Löseth §100), "A vous, Amours ains c'a nului," composed by Kaherdin, and sung to Iseut by a minstrel to plead with her for mercy;
4. *Lai of Iseut* (Löseth §100), "Folie n'est pas vaselage," is Iseut's scornful response to Kaherdin;
5. Last *Lai of Kaherdin* (Löseth §100), "En mourant de si douche mort," composed by Kaherdin as he dies of his hopeless love, sung to Iseut by a minstrel.

Still mad, Tristan returns to Cornwall, where he is cured by Iseut and then banished. He then goes incognito to Arthur's court, where he meets

26. Cf. E. Löseth, *Le roman en prose de Tristan, le roman de Palamède et la compilation de Rusticien de Pise: Analyse critique d'après les mss. de Paris*, Bibliothèque de l'Ecole des hautes études, 82 (Paris: E. Bouillon, 1890–91; repr. New York: Burt Franklin, 1970); the first three volumes of Curtis's edition cover 91 of some 600 paragraphs in Löseth's summary; Ménard's volumes cover §§92–104 and 105–55.

the knight Dinadan. The pair have various adventures together before Tristan returns to Camelot for a tournament. He distinguishes himself, is presented to Arthur's court, and is made a member of the Round Table. King Mark, hearing of Tristan's success, and fearing him, decides to kill his nephew. It is while he is in search of Tristan that Mark overhears the sixth inserted *lai*. This is the *Lai of Lamorat* (Löseth §210), "Sans cuer sui et sans cuer remain," composed and sung by Lamorat, who loves the mother of Gawain and Gaheriet. In his song, he compares his situation to that of Tristan.

After a series of adventures, Mark is imprisoned at Arthur's court. Upon Mark's release, Arthur makes him promise to pardon Tristan, but he continues to worry about Tristan's well-being. Tristan returns to Cornwall and sends *lettres en forme de lai* to Arthur's court to reassure them and to ask for news; he receives replies in the same form from both Lancelot and Arthur. This correspondence constitutes the following series of inserted lyrics (Löseth §§262–63):

7. Verse letter from Tristan to Arthur: "A vous roy qui bien estes roy";
8. Verse letter from Tristan to Lancelot: "A vous amis qui de bontés";
9. Verse letter from Lancelot to Tristan: "A vous Tristan beaux doux amis";
10. Verse letter from Arthur to Tristan: "A vous Tristan par prouesce."

Arthur also writes a letter in prose to Mark threatening him if anything happens to Tristan. In retaliation, Mark writes both to Arthur (in prose) and to Guinevere (in verse) about the queen's adultery. The latter, "Salue vous com le doy faire" (Löseth §266), is the eleventh insertion. Although Arthur fails to understand Mark's oblique hints, the letter to the queen suggests that her affair with Lancelot is common knowledge, and causes her great anxiety. The knight Dinadan decides to punish Mark for his ungallant conduct, and he composes the twelfth insertion, the *Lai Voir Disant* (Löseth §280), "Tant me suis de dire teüs." Dinadan sends a minstrel to perform the song, actually an extended insult, before King Mark at his court.[27]

While Tristan remains at the Cornish court, Mark's jealousy increases, until he secretly imprisons his nephew. Tristan is freed by Lancelot and embarks on a series of adventures interlaced with those of Arthur's knights, including Lamorat, who is killed by Gawain. Once freed by Perceval from

27. This *lai* is discussed in Chapter 3, under "Songs as Characterization."

another captivity, Tristan takes Iseut from Cornwall and goes with her to Camelot, and then to the Joyeuse Garde. He participates in the tournament at Louvezerp, where he is victorious and Iseut is received with approval. Palamède watches Tristan's success with a growing despair that he expresses in song in the thirteenth insertion, the *Lai of Palamède* (Löseth §384), "D'amours viennent li dous penser."

The description of Arthur's plenary court at Pentecost contains two insertions. Just before the banquet a knight arrives with a verse letter, "A toi rois Artus qui signeur" (No. 14, Löseth §393), predicting shame for the king. The knight then sings a final song ("Riens n'est qui ne viengne a sa fin," No. 15, Löseth §393), before killing himself in order to deny that satisfaction to his enemy, who has just arrived at the court.[28]

During the banquet Galahad takes the Siege Perilous; when the Grail quest is proclaimed, Tristan vows to participate for one year. At the end of this period, he overhears a *lai* sung by Helys, the son of the king who invaded Cornwall and was killed by Tristan. This *lai*, "Amours de vostre acordement," (Löseth §399), is the sixteenth insertion.

Although the term of his quest has passed, Tristan is waylaid by another adventure, and does not dare to visit Iseut until he has completed it. As he passes the Joyeuse Garde where they once lived together, he sings the *Lai of Tristan* (Löseth §404) "Lonc temps a que je ne vi chele," the seventeenth *lai*. Tristan falls ill, and when he does not return as he had promised, Iseut sends a verse letter (No. 18, "A vous, Tristran amis verai," Löseth §408) that is quoted when Tristan reads it. He sends her a message, but must finish the affair upon which he is engaged. The story of Erec is inserted at this point, then the narrative returns to Tristan, who encounters Palamède, after which the pair travel together. Near a fountain, they meet the wounded Knight of the Red Shield who insists upon jousting with them, even though he is too weak for a sword-fight. A few days later, as they cross the forest, they hear singing. The song is the *Lai of the Knight with the Red Shield*, "Vos qui n'amez traiez vous sus,"[29] (Löseth §453), the nineteenth insertion.

Tristan and Palamède have more adventures, then part company. Tristan travels incognito to a castle, and two *lais* are inserted into the description of his sojourn. The first, the *Lai de Victoire* ("Aprés chou que je vi

---

28. This incident has been published according to Paris, B.N., fr. 757 and fr. 336 by Colette-Anne van Coolput, *Aventures querant et le sens du monde. Aspects de la réception productive des premiers romans du graal cycliques dans le* Tristan en prose, Médievalia Lovaniensia, série. I.xiv, (Leuven: Leuven University Press, 1986), pp. 225–55.

29. This *lai* is preserved in Paris, B.N., fr. 757, f. 210.

victoire," No. 20, Löseth §469) is played by a female musician who discusses Tristan's compositions. In reply, Tristan sings the twenty-first insertion, the *Lai du Boire Pesant* ("La u jou fui dedans la mer," No. 21, Löseth §469) Upon hearing the song, the minstrel guesses his identity, but no one believes her.

Tristan finally arrives at the Joyeuse Garde and is reunited with Iseut. He leaves to release Palamède from captivity, meets Galahad, and undergoes a series of adventures. Mark invades Arthur's kingdom, abducts Iseut, and at Camelot, attacks Arthur, who is badly weakened by the deaths of knights during the Grail quest. Mark is finally defeated, but has already sent Iseut to Cornwall. Tristan sets off in pursuit, then rests at a castle where a young woman sings the *Lai mortel of Iseut*. Tristan answers with another, the *Lai of Tristan* (No. 22, Löseth §538) "D'amours vient mon chant et mon plour."[30] Tristan reaches Cornwall and manages to see Iseut, to whom he sings a *lai* not quoted. Andret overhears Tristan's song and alerts Mark. The king surprises the lovers and mortally wounds Tristan.

The most famous of Tristan's various *lais* (especially the *Lai de Boire Pesant* and the *Lai de Victoire*) will be discussed in Chapter 4 in terms of their role in the plot, but several others are of interest primarily as expressions of emotion. As in *Guillaume de Dole* and the *Violette*, the expressive *lais* in the *Tristan en Prose* are provoked by the *thought* of the beloved, but here the verb *penser* connotes intense and unhappy meditation. The context of Tristan's *Lai Mortel* is perhaps an extreme example, but worthy of attention; as the first song included in the romance, this *lai* sets a pattern for several others, including those sung by Kaherdin (3, 5), Lamorat (6), Palamède (13), and Helys (16).

The first *lai* is part of Tristan's response to his misinterpretation of Iseut's consoling letter to Kaherdin. Tristan leaps to the (false) conclusion that he has lost her love and flees to the forest in a state of despair that will lead to madness.[31] The state of sorrowing absorption that begins this descent is described at considerable length, but only in terms of its external signs.[32] A *demoiselle* who would like to console Tristan, is his only witness:

---

30. This *lai* has been printed by E. S. Murrell, "The Death of Tristan from Douce MS. 189," *PMLA*, 43 (1928): 343–83.
31. Renée L. Curtis has discussed this episode in "Tristan *Forsené*: The Episode of the Hero's Madness in the *Prose Tristan*," in *The Changing Face of Arthurian Romance: Essays on Arthurian Prose Romances in Memory of Cedric E. Pickford. A Tribute by the Members of the British Branch of the International Arthurian Society*, ed. Alison Adams et al. Arthurian Studies, 16 (Cambridge: D.S. Brewer, 1986), pp. 10–22.
32. On the love meditation, see E. M. Kennedy, "Royal Broodings and Lovers' Trances in the First Part of the Prose *Lancelot*," in *Mélanges de philologie et de littérature offerts à Jeanne*

> [elle] s'en vient devant Tristan et voit qu'il pensoit si durement qu'il n'entendoit a riens fors a ce solement d'ou son corroz li vient. La demoisele est devant li une grant piece, mes il ne la voit mie, ne ele ne li ose dire mot qu'il ne se corroçast. Il plaint et pleure au chief de piece, et sospire soventes foiz et detort ses mains. Et quant il a esté une grant piece en tel maniere sanz dire mot, il dit trop correciez durement: "Haro! Diex; com je suis morz! Fu onques mes nus hons si vilainement trahiz com je fui a ceste foiz?" Et quant il a dite ceste parole il se test, et recomence a penser. (Curtis, vol. III, p. 162, no. 861)

> [she comes before Tristan and sees that he was thinking so deeply that he perceived nothing but only what caused his trouble. The girl is before him a great while, but he does not see her, nor does she dare to say a word to him, lest he become angry. He laments and weeps for some time, and sighs often and wrings his hands. And when he has been like that for a long time without saying a word, he says, sorely afflicted, "Oh God! how I am dead! Was ever a man so betrayed as I have been this time!" And when he has said this, he becomes silent and begins again to think.]

The girl notes his insensibility to distraction, his pallor, tears, and sighs, but of his mental state she can only observe "il pensoit." This "thought" is clearly dangerous: "Je voi bien apertement que cest penser vos grieve tant que bien vos metroit a la mort" (Curtis, vol. III, p. 164, no. 862; "I see clearly that this thought grieves you so that it would bring you to death"). Tristan himself tells her: "Cest pensé qui au cuer me tient est si fort enbatuz en moi qu'il n'en porra jamés issir devant la mort" (ibid.; "This thought which holds my heart is so strongly rooted in me that it cannot leave before I die"). In trying to escape his would-be helper, Tristan rides through the forest until he comes to a fountain, where he once fought Palamède and spent three days with Iseut. These memories push him into a state of insensibility now called "duel" (Curtis, vol. III, p. 165, no. 865). Despite the melancholy nature of his meditation and his obvious pain, Tristan resents intensely any effort to rouse him. He persists in his reflections for eight days without food or drink, until the girl at last attracts his attention by playing the harp. The music rouses him, they discuss the *lais* he has composed to commemorate the great moments of his love affair, and the girl sings each of them in turn.[33] Tristan promises to sing for her the next day, then falls silent and "comence mout durement a penser" (Curtis, vol. III, p. 169, no.

Wathelet-Willem (Liège: Marche Romane, 1978), pp. 301–14. For the background, see D. R. Sutherland, "The Love Meditation in Courtly Literature: A Study of the Terminology and Its Development in Old Provençal and Old French," in *Studies in Medieval French Presented to Alfred Ewert in Honour of his Seventieth Birthday* (Oxford: Clarendon Press, 1961), pp. 165–93.

33. See below, Chapter 4, under "Song as Narration," for an account of this discussion.

869; "begins to think most grievously"). The *lai* is the product of these thoughts, for he has composed it:

> tot novel de la moie dolor et de ma mort. Et por ce que je l'ai fait encontre mon definement, l'ai je apelé Lai Mortel; de la chose li trai le non. (Ibid., no. 870)
>
> [newly from my sorrow and my death. Because I have made it at my death, I have called it the *Lai Mortel*. From the fact I took the name.]

He begins his *lai* by repeating the announcement that it will be his last, and links the themes of Love and Death. These themes run through the song, emphasized by the play on the words *mors* and *amors*. The love which he has treasured is now killing him and he compares it to the bite of a serpent:

> D'amors m'est ensi avenu
> Com a celi qui a tenu
> En son seig le serpent tout nu
> Et puis en est a mort venu.[34]
>
> [From love has it happened to me as to the one who held a snake to his naked breast, and then died from it.]

The image evokes his sense of betrayal by the two people he most trusted. In the last third of his song, Tristan bids farewell to Iseut, his "douce anemie," and asks not to be forgotten.

Upon finishing his song, Tristan relapses into his painful meditation: "il se test tout maintenant que plus ne dit; et recomence son duel ausi grant com il avoit fait autre foiz" (Curtis, vol. III, p. 173, no. 871; "He falls silent and says no more, and begins again his sorrowing as intensely as he had done before"). He tries to kill himself, but cannot find his sword, and when he wanders madly into the forest, the girl gives him up for dead.

The scene is without parallel in the romance—no other character experiences a grief so profound, nor endures it for so long—but many of its features are repeated in other contexts. Kaherdin, Lamorat, Palamède, and Helys, like Tristan, sing *lais* while resting at a fountain. Although performed by secondary characters, each of these *lais* refers in some way to the central love affair. Kaherdin's, of course, is also inspired by his love for

---

34. This *lai* appears on pp. 170–73 of Curtis's edition, vol. III; quoted passage, p. 171, xii. It is also printed by Tatiana Fotitch and Ruth Steiner, *Les lais du roman de Tristan en prose*, pp. 19–30 and Bec, *La Lyrique française*, II, pp. 142–45.

Iseut. Unlike Tristan's, Kaherdin's *lai* is literally *mortel*, and he arranges for it to be sung to Iseut after his death. Lamorat, whose song is overheard by Mark, compares his own unhappy love affair with Tristan's. Tristan himself eavesdrops on the *lai* of Helys, which is inserted in the narrative after a description of Tristan's melancholy thoughts of Iseut. The verb used to describe the mental state of these singers is always "penser," and though it does not indicate such profound despair, their thoughts are always sorrowful. As in Tristan's case, the subject of these thoughts is expressed only in the *lai*, the fruit of the singer's reflection.

There is also some similarity between the context of certain of Gerart's songs in the *Violette* and those established for the *lais* of Lamorat, Palamède, and Helys, as well as the later one of Tristan. None of these songs is *mortel*, and each is inspired, during a period of separation, by the thought of the beloved. Tristan, responding to the springtime beauty of the forest, thinks of Iseut; in contrast to his *Lai Mortel,* there is here some description, both of his thoughts and of his emotions:

> Tristan va penssant a sa dame et recordant que par temps sera aconpli li ans qu'il ne la vit. Trop a esté dur et felon et de cuer orgueilleux qu'il a si longuement laissé qu'il ne la vit, ne pou ne grant. Or s'en reprent de tout son cuer; orendroit est il tant courouciés qu'il ne scet qu'il doie dire. Or est tout desesperés et nicement se reconforte, car il dit bien a soy meismes que desoremés retournera il assés tost et verra sa dame gente qui est beauté de tout le monde. (Paris, B.N., fr. 336, f. 127a)

> [Tristan goes thinking of his lady, and remembering that soon it will be a year since he has seen her. He had been too hard and cruel and proud of heart, for he had gone so long without seeing her at all. Now he repents of it with all his heart; now he is so afflicted that he does not know what he should say. He is now despairing and foolishly consoles himself, for he says to himself that now he will return soon and will see his gentle lady, who is the beauty of the whole world.]

As a result of Iseut's beauty, he composes verses "delictables a ouïr." In the short *lai* that follows, Tristan regrets his long absence:

> Lonc tans a que il ne vit chele
> Qui toute riens vaint de biauté.
> Pour coi que io [di] que se ele
> Me reprenoit de cruauté
> Raison seroit et loiauté.
> Elle est, madame et m'anchele.

Un an ai fait desloiauté
Se diex m'aïst, ceste durté
M'a mis lonc tans en obscurté.[35]

[It has been a long time since he has seen her who conquers everything with beauty. For this reason I say that if she reproaches me for cruelty, it would be right and loyal. She is my lady and my handmaid. For a year have I been disloyal, God help me; this hardness has for a long time embarrassed me.]

From this brief survey, it should be clear that most of the *lais* inserted in the prose *Tristan* are used (in combination with trance-like states) in much the same way that lyrics were used to replace monologues in the verse romances. In each case, the precise expression of emotion is confined to the quoted song, while the passage introducing it prepares for the quotation by describing the setting, often in terms derived from lyric poetry, particularly the "nature introduction." The song itself is prompted by the thought or remembrance of the loved one, and so serves as the expression of that thought.

La Chastelaine de Vergi

Composed near the middle of the thirteenth century, the *Chastelaine de Vergi* is unique in the way it employs its only lyric insertion.[36] Closer in form to *Guillaume de Dole* and the *Roman de la Violette* than to the prose *Tristan*, this short narrative poem contains the most striking example of a lyric quoted in order to describe a character's state of mind. The anonymous work uses a single insertion—a stanza from a *chanson* by the Châte-

---

35. No. 17 of my list; Fotitch and Steiner, p. 106–7. I have made the emendation suggested by the editors in their note to line 3.

36. Gaston Raynaud, ed., *La Chastelaine de Vergi: Poème du XIIIe siècle* (revised and corrected by Lucien Foulet), CFMA (Paris: Champion, 1921); Frederick Whitehead, *La Châtelaine de Vergi* (Manchester: Manchester University Press, 1944, 2nd ed., 1951); R. E. V. Stuip, *La Chastelaine de Vergi: Edition critique du ms B.N. f. fr. 375* (The Hague and Paris: Mouton, 1970). Attempts to date the work on the basis of historical events at the court of Burgundy in 1270 (Emil Lorenz, *Die altfranzösische Versnovelle von der Kastellanin von Vergi in spätern Bearbeitungen* [Halle, 1909]) have fallen into disrepute. For studies, see Paul Zumthor, "De la chanson au récit: 'La Châtelaine de Vergi,'" in *Langue, texte, enigme* (Paris: Seuil, 1975), pp. 219–36; Jean-Charles Payen, "Structure et sens de la 'Châtelaine de Vergi,'" *Le moyen âge*, 79 (1973): 209–50; and André Maraud, "Le lai de Lanval et la Châtelaine de Vergi: la structure narrative," *Romania*, 93 (1972): 433–59.

lain de Couci—to exemplify the emotional situation of the central character. Unlike the majority of lyric insertions, this stanza is not sung, or even recited by one of the characters in the story, but is cited by the author in an analytical passage. The stanza thus illustrates the emotions of a character who does not sing it, and forms part of the author's commentary on the story. Even though the author pays no attention to the musical character of the lyric, the quotation's status as part of a *chanson* is important, because that status is the source of its authority.

The plot of the *Chastelaine* is based on the folkloric motif of "Potiphar's wife" and contrasts strongly with the courtly ethos invoked by the author in the prologue. The hero, the accepted lover of the Châtelaine of Vergi, finds himself obliged to rebuff the amorous suggestions of the wife of his feudal lord, the Duke of Burgundy. The angry duchess complains to her husband of the knight's "improper advances." Confronted by the duke, the knight promises to do whatever is necessary to acquit himself. When asked to reveal the name of the lady he loves, he is caught between conflicting duties, for he has sworn, as proof of his love for the Châtelaine, to guard her secret. While trying to reach a decision, he thinks of his love for her:

> Et por ce qu'adés li sovient
> de la grant joie et du solaz
> q'il a eü entre ses braz,
> si se pensse, s'il la messert
> et s'il par son mesfet la pert,
> quant o soi ne l'en peut mener,
> comment porra sanz li durer.
> Si est en tel point autressi
> com li chastelains de Couci,
> qui au cuer n'avoit s'amor non,
> dist en un vers d'une chançon.
> (vv. 284–94)

[And because he remembers continually the great joy and solace that he had in her arms, he thinks to himself, if he fails in service to her, and if he loses her through his misdeed, when he cannot take her with him, how could he live without her. He is in the same situation as the Châtelain de Couci, who with nothing but love in his heart, said in the stanza of a song.]

In the quotation that follows, the poet regrets the necessity of parting from his lady, and wonders how he will survive the separation:

> Par Dieu, Amors, fort m'est a consirrer
> du dous solaz et de la compaingnie
> et des samblanz que m'i soloit moustrer
> cele qui m'ert et compaingne et amie:
> et quant regart sa simple cortoisie
> et les douz mos qu'a moi soloit parler,
> comment me puet li cuers ou cors durer?
> Quant il n'en part, certes trop est mauvés.
> (vv. 295–302)

[By God, Love, it is hard to do without the sweet solace and the company and the appearance that she used to show me, she who was my companion and my beloved; and when I consider her simple courtesy and the sweet words she used to say to me, how can my heart remain in my body? If it does not leave it, it is certainly too bad.]

Both the knight and the poet to whom he is compared enjoy a requited love threatened by separation. But while the poet speaks of his lady in the past tense ("ert"), the knight has a difficult choice before him. If he respects the Châtelaine's secret, he will be banished from the duchy and never see her again; if he speaks, he risks losing her love. In fact, he agonizes over the decision until the duke takes umbrage at his hesitation, which he interprets as a lack of confidence in his own discretion. Given this additional pressure, the prospect of separation from his lady impells the knight to speak. Unable to face exile without her, he takes a calculated risk and reveals his secret, trusting the duke to keep it.

The quotation of a stanza from the courtly repertoire has a significance in the new context beyond the meaning of its words. The author establishes a comparison between his hero and a famous poet-lover, and thus places him in the context of *fin' amors*. The song is a sign of the ideal to which the knight aspires, but at the same time, it moves him to betray that ideal. Like Gerart de Nevers and the emperor Conrad, who borrow *chansons* on their own behalf, the hero of the *Chastelaine de Vergi* is placed in an ironic relationship with a song that is said to suit his feelings. Though all three heroes betray their courtly ideal, only here is the outcome tragic, for the knight is betrayed by the duke and the duchess, and his lady kills herself.

Conte du Cheval de Fust, or Meliacin

Girart d'Amiens made more sophisticated use of lyric insertions in his *Conte du Cheval de Fust* (commonly called *Meliacin*, composed around 1290) than in his earlier *Escanor*.[37] *Meliacin* contains no fewer than twenty-four insertions: two *rondeaux*, one *refrain*, seven motets, and thirteen stanzas from *chansons* (four anonymous, the rest by known authors), as well as one complete *chanson* which may have been composed by Girart himself.[38] All but two of these insertions are attributed to the central couple, Meliacin and Celinde, though the heroine sings only four times. Most of Meliacin's eighteen songs are used to express his sentiments, including three sung at the request of minor characters and one which forms part of a speech to the Duke of Galice. Girart differed from his predecessors in abandoning completely the insertion of lyrics in descriptions of court life, and in developing a much more flexible treatment of songs as expressions of emotions. Like Jean Renart and Gerbert de Montreuil, Girart occasionally used songs to replace monologues. In other instances, he used monologues as settings for the lyric insertions, which might occur in the middle of the passage or provide a conclusion to it.

The plot of *Meliacin* is virtually identical to that of *Cleomadés* (probably composed somewhat earlier)[39]: The magician Clamazart, who is an ugly dwarf, presents a mechanical flying horse to Nubien, King of Ermenie. In return, the magician asks for the hand of Gloriande, the king's youngest and most beautiful daughter. Gloriande's brother Meliacin persuades their father not to allow the match, and the outraged Clamazart causes Meliacin to be carried away on the horse. Meliacin eventually discovers the levers that control the horse, and lands on the tower of a castle where, in a guarded room, he discovers Celinde. The pair promptly fall in love, but Meliacin is caught and imprisoned. Shortly after his escape, he elopes with

---

37. See below, Chapter 3, under "The Music of the Court," for a discussion of Girart's insertion of *refrains* in a passage of description in *Escanor*. The edition of Antoinette Saly, *Girart d'Amiens, Meliacin, ou le Cheval de Fust: Edition critique*, Senefiance, 27 (Aix-en Provence, 1990) replaces a partial edition by Paul Aebischer, *Girard d'Amiens, Le Roman du cheval de fust ou de Meliacin: Extraits publiés d'après le texte du ms. dans la Biblioteca Riccardiana de Florence avec une introduction et un glossaire réduit*, TLF, 212 (Geneva: Droz, 1974). The songs were first published in context by F. Stengel, "Die Liedercitate aus Girardin's d'Amiens *Conte du cheval de fust*," ZRP, 10 (1886): 460–76; the text of the songs was republished by A. Saly, "La chanson dans le *Meliacin*," *TLL*, 23. 2 (1985): 7–23. See also Gerard J. Brault, "Les Manuscrits des oeuvres de Girart d'Amiens," *Romania*, 80 (1959): 433–40.

38. Antoinette Saly, "La chanson du duc de Galice (*Meliacin*)," *TLL*, 12.2 (1974) 7–16.

39. See below, Chapter 4 for the plot of *Cleomadés*. On the relationship between the two romances, see Gaston Paris, HLF, 31 (1893), pp. 151–205.

Celinde, but she is abducted by Clamazart just before meeting Meliacin's family. After four years of adventures, Meliacin finally rescues Celinde, who has been feigning madness in order to evade the attentions of her protector, the Duke of Galice. The couple return to Ermenie, where all of the principal characters are married.

The first three *chansons* in *Meliacin* serve as the only clue to the sentiments of the singers at this early stage of the romance. Before the first *chanson*, Meliacin notices (vv. 2120–23) the "tans bel," and states that "fine amour" makes him sing for "la bele plaisant e sage" (Celinde), whom he has just met. His reaction to meeting Celinde is revealed only in the stanza: "Et pour ce i ai je mon cuer mis, / Car a nul plus plaisant mestier / Ne le sai aillors emploier" (vv. 2136–38; "And for this have I put my heart into it, for I know of no more pleasant occupation elsewhere"). On the second occasion, as he sets out to rejoin the lady, the thought of her reminds him of a *chant* by Gace Brulé,[40] in which he gives voice to his determination. It is Celinde who sings the third insertion, in a context similar to that of Meliacin's first song: "Amors" (v. 3680) makes her notice the "tans et bel et cler" (v. 3689) that causes her to think of a "ver" (v. 3692) of Perrin Angicourt. The song echoes the description of spring in the text, but goes on to voice Celinde's fear that she might have missed her chance to love:

> Comme oisel laissent lor cri
> Et lor chanter par froidure,
> Ai je longuement langui
> En pauour d'avoir failli
> A la grant bone aventure
> Dont Amors me rassegure.
> (vv. 3700–3705)

[As the birds leave off their chirping and their song in the cold, I have languished for a long time in the fear of having failed at the great adventure of which Love gives me confidence.]

As in the *Roman de la Violette*, the repetition of the motif by the heroine establishes an equality between the lovers and unites them even before they have declared their love. In yet another way, this song brings the pair

---

40. Vv. 3598–3607, "Cil qui d'Amours me conseille." This same stanza was used in the *Violette* by the Duke of Metz to express a similar idea; see above, under "*Roman de la Violette*."

together, for Meliacin overhears it and Celinde discovers him when he reacts to it in the fourth song.

Meliacin prefaces this song with a long monologue in which he regrets that Celinde's affections are already engaged (as he thinks) elsewhere. He cannot decide whether to approach her. At the end of this passage, he finds comfort in "le tans bel et la saison" (v. 3837) and declares: "ai esperance / k'Amours me face aucun tans riche" (vv. 3843–44; "I hope that Love will someday make me rich"). His changed mood is reflected in the song:

> Esperance d'amour que j'ai
> Et desir d'avoir amie
> Me font amoureus et gai.
> (vv. 3869–71)

> [The hope of Love that I have, and the desire to love a beloved, makes me loving and gay.]

As these quotations demonstrate, the *chanson* repeats in summary form the hopeful theme of the monologue at the same time that it serves to reunite the pair, who quickly resolve their misunderstanding and elope happily on the magic horse, exchanging songs as they fly.[41]

It is not until he discovers Celinde's abduction by the evil magician that Meliacin once more gives vent to his feelings in a song, this time combined with a monologue. Meliacin withdraws from the scene in a state of shock and begins to lament the loss of his love in terms that resemble those commonly used in courtly lyrics to describe the pain of unrequited love:

> Ha! faisoit il, tres douce amie,
> Comme pour vous sui esbahis!
> Tant en sui et mors et traïs
> Qu'a petit li cuers ne me fent.
> (vv. 5724–27)

> ["Ah!" he said, "most sweet lady, how I am frightened for you; so much am I wounded and betrayed by it that my heart almost breaks."]

---

41. See below, Chapter 5, for a discussion of songs used in dialogue.

The complaint gradually turns into a pledge of undying love, the thought of which reminds him of Celinde's perfection, and he lists her virtues. Once more he bewails her loss, but this time vows to search for her, inspired by hope, without which he would die. This hope reminds him of the god of Love, in whose favor he places his confidence. He ends the monologue with a vow of loyalty to Love, in return for success in his quest. The hopeful note on which he ends the monologue introduces his song:

> Bone aventure aviegne a fol espoir
> Qui vrais amans fait vivre et esjoïr!
> Desperance fait languir et doloir,
> Et mes fox cuers me fait cuidier garir;
> S'il fust sages, il me fesist mourir.
> Pour ce fait bon de la folie avoir,
> Qu'en trop grant sens voit on bien mescheoir.
> (vv. 5794–5800)

> [May good fortune come to foolish hope, which makes a true lover live and rejoice. Despair makes me languish and sorrow and my foolish heart makes me think I am cured. If it were wise, it would make me die; for this reason it is good to be foolish, for with too much sense one can come to grief.]

The stanza restates and sums up the major themes of the monologue: the despair caused by his loss; the necessity of hoping even in unpromising circumstances; the recognition that despair will surely result in failure; and the wish that his hope may be rewarded.

Meliacin's state of mind changes as a result of the monologue. If at the beginning he is stunned by the trick of fate, at the end he declares his intention of hoping against hope and enlists the aid of the god of Love. This alteration of mood, brought about by a close association of ideas, introduces the hopeful confidence expressed in the song. Both the monologue and the song reflect the ambivalent state of Meliacin's mind: full of hope, as he must be in order to accomplish his quest, yet susceptible to despair because of his grief. At the end of his song, Meliacin is no longer paralyzed by the enormity of his loss; motivated by "fol espoir," he is ready to pursue Celinde and undertake her rescue.

Girart varied the pattern slightly for the insertion of the tenth lyric, sung at the outset of the quest. As before, Meliacin responds to the vernal beauty around him, but as in many *chansons*, the joy of nature highlights the lover's misery, and his gloomy reflections rise to the surface: "Las, trop me fu tranchans / Li meschiés par coi je perdi / Ma dame" (vv. 5900–5902; "Alas, too wounding was the mischance by which I lost my lady"). After dwelling on Celinde's beauty, the joy she gave him, and her glance when he last saw her, Meliacin concludes by repeating his determination to regain his earlier happiness. His song echoes the motif of the parting glance and sums up the main ideas of the monologue:

Diex! La reverrai je ja,
La bele au cors gent,
Qui tant debonairement
Au partir me regarda?
Ains puis mes cuers n'oublia
Son tres douc acointement.
Et se je n'i sui souvent,
S'est tous jours mes penssers la,
Car doucement navré m'a
La bele qui mon cuer a.
(vv. 5984–93)

[God! Shall I ever see her again, the beauty with the fine figure who looked at me so sweetly at parting? Never can my heart forget her most sweet welcome. And if I am not with her often, my thoughts are always there, for she has sweetly wounded me, the beauty who has my heart.]

In this sequence of description of landscape, monologue, and song, Girart has used three types of discourse to treat the conventional themes of the courtly lyric. While the descriptive passage serves as the *introduction printanière*, and the hero articulates the relationship between his mood and his surroundings, the love and desire which are the natural conclusion of the sequence are expressed in the lyric form itself. Girart's originality in adapting the lyric insertion technique lies in achieving a narrative version of the movement of a *chanson d'amour*.[42]

[42]. Girart did not use lyric insertions exclusively in combination with monologues, and the eleventh and thirteenth songs are used in essentially the same way as those in the *Violette*. In each case the hero's response to the beauty of spring is to think of his lady and to comfort

Girart made the relationship between lyric and narrative, already close in the treatment of combinations of song and monologue, still more explicit in his treatment of the fifteenth insertion. In this passage Meliacin comes upon two girls singing as they make rose garlands, and he thanks them for the comfort they have given him. Although no songs occur in this passage, Girart has rendered narratively the situation found in many *reverdies*.[43] The girls engage him in conversation, and comment on his singing:

Vous avés hui .ii. chançons dites;
Je ne sai se vous les fesistes,
Mais trop en est plaisans li sons,
Et se nous savons vos chançons,
Trop volentiers les chanterommes:
Au mains, quant nous ne vous verrommes,
S'avrons nous tant de ramenbrance,
Et nous sera grant alejance.
Et vous chantés si gaiement,
Et si cler, et si doucement,
Et d'une si entire alaine
C'on ne trouveroit en cest raigne
Ame qu'a vous se peüst prendre.
(vv. 8990–9002)

[You have sung two songs today; I do not know if you composed them, but their melody is most pleasant, and if we knew your songs we would sing them willingly. At the least when we see you we will have so much remembrance and it will give us great consolation. And you sing so gaily, so clearly and so sweetly and with such good breath, that one could not find anyone in the kingdom to rival you.]

It is clear that Meliacin's performance, despite its melancholy inspiration, gives pleasure to his audience, who request another song as well as instruction from him. His singing is thus not simply an expression of his feelings,

---

himself in song. The passages introducing these insertions are all in the third person and confined to describing the hero's surroundings. His thoughts and feelings are indicated only in the songs he chooses. The fourteenth song, on the other hand, is introduced in the same way as the two just discussed, but is followed by a monologue devoted to Celinde's beauty. The twelfth song is used with a monologue, while the nineteenth comes at the conclusion of a long speech to another character.

43. On this genre see Bec, *La lyrique française*, pp. 136–41.

but has become an aspect of his public personality. Meliacin, like Tristan before him, has acquired authority as a singer. Although he feels little desire to sing, Meliacin is reluctant to disappoint his listeners, and performs a stanza by Richart de Fournival. In this episode, the lyrics take on a new role in the romance and are accompanied by a literary discussion, a type of metadiscourse reminiscent of Tristan's discussions of his own compositions. As a result, the songs are more firmly rooted in the enclosing text.

The sixteenth and seventeenth songs are quoted in similar circumstances. Meliacin, recovering from a wound, is engaged in conversation with a girl who asks him to sing. He obliges, choosing a song he has not sung before, one that may serve as a model to lovers:

> Ainsçois orrés toute premiere
> Un chant c'onques mais ne chantai,
> Car n'a gaires que le chant ai,
> Mais mout me plaist e me doit plaire,
> Quar d'Amour en tieng l'essamplaire,
> Dont ja iour n'ere recreüs.
> (vv. 10843–48)

> [Thus you will hear first a song that I have never sung before, for I have not had the melody for long, but it pleases me completely, for I consider it the model of love which I will never renounce.]

He goes on to say that he will serve his lady, through deeds and by composing songs, before performing a stanza attributed to Gerardin de Boulogne. At the end of his song, he tries to explain his feelings to his listener: there is no remedy for his sorrow and so he must take comfort in it. These reflections prompt him to sing once more, and he chooses a motet, "un chant / ke j'ai fait pour ma douce dame."[44] Here again, Meliacin is presented not merely as a character who (like the protagonists of earlier romances) expresses his feelings in songs borrowed from the current repertoire, but as a lover and poet. This portrayal of Meliacin may have been modeled on the legendary lover-singer Tristan; there are striking similarities between the two characters even if Meliacin's situation is not as desperate as Tristan's. The idea of telling the story of a poet-lover was

---

44. Vv. 10928–29. The actual authorship of the quoted songs is less important here than the way the author presents the hero.

developed more fully by Jakemés, who chose the celebrated *trouvère*, the Châtelain de Couci, as the hero of his romance. The Châtelain in turn anticipated the figure of the lover-poet-narrator of the *dit*, which dominated the fourteenth century.

In addition to the flexibility with which he manipulated the lyric insertion device, and the variety of contexts he created for his quotations, Girart distinguished himself from his predecessors by his attitude toward the songs. Whereas Jean Renart and Gerbert de Montreuil seem to have exploited more or less systematically the ironic potential of their quotations, irony is conspicuously absent from *Meliacin*. The songs occur in contexts so carefully prepared that they always seem appropriate to the hero's situation and state of mind. Meliacin, unlike Conrad and Gerart, comes close to living up to the ideal of love that he espouses in his songs. Girart's hero seems to announce the Châtelain de Couci, for the songs of both are emblems of their fidelity to love.

Roman du Castelain de Couci et de la Dame de Fayel

The sixth narrative work we shall consider here, the *Roman du Castelain de Couci et de la Dame de Fayel*, was composed by Jakemés Sakesep about a decade after the appearance of *Meliacin*.[45] Jakemés chose as his hero the *trouvère* of the title and wove a romance around the few biographical indications in the *chansons* of his composition that had survived. Much of the plot of the romance is constructed to account for the composition of the songs. The songs, therefore, are for the first time central to the story. Indeed, they are its very source, and consequently are generally quoted in their entirety. The romance contains ten insertions: six *chansons* and one *virelai* attributed in the romance to the Châtelain de Couci, and three *rondeaux*. The attribution of one of these lyrics (the first *chanson*, vv. 362–406) is doubtful, while another (the fourth *chanson*, vv. 5952–91) is certainly the work of Gace Brulé; the *virelai* and two of the *rondeaux* are *unica* that may well be the work of Jakemés himself.[46]

The choice of a poet as hero had important consequences for the

---

45. Maurice Delbouille and John E. Matzke, eds., SATF (Paris and Abbeville: F. Paillart, 1936). See p. lxxiv for a discussion of the date: after 1285, at the end of the thirteenth or the beginning of the fourteenth century.
46. On the attribution of the songs see A. Lerond, ed., *Chansons attribuées au Châtelain de Couci* (Paris: Presses Universitaires de France, 1964), pp. 36–44.

romance, for it altered the relationship between the singer and his songs, as well as that between the two modes of discourse. When Conrad, Gerart, and Meliacin chose songs from the repertoire, and in so doing declared their adherence to an ideology of love, they appropriated the emotional expressions of others. Both Jean Renart and Gerbert de Montreuil exploited the resulting ironic potential fairly consistently. Girart's Meliacin, on the other hand, was successful in living up to his ideal, and became a poet himself by the end of the romance. By contrast Renaut, the Châtelain de Couci, created *chansons d'amour* in response to his passion for the Dame de Fayel. From the beginning of Jakemés's romance he is not merely an adherent of *fin' amors,* but an exemplar of it. Since the songs are supposed to grow out of the development of the plot, it is important that they be quoted in full.[47] This necessary, logical connection between song and story is, of course, only notional, and Jakemés apparently found himself obliged to select, as had his predecessors: he did not include the whole corpus of the Châtelain's poems, and as we have noted, he substituted at least one by another poet, and others perhaps of his own composition.

Although the outline of the plot appears to be based on the few events known of the life of Gui de Thourotte, Châtelain de Couci from 1186 to 1202, it was greatly embellished by the folkloric motif of the *coeur mangé*. Renaut, the fictional hero, a worthy, courtly knight of small estate, falls in love with the Dame de Fayel, the most noble and beautiful lady of the region and the wife of his neighbor. One day Renaut goes to visit her, but is so overcome with emotion that he can scarcely speak. When he explains his distress, she rebuffs him, declaring that she will remain faithful to her husband. Nevertheless, she is touched by his sincerity and follows his career with interest. He decides to address her again, but this time in a song which he has a minstrel perform for her.

Renaut has two ends in view in composing the first song: the service he owes to Love and his wish to inform his lady of his desire. The song is not presented as the immediate response to an overmastering emotion. Jakemés attributes the song to his hero's desire to serve Love completely, but does not provide any further details about his state of mind. It is the song itself, and not the context into which it is set, that must explain his emotions. While intended to convince the Dame de Fayel of his passion and his good faith, this song also demonstrates Renaut's skill as poet and

---

47. As opposed to single stanzas quoted by a character because they happen to be (or are said by the author to be) appropriate, as in earlier verse romances. The *lais* in the *Tristan en Prose* were quoted in full and may well have been composed for their contexts.

establishes him as a *fin' amant*. Unlike false lovers who "se plaignent sans dolour" (v. 369; "complain without sorrow"), he is moved by Love itself to admire her for her great merit:

> Bien m'a amours atournee
> Douce painne et douc labour,
> Ne ja pour riens qui soit nee
> N'oublierai ceste honnour
> D'amer toute la meillour
> Que par les boins soit loee.
> (vv. 386–91)

[Truly has Love prepared sweet pain and sweet labor for me, nor shall I ever, for anything born forget this honor of loving the best, may she be praised by the good.]

He ends, as he began, by distancing himself from "li autre enquerreour" (v. 398; "the other suitors") who turn joy into sorrow, and he confines his actual request to the *envoi*. Jakemés goes on to recount the "publication" of the song: Renaut teaches it to a "menestrel" (v. 407), who is to sing it wherever he can until he is able to perform it for the Dame de Fayel. This first song serves as an emblem of Renaut's love, but at the same time establishes his credentials as a working poet as well as a lover.

The remaining five *chansons* mark the progression of the love affair and are composed in reaction to its principal events: Renaut's second meeting with the lady, her failure to admit him to a promised nocturnal interview, their exposure, separation, and death.

After a more successful interview with the lady, in which she gives him a sleeve to wear on his lance, the Châtelain composes a second *chanson* that replaces any other statement of his feelings, whether in monologue or description. On the contrary, it is the lady's sentiments that are analyzed in the passage preceding the lyric. The Châtelain's song is introduced only indirectly, by an examination of his lady's inner debate and her efforts to resist her growing love. His song counterbalances and contrasts with the preceding analysis. His reason for singing, not indicated in the narrative, is stated in the first stanza:

> Or ai talent que canch pour resbaudir;
> Bien doi canter, puis qu'il vient a plaisir

Celi qui j'ai fait de coer liet hommage;
Si doi avoir grant joie en mon corage,
S'elle me voet a son oés retenir.
(vv. 819–23)

[Now I wish to sing in order to rejoice. Indeed I must sing, because it pleases her to whom I have done homage with my heart. So I must have great joy in my spirit, if she wishes to retain me for her bidding.]

As we have seen, the lady has indeed found his song pleasing, for she has given him encouragement. The stanza thus coincides perfectly with its context. Renaut goes on to describe the effect of her beauty on him, and in the third stanza compares himself with Tristan: "C'onques Tristans qui but le buverage / Si loiaument n'ama sans departir" (vv. 834–35; "For never did Tristan, who drank the love potion, love so loyally without division"). With the reference to the "buverage" he claims superiority even to this legendary lover, for he is completely devoted to love without benefit of magic. This allusion and his fear of the "fole gent volage," (v. 850) cast a shadow over his joy and foreshadow the end of the romance.

The third song, composed in response to being tested by the Dame de Fayel, is the only one to be combined with a monologue, albeit a very short one. Having promised him admission to her room, she decides instead to leave him standing at the gate in the rain. Renaut complains of her caprice in a brief speech (seven lines): "Las! je cuidoie avoir amie, / Mais g'i ai bien dou tout fali!" (vv. 2577–78; "Alas, I thought I had a lover, but I have failed completely"). Jakemés then asserts a change of mood: "Mais Esperance l'esvigure" (v. 2584; "but Hope invigorates him"), and then Renaut composes a song "selonc çou ke son coer sentoit" (v. 2589; "according to what his heart feels"). The three stanzas quoted reflect the shifts of emotion just described. The opening contrast between the joy of spring and his pain leads to a pledge of perseverance despite the apparent folly of this course, for "en la fin iert grans li guerredons" (v. 2613; "in the end the reward will be great").

The next song does not occur until the love affair has been guessed by the Dame de Vermandois and disclosed to the lord of Fayel. The lovers are separated for some time, but the Châtelain manages to retaliate by humiliating the Dame de Vermandois. The song that follows this account is scarcely introduced at all. Hope sustains the hero, who "son tamps emploie en honnesté" (v. 5951; "employs his time honestly"); the quotation follows immediately, and seems ill-suited to its context. Although the complaints of his sufferings and his fear that the "conseil de la fausse vilainne" (v. 5965; "advice of the false traitoress") might end the affair are appropriate enough, the admonitions to his lady to take pity on him are surprising here. This song, though it comes in the middle of the affair, marks the end of their security. Henceforth, their meetings are achieved by means of ruses and disguises worthy of Tristan, and are overshadowed by the growing jealousy of the Sire de Fayel.

Eventually, the jealous husband tricks his rival into pledging to undertake a crusade. Renaut does so because he thinks that the Sire de Fayel is to do likewise, and he sings a single stanza of a *chanson* in happy anticipation of a quick end to the separation. His wish at the end of the stanza is ambiguous because Renaut does not anticipate a definitive separation:

Or me laist Dieus a tel honnour monter
Que celle k'aim entre mes bras nuette
Tiengne une fois ains que voise outre mer!
(vv. 7009–11)

[Now may God let me rise to such honor that I may hold the one I love naked in my arms once before I go abroad.]

It takes on an added poignancy as the reader realizes the true state of affairs. Once Renaut is aware of the trick, he takes his leave of his lady and sings again in a different vein. This song, with its allusions to the "vilains" (v. 7376) who separates the lovers, and to the "fol losengeour" (v. 7379), translates accurately the Châtelain's grief and anger, and the last stanza repeats the leave-taking that has just occured: "Jou m'en vois, dame! A Dieu li creatour / Vous commanch jou, en quel liu que je soie" (vv. 7387–88; "I leave you my lady, I commend you to God the creator wherever I may be"). Neither of these songs accompanies a monologue or a passage of analysis. The first follows the brief notation that the singer's heart was "deduisant et liet" (7002; "delighted and happy"), while before the second Renaut is pensive and silent (v. 7341). Both, however, are responses to the thought or memory of the beloved.

As we have seen, Jakemés inserted the *chansons* in the *Castelain de Couci* in essentially the same manner established by Jean Renart: they are juxtaposed to the narrative text and are introduced only by a short transitional passage. The spare indications of the singer's frame of mind are made precise by the quoted stanzas themselves. The novelty of Jakemés's technique is his almost consistent use of complete songs: only once does he content himself with a single stanza. Where Girart d'Amiens used passages of interior monologue to replace parts of the lyric movement and to account for the use of the song, Jakemés used a complete song and dispensed with the monologue. Since his hero was a poet, what could be more natural than for his emotional expression to be cast in *chanson* form? Furthermore, the sheer length of the quoted passages gives considerable scope for expression and makes it a more than adequate replacement for a monologue.

There are two songs (the second vv. 816–55, and the third vv. 2591–2614) that *are* associated with monologues, but Jakemés's technique in associating the two elements differs markedly from that of his predecessors. Instead of growing out of the monologue as its logical conclusion, the Châtelain's third song is a hopeful reply to the despair and disappointment expressed in his monologue. His second song is used in a yet different manner, as it balances and contrasts with a monologue by his lady.

However innovative and effective we may find Jakemés's manipulation of lyric insertions on a technical level,[48] inconsistencies remain between the plot and the songs it is supposed to explain. It is clear that the *Castelain de Couci* is not a biography, but a work in the tradition of Jean Renart's *Roman de la Rose*, the *Roman de la Violette*, and *Meliacin*: it is a *roman d'aventures* that incorporates lyric insertions. While casting the hero as a poet accounts for the insertions, the two elements remain separate. It is not until the poet himself tells the story of the songs in the *dit amoureux* that they blend together.

Meliador

A gap of six or seven decades separates the *Castelain de Couci* from the next work to make significant use of inserted lyrics for expressive purposes, the *Roman de Meliador* of Jean Froissart. This a very different sort of narrative. Froissart, in incorporating lyric insertions into his romance, confronted a situation unparalleled in the corpus. He seems, in 1382–83, to have revised a

---

48. M. Delbouille, in the introduction to his edition (p. lxiv), was not convinced of the effectiveness of the songs attributed to the Châtelain: "les pièces n'ont, par leur contenu, que des liens souvent fort lâches avec l'épisode où elles sont introduites." Most of his skepticism, however, is provoked by the last insertion, the *virelai* said to be composed by the dying hero. Unrecorded elsewhere, this piece may well be the work of Jakemés, but it accords poorly with the context in its form (a dance song) as well as in its content.

work composed earlier, and to have used it as a setting for the poems of his patron Wenceslas de Luxembourg, Duke of Brabant.[49] His decision to include *all* of Wenceslas's songs meant that he could not, as had other poets using borrowed songs, choose what he needed from the repertoire.[50]

The second *Meliador*, as Dembowski has demonstrated, was in fact the result of a collaboration between Froissart and Wenceslas, and consequently it is important to examine the relationship between poet and patron. If others of his patrons encouraged Froissart as a chronicler, it was Wenceslas who most shared his poetic interests. As Duke of Brabant, Wenceslas maintained at Brussels a splendid court noted for its feasts and tournaments. He shared Froissart's view of chivalry as a constant search for glory and honor acquired through knightly exploits and celebrated by poetry. Other aspects of this relationship, exemplified in Froissart's *Prison Amoureuse,* will be discussed in Chapter 6, but for *Meliador*, it is the mutual belief in chivalric poetry that is of central importance. Whatever criticism may be directed at Wenceslas's poetic skill,[51] Froissart paid Wenceslas the

---

49. Auguste Longnon, ed., *Meliador par Jean Froissart: Roman comprenant les poésies lyriques de Wenceslas de Bohème duc de Luxembourg et de Brabant*, 3 vols. SATF (Paris: Firmin Didot, 1895–99); see pp. xliii–lii on the two redactions, and pp. lii–lxxiv for the date. He placed the first version shortly after 1365 and the revision between 1370 and 1383. There is some controversy about the dating of the two versions. G. L. Kittredge, "Chaucer and Froissart (with a Discussion of the Date of the *Meliador*)," *Englischche Studien*, 26 (1899): 321–36, argued that the revision was made after 1388. Michel Zink, "Froissart et la nuit du chasseur," *Poétique*, 41 (1980): 60–77, agrees with Kittredge, while Peter F. Dembowski, *Jean Froissart and His Meliador: Context, Craft, and Sense* (Lexington, Ky.: French Forum, 1983), pp. 58–59, accepts the probability of Longnon's hypothesis. Likewise, A. H. Diverres, "Les aventures galloises dans Meliador de Froissart," *Melanges Charles Foulon*, 2 vols. (Rennes: Institut de Français, Université de Haute-Bretagne; Liège: Marche Romane, 1980), II, pp. 73–79, states that a version of the romance was in circulation from 1368 (p. 73). In a more recent article, Diverres takes up again the question of the two versions, and carefully analyzes the relationship between the fragments and the published edition. He argues convincingly that Froissart probably carried out in 1382–83 the revision of a romance that he had composed around 1367, although it may have been started before 1365, and perhaps as early as 1362; "The Two Versions of Froissart's *Meliador*," *Studies in Medieval French Language and Literature Presented to Brian Woledge in Honour of his 80th Birthday*, ed. Sally Burch North, Publications romanes et françaises, 180 (Geneva: Droz, 1987), pp. 37–48. For other studies of *Meliador*, see the series of articles by A. H. Diverres, "Froissart's Journey to Scotland," *Forum for Modern Language Studies*, 1 (1965): 54–63; "The Geography of Britain in Froissart's *Meliador*," in *Medieval Miscellany Presented to Eugène Vinaver* (Manchester: Manchester University Press, and New York: Barnes and Noble, 1965), pp. 97–112; "The Irish Adventures in Froissart's *Meliador*," *Mélanges de langue et de littérature du moyen âge et de la renaissance offerts à Jean Frappier, professeur à la Sorbonne* (Geneva: Droz, 1970), pp. 235–51.

50. Cf. the *Dit du Florin*, vv. 300–304 and the *Chroniques de Jean Froissart*, XII, ed. E. Mirot, S.H.F. (Paris, 1931), pp. 75–76; also ed. by A. H. Diverres in *Froissart, Voyage en Béarn* (Manchester: Manchester University Press, 1953), pp. 65–66. As Wenceslas's poems do not survive elsewhere, it is impossible to know if Froissart did incorporate all of them in *Meliador*; see Kelly, *Medieval Imagination*, pp. 243–53, on Froissart's use of these poems.

51. See Dembowski, *Jean Froissart and His Meliador*, p. 93.

68   Chapter 2

compliment of treating his compositions as worthy expressions of love. Thus of the seventy-nine songs in the romance as it now exists,[52] some fifty-seven are sung or written (eight are sent as messages) under the inspiration of *amours*.

The plot of this enormously long romance is complex, but a brief summary will be useful here. The work is punctuated by four major tournaments. Hermondine, daughter of King Hermond of Scotland, meets the knight Camel while visiting her cousin Florée, daughter of Loth of Mongriès. Camel, who wishes to marry Hermondine and suspects Florée of working against him, kidnaps Loth and threatens to kill him if Hermondine does not accept him. Hermond, meanwhile, is anxious for his daughter to marry. In order to gain time, Hermondine, on Florée's advice, announces that she has vowed to marry the knight of Arthur's court who is acclaimed as the best after five years of testing. Her vow is announced at the tournament at La Garde, and Meliador is introduced. He defeats a series of knights, and Florée (thinking him able to overcome Camel) recommends him to Hermondine. Meliador in fact succeeds in killing Camel and emerges as the most outstanding of the knights. His only serious rival, Agamanor, conveniently falls in love with Meliador's sister Phenonée at the second tournament (Tarbonne), and thereafter loses interest in Hermondine. In the last section of the romance an Irish knight, Sagremor, not a contestant, is introduced, but he is paired with the lady Sebille. At the end of the work there is a tournament at Monchus in Scotland, where Meliador is proclaimed the winner of the whole contest. Following that tournament, Meliador and Agamanor marry their ladies, as do the lesser knights Tangis, Dagoriset, and Gratien. A husband is found for Florée, and only the romance of Sagremor and Sebille remains incomplete.

Although Froissart, of necessity, grants lyric expression to a great number of his characters, the motivation for the songs is similar to that in the earlier verse romances. The knights sing for love of their ladies, from whom they are separated by the terms of the quest. The verbs *penser* and *souvenir* figure prominently in the transitional passages:

---

52. *Meliador* as it survives is incomplete; two folios containing 136 lines each were torn from the manuscript, which also lacks the end. Longnon in the introduction to his edition (p. xlvi) and Dembowski, *Jean Froissart and His Meliador* (p. 19 and n. 15), estimated that this final section contained 2720 lines. Given the lacuna, it is uncertain how many songs the complete text might have contained.

Souvenirs d'amours si l'argüe,
Et Plaisance avoecques Jonece,
De canter par droite liece
.I. rondelet biel et joli.
(vv. 3603–6)

[The memory of love thus presses him, with Pleasure and Youth, to sing happily a beautiful and charming little *rondeau*.]

Et Melyador, qui pas n'ist
De son penser, pense et repense.
En pensant illuec il s'apense
Qu'il fera la une balade,
De coer tout pesant et malade,
Pour ce qu'il n'a mies espoir
De sa dame plus reveoir,
Se ce n'est fortune trop grande.
(vv. 12528–35).

[And Meliador, who does not leave his meditation, thinks and thinks again. While thinking, he decides then that he will compose a *ballade*, with a heart all heavy and sick, because he has no hope of seeing his lady again, if fortune is not great.]

Like that of Conrad in *Guillaume de Dole*, Meliador's love is an *amour lointain*, for he comes to love Hermondine by hearsay:

Un sentemens gais et jolis
Qui li fist faire, ce m'est vis,
.I. virelai tres amoureus
En pensant, comme gratieus,
A la belle qu'il ne vit onques.
(vv. 6525–29)

[A gay and charming feeling which makes him compose, so I think, an amorous *virelai*, while thinking graciously of the beauty whom he had never seen.]

In contrast to the emperor, however, Froissart's hero is not troubled by obstacles to marriage: the central pair reach an understanding halfway through the romance, even though they must wait until the end of the five-year quest for public recognition of their love. Such straightforwardness is characteristic of *Meliador*; as Peter Dembowski has pointed out, "Froissardian heroes do not live through any real psychological dramas, indeed, they rarely confront any true moral dilemma."[53] The necessary corollary of this simplification of the romance world is an absence of emotional development and psychological analysis. Consequently, when Wenceslas's poems are used as expressions of love, their function is decidedly different from those in *Guillaume de Dole*, for example, which marked the hero's growing entanglement. In Froissart's romance, the songs appear characteristic of the singers—the knights are courtly, and so such forms are only to be expected of them.

After he has met Hermondine, Meliador is obliged to continue his quest for honor and glory in order to be sure of winning her in the end. Separated from his lady, he continues to sing for love of her:

> Pour l'amour de ma souverainne,
> La fille au gentil roy d'Escoce
> Amours voelt que droit ci j'approce
> A faire .I. rondelet joli,
> Et je voir, pour l'amour de li,
> Li ferai tout presentement
> Et canterai de sentement.
> (vv. 18448–54)

[For the love of my sovereign lady, the daughter of the noble king of Scotland, Love wishes that I here begin to compose a pretty little *rondeau*, and indeed, for love of her, I shall do it shortly, and sing it with feeling.]

His attitude is closest to that of Meliacin, for his lady is absent through no fault of his own, and none of his songs is susceptible to irony. Yet the urgency of Meliacin's quest is lacking in *Meliador*, because the limits of the quest were established at the beginning, and the rules agreed to by the

---

53. Dembowski, *Jean Froissart and His Meliador*, p. 98.

participants. A further difference between the two romances lies in the quality of the songs themselves. At least some of Meliacin's songs were composed by poets of the first rank, while those of Wenceslas have attracted little but adverse criticism from modern scholars.[54] The poems are probably best seen as ephemeral pieces of improvisation,[55] and although Froissart claimed for them a conventional expressive value, he acknowledged their real function in the romance: "Pour ses pensées mieulz pollir / Commença la .I. rondelet" (vv. 18823–24; "In order to polish his thoughts, he composed a little *rondeau*"). The songs are thus part of the elegant style of the romance, and, true to the ideal of the middle style, enhance its eloquence.

Nevertheless, the role of the lyrics cannot be reduced to simple eloquence. The songs do express a kind of love, and in singing them, the characters declare their adherence to its ideal. If that ideal is not *fin' amors*, the difficult and melancholy joy of the troubadors and the *trouvères*, it is nonetheless a "courtly love," a love informed by the rules of refined society and courteous behavior. Unlike *fin' amors*, the love in *Meliador* is essentially optimistic.[56]

In part because the singing is so widespread, and in part because of the lack of psychological development, the songs in *Meliador* create an effect very different from those in the early romances. Rather than convincing the audience of the heroes' intense emotions, the songs of Wenceslas serve the same purpose as the *rondets de carole* in *Guillaume de Dole*. In the words of Jeanne Lods: "Le chant fait partie de la vie, on peut dire de la civilisation dans laquelle sont replacées les aventures arturiennes."[57] As a result, songs ostensibly used for the expression of emotions come to enhance the décor. Nevertheless, this is true only of the cumulative effect of the songs throughout the whole romance. On the level of the episode, they serve as reminders of the love interest that is the source and inspiration as well as the reward of all the knight-errantry. They also draw attention to Wenceslas, the collaborator, patron, and implied audience of the romance. Froissart's patron was able to watch the embodiments of his ideals perform songs of his own

---

54. Cf. Longnon, ed. cit., p. lxiv; Alexandre Micha, "Meliador," *Dictionnaire des lettres françaises: Le Moyen Age* (Paris: Fayard, 1964), p. 506; and Dembowski, *Jean Froissart and His Meliador*, pp. 93–94.

55. Poirion, *Le Poète et le prince: L'évolution du lyrisme courtois de Guillaume de Machaut à Charles d'Orléans* (Grenoble: Publications de la Faculté des Lettres et sciences humaines, 35, 1965; repr. Geneva: Slatkine, 1978), p. 147.

56. Cf. Dembowski, *Jean Froissart and His Meliador*, p. 110.

57. "Les Poésies de Wenceslas et le *Meliador* de Froissart," *Melanges Charles Foulon*, I, p. 216. This aspect of the songs in *Meliador* will be discussed more fully in the next chapter.

composition and no doubt derived considerable satisfaction from the spectacle.

Ysaÿe le Triste

If *Meliador* is essentially a revival of the Arthurian verse romance, the last work we shall examine in this context, *Ysaÿe le Triste*, is a continuation of the Tristan legend.[58] The romance was composed at the end of the fourteenth century or at the beginning of the fifteenth and is roughly contemporary with *Meliador*, although it bears little resemblance to Froissart's work. The title given in a colophon of the Darmstadt manuscript gives an indication of its breadth: "Li romant de Ysaye le Tristre et du Marc Essilliet son fil." The plot can be divided fairly easily into three parts: the *enfances* of Ysaÿe, the son born to Tristan and Iseut in the Morois; the childhood of his own son Marc; and finally, Marc's adventures in foreign countries. Twenty-three songs are quoted in the romance: thirteen *rondeaux* sung in the context of a banquet,[59] and ten *lais* and *rondeaux* composed by the heroine Marthe, the *amie* and eventual wife of Ysaÿe and the mother of Marc.[60] Ysaÿe seems not to have inherited his father's talent, for it is only Marthe who expresses herself in song.

Though she has never met him, Marthe falls in love with descriptions of Ysaÿe and takes the initiative in the affair. Her written declaration of her love eventually receives an encouraging answer. Soon afterward, her uncle Yrions finds her in a state of extreme concentration:

---

58. My analysis was based on examination, at the Institut de Recherche et d'Histoire des Textes in Paris, of microfilms of mss. 2524 of the Hessische Landes- und Hochschulbibliothek in Darmstadt, and ms. 688 of the Herzogliche gothaische Bibliothek, and the sixteenth-century printed edition by Galliot, *Ysaie le triste, filz Tristan de Leonois* (Paris, 1522). I have verified the quotations with the edition by André Giachetti, *Ysaÿe le triste: Roman arthurien du moyen âge tardif*, Publications de l'Université de Rouen, 142 (Rouen: Presse Universitaire de Rouen, 1990). The analysis by Julius Zeidler, "Der Prosaroman Ysaÿe le Triste," *ZRP*, 25 (1901): 175–214, 472–89, and 641–68, is also useful. For dating, see André Giachetti, "Ysaÿe le Triste et l'Ecosse," *Bulletin Bibliographique de la Société Internationale Arthurienne*, 15 (1963): 109–19. On the organization of the romance, see Barry Beardsmore, "Les *Enfances Auberon* dans *Ysaïe le Triste* et leur importance dans la structure du roman," *Mélanges de langue et littérature françaises du moyen âge offerts à Pierre Jonin*, *Senefiance*, 7 (1979): 103–13.

59. Cf. below, Chapter 3, n. 20 on this passage.

60. On the *lais* see André Giachetti, "Une nouvelle forme du *lai* apparue à la fin du XIVe siècle," *Etudes de langue et de littérature du moyen âge offertes à Félix Lecoy* (Paris: Champion, 1973), pp. 147–55.

sy le trouve faisant ung escript. Lors le salue et elle ne dist mot, car sy grant entente avoit a ce qu'elle n'entendoit point a che qu'il disoit. . . . Yrions s'approche de ly, et quant elle le perchut, sy tressaly. "Bielle nieche," fait Yrions, "a quoy pensés vous sy fort?" "Sire," fait elle, "c'est a une canchonette que je faisoye; regardés s'elle est bien faitte." (Giachetti, p. 105, §122)

[So he found her writing a long piece. Then he salutes her, and she says nothing, for she had such a great work that she did not hear what he said. . . . Yrions approaches her and when she notices him, she shudders. "Fair niece," says Yrions, "What do you think about so deeply?" "Sir," she says, "It is about a song that I was writing; see if it is well done."]

The composition is designated "canchonette," yet the author stresses the status of the song as "writing." Yrions is asked to *look* at it and judge it, and he reads it aloud. This is in striking contrast to Tristan's *lais*, all sung without reference to texts, although other characters, such as Kaherdin, composed in writing.

In this first song, Marthe acknowledges the risk she takes in loving, and cites Ysaÿe's perfection as the source of her passion:

J'ameray mal gré dangier
    Le Dangereus
Car je l'ay et bel et bon,
    Sy est mes ceurs.
Et quant il est sy parfais,
Qu'iroie ge plus atendant
Qu'en dis, en pensés, et en fais
N'iroit un mileur trovant.
(Ibid)

[I will love the dangerous one despite the danger, for I have it well and good, thus is my heart. And when he is so perfect, why should I wait longer? I should never find a better one, in words, in thoughts, and in deeds.]

The author of the romance made a clear allusion to the traditional *amour lointain*, but has varied the theme in attributing the love to his heroine. Marthe herself breaks with tradition in taking control of events, in the manner of Machaut's Toutebelle in the somewhat earlier *Voir Dit*.

Marthe sings again as she waits for Ysaÿe's arrival to be announced, in anticipation of their first meeting. As before, there is no discussion of her feelings in the narrative. It is the song alone that reveals her emotions:

> Trop demeure mon amy, ce poise moy
> Sy en cante par amours et par anoy;
> Se j'en cante par anoy, ce n'est mie sans raison:
> Onques ne le vy, et sy voy que ja n'array garison
> Ou mal qui me contralie. Ce fait dangier que me lie
> Dont j'en sui en effroy. S'y ne vient je m'ochiray,
> Pour perdre arme et foy. Trop demeure mon amy.
> (Giachetti, p. 123, §154)

> [Too long tarries my lover, this pains me, so I sing for love and for distress. If I sing for distress, it is not without reason: I have never seen him and so I see that I shall never be cured of the pain that assails me. This makes a danger that binds me, which I fear. If he does not come, I shall kill myself to lose soul and faith. Too long tarries my lover.]

Her impatience is a cliché—Celinde and Clarmondine sing to the same effect,[61] with as little justification—but references to "onques ne le vy" tailor the song to her situation, as well as anticipating some of the *rondeaux* in the *Voir Dit*.

Ysaÿe returns her love, but is obliged before long to leave to answer a challenge. During his absence, she bears a son, and then decides to set out in search of her lover. She composes the third song in the course of reaching this decision. This *lai* is one of the longest in the romance, consisting of some 175 lines. Unlike the first two songs, this one is preceded by a monologue in which Marthe regrets the long separation, and reproaches her lover for his absence:

> Et Ysaÿe, tres loyaus cuers d'amy, te souvient il plus de ceste lasse qui meurt pour l'amour de toy? Ore y a il pres de deux ans que je ne te vey. Certes je t'achointay de malle heure quant je meurch pour l'amour de toy! . . . A! lasse, dolente, ayme on pour ainsy faire? Aime on pour laissier s'amie? Ayme on pour lui faire detourbier? Ayme on pour lui faire hissir hors du sens? (Ibid., p. 166, §251)

> [Ah! Ysaÿe, most loyal heart of a lover, do you remember any more this miserable creature who dies for love of you? It is now nearly two years since I

---

61. See below, Chapter 4, under "Song as Action."

have seen you. Indeed, I met you in an evil hour, when I die for love of you. . . .
Ah! wretched, sorrowful, does one love in order to do this? Does one love to
abandon his beloved? Does one love in order to cause her distress? Does one
love to make her lose her mind?]

Her song is not spontaneous, for she devotes considerable effort to its
composition; only then does she sing it. The first eight lines form a *rondeau*
that announces her intentions:

> Je veul faire ung joly lay
> Pour l'amour de mon amy.
> Yrion mon oncle lay,
> Je veul faire ung joly lay.
> Et s'iray sans nul delay
> Lui querant qu'il est a my.
> (Ibid., p. 167, §252)

> [I wish to make a pretty *lai* for the love of my beloved. I leave Yrion my
> uncle, I wish to make a pretty *lai*; And so I shall go without delay,
> seeking the one who is my beloved.]

She restates her decision in another verse form before going on to explain
that her quest is urgent: a longer separation will surely kill her. In spite of
her determination, her song makes it quite clear that she is far from
sanguine about the outcome:

> Je sui quetive et dolente et mescans . . .
>
> Or m'en iray et par bos et par camps
> Remplie d'ire et de divers pensé
> En aventure serray me vye usans
> La gist beaux cans, ce dient ly sené;
> Se je devie sy en ert occuppé
> Cellui que j'aime et que tant m'est haans.
> Mais plus perdroit que il n'a empensé
> Sy prie Dieu qu'i me soit secourans.
> Sans lui ne puis en vye estre durans.
> (Giachetti, p. 169, §256)

> [I am miserable and sorrowful and worse off . . . Now I will go through
> forests and fields, filled with anger and other thoughts; I will use up my

life in adventure—beautiful songs are found there, so say the wise men; if I die, then he will be concerned, the one whom I love and who is such pain to me. But he would lose more than he thought, so I pray God that he rescue me. Without him I cannot endure in life.]

As with the first "song," the author insists on the written quality of the *lai*. After singing, she reads it over, puts the copy in her bodice, and dons her disguise.

Marthe actually sings the eighth song in the presence of Ysaÿe, but does not recognize him. He is attending a wounded knight when Marthe arrives and sings to them in her capacity as minstrel. This song also begins with a *rondeau,* and contains references to her story, but they are vague enough not to reveal her identity:

Et se muir en cest voiage
Je prenderay la mort en gré;
Je languis, cante et esrage . . .

Nieche de Roy
En tel aroy
Ne vit ains nulx.
Mes or m'en croy,
Men mal acroy,
N'en ait tel nulx!
(Giachetti, pp. 180–81, §279)

[And if I die on this voyage, I will take death willingly. I languish, sing and go mad . . . No one has yet seen a king's niece in such a state. But now I think my pain increases. May no one have such (pain)!]

The song occasions an interesting exchange between the lovers:

Quant Ysaye ot oÿ si dist que oncques mais n'avoit oÿ de bouche mieulx chanter ne aussi gracieusement. Et pour ce luy demanda en l'heure qui ceste chanson luy avoit apprinse. "Sire, chevalier," fait elle, "la nieche du roy Irion la m'a apprinse" . . . "Et pourquoy la fist elle?" fait il. Elle respond, "Pour l'amour d'ung chevalier qu'elle aymoit lequel estoit nommé Ysaÿe le Triste." "Dictes moy comment il luy est." "Par ma foy," fait Marthe, "je croy qu'il luy soit maulvaisement. Car elle se partit en l'heure de minuit toute seulle pour aller querre son amy Ysaÿe, ne on ne sçait quelle part elle est allee." (Ibid. pp. 183–84, §281)

[When Ysaÿe had heard her speak thus, he said that he had never heard anyone sing better or more gracefully. And for this reason he asked her then who had taught her this song. "Sir knight," she says, "the niece of King Yrion taught it to me." . . . "And why did she compose it?" he asks. She answers, "For the love of a knight that she loved who is named Ysaÿe le Triste." "Tell me how she is." "By my faith," says Marthe, "I think that she is poorly. For she left at midnight all alone to go seek her lover Ysaÿe, and no one knows where she has gone."]

The author develops fully the irony of the situation. Marthe behaves as she has before, freely admitting both the authorship and the inspiration of the song, suppressing only her own identity. Her defense becomes an obstacle and delays the lovers' reunion.

Disguised as a minstrel, Marthe performs one song on request and another to pay her passage on a boat. Nevertheless, these pieces reflect her sentiments:

Remplye d'ire plus que je ne puis dire
M'en fault aller querir le mien amy . . .
Lasse, dolente, quetive, que ferai ge?
Anuis me tire que par trop mal matire.
(Ibid., p. 174, §268)

[Filled with more anger than I can tell, I must go seek my lover . . . Miserable, sorrowful, wretched, what shall I do? Trouble draws me, which pains me badly.]

Indeed, these songs are her only form of emotional expression, for the passages surrounding the insertions are confined to noting events and offer no comment on the heroine's state of mind.

The similarity between Marthe's role in the romance and that of heroes of earlier romances is striking. Here it is the lady who searches for her lover and who reveals the inspiration of her love in songs throughout her journey. Marthe is the character to whom the love affair is most important, and it is fitting that she should sing the songs which are the principal embodiments of it. In this respect, Marthe resembles the male heroes Gerart, Meliacin, Meliador, and the Beau Chevalier, while her disguise had precedents in those of Fresne in *Galeran de Bretagne*, of Nicolette in *Aucassin et Nicolette*, and of Coeur d'Acier in *Perceforest*.[62] Unlike her predecessors'

---

62. See below, Chapter 4, under "Song as Action."

songs, however, Marthe's songs form part of her camouflage, while the earlier heroines sang to reveal their identity.

In concluding this chapter, it will be useful to reflect briefly on what it has revealed about the use of inserted lyrics to express emotions, on the problems that this use raised for authors, and on the variety of solutions they found. I shall begin with the basic question of the effective relationship established between the inserted songs and the emotions they purport to express.

The relationship between song and emotion in the eight romances just studied can be arranged in a spectrum. At one end would be the more traditional use of lyric motifs borrowed from the *chansons* but arranged discursively in a monologue. The character speaks directly in a language borrowed from the *chanson*, but does not sing. At the other end, we have the situation of *Guillaume de Dole* and the *Tristan en Prose*, where the song is the only explicit expression of emotion. In between is the technique employed in romances such as *Meliacin*, in which both monologue and lyric are combined in a single passage, and the *Chastelaine de Vergi*, whose author makes similar use of a descriptive analytical passage. The function of the song is to crystallize the emotional reaction to thought or remembrance ("penser," "souvenir," "memoire") of the lady. The consoling "doux penser" of the *chanson* thus becomes the cue for the insertion of a song. Structurally, the lovers of these romances are separated for much of the plot, and the periodic insertion of *chansons* keeps the motivating love affair before the audience while it simultaneously establishes the lovers' claim to a particular type of love, that of *fin' amors*.

The relationship between the singer and the song also varies significantly in these romances. Singers, and even lovers, who are not poets seem unable to bear comparison with the poet-lovers of the troubadour and *trouvère* tradition. Hence we see the irony of the *chanson* stanzas quoted in *Guillaume de Dole*, the *Roman de la Violette*, and the *Chastelaine de Vergi*. The hero of *Guilluame de Dole* sings emotions quite different from those he feels, and in the *Roman de la Violette* a song signals the hero's betrayal of his lady and calls his behavior into contrast with hers.

The sentiments expressed in the songs of Meliacin and the Châtelain de Couci generally correspond to what they might be expected to feel in the particular situations in which they are quoted or sung; certainly the descrepancies are not exploited ironically. These songs are for the most part presented as direct responses to specific events. Meliacin sings for himself, but the Châtelain composed for an audience—the Dame de Fayel—and we see him making arrangements for the transmission of his song. Meliacin is an especially interesting figure, representing a point of transition between Conrad and Gerart, who sing only borrowed songs, and the Châtelain, who is a poet cast as the hero of his own story. Meliacin begins by using songs from the standard repertoire, but is presented as a poet at least once, composing a new song under the inspiration of his own passion. The poet-lover-hero of these romances is the ancestor of the poet-lover-narrators who dominate the fourteenth century in the *dits amoureux* that are the subject of Chapter 6.

The songs in *Meliador* are vague enough, and the various affairs similar enough that Wenceslas's songs are appropriate to their context, if not truly expressive. Whereas borrowed songs had been chosen from the repertoire (even the songs in the *Castelain de Couci* include some not composed by the poet), Froissart used those of a single poet. In so doing, he flattered his patron by putting his songs on the same level as the famous *chansons* of the *trouvères* of earlier generations.

When the singer is a poet, temporal questions become increasingly acute. The manner of dealing with the space between composition and performance is particularly significant in the *Tristan en Prose*. Several of Tristan's *lais* were supposed to have been composed at critical moments in his affair with Iseut, yet there is no mention of them at these points, and they are sung only much later in the romance. The text indicates clearly that his *lais* were in circulation, for several of them are performed and discussed by the female minstrels he encounters during his travels, yet Tristan seldom arranges for the transmission of a *lai*. The *lettres en forme de lai*[63] seem to have been sent as letters—no mention is made of anyone singing them, although some of them have notations in the manuscripts. Kaherdin, on the other hand, wrote down his *lai mortel*, and taught it to a minstrel in order to insure its performance before Iseut. Similarly, the Châtelain de Couci taught his first song to a minstrel so that it could be sung to the Dame de Fayel. Marthe, although uninterested in sending her songs, frequently composed with pen, rather than harp, in hand, and the portrayal of her action intensifies the contrast between composition and performance. The problems of composition, transmission, and performance will become explicit in the *dits,* and particularly in Machaut's *Voir Dit*, as we shall see in a later chapter.

---

63. See below, Chapter 5.

3. Songs as Description

The descriptive use of inserted songs is coeval with the expressive use just examined, and just as common in the narratives of our period. The complex relationship between the songs inserted for descriptive purposes and the nonlyrical passages of description they were used to supplement is similar in some respects to that between the songs inserted for expressive purposes and the monologues they either supplemented or replaced.

In general, descriptive passages in medieval French romances fulfill one of two distinct functions. Some establish the background against which the events take place and thus set the tone of the text, while others delineate the portrait of a particular character or object.[1] Passages of the first type usually deal with the castle and court, the place from which the knight sets forth, or else the forest or wilderness, the *locus* of adventure. Songs could be and were inserted into passages of both types, but for obvious reasons the vast majority were employed in passages describing the life of the court. While music had no particular relevance to most characters or objects, and was rarely to be heard in the wilderness, music normally accompanied most of the activities of the court: banquets, processions, tournaments, and similar festivities. Since this music was often mentioned explicitly in the narrative of romances from the twelfth century onward, the step from reference to quotation in this context was a natural one.[2] Indeed,

---

1. On the dual role of descriptions, see Paul Zumthor, *Essai de poétique médiévale*, pp. 353–54; on description in romance, see Erich Auerbach, *Mimesis: The Representation of Reality in Western Literature*, trans. Willard R.Trask (Princeton: Princeton University Press, 1968), p. 131. For a general theory of descriptions, see Philippe Hamon, "Qu'est-ce qu'une description," *Poétique*, 12 (1972): 465–85; and *Introduction à l'analyse du descriptif* (Paris: Hachette-Classiques, 1981). The effect of descriptive passages of any sort is similar to the one we have observed for lyric insertions, for they, too, interrupt the flow of narrative development. The descriptions of scenes, and particularly of those of the pageant of court life, are composed of a series of actions and constitute miniature narratives. Nevertheless, like simpler descriptive passages, these scenes give the impression of being "inserted" into the larger narrative. Cf. Hamon, "Qu'est-ce qu'une description," pp. 465–66; and Gérard Genette, "Frontières du récit," *Figures*, II (Paris: Seuil, 1969; repr. Collection Points, 1979), pp. 49–69, esp. p. 59.

2. Singing and dancing are mentioned in such passages even where lyrics are not quoted: e.g., *Erec et Enide*, vv. 1987–2000, 6131–37, 6327–35; *Yvain*, vv. 2348–56; *Panthere d'Amors*, vv. 157–75, 214–45; *Guillaume de Dole*, vv. 364–416; *Cleomadés*, vv. 2875 ff., 7229 ff., 17281 ff; *Sone de*

when Jean Renart at the beginning of the thirteenth century inserted several *rondets de carole* and *refrains* into his descriptions of the activities of the emperor's court in his *Roman de la Rose*, he did no more than amplify the references to musical performance that were already conventional in the representations of those scenes punctuating most romances. The great majority of the songs quoted in his *Roman de la Rose* are in fact included in such scenes, and this repeated use of lyric insertions established them firmly in the repertoire of descriptive techniques.

Many later thirteenth-century authors imitated Jean Renart's technique, but none was as lavish in his quotations. Even Gerbert de Montreuil, his earliest imitator, used an extended description embellished with several songs only at the beginning of his *Roman de la Violette*. The musical scene augmented with quoted songs seems to have become conventional very rapidly, and many thirteenth-century authors contented themselves with a single quotation. Once the convention was established, a song cited in a musical description could be made to serve other narrative purposes at the same time. In *Ysaÿe le Triste*, for example, Marthe is able to express herself in quoted songs in full court because she is disguised as a minstrel, and in the *Castelain de Couci*, as we shall see, a lyric inserted into the description of a courtly scene influences the plot.

Most of the songs quoted in the context of scenes at court are *rondets de carole*, *refrains*, or *rondeaux*, and they are often presented as accompaniments to dancing. Both in their genre and their content they belong to the register referred to by Zumthor as that of "la bonne vie."[3] These songs celebrate reciprocated love or advise the abandonment of unhappy love. Their tone is lighthearted, and they contribute to the creation of an impression of gaiety and elegance. In Jakobson's terminology, their function, for the reader/listener is connotative, even if it might be communicative for the singers in the romance. The one genre *not* generally quoted in this context is the *chanson courtoise*, whose ideology is not notably cheerful.

The role of these elaborate scenes in the narrative is not simply to provide atmosphere or background, although they do that. They are social occasions, and give us an opportunity to view the characters of romance behaving within the hierarchy of their society, and not confined to the

---

Nansai, vv. 129 ff., 289 ff., 2027 ff., 14741 ff.; *Escanor*, vv. 6090 ff., 6324 ff., 12902 ff., 23173 ff., etc. Cf. also descriptions of feasts in Froissart's *Chroniques* IV, 1 and 16. On the rhetorical principle of *amplificatio*, see Faral, *Les arts poétiques*, pp. 61–85, and de Bruyne, *Etudes d'esthétique*, II, pp. 16–17.

3. Zumthor, *Langue et technique*, p. 156–58.

isolation of the individual adventure. The different scenes permit the characters to appear in different lights, and the use of the various types of song appropriate to these scenes allows the authors to play with contrasts of register.

Toward the end of the thirteenth century, the descriptive use of the insertion device reappeared in its fullest form (in *Renart le Nouvel* and the *Court de Paradis*), but in contexts that are clearly parodies of earlier works. In the fourteenth century the device continued to be used as an element of description in the way it had been in the earlier part of the thirteenth century, but its use decreased. The decline in its use was probably due to the displacement of the traditional romance by the *dit* in this period. The only significant use of the insertion device for descriptive purposes in the second half of the fourteenth century was in Froissart's romance *Meliador*. At the beginning of the fifteenth century, however, Christine de Pizan varied the convention by applying it to a another kind of description. She used *refrains* of the traditional type to enliven her idyllic portrait of the pastoral life in the *Dit de la Pastoure*, but maintained a distinction of genres similar to that found in earlier works.

Songs were also used in descriptive passages of the second type—those used to delineate character—but this use was relatively rare. In fact, I have found only four examples of explicit characterization by means of songs, three from the thirteenth century and one from the fifteenth. In the *Tristan en Prose*, the *Mariage des Sept Arts*, the *Ludus-Anticlaudien*, and Christine de Pizan's *Dit de la Rose*, we find examples of characters who sing outside the context of a descriptive scene. In the last three of these works, it is an allegorical figure who expresses herself in song, either partially or entirely. To some extent, it is the simple act of singing that distinguishes a character like Music in the *Mariage* from her companions, although the genre, register, and content of the quoted song also contribute to the characterization.[4]

The rest of this chapter will present a more detailed examination of the descriptive use of inserted songs in the principal exemplars, arranged in four sections: one concerned with the orthodox use of songs in the description of court scenes, one with their satirical use for anti-courtly scenes, and

---

4. Of course, the fact that a character chooses to sing a particular type of song, such as the *chanson d'amour*, associates him with a poetic tradition, e.g. that of the courtly poet-lover, while the particular songs he sings serve to characterize him in the same way as his speeches and monologues, though the use of songs in these ways is not primarily descriptive.

one with their use in uncourtly pastoral scenes. The final section will deal with lyrics as explicit elements of characterization.

The Music of the Court

ROMAN DE LA ROSE OR *GUILLAUME DE DOLE*
Most of the lyric insertions—some thirty-five of the total—in Jean Renart's groundbreaking *Roman de la Rose* appear in the context of scenes of court life. The romance opens with a description of the Emperor Conrad, a paragon of courtly virtues, whose refinement is reflected in the splendor of his court. Conrad convokes a *fête champêtre*, summoning illustrious vassals and beautiful ladies. The emperor takes the more jealous members hunting, while the others amuse themselves by singing and dancing. Six songs—*refrains* and *rondets de carole*—are quoted in the context of their dalliance.

The songs play on the themes of love, spring, and joy and reflect the singers' surroundings. Courtiers returning from a spring are mentioned in two of the songs, while others refer to the forest and the month of May; the singing is thus connected to the narrative by allusions to the context. Some of the singers are identified by title if not by name: the sister of the Duke of Mainz (v. 308), the Count of Savoy (v. 316), the Count of Luxembourg (v. 323). The latter, according to the text, sings his *rondet* for the love of a lady who is herself a beautiful singer. Even when we learn no more of their story, the allusion adds a note of dramatic interest to the description. The scene as a whole creates an impression of elegant merriment which echoes the portrait of the emperor.

After dinner that evening, four songs are performed to accompany the *carole*.[5] The first of these contains an invitation to dance:

C'est tot la gieus, enmi les prez,
Vos ne sentez mie les maus d'amer!

---

5. For bibliography on the *carole*, see Bec, *La lyrique française*, I, pp. 220–21. Bec published some of the songs with commentary: vol. II, pp. 150–51, 158–60. Others were published by Friedrich Gennrich, *Rondeaux Virelais und Balladen*, 2 vols. Gesellschaft für romanische Literatur, 43, 47 (Dresden, Halle: Niemeyer, 1921–27), and *Das altfranzösische Rondeau und Virelai im 12. und 13. Jahrhundert*, vol. III of *Rondeaux Virelais und Balladen*, Summa musicae Medii Aevi, 10 (Langen-bei-Frankfurt, 1963).

Dames i vont por caroler,
Remirez voz braz!
(vv. 514–17)

[Way down there, in the meadows. You do not feel the pains of love! Ladies go there to dance, watch your arms!]

The other lyrics allude to pairs of lovers (Robin and Mariete, Aeliz and Emmelot) and create an impression of an easy sort of love, a pleasant dalliance far removed from the difficult ideal of *fin'amors*. This detailed opening scene, with its evocation of luxury—rich food, fine wine, silver cups, silks and furs as well as music—is not essential to the plot, but it sets the tone of the romance. The luxurious and brilliant background it provides for the characters reflects their indulgent and pleasure-loving nature, and reveals the emperor's superficiality in his choice of companions.[6]

Two other passages in the romance recall the gaiety and richness of the first scene and make similar use of lyric insertions. The party Guillaume gives for his friends after his arrival at court in Tref-sur-Meuse (vv. 1704–1861) illustrates his generosity, for it exemplifies, on a smaller scale, the virtues of the emperor cited at the beginning of the work. That the two scenes are indeed comparable is evident from the techniques of description, which are identical.[7] The next passage (vv. 2218–2421), a panorama of the entrance of Guillaume and his friends to St. Trond, and the cavalcade of knights riding to the tournament, characterizes Guillaume in a more general way. He is shown attracting the admiration of the crowd of spectators. The reader sees Guillaume moving successfully into his new environment. His reception into this elite society proves more effectively than mere assertion that he is worthy of his elevated status. These passages serve, in addition, to bolster the characterization of Guillaume as the brother of Liénor, the heroine of the romance. A very carefully chaperoned young woman, she does not appear at the court until the last stage of the story. Her brother functions in effect as her deputy by winning the favor of the emperor.

6. Faith Lyons, *Les éléments descriptifs dans le roman d'aventure au 13e siècle (en particulier Amadas et Ydoine, Gliglois, Galeran, l'Escoufle, Guillaume de Dole, Jehan et Blonde, Le Castelain de Couci)*, Publications romanes et françaises, 84 (Geneva: Droz, 1965). The songs in this first scene were analyzed in detail by Eric M. Steinle in "'La graine as dras': Jean Renart and the Lyric Romance," read at the meeting of the Medieval Academy of America in Toronto, April 1986.

7. Lyons, *Les éléments descriptifs*, p. 109.

These scenes of elegant amusement, complete with their quoted songs, occupy a considerable part of the whole work, and together they reinforce Conrad's image as a courtly paragon, even as they provide a background against which to examine the emperor's behavior in the plot. When Conrad (as we saw in Chapter 2) proclaims the difficult ideals of *fin'amors* in stanzas of *chansons courtoises*, he sets himself apart from "la bonne vie" celebrated by his courtiers. The *refrains* and *rondets* are the setting for the *chansons*, the context in which its ideal must be attempted. The juxtaposition of registers is imposed on the reader/listener, who must wonder how the hero can reconcile them.

In the end it is not the hero, but the heroine, Liénor, who resolves the impasse, although she appears infrequently in the romance. Like Conrad, she is introduced in a characteristic setting. When the emperor's messenger first comes to Dole, Liénor and her mother entertain him by singing *chansons de toile*.[8] One song in particular corresponds to the situation of Liénor and her mother, who are embroidering religious vestments:

> Fille et la mere se sieent a l'orfrois,
> a un fil d'or i font orïeuls croiz.
> Parla la mere qui le cuer ot cortois.
> Tant bon'amor fist bele Aude en Doon!
> "Aprenez, fille, a coudre et a filer,
> et en l'orfrois orïex crois lever.
> L'amor Doon vos covient oublier."
> (vv. 1159–65)

[Daughter and mother sit embroidering, with a thread of gold they make golden crosses. The mother spoke with courteous heart. Such good love had beautiful Aude for Doon! "Daughter, learn to sew and spin and to raise a golden cross in embroidery. You must forget the love of Doon."]

The songs reveal nothing of Liénor's personality or thoughts, but the scene as a whole gives some idea of the life she leads. Her skill in singing,

---

8. See Michel Zink, *Belle: Essai sur les chansons de toile, suivi d'une édition et d'une traduction*, musical transcriptions by Gérard Le Vot. Collection Essais sur le Moyen Age, 1 (Paris: Champion, 1978).

86   Chapter 3

moreover, adds to the charm of a girl whose beauty has been described in some detail.⁹

All of the lyrics inserted in the passages discussed to this point are expressions of gaiety. Since the impression is created by the mere act of singing, the words of the songs need not always reflect the same mood; the fact that some songs deal with unhappy love does not mar the occasion. Since they are performed in public, there is no explicit expression of any emotion other than gaiety. The social, impersonal character of festive singing would be exploited by later writers to allow their characters to hide their feelings at the same time as they express them, but there is no suggestion here of *double entendre*.

Two songs quoted in the description of the May festival at Mainz serve to reveal Conrad's feelings indirectly. When he overhears his joyful subjects sing gaily in the streets, the words of their song—"Amours a non ciz maus qui me tormente" (v. 4587; "Love is the name of the pain that torments me")—contrast with the jollity of the singers, but suit the emperor's mood very well. A little later, as Conrad listens to proclamations of the joys of spring, the author describes the effect of the song upon him:

> A poi li rois ne forsane
> en l'autre sale ou il estoit;
> nule riens ne le confortoit
> qu'en li die, n'en fet n'en chant.
> (vv. 4660–63)

> [The king almost went mad in the other room where he was; nothing consoled him, whatever one said to him, whether in speech or in song.]

The indirect portrayal of Conrad's emotions is rendered still more effective, for the song is shown to have a similar effect upon Liénor, who overhears it in another part of the castle. In this way, the two unhappy lovers are linked by a song even before they meet. Thus, if the *refrains* sung in the opening scenes mark the initial state of the main characters, their sentiments as they become involved in the plot are reflected in their changing reactions to the later *refrains*.

---

9. Grace Frank, "*Le Roman de la rose ou de Guillaume de Dole* ll. 1330 ff.," *Romanic Review*, 29 (1938): 209–11, argued that the epic *laisse* is sung at Liénor's request and contributes to the energetic and decisive portrayal of her.

The romance ends with a description of Conrad's wedding, a passage which counterbalances the opening scene. As before, a series of songs—a Provençal *canso*,[10] a *chanson de toile*, and several *rondets*—are sung as part of the festivities. Conrad's last song, a *rondet de carole*, constitutes his proposal: "Que demandez vos / Quant vos m'avez?" and supplies the answer: "Ge ne demant rien / se vos m'amez bien" (vv. 5106–7, 5110–11; "What do you ask, when you have me?" "I ask nothing if you love me well"). It is his only *rondet*, and as we saw in Chapter 2,[11] the change in genre signals his abandonment of the *chanson d'amour* and its ideal of *fin' amors* that the narrative has shown to be both impossible and inappropriate for him. In contrast, the lighthearted dance song suits both his character and his newfound happiness. The courtly songs celebrated the unrequited ideal love that Conrad is not capable of attaining. The change of genre marks Conrad's move from the status of lover to that of husband, and the romance ends with a wedding, a public celebration of requited love.

Roman de la Violette

The second author to make use of the insertion device in a descriptive way, Gerbert de Montreuil, modeled the opening scene of his *Roman de la Violette* closely on the beginning of *Guillaume de Dole*. Gerbert described the celebrations of the Easter court of King Louis, whose attendants take turns singing *refrains* at the end of the meal. The passage in question quotes no fewer than ten songs—nine *refrains* and a single stanza of a *chanson d'amour*, and it is significant that this is exactly the number quoted in the corresponding scene of Jean Renart's work. The stanza and two of the *refrains* are sung by Gerart, the hero of the romance, who is the last of the company to sing.

If Jean Renart's hero is characterized by descriptions of the elegant court he sponsors, the hero of the *Violette* defines himself rather differently. Gerart distinguishes himself from his companions by outdoing them with his songs, and it is his boastful speech framed with songs that triggers the plot. When Gerart is asked to sing, he chooses a stanza by Gace Brulé. His song opens with a reference to the invitation to sing and goes on to denounce those who envy lovers:

10. See Fabienne Gégou, "Jean Renart et la lyrique occitane," *Mélanges de langue et de littérature médiévales offerts à Pierre LeGentil* (Besançon: Jacques et Demontrond, 1973), pp. 319–23.

11. See above, Chapter 2, under "Guillaume de Dole."

88   Chapter 3

> Ne ja ne quier k'envïeus mot en die,
>   Car onques nes amai,
>   Ne ja nes amerai;
>   Et kis aimme, bien sai
>   K'il fait cruël folie,
> K'envïeus sont molt plain de felonnie.
> (vv. 193–98)

[Never have I wished the envious to say a word, for I never loved them, nor shall I ever love them; And whoever does love them, I know well that he commits a cruel folly, for the envious are full of treachery.]

Gerart, like Conrad, proclaims adherence to an ideal of love different from that of the court, and one that he proves himself unable to live up to, as we saw in the previous chapter, for he was deceived by the envious Lisiart. These lines are prophetic, for at the end of the scene Lisiart, who is truly "plain de felonnie," challenges Gerart, and later slanders the heroine.

Gerart follows the song with a long, bragging description of his lady which he opens and closes with *refrains*:

> J'ai amours fait a mon gré,
> Miels en vaurra ma vie.
> (vv. 204–5)

[I have a love to my taste, my life will be better for it.]

> Dont n'ai jou droit que m'envoise,
> Quant la plus biele amie ai?
> (vv. 237–38)

[Haven't I the right to rejoice when I have the most beautiful lady?]

Though the songs are boastful enough, they might have been unobjectionable if not supplemented by the speech, for they would not have been essentially different from the *refrains* sung by the other members of the court. In expressing his arrogant confidence in his lady's love in two *refrains* and a *chanson* stanza, Gerart breaks the rules of courtly etiquette. Although his appropriation of the *chanson* proclaims him to be a *fin'amant*, his boastful use of *refrains* sends a mixed message. He aspires to a courtly ideal while enjoying the register of "la bonne vie." Here, as in the case of Jean Renart's *Rose,* the audience is invited to place the hero's actions within the context of a poetic register, and not necessarily the one invoked by him. Gerbert's opening passage is carefully tied to the plot structure and gives his romance its thematic unity, in its clear exploitation of registral contrast.

ESCANOR

Much later in the thirteenth century, the poet Girart d'Amiens inserted lyrics into two works, but only *Escanor* concerns us here. In contrast to the two romances we have already examined, this work, composed between 1277 and 1282, contains only four songs, all of which are *refrains* quoted in a single descriptive passage.[12] These insertions embellish the account of Escanor's progress toward Arthur's court, where he is to meet Gawain in combat, and serve an essentially augmentative purpose.

The approach of the cortege is presented from the point of view of Galantinet, a friend of Gawain's squire Giflet. Both young men are dismayed by Gawain's inexplicable depression over the approaching contest, and Galantinet leaves the court with the intention of rescuing Gawain by ambushing Escanor.[13] Although the general content of the description is reminiscent of that of the tournament of St. Trond in *Guillaume de Dole,* the context here casts a sinister shadow that is absent from the earlier romance.

Galantinet meets successive groups of maidens and retainers, all singing gaily as they ride. When questioned by the squire, the first group of young men announce that they have come from the Blanche Montagne (Escanor's stronghold) to watch the contest. Galantinet's reaction is revealing:

Quant li escuiers entendi
l'affaire c'on li despondi,

---

12. H. Michelant, ed., *Der Roman von Escanor von Gerard von Amiens,* Bibliothek des literarischen Vereins in Stuttgart, 178 (Tübingen: H. Laupp, 1886); corrections by A. Tobler, "*Der Roman von Escanor von Gerard von Amiens,* herausgegeben von Dr H. Michelant," *ZRP,* 11 (1887): 421–29. For the date, see Gerard J. Brault, "Arthurian Heraldry and the Date of Escanor," *Bulletin Bibliographique de la Société Internationale Arthurienne,* 11 (1959): 81–88: "Sometime between these two dates, perhaps in connection with the Round Table held at Warwich in 1281" (p. 88); he also discussed the date in his dissertation, "A Study of the Works of Girart d'Amiens," (Ph.D. Diss., University of Pennsylvania, 1958), pp. 77–85.

13. See Gaston Paris, "Girart d'Amiens" in *HLF,* 31 (1893): 151–205, especially pp. 154 and 162, on Michelant's erroneous attribution of the episode to Giflet.

> outre en ala grant aleure,
> et dist bien, de ceste aventure
> ne set que dire ne que faire....
> s'il em peust l'orgueil abatre,
> bien li pleust por son seingnor,
> car doutance onques jor greignor
> n'ot de son seingnor en sa vie.
> (vv. 7964–68, 7971–74)

> [When the squire heard the affair explained to him, he rode on at great speed and said that he knew neither what to say or do about this situation.... If he could beat down the pride (of Escanor), he would be well pleased for his lord, for never had he greater fear for his lord in his life.]

Galantinet interprets the young men's singing as *orgueil*, and on the assumption that such overweening confidence must be well-founded, becomes even more doubtful of Gawain's ability to defeat Escanor. His concern increases when he meets a second group of singers: girls who praise their lord in such glowing terms as to give the squire pause. He is greatly impressed that the foreigner should have such loyal and confident supporters. The third group, made up of splendidly dressed ladies, so dazzles Galantinet that he cannot approach them. Indeed, he thinks himself bewitched:

> li escuiers qui vit l'affaire
> le tint a grant enchantement....
> mout forment se prist a debatre
> en son cuer conment cheviroit
> n'en quele maniere ouvrerroit.
> (vv. 8142–43; 8148–50)

> [The squire who saw the affair took it for a great enchantment.... He began to debate strongly in his heart how it would end and what he should do.]

When he finally questions the ladies, their praise of their lord knows no bounds, a fact which does little to allay Galantinet's fear for Gawain.

A change of scene at this point returns the action to Arthur's court, where Gawain's continued melancholy is cause for great concern, and contrasts sharply with the description of the gaiety and confidence of Escanor's brilliant court. As the scene returns again to the approaching procession, the last *refrain* is sung by Escanor himself and his lady:

> "Ainsi doit entrer en vile
> qui amours maine."
> Li Biauz Escanors deduisant
> s'aloit ainsi qui doulousant
> ne s'aloit de nule aventure.
> La pluz tres douce creature
> du monde par la main tenoit;
> et cele pour lui demenoit
> par son plaisir joie et revel.
> (vv. 8340–48)

["So should he enter the city, the one whom love leads." The handsome Escanor went thus rejoicing, who was not going to sorrow for any adventure. He held the sweetest creature in the world by the hand, and she for his pleasure showed her joy and celebration.]

The *refrain* is one used frequently in processions, and is clearly a sign of Escanor's mood of cheerful confidence as he rides to confront Gawain. Marked by a series of encounters, the effect of the procession is cumulative, and the eager anticipation of Escanor and his retainers, coupled with Gawain's uncharacteristic melancholy, strengthen Galantinet's decision to carry out his ambush. Although the squire had decided on his course of action before meeting the cavalcade, the spectacle of such aplomb increases his fear for Gawain and strengthens his resolve. Every aspect of the procession impresses the squire: the number of supporters, their beauty, the richness of their attire, as well as the air of celebration and anticipation that they express in their songs. The lyrics, then, function as one element of a detailed descriptive passage, the whole of which makes an important impression upon the audience as well as upon the squire.

Considered within the context of the episode, the gaiety of the songs contrasts quite effectively with the squire's growing dismay and with Gawain's despondency. It is, however, harder to account for the episode within the romance as a whole.[14] After this build-up of suspense, the meeting of Gawain and Escanor is forestalled by Galantinet's ill-advised and underhanded ambush. When he eventually recovers from the attack, Escanor is handily defeated by Gawain, whose crisis of confidence is never satisfactorily explained. Girart in this early work thus shows himself as a gifted raconteur who is not always able to combine striking scenes into a coherent whole. What is evident, however, is his skill in exploiting songs in a descriptive passage for the purpose of revealing a character's state of mind. There is no element of psychological exploration in the songs; on the contrary, it is the character's reaction to their innocent cheerfulness that is revealing.

Tournoi de Chauvenci

The *Tournoi de Chauvenci*,[15] written by Jacques Bretel in 1285 to commemorate an actual tournament held by the Comte de Chiny, is the quintessential exemplar of a narrative containing lyric insertions used descriptively. All of its thirty-five *refrains* are sung in social settings, and indeed, the whole work is a patchwork of celebrations and jousts accompanied by music. The company sings on its way to the tournament, on entering the lists, while returning to the castle in the evening, during meals, and to accompany dancing.[16] The activities of the tournament are spread over five days and all except the actual fighting are punctuated by songs. The match begins on Monday with seven jousts; the company then adjourns to the castle singing three *refrains*; after dinner three more songs accompany the dancing. This pattern is repeated with some variation on Tuesday: three of the knights participating in the ten jousts sing *refrains* as they take their places, and two more are sung as the group moves indoors, where they sing six more *refrains* while they dance. Wednesday, devoted to organizing the tournament proper, is described only briefly, but Thursday's events follow the earlier sequence: the ladies dance among themselves in the morning (one *refrain*), and then process with their knights to the field singing four more songs. They watch the tournament (vv. 3335–4114) and perform one song as they return, while ten more accompany the "jeu de chapelet." On the

---

14. Ladd, "Lyric Insertions," pp. 99–100, argued that the passage is meant to characterize Escanor. While true, this interpretation ignores the effect that the whole scene seems calculated to produce upon Galantinet. It should also be borne in mind that Escanor is not the hero of the romance, which is primarily devoted to the adventures of Kay and Gawain. Because the beginning of the work had been lost, the title was the choice of the editor.

15. Maurice Delbouille, ed., *Jacques Bretel: Le Tournoi de Chauvency: édition complète* (Paris: Droz & Liège: H. Vaillant Carman, 1932); for date, see p. lvi.

16. Ibid., p. lxv.

following morning, one song is quoted as the ladies dance and another as the group departs. It is characteristic of Jacques's descriptive technique that the songs occur in groups of at least three or four, and alternate with passages devoted to descriptions of chivalric prowess.

Rather than analyze every insertion in this work, I shall limit my discussion to a few examples, and concentrate on the impression created by the songs. The second dance, performed after dinner on Tuesday evening, is accompanied by several songs:

> Par le doi tint Renaut de Trie
> Qui n'estoit pas mains biaus de li.
> Il comença de cuer joli
> A chanter sans trop grant proiere,
> Ne paroit mie a sa chiere
> Qu'il eüst point le cuer tourblé:
>   Hé, tres douce Jehannette,—Vos m'avéz mon cuer emblé!
> Jehenne d'Auviler l'esgarde,
> Qui n'estoit nice ne couarde,
> Mais teile com j'ai devisé.
> Un petitet l'ai avisé,
> Le bras estent et puis se torne,
> A chanter lïement s'atorne
> Et a commencié sans delai:
>   Onques mais n'amai!—He Diex, bone estrainne:—
>   Encommencié l'ai!
> En mon cuer pansai: "Se me samble,
> Dont avenéz vos bien ensamble."
> (vv. 2448–64)

[By the hand she held Renaut of Trie, who was no less beautiful than she. He began with merry heart, to sing without much asking, nor did it seem to his beloved that he had a troubled heart: "Eh! most sweet little Janet—you have stolen my heart!" Jeanne of Auvilier, who was neither foolish nor cowardly, but such as I have described, looks at him. I looked at her a moment, she extends her arm, then turns, prepares to sing gaily, and she began without delay: "Never before have I loved—O God! good fortune: I have begun!" In my heart I thought: "It seems to me, you suit each other well."]

Bretel's descriptive technique in this passage is quite similar to that of Jean Renart: there are references to the gaiety, grace, and beauty of the singers, who are identified here by name rather than by title alone. The individual performances hint at relationships among the participants, and the songs are, as here, often paired to respond to each other, although none of the relationships is developed in the narrative. The attribution of the songs to characters who are named but not otherwise described is another way of adding specificity to the scene. The description is embellished with little dramatic interludes which hint at narrative possibilities not pursued.

At the end of the tournament, the contestants forget their wounds and join happily in the singing as the company adjourns to the castle:

> Et li chevalier tuit monté,
> Detaillié et haligoté,
> Blecié de cors et de visaiges,
> Si d'armes en est li usaiges,
> Les enmaignent, joie faisant.
> Une chançon douce et plaisant
> Chantoient tuit par grant deport:
>   Je taig par le doi m'amie,—Vaigne avant cui je en fas tort!
> Del champ se partent sanz tristesce,
> A grant joie et a grant l'iesce,
> Cil qui avoient gaaignié.
> (vv. 4123–33)

[The knights all mounted, cut and torn, wounded in body and face, they bring them joyfully. They sang a sweet and pleasant song for entertainment. "I hold my lady by the hand,—he whom I wrong, come forth!" They leave the field without sadness, but with great joy and happiness, those who have won.]

The quotation of this song is an effective way of conveying the lighthearted mood of the contestants, despite the pain of their wounds.

Because the description of the tournament at Chauvency is not set into a larger narrative framework, but constitutes the whole of the narrative, the *Tournoi* is an example of the descriptive use of lyrics in its purest form. The narrator (a herald or minstrel?) remains a detached observer of the scene: he declines to participate in the singing because he is not of noble birth. His attention is not focused on any individual, for he is intent upon conveying the panoramic view of the whole spectacle. The songs, which convey quite vividly a mood of gaiety and excitement, are used in settings essentially similar to those of *Guillaume de Dole* and its successors. But because the author's intent is almost purely descriptive, the songs do not have any of the secondary functions discernible in the earlier works. They do not motivate the plot or have a psychological effect on a character, nor are they related to a thematic structure. On the other hand, because the narrative is so straightforward, the possibilities for tension between songs and context are all but eliminated.

Bretel's account of an historical tournament is particularly interesting in its use of songs. We have here an eyewitness account of the behavior of real people rendered with the techniques employed in fictional accounts of similar events. When Jean Renart explained his use of quotations, he pretended to a desire to preserve the songs from oblivion. Yet some sixty years later, an actual tournament was recounted by means of identical techniques using songs that are similar to, if not in fact the same as, those used by Renart.[17]

Roman du Castelain de Couci

Near the end of the thirteenth century, Jakemés Sakesep used three songs in his *Roman du Castelain de Couci et de la Dame de Fayel* in a way reminiscent of the opening scene of the *Roman de la Violette*. As in the earlier romance, the two passages containing songs describe baronial feasts which end in dancing, and the quoted lyrics provoke developments in the plot. Jakemés differed from his predecessor in relating the songs to the emotional state of his hero and heroine, as well as to the plot. The two scenes occur near the beginning of the romance, where the courtly festivities provide opportunities for the lovers to meet.[18] The first *rondeau* is sung on one such occasion. After dinner on the eve of a tournament, the guests begin a *carole*:

---

17. Cf. Poirion, *Précis de littérature française du Moyen Age*, p. 118. There are occasional instances of *rondeaux* or *refrains* inserted into descriptions of feasts or dancing in the several continuations of the Roman des Sept Sages: *Roman de Laurin, fils de Marques le Seneschal*, ed. Lewis Thorpe (Cambridge: W. Heffer & Sons, 1960), pp. 94–95, 134–35; *Roman de Cassidorus*, ed. Joseph Palermo, 2 vols., SATF (Paris, 1963–64), pp. 48, 193–94. *Peliarmenus* and *Kanor* are as yet unpublished, although Meradith McMunn is completing an edition of the latter; in the absence of editions, I have read the romances in manuscript: see London, B. L., Harley 4903, ff. 103d, 198d; and Paris, B. N., fr. 22550, ff. 19, 122. Thorpe assigns *Laurin* to the "fifties or sixties of the thirteenth century" (p. xvii), while Palermo (p. lv) gives ca. 1270 as the date of *Cassidorus*; McMunn places *Kanor* ca. 1278–92.

18. See Lyons, *Les éléments descriptifs*, p. 155.

96   Chapter 3

> Quant on ot siervi a plenté,
> De toutes pars se sont levé;
> Dont veïssiés carole prise.
> Errant a une dame emprise
> Ceste cancon mygnotement:
> > Toute nostre gent
> > Sont li plus joli
> > Dou tournoiement;
> > S'aimment loiaument
> > Toute nostre gent.
>
> (vv. 984–93)

[When they had been served plentifully, they rose on all sides and began a *carole*. Straightaway, a lady sang this song gracefully: "All our people are the most handsome of the tournament. They love loyally, all our people."]

The *rondeau* of the *carole* is not only effective in evoking the festive atmosphere of the gathering, but is very neatly inserted into the context. The mention of loyal love reflects the main interest of the romance, and the occasion for the song is indeed a tournament. The scene also contrasts nicely with the Châtelain's state of mind as he watches for a chance to slip away to meet his lady and receive the sleeve she promised him. This song, like the two other *rondeaux*, contrasts with the register of most of the songs in the romance. Whereas the *chansons* composed by the Châtelain belong to the courtly register of *fin'amors* and celebrate his sufferings, these dance songs evoke a happier sentiment which is not possible for the hero.

The two remaining *rondeaux* in the romance are inserted in a later passage describing a summer festival in the Vermandois—the last occasion when the Châtelain and his lady appear in a social context. This scene is also one of the major turning points in the narrative, for it is here that their liaison is first exposed. The Dame de Vermandois notices the Châtelain's unhappy mien and comments on it. Intercepting his glance at the Dame de Fayel, she guesses the cause and sings:

> Cescuns se doit esbaudir
> > Mignotement,
> Qui vit amoureusement;
> Sans plaindre et faire souffrir.
>
> (vv. 3832–35)

[Everyone should rejoice graciously who lives lovingly; without complaining and causing suffering.]

Her song seems to an admonish the Châtelain, and justifiably: had he better disguised his suffering, he would not have betrayed his secret. The final *rondeau* is sung by the Dame de Fayel herself as she leads the dancing:

J'aim bien loiaument,
Et s'ai biel ami
Pour cui di souvent
J'aim bien loiaument.
(vv. 3857–60)

[I love very loyally, and I have a lover for whom I say often, I love very loyally.]

The song seems apt, but in the circumstances most unfortunate, for it confirms the suspicions of the Dame de Vermandois. On another level, however, the *rondeau* is inappropriate, for her relationship with the Châtelain belongs to a mode more characterized by suffering than by cheerful enjoyment.

The three *rondeaux* in the *Castelain de Couci* inserted into descriptive passages do therefore contribute to the festive mood of a celebration, but in each case their significance goes beyond the superficial meaning of the words. This deeper significance is apparent to the reader, but hidden from most of the characters—a situation that adds ironic overtones to the scene. Jakemés has taken advantage of the apparently impersonal quality of social singing to allow his characters to play out a personal drama in public. Once the love has become known, however, such a game is no longer possible, and the Châtelain and his lady never again appear in such surroundings.

COURT D'AMOURS

The next innovation in the descriptive use of lyric insertions in courtly scenes was its incorporation into a new genre of narrative, the allegory. The continuation of the *Court d'Amours*,[19] composed around 1322, contains an

---

19. Terence Scully, ed., *Le Court d'Amours de Mahieu le Poirier et la Suite anonyme de la "Court d'Amours"* (Waterloo, Ontario: Wilfred Laurier University Press, 1976). The continuation is preceded in the manuscript by another short work, the *Ju de le Capete Martinet*. H. R. Jauss, "Entstehung und Strukturwandel der allegorischen Dichtung," *GRMLA,* VI.1 (1968):

account of a celebration held by the forces of Love while besieging the castle of Envy. Thirty-three *refrains* are inserted into the description of this single night of singing and dancing before the fighting is resumed.

The *Court d'Amours* opens with a judicial scene: problems of love are argued before the god of Love and are judged by him. During the course of the narrative, thirty-two cases are presented. The business of the court is interrupted by Envy, who attempts to seize the castle of Love by force. This part of the work ends with the retreat of Love and the occupation of the castle by Envy. The *Continuation* opens with a description of Envy's court and her adherents boasting of their successes in separating lovers.

After several initial encounters with the *mesdisans* (the supporters of Envy), the disciples of Love begin their final effort to reclaim the castle. Their attack is interrupted by nightfall and, exhilarated by the prospect of victory, they spend the night in revelry, taking turns singing:

> Aprés cheste canchon jolie
> conmencha par se courtoisie
> une dame qui fu de Mons
> en Hainnaut, et pour les barons
> ensanier si leur dist ainssi
> en cantant de lié cuer joli
> cheste canchon moult liement,
> conment qu'il voit, chertainnement:
> > Nus n'iert ja jolis,
> > s'il n'aimme.
> Cascuns repondi a sen tour.
> (Scully, p. 199, vv. 3382–89, including 3388, bis, a, b)

[Afterward, a lady from Mons in Hainaut began this pretty song, and in order to teach the barons, she said to them, singing this song lightheartedly and happily, although he sees, certainly: "No one will ever be handsome if he does not love." Each one replied in turn.]

The tone of the passage is gay, but the singers make some allusions to their

---

146–244, esp. p. 240, thought that the three texts form a single composition by one author; cf. Scully p. vi, n. 8. For the date, see ibid., p. xxii. For corrections to part of the edition, see Jean-Marie d'Heur and Michel Zink, "Pastourelle et Courtoisie: Sur un arrêt inédit de 'Le court d'amours' de Mahiu li Poirier," in *Mélanges de philologie et littérature offerts à Jeanne Wathelet-Willem* (Liège: Marche Romane, 1978), pp. 126–42 and 741–52.

situation. Several of the songs refer to the slanderers, the supporters of Envy:

> Amours, par vo grant signourie
> et pour vo conseil que j'ai prest,
> gais et jolis suis pour m'amie:
> des mesdisans a riens ne m'est.
> (Scully, p. 198, 3368a–d)

["Love, by your power and your advice that I have taken, I am gay and handsome for my lady: the slanderers are nothing to me."]

> Mesdisant creveront, ja n'en saront
> le joie que j'ai.
> (Scully, p. 206, vv. 3617a–b)

["The slanderers will die, never will they know the joy I have."]

Such references to slanderers are common in *refrains,* but they are particularly appropriate in the context of a lull in the battle between Envy and the forces of Love.

The scene as a whole reflects the sentiments of the lyrics—a joyful celebration in defiance of Envy. It is clear even from these few quotations that the device is applied to its new context without alteration; the pattern found here is essentially that of *Guillaume de Dole.* What differs is the relationship between singer and song. In the romances discussed so far, *refrains* and *rondeaux* are used impersonally, that is, the singer may choose any song of the requisite genre without thought for the appropriateness of its words either to himself or the occasion. Those songs which do suit a particular character are not usually perceived as such by his companions. Here, however, the relationship of the songs to their performers is much more direct. It is as if the songs had come to life and sung themselves, for the cast of courtly virtues participates in the performance.[20]

---

20. The applications of this conventional mode of description became much more mechanical in the remaining works of the fourteenth century. In Jean Le Court's *Restor du paon,* the single *rondeau* in the work is sung as the peacock is carried in procession through the hall (*Jean le Court, dit Brisebare Le Restor du paon: édition critique,* ed. Richard J. Carey, TLF, 119 [Geneva: Droz, 1966]; see pp. 210–12 on the *rondeau* and its music). The late fourteenth-century prose romance *Ysaÿe le Triste* contains an episode similar to that in the *Restor.* See

100   Chapter 3

MELIADOR

As we have seen in Chapter 2, most of the songs inserted by Jean Froissart into his *Meliador* are used expressively.[21] The vast majority of the seventy-nine pieces in *Meliador* are sung by characters in solitude or enclosed with letters, and serve as expressions of their emotions; despite the fact that the plot of the romance is organized around four major tournaments and is punctuated with descriptions of court festivities, only fifteen songs are quoted in the context of celebrations at court.[22]

As in *Guillaume de Dole,* the descriptions of the aristocratic life — the sumptuous dinners and celebrations that accompany the tournaments and jousts—form an elegant backdrop for the action, whose point is to show the virtues of the chivalric class in action. Froissart's emphasis in the tournaments is on the fighting rather than the feasting, so that although music is always mentioned, songs are quoted in connection with only two of them. The first occasion, the tournament at Tarbonne (vv. 12659–13442), invites comparison to *Escanor* in its use of songs to highlight the emotional state of a particular character.

The songs sung at Tarbonne occur in circumstances that are by this time completely conventional, but the purpose of the scene is to dramatize the change of heart of Agamanor, Meliador's chief rival. Agamanor has been competing for the hand of Hermondine, but at Tarbonne he sees and falls in love with Meliador's sister Phenonée. Agamanor notices Phenonée dancing the *carole* to the accompaniment of songs performed by two minor characters. The scene is not described objectively, but presented from Agamanor's point of view.

The first *rondel* interrupts his thoughts as he watches Phenonée with growing interest:

> Adont se desrompent ces routes
> Et commencent a caroler:

---

above, Chapter 2, under "*Ysaÿe le Triste*" and n. 58 for a fuller discussion of this romance. The passage in question contains thirteen *rondeaux* sung in the context of a banquet during which vows are made. Cf. Zeidler, "Der Prosaroman 'Ysaÿe le Triste,'" *ZRP,* 25 (1901): 175–214, especially pp. 179–80.

In Guillaume de Deguileville's *Pèlerinage de l'âme* (ed. J. J. Stürzinger, London: The Roxburghe Club, 1895), several processions are described as accompanied by songs. Souls sing as they leave purgatory, in purgatory, and in paradise, but the songs are not set off in any way from the body of the text in octosyllabic couplets. On this work see Alfred Jeanroy, "La Passion Nostre Dame et 'Le Pèlerinage de l'Ame' de Guillaume de Digulleville," *Romania,* 36 (1907): 361–66.

21. See above, Chapter 2, under "*Meliador.*"
22. Dembowski, *Jean Froissart and His Meliador,* pp. 62–63.

La veïssiés moult bien aler,
A ces caroles qui sont belles,
Signeurs avoecques damoiselles.
Agamanor, qui en la presse
Estoit, voit c'une dame presse
Au canter, de bon sentement,
.I. rondelet presentement,
Qui fist les aultres resjoïr.
Le rondelet porés oïr.
    Ou que je soie, doulz amis,
    N'aiés ja doubte de moi.
    Mes coers n'iert ja de vous partis,
    Ou que je soie, etc.
    Je vous seray loyaus toutdis,
    Et vous jure par ma foy,
    Ou que je soie, etc.
Tantost reprist uns chevaliers
Au chanter, qui fu biaus parliers,
Frices, gracieus et courtois,
Et canta a jolie vois
Qui fu moult volontiers oÿe.
Et lors se taist la compagnie,
Quant cilz commença a canter,
Jusques a tant qu'il pot cesser.
Tous en est au coer resjoïs
Agamanor, quant a oÿs
Parlers si doulz, et dist sus s'ame,
En regardant dessus ma dame
Phenonée, qui tant est belle:
"Au coer me point une estincelle
D'Amours . . ."
(vv. 13294–326)

[Then the groups break up and begin to dance the *carole*. There you would have seen them go well in these dances that are so beautiful, lords with ladies. Agamanor, who was in the crowd, sees that a lady hastens to sing, with good sentiment, a *rondelet*, which makes the others rejoice. You shall hear the *rondelet*: "Wherever I may be, sweet friend, do not doubt me. My heart shall never be parted from you. Wherever I may be etc. I shall always be loyal to you, and I swear to you by my faith, wherever I may be etc." Then a knight begins to sing, who was well-spoken, galant, graceful and courteous, and he sang with a pretty voice that was heard most willingly. And then the company fell silent when he began to sing until he had stopped. Agamanor was completely overjoyed at heart when he heard such sweet speech, and said upon his soul, looking at lady Phenonée, who is so beautiful: "A spark of love pierces my heart . . ."]

The passage immediately following the first lyric announces the second song, which is not inserted until fifty lines later, and the delay is occasioned by a monologue exploring Agamanor's state of mind. The monologue continues for another fifteen lines, but after this interruption, the author returns to his description of the *carole* and quotes the second *rondel*:

Mais Agamanor, sachiés bien,
Ne le volsist pour nulle rien,
Ançois se cuevre et si se boute
Toutdis ou plus fort de le route,
Et entent ce c'on dist et cante.
Bien a retenu, je m'en vante,
Le rondelet dou chevalier.
Il ne fait pas a oubliier,
Car il est jolis et courtois
Et chantés d'une belle vois.
    Mon coer est lié plus c'onques mes.
    De ce, dame, je vous merci.
(vv. 13352–63)

[But Agamanor, know it well, wished for nothing, and so covers himself and pulls himself completely out of the way, and hears what they say and sing. He well remembered, so I claim, the knight's *rondelet*. He does not forget it, for it is pretty and courtly, and sung in a beautiful voice: "My heart is happier than ever before. For this, lady, I thank you."]

Since Froissart does not usually quote songs that accompany dancing, his decision to do so here calls for some comment. The scene is, of course, crucial to Agamanor's development: this knight, who so far has been Meliador's most ardent rival for the hand of Hermondine, realizes here that he is no longer interested in her, but in Phenonée. The song he overhears actually describes what has happened to him, although he does not quite realize it. As in *Escanor,* the song itself is less important to the singer than to the eavesdropper. But while the *rondel* quoted here marks the change in Agamanor, it does not effect that change.

The only other description of a feast that includes lyric insertions is the final tournament at Monchus, where the leading knights of the romance are married to their ladies. The last section of the romance as it now exists (roughly one thousand lines) contains eight songs spaced fairly regularly through the passsage and quoted in the context of several banquets. Once again, Froissart seems to have departed from his normal practice, but considering the occasion for these celebrations may explain it. In general, as we saw in Chapter 2, the songs in *Meliador* express the theme of love, while the narrative concerns itself with prowess. The tournament of Tarbonne, which displayed Agamanor's skill to advantage, was also the occasion on which he fell in love with Phenonée. While he did not sing, the use of songs to frame his change of heart was most fitting. Likewise, the account of the weddings at the end of the romance is an occasion for the author to unite his two themes and show the crowning of chivalry by love. Froissart was consistent in reserving the lyric mode for the expression of love, and used songs in his descriptions of celebrations only when the theme of love was of paramount importance.

Music of the Anti-Court

In the works discussed so far in this chapter, songs have been quoted straightforwardly as elements of description, even where they also serve other artistic purposes. Most of the passages are quite similar, the chief variations being the number and genre of the songs. Such conservatism may well have arisen from the nature of the technique, essentially a kind of *reportage*. Since the device itself remained unchanged, the principal modifications in its use resulted from attempts to make such scenes serve more than one purpose. During the period in which the device became conventional (the later thirteenth and early fourteenth centuries), three authors produced parodies of courtly musical scenes. Each assumed the use of lyric insertions as a conventional element of description, and distorted it to comic effect. The incongruity of saints (The *Court de Paradis*), bourgeoises (*Les Trois Dames de Paris*), and animals (*Renart le Nouvel*) aping the behavior of courtly aristocrats is risible.[23] In the last instance, the device is multiplied to the point of ridiculous exaggeration, while in all three works its transposition to a different social class leads to a comic dislocation.

The *Court de Paradis* is a description of the heavenly kingdom in terms usually applied to earthly ones. Composed in the second half of the thirteenth century, the poem describes Christ's plenary court on the Feast of All Saints.[24] The anonymous author concentrates on the procession of arriving guests, who sing eighteen *refrains* as they enter the hall.

After a brief prologue, the author describes God's decision to hold full court on All Saints' Day. Simon and Jude are sent to fetch heaven's inhabitants. The angels arrive first singing the *Te Deum*; they are followed by the patriarchs, and the poem's propriety disappears as they sing the *refrain* of a secular dance song: "Je vi d'amor / En bone esperance" (vv. 259–60; "I live by love in good hope"). This first *refrain* is typical of the remainder. Fourteen mention love directly, or by implication, and the remaining four refer to "joie." In all but two of the *refrains* love is presented in positive terms.

The procession continues with Apostles, Martyrs, and Fathers of the Church, all of whose songs are about love. The song of the Holy Innocents "Vrais Diex, la joie que j'ai / Me vient de vos" (vv. 318–19; "True God, the joy I have comes to me from you") is unobjectionable in the context, but it is clearly a variation of a secular song.[25] As in other court festivals, the celebration continues with dancing; Mary Magdalene sings a *refrain* that invites the others to dance:

> La Madelainne o li apele,
> Si l'a prise par la main bele,
> Et vont chantant par grant soulaz:
> > Tout cil qui sunt enamoraz
> > Viegnent dancier, li autre non.
> A cest apel vienent pucelles,

---

23. See Zumthor, *Essai*, p. 105, on this technique.
24. E. Vilamo-Pentti, ed., *La Court de Paradis*, Annales Academiae Scientiarum Fennicae, B. 79, 1 (Helsinki: Société de Littérature Finnoise, 1953); see p. 43 for date. The *refrains* were examined by D. L. Buffum, "The Refrains of the *Court de Paradis* and of a *Salut d'Amour* (Jubinal, 235)," *Modern Language Notes*, 27 (1912): 5–11. In one manuscript (Paris, B. N., fr. 25532), all the *refrains* have musical notation.
25. Vilamo-Pentti, pp. 63–64. The same is true of the *refrain* (vv. 504–5) sung by the whole company; see pp. 76–77.

Virges, dames et damoiseles,
Apostre, martir, Innocent.
(vv. 409–16)

[The Magdalene calls to her, and so took her by the hand, and they go singing with great pleasure: "All those who are in love, come dance, the others no." To this call come girls, virgins, married ladies, unmarried ladies, Apostles, Martyrs, and Innocents.]

Her song is of the type which is usually used to begin a *carole*. All of the songs except the *Te Deum* are dance songs, and to that extent appropriate for the performance of the dance. Near the end of the poem, we learn the reason for all the jubilation: the saints are joyous because they live in the presence of God, who redeemed them by his death, rose again, and ascended into heaven.

Pour ce sunt de chanter engrant,
Si chantent tuit communalment
De fine amor qui les mestroie
Et chascuns chantoit endroit soi:
    Touz li cuers me rit de joie
    Quant Dieu voi.
(vv. 500–505)

[For this they wish to sing and so sing all together of fine love which rules them and each one sang in his own way: "All my heart laughs with joy when I see God."]

The inhabitants of heaven celebrate the joy of redemption, but do so with songs that belong to the register of "la bonne vie." It is the juxtaposition of secular song of the most worldly type to religious doctrine that produces the shock of suprise typical of the work. While the insistence on heavenly joy is not unreasonable,[26] its expression in the songs of the god of Love is incongruous, and creates a tone of lighthearted irreverence.

The parody of the convention is clearer still in Jacquemart Gielée's *Renart le Nouvel*, composed around 1289.[27] The work, intended as a satirical

---

26. Cf., for example, Psalms 148.2, 149.3.
27. H. Roussel, ed., *Renart le nouvel par Jacquemart Gielée* (Paris, 1961); for date, see John

attack on the vices of society, is an allegorical transformation of the Reynard material in which the fox has become the symbol of evil incarnate. The lion-king Noble besieges Renart's castle at the urging of the fox's victims, but is unable to capture it. Renart in the meantime carries off Orgueil, the king's son, crowns him king of the vices, and frees Noble's prisoners. The fox then seeks reconciliation with the king, who appoints him seneschal. Once more outraged by Renart's misdeeds, Noble seizes his castle but the fox escapes on the ship of vice, taking with him the wives of the king, the wolf, and the leopard. Noble plans to pursue him in the ship of virtue, but fails to do so, and is once again reconciled with the fox. Noble's ship then disappears, and he is obliged to embark with Renart, whose triumph is complete. The tale ends with the reunion of all the animals at a feast in Renart's castle.

As presented in the modern edition, *Renart le Nouvel* contains sixty-six insertions, including one liturgical piece in Latin (*Asperges*, v. 5304); the remainder are *refrains,* three of which are repeated in the text. Not included in this figure are the incipits of liturgical pieces (*Te Deum*, vv. 2469, 6946 and *Veni creator*, v. 5291).[28] One difficulty that arises in studying the lyric insertions in this work is that the four manuscripts agree on only forty of the insertions; the remainder are replaced by different *refrains* in the different manuscripts. Although these variants would seem to require four different readings of the text, the variant songs are usually equivalent in sense and tone. Since the genre and general sense of the songs are more important than the particular words, it is possible to analyze the work on the basis of one manuscript without misrepresenting it significantly. One critic, in fact, has suggested that the four manuscripts represent four "performances" of the work, and that the substitutions reflect differences in the particular occasion and the preferences of the performers.[29]

The occasions for singing in *Renart le Nouvel* are those that we have observed in other romances: processions (vv. 1732–51, two *refrains;* vv.

Flinn, *Le Roman de Renart dans la littérature française et dans les littératures étrangères du moyen âge* (Toronto: University of Toronto Press, 1963), pp. 246–363, esp. 246, 251. See also R. Bossuat, *Le Roman de Renard*, Connaissance des Lettres, 49 (Paris: Hatier, 1967).

28. The songs have been studied by H. Roussel in an unpublished thesis, *Etude sur Renart le Nouvel du poète lillois Jacquemart Gielée* (Thèse, Faculté de Lettres, Paris, 1956), chapter 5, pp. 312ff; by Jean Maillard, "Les refrains de caroles dans Renart le Nouvel," and by N. H. J. van den Boogard, "Jacquemart Giélée et la lyrique de son temps," in *Alain de Lille, Gautier de Châtillon, Jakemart Giélée et leur temps*, ed. H. Roussel and F. Suard, Actes du Colloque de Lille Oct., 1978 (Lille: Presse Universitaire de Lille, 1980), pp. 277–93 and 333–53, respectively. Maillard printed the notation for *refrains* 23–31.

29. Boogaard, "Jacquemart Giélée," pp. 351–52.

2336–63, one *refrain*), celebratory feasts (vv. 2400 ff., 1 *refrain*; vv. 6229–6320, three *refrains*; vv. 6947–74, one *refrain*); to accompany the *carole* (vv. 2528–61, four *refrains*). The final scene of the work when the animals assemble is a musical explosion with forty-five *refrains* inserted in a passage of three hundred lines (vv. 6621–6938).

The outrageous exaggeration of the final scene is exploited to comic effect by the dislocation of the scene—the substitution of animals for people—and by the literal application of the words of the songs. For instance, the monkey sings an invitation to her lover:

> Chapelet de venke
> Et nouvel ami ferai.
> Tout si en cantant descendi;
> Symons, li mainmonnés, l'oï,
> Qui l'avoit amee grant tans;
> Acolee l'a par les flans,
> Si le mist jus del palefroi,
> Car li l'amoit en boine foi
> Et pour l'amour qu'il ot a li
> Dist en haut che motet joli,
> Con chius qui aime de grant foi:
> A ma dame servir
> Ai mis mon cuer et moi.
> (vv. 6768–78 [regardless of length, refrains are numbered as single lines])

["Periwinkle garland, and I will take a new lover." While singing she alighted. Simon the macaque heard her, who had loved her for a long time; he grasped her flanks and put her down from the horse, for he loved her in good faith and for the love he had for her he sang out loud this pretty motet like one who loves with great faith: "To serve my lady have I set my heart and myself."]

Overhearing this blatant exchange, the husband rues his marriage:

> Quant Cointeriaus li singes l'ot,
> Dedens son cuer grant doel en ot;
> Samblant fait que n'en veïst mie
> Et, pour lui couvrir, par boisdie

> Canta en aus tournant le dos:
>> Dieus! je me mariai trop tos.
>> De moi marier fis que fols.
> (vv. 6779–84)

[When Cointeriau the monkey heard him, his heart was very sorrowful. He pretended that he saw nothing, and, to cover up by ruse, he sang turning his back on them: "God! I married too soon. I acted like a fool in marrying."]

The three songs form a sort of narrative interlude in the midst of the long description. But by using the *refrains* in this way, Jacquemart broke with tradition. For it is characteristic of a lyric used "descriptively" that the words have nothing to do with the singer; on the contrary, the mere act of singing expresses gaiety. Here, however, a "lady" and her lover exchange public declarations, while the betrayed husband is left to make the best of the situation.

This adaptation of the traditional device appears elsewhere in the work. In a similar passage, the marten sings:

> Ja ne lairai pour mon mari a dire,
> Li miens amis jut anuit avoec moi.
> Quant ses maris l'a entendue,
> Il l'aerst et dont l'a batue
> Disant ce, car plains d'aïr fu:
>> Ameras me tu, tu, tu,
>> Ameras me tu? (vv. 6846–50)

["I shall not, for my husband's sake, stop saying, my lover lay with me this night." When her husband heard her, he seized her and struck her saying this, for he was full of hate: "Will you love me, you, you, will you love me?"]

The drama is the same, although the outcome is different: this "lady" is less fortunate, for the husband is less complaisant. The linking of *refrains* is developed at some length in another segment of the scene (vv. 6795–6840), where the bull Bruiant courts two cows, Blere and Masquerelle, simultaneously, the three voices blending in a comic trio punctuated with seven *refrains*. The scene ends with the entire scurrilous group joining in the *Te Deum* (v. 6946). This appropriation of a sacred hymn by the forces of vice suggests that worldly success is blessed by corrupt churchmen.

Songs as Description 109

These examples serve as illustrations of Jacquemart's technique throughout the work. The seductions, betrayals, and reprisals which constitute the plot of *Renart le Nouvel* are here summarized and reenacted in miniature within the frame of the courtly procession. There is a decided comic element in the scandalous behavior of the animal courtiers, but the satire of the court society is clear: the animals make explicit tensions which normally remain hidden in polite society.

The genre of the insertions contributes to the social satire of the work. The courtly pretensions of the characters are belied by their actions, and their failings are revealed in their proclamation of the register of "la bonne vie," which has degenerated in this context into adultery and deceit. The liturgical pieces are in turn degraded, for they, like the ecclesiastical bodies attacked by the work, cast a blasphemous approval on a vicious social order.

Watriquet de Couvin parodied the motif of the court banquet, not by exaggeration or literalism, but by the dislocation of its activities to a lower social class. All the elements of the traditional description of a banquet (including the inserted songs) are applied to an orgy of three *bourgeoises* in the *Trois Dames de Paris*.[30] The title sets the ironic tone of the work, for the cast of characters includes no ladies. Two of the "dames" (Margue and her niece Maroie Clippe[31]) stop at a tavern on their way to the market, where they meet Dame Tifaigne. The latter praises the tavern's fare, and suggests a picnic by the riverbank where no one can see them. After charging the food and wine to their husbands' accounts, the three set off, with a waiter (Druins) to serve them. At midnight, quite drunk, they dance naked in the street and collapse in a stupor. The next morning they are discovered still comatose, presumed dead, and buried. They awaken at midnight on the second night and dig themselves out, but faint with the cold. Their neighbors are amazed to find the bodies returned from the grave, but the mystery is solved when Tifaigne shouts for drink.

The *dit* contains two songs, both *refrains*, which are inserted into the description of the orgy. The first is sung at the height of the feast, which is a travesty of an elegant court banquet:

Lors comença Margue à suer
Et boire à grandes henapées;

---

30. Auguste Scheler, ed., *Dits de Watriquet de Couvin, publiés d'après les manuscrits de Paris et de Bruxelles et accompagnés de variantes et de notes explicatives* (Brussels: Victor DeVaux, 1863), pp. 381–90.
31. Three forms of this name—Maroie Clippe, Maroie, and Maroclippe—occur in the text.

110   Chapter 3

> En poi d'eure erent eschapées
> .III. chopines parmi sa gorge.
> "Dame, foi que je doi saint Jorge,"
> Dist Maroclippe sa commere,
> "Cis vins me fait la bouche amere,
> Je veul avoir de la garnache,
> Se vendre devoie ma vache;
> S'en aurai jà au mains plain pot."
> (vv. 72–81)

> [Then Margue began to sweat and to drink in great gulps; very quickly three pints disappeared down her throat. "Lady, by my faith in St. George," said her companion Maroclippe, "this wine makes my mouth sour; I want some wine from Grenada, if I have to sell my cow; I will have at least a full pot of it."]

The passage continues with a description of their surroundings, the various dishes they consume, and their beverages. When the provisions give out, the waiter is sent to fetch more. While waiting, Maroie sings:

> Commere, menons bon revel,
> Tiex vilains l'escot paiera,
> Qui jà du vin n'ensaiera.
> (vv. 94–96)

> [Friend, let's celebrate, the lout will pay the bill who will never taste the wine.]

The song is perfectly appropriate in the context; the women are indeed having a "bon revel" for which their husbands will have to pay. In addition, the insertion of a *refrain* in such a scene makes the allusion to other, more refined, feasts more explicit.

As in descriptions of the court, dancing follows the banquet, and the three "dames" provide their own accompaniment:

> "S'irons treschier parmi la rue."
> Atant chascune à terre rue
> Son corset et son chaperon;
> Escourchié furent li geron

Des cotes desus la pelice,
Et Druins hors de l'uis les glice.
Chantant chascune à haute vois:
"Amours, au vireli m'en vois!"
(vv. 157–164)

["Let's go dance in the street." Then each one throws down her cloak and hood; the tunics were peeled off from the dresses above their skin, and Druins slid them out the door. Each one singing out loud, "Love, I go to the *virelai*."]

In addition to the songs, we note the same elements of description: the details of food, wine, dancing, and the suggestion of festivity. In a courtly description there is an impression of panorama, of many participants. Here the similar impression of movement and activity is confined to the three participants, and is frenzied indeed. The scandalous nature of their *carole* makes the scene extremely funny, and much of the comic effect is derived from the clear parody of a familiar convention.[32]

In all three works in which the lyric insertion device is used parodically, the characters appear ludicrous by their appropriation of behavior that does not properly belong to them. The humor in the *Court de Paradis* arises from the humanizing of figures normally considered indifferent to frivolous amusement. But from another point of view, the portrayal of the heavenly court is appropriate, for it is supposed to be a "court of joy"; the only incongruity arises from interpreting the joy in such earthly terms. The humor of the other two works, on the other hand, is satirical. In both *Renart le Nouvel* and the *Trois Dames de Paris*, it is not merely the characters aping their betters who are mocked; the imitated behavior itself appears ridiculous. Removed from its normal sphere, the courtly ideal is exposed to criticism.

The Song of the Shepherdess

Lyric insertions had been introduced into the evocation of pastoral scenes as early as the mid-thirteenth century, when Adam de la Halle employed

---

[32]. Watriquet used *refrains* in similarly incongruous contexts in his "Fatras"; cf. Eglal Doss-Quinby, *Les refrains chez les trouvères du XIIe siècle au début du XIVe*, American University Studies, Series II: Romance Languages and Literature, 17 (New York, Bern, Frankfurt-am-Main: Peter Lang, 1984), p. 260.

them in his play the *Jeu de Robin et Marion*. They are not found in a narrative work of the pastoral genre until the end of our period, when Christine de Pizan used them in her *Dit de la Pastoure*.[33] The function of the device is essentially the same in Christine's *dit* as it was in the descriptive passages of two centuries earlier in *Guillaume de Dole*, but as in the *Trois Dames de Paris*, the singers belong to another order of society. Instead of emphasizing the brilliance and elegance of a royal or aristocratic court, two songs in the *Dit de la Pastoure* evoke the idyllic pastoral life of the shepherdess.[34] Their function is thus quite different from that of the lyrics in the *Trois Dames* and the other works discussed in the last section.

As the work opens, the shepherdess explains that love has made her unhappy, and recalls her carefree life before she fell in love. She describes in some detail her duties and responsibilities, but also the pleasures of her life, particularly music and dancing. According to the shepherdess, picnics by a stream were often occasions for lighthearted celebrations:

> La a cotes de buriaulx
> Vous veissiés ces pastoreaulx
> Mener feste a desmesure,
> Pour attaindre a la mesure
> Fraper du pié en dançant,
> Gautier emprès Helissant
> A cloche pié faire un sault,
> Si comme amours les assault,
> Huer, crier, rigoler
> Et ensemble entr'acoler:

---

33. This is the only pastoral narrative composed in our period in which lyrics were inserted, but they were also used in the *Pastoralet*, a fifteenth-century piece of Burgundian propaganda against the House of Orléans; Joël Blanchard, ed., *Le Pastorale, édité avec introduction notes et glossaire*, Publications de l'Université de Rouen (Paris: Presses Universitaires de France, 1983). Courtly and pastoral elements are joined in this work: the shepherds in the story represent the members of the court of Charles VI in a roman à clef. Music is said to be an essential part of the pastoral life (vv. 265–74; 347–49, 428–33), but no songs are quoted until the lyric contest. Although the passage is meant to suggest an idyll, the insertion of sophisticated songs betrays the disguise of the shepherds. I have not discussed this work in detail because it is less a work of fiction than of political propaganda, and the pastoral disguise of the aristocratic characters is unconvincing.

34. Maurice Roy, ed., *Les Oeuvres poétiques de Christine de Pisan*, 3 vols. SATF (Paris: Firmin Didot, 1886–96); vol. 2, pp. 223–94. See also Joël Blanchard, *La pastorale en France aux XIVe et XVe siècles: Recherches sur les structures de l'imaginaire médiéval*, Bibliothèque du XVe siècle (Paris: Champion, 1983). The songs of the shepherdess after she falls in love with the knight are discussed in Chapter 6.

> Est ce vie vie vie?
> Qui jamais a d'autre envie?
(vv. 209–20)³⁵

[There in woolen tunics you would see these shepherds celebrate enthusiastically, and stamp their feet to keep time in dancing. You would see Gautier next to Helissant jump with a lame foot, as love assaults him, shout, cry out, laugh and embrace each other: "Is this life, life, life? Who has any other wish?"]

The songs of her companions serve not only to accompany dances, but to express contentment in requited love:

> En celle lande champestre,
> De flours couverte a tous tours,
> Sont ilz aise ces pastours
> Berbis gardans par sillons,
> Et ces jolis oysillons
> Qui les cuers leur resjoïst!
> En celle place on oÿst
> Chanter Parrot et Margot:
>> "Larigot va larigot,
>> Mari, tu ne m'aimes mie,
>> Pour ce a Robin suis amie."
(vv. 236–46)

[In this rural country, covered with flowers on every side, these shepherds are at ease, guarding their sheep in rows, and these pretty little birds who gladden their hearts. In that place, one hears Parrot and Margot singing: "Larigot va larigot, Husband, you do not love me, so I am Robin's lover."]

The effect of the whole scene, of which the two songs are only a small part, is to set forth a picture of peace and happiness, which is disrupted by the arrival of the knight with whom the shepherdess falls in love. After his

---

35. Verses 219–20 and 244–46 are not identified by Roy as *refrains*, but appear to belong to the genre. I have replaced the semi-colon at the end of line 218 with a colon to set off the lines of the *refrain* more clearly.

arrival, the lightheartedness of her former existence is lost to her, and she recalls it with nostalgia.

Songs as Characterization; The Allegorical Singers

As I noted in the introduction to this chapter, examples of explicit characterization by means of songs are rare in the corpus of works with lyric insertions. Indeed, only four narratives contain lyrics employed for this purpose. In three of these narratives, the inserted songs are employed in an essentially similar way: an allegorical character (Music in both the anonymous *Mariage des Sept Arts* and the *Ludus-Anticlaudien*, Loyauté in Christine de Pizan's *Dit de la Rose*) uses song rather than speech as a means of expression, and does so to portray her own nature. In the one remaining work, the *Roman de Tristan en Prose*, the inserted lyric is used rather differently: a *lai* composed by someone else is used to characterize King Mark.

In the prose *Tristan*, King Mark's malice and deceit are exposed in a *lai* composed by Dinadan, the most cynical member of his court. Angered by King Arthur's defense of Tristan, Mark decides to take revenge on Guinevere. He sends her a *lai* describing in crude terms her relationship with Lancelot, and attempts to make her think that the song has been widely circulated. Dinadan, wishing to punish the king in like manner, arranges for a musical denunciation of the king, the *Lai Voir Disant*, to be performed in Mark's presence.[36] In the sixteen quatrains of this extended insult, the king, "Rois March, dolans viex et chaitif" (IV, 1; "King Mark, sad, old and miserable"), is accorded all the chivalric and courtly vices: "Deshounour, vergoigne et laidure" (VI, 2; "Dishonor, shame, and ugliness"), "Faillis de cuer, couars, renois" (XII, 1; "faint-hearted, cowardly, treacherous"), and "Mesdisant" (XVI, 1; "slandering"). As if this were not enough, he is said to have "murder in his heart" (VIII, 3). This catalogue of invective indicates the low esteem enjoyed by Mark in the eyes of his own court, and simultaneously contributes to his ill-repute.

The *Mariage des Sept Arts* is narrated by a lovelorn poet who falls asleep

---

36. This is the twelfth *lai* inserted in the romance; Löseth, §280. Fotitch and Steiner, eds., *Les lais du roman de Tristan en prose*, pp. 78–84; also printed in Bec, *La lyrique française*, II, pp. 140–42. For the context, I have relied on the manuscript, Paris, B. N., fr. 336, f. 1b. See above, Chapter 2, n. 21 for bibliography.

in an orchard and dreams of seven ladies, the Arts.[37] They enter in turn, and each announces her intention of marrying one of the seven virtues. *Musique,* the fifth of the Arts to speak, is described simply as "envosie" (v. 151). Her sisters are not more fully described by the narrator, but proclaim themselves and their abilities. *Grammaire* calls herself the source of all "clergie" (v. 26), and the fountain of the arts (v. 41). *Dialectique* admits to being pale and yellow with study (v. 72). *Geometrie* boasts of having measured everything (vv. 129–36). *Musique,* however, says nothing of herself; she enters singing, and announces that *Orison* is her choice for a husband. She breaks into song twice more during her speech and defies those who might oppose her choice: slanderers and her mother are both dismissed in these *refrains*:

> Je vodroie que mesdisant
> Fussent sourt et aveugle et mu.
> (vv. 159–60);

["I wish that the slanderers were deaf and blind and dumb."]

> Deshait ait qui lara
> Por chastoi de meire
> Son ami qui l'a.
> (vv. 173–75).

["Damned be she who would leave the lover who has her, for a mother's warnings."]

The idea of the latter song is developed in the following stanza, where *Musique* threatens to live with her lover if not allowed to marry. The last *refrain* is *Musique*'s response to her mother's consent: "La rose m'est donneie / Et je la prenderai" (vv. 184–85; "The rose is given to me and I shall take it"). Her songs serve not only to express her point of view, but to characterize her. Rather than speak of her accomplishments, she demonstrates them to the audience.

---

37. Arthur Långfors, ed., *Le Mariage des sept arts par Jehan le Teinturier d'Arras suivi d'une version anonyme; Poèmes français du XIIIe siècle,* CFMA 31 (Paris: Champion, 1923), pp. 11–26. The editor did not try to narrow the dating of either of the poems. The anonymous version is preserved in a manuscript of the late thirteenth century (p. iv).

All three *refrains* seem to assume a love requited, and in the last two, the singer defiantly declares her determination to be true to love. The tone of the songs is at variance with the didactic tenor of the work. Indeed, when *Physique* arrives in hopes of marriage, she is chased away by the others, a scene interpreted by Långfors as an exclusion of physical love.[38] On the other hand, the whole account is set within the framework of a dream inspired by the poet's meditation on his own affair, and once the arts are established, he asks their counsel. Although *Theologie*, in keeping with the moral tone of most of the poem, recommends renunciation and devotion to God, it is *Musique* who has the last word, for she composes a *chanson* for the poet to sing to his lady. *Musique* thus represents a contrary, perhaps even subversive tendency in the poem. She distinguishes herself not only by her mode of expression, but by her attitudes. The fact that the poem ends with her song, which is meant to win a lady's favor for the poet, undermines the didactic and moralizing stance of the rest of the work.[39]

The characterization of the goddess *Musique* in the *Ludus-Anticlaudien*, another allegory translated from Latin before 1286, is much less disruptive.[40] In this work, it is the act of singing, rather than the choice of songs, that distinguishes *Musique* from her sisters. Her song is a *rondeau* about the god of Love, who is identified with Jesus Christ:

> Le Dieu d'Amours, qui ne set dechevoir,
> doit on amer sur tous principaument;
> chou que j'ai vient de li, s'ameray voir
> le Dieu d'Amours, qui ne set dechevoir:
> ch'est Jhesu Crist ou on prent sens pooir.
> (vv. 1413–17)

[The god of love, who does not know how to deceive, should be loved

---

38. Långfors, *Mariage*, p. xi.
39. Cf. Anne Ladd, "Attitudes Toward Lyric in the *Lai d'Aristote* and Some Later Fictional Narratives," *Romania*, 96 (1975): 194–208.
40. Ed. P. H. Rastatter, "'Ludus-Anticlaudien': A Thirteenth Century Translation of the *Ludus Super Anticlaudianum* of Adam de la Bassee by 'A Monk from Cysoin,' edited for the first time with Introduction, Notes, and Glossary" (Ph.D. Diss., University of Oregon, 1966); the date is discussed on pp. xiv, xxxvi. On the French work and its model, see Marc-René Jung, *Etudes sur le poème allégorique en France au moyen âge* (Bern: Francke, 1974), pp. 93–104; and Robert Bossuat, "Une prétendue traduction de l'Anti-Claudien d'Alain de Lille," *Mélanges de linguistique et de littérature offerts à M. Alfred Jeanroy* (Paris, 1928), pp. 265–77; for a comparison of the two texts, see the edition of the *Ludus super Anticlaudianum*, ed. Paul Bayart (Tourcoing: G. Frère, 1930), pp. lxxix–cvi.

above all from the beginning; what I have comes from him, so shall I truly love the god of love who does not know how to deceive. It is Jesus Christ from whom one takes power.]

A second *rondeau,* "Dame ou fort jour du destroit jugement" (v. 1421) is a prayer to the Blessed Virgin for her intercession with Jesus Christ. Neither the *rondeau* nor its refrain is attested elsewhere, but it is likely that the songs were adapted to suit the context in the same way as the two "pious" *refrains* in the *Court de Paradis.* The content of the songs is thus assimilated to the moralizing tone of the work, and despite the surprise of the form, there is no comic effect in their use.

At the beginning of the fifteenth century, we find still another example of poetic form serving indirectly as characterization in the *Dit de la Rose.* Christine de Pizan composed her poem on 14 February 1402 as a riposte to her opponents in the *Querelle de la Rose,* and dedicated it to the Duke of Orléans.[41] The *Dit* recounts first the founding of an order of chivalry by the god of Love at the court of Orléans, while in the second part, Christine describes a dream which explains the true meaning of the foundation. The setting of the poem could not be more conventional: Christine's description of the banquet refers to the magnificence of the meal, the elegance and refinement of the guests, and the gaiety of their songs, although none of these is quoted. Here, as in the *Tournoi de Chauvenci,* a real event is cast in a literary form, for Christine's poem is the record of an actual feast.

Loyauté, the messenger of Love, arrives accompanied by nymphs who sing a motet that is described but not quoted. When she addresses the company, on the other hand, *Loyauté*'s speech is cast as a pair of *ballades.* In the first, she announces that she is Love's messenger and that she brings news. The second, which follows immediately, offers the rose as an emblem to all who vow to uphold the honor of ladies, and proclaims the foundation of the Order of the Rose. *Loyauté* administers the oath that marks admission to the order, an oath which the knights at Orléans repeat with enthusiasm. Gratified by this support for the chivalric defense of ladies, *Loyauté* gracefully takes her leave in a quoted *rondeau,* returning to Love with her

---

41. Roy, ed., *Oeuvres de Christine de Pisan,* II, pp. 29–48. Cf. Charity Cannon Willard, *Christine de Pizan: Her Life and Works* (New York: Persea Books, 1984), pp. 167–69; and Daniel Poirion, *Précis de la littérature française au moyen âge* (Paris: Presses Universitaires de France, 1983), p. 267. For a summary of Christine's role in the *Querelle,* see Régine Pernoud, *Christine de Pisan* (Paris: Calmann-Lévy, 1982), pp. 104–33.

good news. But while *Loyauté* speaks only in lyric form in public, she addresses a long explanation to Christine in nonlyric octosyllabic verse in the privacy of a dream.

The "songs" used by *Loyauté* are essential to the plot, because the information they contain is not conveyed to the court by other means, though it could well have been. Christine's choice of lyric forms for the communication of the message draws attention to the form, and this in turn to the speaker. The lyric forms are identified with Love itself, and their use by the god and his deputy could not be more fitting. By her use of *ballades* and a *rondeau*, *Loyauté* demonstrates her grace and courtesy, as well as her close adherence to Love. She manages, in addition, to distinguish herself in a company whose refinement is unimpeachable. Her songs place her firmly in the courtly tradition whose values she seeks to reestablish.

When songs are quoted in the description of a celebration as examples of the music used to accompany it, they fill in detail, make the description specific, and enhance the impression of "reality." In short, they conform to the rhetorical principle of *amplificatio*, and are thus similar to other details of description. The particular song may be less important than the act of singing, but the type of song chosen is always of great importance. Omission of the quotations would make the description less specific and less exact, and would diminish its impact; more importantly it would also change its nature.

As we have seen, once introduced by Jean Renart, quoted songs quickly became a conventional element of the description of court life in French romances whether in verse or in prose, and most authors who employed it not only used fewer songs to create the effect, but made them serve some additional purpose. On occasion, the characters take advantage of the opportunity to express themselves in a context where expressivity is not expected, and is thus unrecognized by their companions. The songs inserted into these descriptive passages were thus more fully woven into the plot structure. In these instances, the particular song chosen may be more important than the act of singing itself. The words are important for reasons other than their decorative or evocative value; therefore the extraneous insertion is more fully integrated into the work. At the same time, the genre and register of the song are just as important as its content. In Bakhtin's terms, the songs constitute another image of language, distinct from that of the narrative, and the two enter into different relationships. In *Guillaume de Dole* there is harmony between the dance songs and the descriptions of celebration. Gerbert de Montreuil's *Violette* begins in imitation of *Guillaume de Dole*, but the chanson inserted at the end of the passage contrasts in register with both the preceding songs and their settings. The *refrains* of the *Court de Paradis*, on the other hand, suit the sprightly style of the narrative, but are deliberately discordant with its setting. Similarly, but to a more extreme degree, the songs of *Musique* in the *Mariage des Sept Arts* flatly contradict the tone and the message of the narrative, resulting in a subversion of its overt meaning.

4. Songs as Plot

Perhaps the clearest way to integrate an essentially non-narrative element like a song into a story is to give it a narrative or "diegetic" function.[1] The simplest way to accomplish this is to attribute the lyric to a character as a form of speech, but the songs used in this way in our corpus commonly have a more important impact on some other aspect of the work, and I have discussed them elsewhere.[2] A second way to integrate lyric insertions into the plot is to make them part of the chronological or causal sequence of events.[3] As we shall see, some songs attributed to characters do indeed serve as substitutes for actions (as in the *Lai d'Aristote*) or convey information that would otherwise remain secret, and which in turn provokes an action that advances or changes the plot (as in *Galeran de Bretagne, Guillaume de Dole*, the *Roman de la Violette, Cleomadés,* and *Sone de Nansay*). Finally, songs can be subordinated to the plot either by emphasizing (even if they do not motivate) major reversals, or by recalling earlier events to the audience's attention (as in the *Tristan en Prose* and *Perceforest*). The last two of these possibilities have the greatest impact on plot and are the subject of this chapter on the narrative function of inserted lyrics.

Song as Action

In *Galeran de Bretagne*, composed by the otherwise anonymous poet Renaut in the first decade of the thirteenth century,[4] an inserted song serves to

---

1. Gérard Genette uses the term "diegesis" as a synonym for "story" (*histoire*), referring to the sequence of events that is the subject of a written or oral discourse (narrative or *récit*); cf. *Narrative Discourse: An Essay in Method*, trans. Jane E. Lewin (Ithaca, N.Y.: Cornell University Press, 1980), p. 27 and note 2; see also his discussion in "Les Frontières du récit," reprinted in *Figures*, II (Paris: Seuil, 1969), pp. 50–56.
2. We have already seen how the *chanson d'amour* functioned as a means of expression, and how songs sung during festivals enhanced descriptions; similarly in the next chapter, I shall examine songs used as modes of communication.
3. See, for example, Tzvetan Todorov, *Les genres du discours* (Paris: Seuil, 1978), p. 64. For a bibliography on narratology, see Wallace Martin, *Recent Theories of Narrative* (Ithaca, N.Y.: Cornell University Press, 1986), pp. 212–38.
4. Lucien Foulet, ed., *Jean Renart [sic]: Galeran de Bretagne. Roman du XIIIe siècle*, CFMA, 37 (Paris: Champion, 1925). For the date, see Rita Lejeune-Dehousse, *L'oeuvre de Jean Renart*, p. 147 and n. 1: before *Guillaume de Dole* (1214, p. 130), and after *Escoufle* (1200–1202,

bring about the denouement of the plot. Renaut borrowed Marie de France's *Lai de Fresne* as a frame for his romance about two children who fall in love.[5] As in the *lai,* the heroine (Fresne) was abandoned by her mother and raised in a convent where Galeran, son of the Count of Brittany, was sent to be educated. The pair fall in love but are separated by the abbess, and Fresne is obliged to leave the convent. Unable to find Fresne, Galeran yields to pressure to marry and chooses Fleuri, actually the twin sister of his beloved. When she learns of the proposed marriage, Fresne comes to the court disguised as a minstrel and sings two songs which reveal her presence to Galeran. Fresne's real identity, however, is established by her mother's recognition of a piece of silk left with her when she was abandoned.

Galeran, separated from the exiled Fresne, and divided from his true self, thinks to find happiness with the "image" or shadow of his beloved.[6] This attempt brings on a crisis of self-doubt, and coming to his senses, Galeran realizes that his marriage would be a "faulce jointure." Without Fresne, he lacks the strength to resist his advisors. Were she there, he would say to them: "Je n'en vueil mie" (v. 6859). Fresne answers his wish with two songs, one quoted, the other only described, and it is the latter that is more important. As she enters the court, Fresne sings a *refrain*:

Et Fresne, sans dire autre chose,
S'en va errant tout a eslaiz,
Ne fine jusques el palays,
Puis chante quant elle est en my:
  "Je voiz aux noces mon amy:
  Plus dolente de moy n'y va!"
(vv. 6972–77)[7]

---

pp. 212–25). This romance was attributed to Jean Renart by Lucien Foulet, "Galeran et Jean Renart," *Romania*, 51 (1925): 76–104, but Rita Lejeune-Dehousse, after reviewing the evidence, decided against the attribution; see *L'oeuvre de Jean Renart*, pp. 28–34. For further discussion, see V. F. Koenig, "The Authorship of *Galeran de Bretagne*," *Modern Language Notes*, 49 (1934): 248–55; and Ernst Hoepffner, "Renart ou Renaut," *Romania*, 62 (1936): 196–231. Although Renaut, the otherwise unknown author of *Galeran de Bretagne*, seems to have anticipated Jean Renart in quoting songs, the latter's claim is justified, because he established the device in the narrative repertoire.

5. Cf. Ernst Hoeppfner, "Les lais de Marie de France dans *Galeran de Bretagne et Guillaume de Dole*," *Romania*, 56 (1930): 212–35.

6. On the conflict of appearances and reality in the romance, see A. M. Plasson, "L'obsession du reflet dans 'Galeran de Bretagne,'" in *Mélanges . . . Le Gentil* (Besançon: Jacques et Demontrond, 1973), pp. 673–89; for a study of the romance, see Ingeborg Dubs, *Galeran de Bretagn: Die Kriese im französischen höfischen Roman*, Studiorum romanicorum collectio Turicensis, III (Bern: A. Francke, 1949).

7. The *refrain* is no. 1151 in Boogaard's collection. It also occurs in a motet. Foulet, in the

[And Fresne, without saying anything else, leaves at once as quickly as possible; she does not stop until (she reaches) the palace, then she sings when she is inside: "I go to my lover's wedding, no one goes there sadder than I."]

This song attracts the attention of the whole court and disturbs Galeran, who has not yet recognized Fresne. She then approaches and sings the song he taught her, the "lay Galeren le Breton":

Par un doulx lay le desconforte;
Les autres laiz, celuy a pris
Que Galeren li a apris.
El dit ne mesprent n'en la note:
De Galeren le Breton note.
Si l'escoutent toutes et tuit;
Des moz n'entent nulz le deduit
Fors que dui; mais li chans est doulx,
Si les fait entendre a li tous.
(vv. 6996–7004)

[With a sweet *lai* she disturbs him; she left the others and took this one, that Galeran had taught her. She mistook neither the words nor the music, she plays (music) about Galeran the Breton. They all listened to it; the pleasure of the words only two understand, but the song is sweet, so it makes them all listen.]

Galeran is thunderstruck by the song, and Fresne asks pointedly if he has been hit by a "lance de fresne" (v. 7025). The described song is a means of private communication in public between the two lovers: the music is sweet, but only the lovers understand the words. Fresne's disguise makes the message possible, for minstrels are expected to sing, while their songs are not supposed to have personal meaning. The *lai* was a secret shared by the lovers. Since Galeran taught it to no one else, the *lai* is a sign of Fresne's identity. The text indicates quite clearly that Galeran has recognized Fresne (vv. 7026–29), and a little later he announces that he will not go through with the ceremony (vv. 7068–72). Therefore it is the described *lai*, rather than the quoted song, that alters the course of events.

---

glossary to *Galeran* (p. 277 v. *note*), identified it as a fragment of a *pastourelle* (K. Bartsch, *Romanzen und Pastourellen* [Leipzig: F. C. W. Vogel, 1870], p. 214).

Despite the importance of this scene, its diegetic function remains ambiguous, for the second recognition scene (in which a piece of cloth rather than a song acts as the trigger) is essential for the happy ending. Fresne's reappearance is sufficient to disrupt the wedding, but her real identity and social position are only revealed in the latter scene, and it is this recognition that enables the lovers to marry and still meet Galeran's responsibilities.[8] Nevertheless, Renaut's use of the *lai* is fundamental to the theme of the romance, which valorizes "le romanesque" at the expense of social reality. The *lai* raises the love of Galeran and Fresne to the level of literature, and enables the two heroes to triumph.

A less ambiguous example of a song determining the course of the plot is found in *Guillaume de Dole*, written some years after *Galeran de Bretagne*. In this romance, the emperor Conrad, as we saw in Chapter 2, sings a series of songs that betray his growing preoccupation with Liénor de Dole. The seventh of these precipitates a major reversal in the plot.

Immediately before Conrad's song there is a description of the seneschal, who is clearly suspicious of Guillaume and spies on him hoping to discover the secret of his favor:

> Il fu toz les jors de sa vie
> assez plus fel que ne fu Keus.
> Il estoit adés ovoec eus
> por engignier et por deçoivre,
> savoir s'il peüst aperçoivre
> por qu'il i a si grant amor.
> (vv. 3163–68)
>
> [All the days of his life he was more treacherous than Keu. He was with them continuously to deceive and to take them by surprise, to know if he could discover why he (Guillaume) had such great love.]

Immediately after this passage, the author reports a conversation between Guillaume and Conrad which is overheard by the wicked seneschal. When Guillaume speaks of his sister and her prospective visit to the court, Conrad answers by singing two stanzas of an anonymous *chanson d'amour*. The eavesdropping seneschal suddenly understands the source of Guillaume's

---

8. See, however, the different interpretations of Ch.-V. Langlois, *La Vie en France au moyen âge de la fin du XIIe au milieu du XIVe siècle d'après les romans mondains du temps* (Paris: Hachette, 1924), pp. 32–33; and Lucien Foulet, "Marie de France et la légende de Tristan," *ZRP*, 32 (1908): 161–83, 257–89, especially p. 269 n.1.

success at court and decides to unmake the match that would seal his rival's good fortune. Given the context, the song is as explicit as an announcement, and the villain has no difficulty drawing the correct conclusion. The song thus motivates the principal reversal in the plot, for the seneschal acts on his knowledge and plans to prevent the marriage by seducing Liénor. After the decorative songs used in the opening scenes and the *chanson* stanzas that are attributed to Conrad, this episode marks an attempt by the author to integrate one of the songs more fully into the plot.[9]

Not long afterward, Henri d'Andeli, in the *Lai d'Aristote*, gave a narrative function to a series of songs by making them serve as actions.[10] The four lyric insertions—two *rondeaux*, a fragment from a *chanson de toile*, and a *refrain*—not only punctuate the movement of the central episode, but are instrumental in bringing about the denouement.

The story is set in the time of Alexander, whose tutor, Aristotle, rebukes him for devoting too much time to love. Miffed by his intervention, Alexander's mistress decides to subdue the meddling philosopher. Her campaign to ensnare him begins with a dance outside his window. The setting, the "vergiers plains de verdure" (v. 285) is echoed in the first *rondeau* that she uses to attract Aristotle's attention:

C'est la jus desoz l'olive.
Or la voi venir, m'amie!
La fontaine i sort serie,
El glaioloi, desoz l'aunoi.
Or la voi, la voi, la voi,
La bele blonde! A li m'otroi!
(vv. 303–8)

---

9. In the opening scene of the *Roman de la Violette*, the hero sings and speaks boastfully of his lady's love and in so doing provokes the villain to try to disprove his claim. But as boastful as the songs are, they might have been unobjectionable if not supplemented by the speech, for they are not essentially different from the other songs in the passage (see Chapter 3, section titled, "*Roman de la Violette*"). The boastful speech is the determining factor, and the diegetic function of the songs is lessened. Several other plot developments in the *Violette* are initiated by songs: a *chanson de toile* (vv. 2303–9) recalls the hero to his quest to his lady. He sings a *chanson* (vv. 3236–43) to console himself, but is overheard by another lady who thinks that he sings for love of her. Aiglente, rebuffed by the hero, sings a *refrain* (vv. 3450–51) asking for a cure for love, and her governess offers her a love potion that entrances the hero. Rather than precipitating a major turn of events, these songs motivate several smaller sequences of events. Their influence becomes pervasive, as they repeatedly accentuate the action.

10. Maurice Delbouille, ed., *Le Lai d'Aristote de Henri d' Andeli d' après tous les mss* (Paris: Société d'édition "Les Belles Lettres," 1951). The work seems to have been composed ca. 1230, though there is some uncertainty as to its date; see p. 29.

[It's down there, beneath the olive tree. Now I see her coming, my beloved! The spring gushes forth clear among the gladiolas, beneath the alder. Now I see her, see her, see her, the beautiful blonde! I give myself to her!]

The song describes what she is doing and the reaction she anticipates from the philosopher. As she intended, Aristotle notices only too well "la bele blonde." At the same time, the song announces in miniature the shape of the narrative, for the last part, "a li m'otroi," anticipates the ending. The girl has awakened a memory "that makes him close his books" (v. 325), and has his undivided attention as she dances, gathers flowers, and sings a second *rondeau*. She then approaches the window and sings a third song in a more sentimental vein:

> En un vergier, lez une fontenele
> Dont clere est l'onde et blanche la gravele,
> Siet fille a roi, sa main a sa maissele.
> En soupirant son doz ami apele:
>   Haï; cuens Guis amis!
> La vostre amor me tolt solaz et ris.
> (vv. 384–89)

[In an orchard, beside a spring whose water is clear and whose stones are white, sits the daughter of a king, her hand at her cheek. Sighing, she calls her dear lover: "Ah! Count Gui, love, your love deprives me of pleasure and laughter."]

Aristotle misses the irony of her choice: the girl in the *chanson de toile* sighs for her young lover, while the singer pretends to sigh for the old philosopher. Though he suspects her intentions, he is unable to resist her suggestion and admits his love. This portion of the poem, then, is essentially a seduction scene; the songs which bring it about both replace and symbolize other more explicitly seductive actions.

Having ensnared her enemy, the girl dramatizes her triumph by bidding Aristotle put a saddle on his back and carry her astride. Her song "Ainsi va qui amors maine" (v. 461; "so he goes, whom love rules") announces her triumph to the hidden Alexander and completes the philosopher's humiliation.

In Adenet le Roi's *Cleomadés,* probably written shortly before 1285,[11] a series of seven *rondeaux* precipitates a major reversal in the plot. Cleomadés, heir to the Spanish throne, is transported on a magic horse to Tuscany, where he falls in love with the king's daughter, Clarmondine. He escapes from her father and returns later to carry her off. At her request, she waits outside Cleomadés's castle while he announces her arrival to his family, but she is abducted by the evil magician Crompart. The remainder of the romance is devoted to the hero's adventures during his search for his lady.

While waiting for Cleomadés to introduce her to his family, Clarmondine sings three *rondeaux* as expressions of love and joy (vv. 5495–96). Despite her avowed inspiration, all three songs deal with separation and impatience for a lover's return:

Dieus! trop demeure mes amis;
Tart m'est que le revoie,
Li biaus, li courtois, li jolis . . .
(vv. 5497–99);

[God! My lover delays too long. It has been a long time since I have seen him, the handsome, the courteous, the charming . . .]

Tant que j'aie Amours avoec moi,
Ne suis je pas seulete.
(vv. 5513–14)

[As long as I have Love with me, I am not alone.]

Revenez, revenez!
Dous amis, trop demorez,
Trop longuement m'oubliez.
(vv. 5533–35)

[Come back, come back, sweet love, you tarry too long, you forget me too long.]

---

11. Ed. Albert Henry, *Les oeuvres d'Adenet le Roi,* V *Cleomadés,* 2 vols. Université libre de Bruxelles, Travaux de la Faculté de Philosophie et Lettres, 46 (Brussels: Editions de l'Université de Bruxelles, 1971); see also Margaret Munroe Boland, *Cleomadés: A Study in Architectonic Patterns,* Romance Monographs Inc. 11, (Jackson, Miss.: University of Mississippi Press, 1974).

Attracted by the sound of her voice, the magician spies the unprotected young lady and sees an opportunity to revenge himself on Cleomadés. He seizes Clarmondine and carries her off on the magic horse.

The impatience of her songs, though exaggerated for the short delay expected, anticipates the lovers' separation for the rest of the romance. The narrative function of the songs, however, has nothing to do with their words; it is their sound that attracts the attention of Crompart. The magician bears a grudge against Cleomadés, who blocked Crompart's marriage to his sister, and the abduction of Clarmondine serves nicely both as revenge and as compensation for his loss of a noble wife.[12]

The remaining *rondeaux* in *Cleomadés* are sung by the hero's family as they go out to welcome Clarmondine into their household. The four songs are performed by Cleomadés and his mother and sisters as they process to greet the waiting Clarmondine. Their songs express their approval of the match, celebrate Clarmondine's merits, and the last, sung by the hero, mentions her by name:

> On doit bien aler liement
> Encontre tel pucele,
> Con est Clarmondine au cors gent.
> (vv. 5915–17)

> [We should indeed go happily to such a girl as the lovely Clarmondine.]

The inclusion of the *rondeaux* at this point delays the discovery of the kidnapping, and the celebratory mood of the scene contrasts strongly with the violence of the preceding one. As a group, the seven songs bracket the principal turning point in the plot and provide a contrasting interlude that highlights its importance. We have already noted how Jean Renart juxtaposed a celebratory scene to a description of the villain's machinations,[13]

---

12. While Clarmondine's songs precipitate the crisis, it is not the songs themselves but the sound of singing that is effective. Since the words convey no information, and it is a mere noise that attracts attention, it would appear that some other means would have served the author's needs just as well. Indeed, while the heroine of the *Conte du Cheval de Fust (Meliacin)*, a romance modeled on *Cleomadés*, sings a song remarkably similar to those of Clarmondine, inspiration for the abduction in that romance is explicitly attributed to the sight of the horse (*Meliacin*, vv. 3528–59).

13. Vv. 3390–3435.

and the songs in *Cleomadés* are similar in function. In each case the lyric interlude intensifies the real or projected violence and heightens the suspense of the plot.[14]

Sone de Nansay,[15] composed near the end of the thirteenth century, contains a *lai* which helps to determine the course of events, and two *rondets* inserted into an episode that marks a turning point in the romance. The hero's adventures begin when he is unable to win the love of his lady Yde. Quite successful in his quest to win fame and glory, Sone returns periodically to press his suit with Yde. Eventually he enters the service of the King of Norway, whose daughter Odée falls in love with him. Still preoccupied with Yde, Sone remains unaware of Odée's feelings, and decides to return home. When Odée comes to his ship to bid him farewell, a sudden storm carries the ship out to sea and then to Ireland. They share a series of adventures and manage at last to return to Norway. Sone then returns to France and resumes his interrupted courtship of Yde. During the tournament at Châlons, Yde at last shows signs of relenting, largely because of the match-making efforts of the Countess of Champagne and Sone's uncle the Count of Brabant, but Sone rather surprisingly fails to press his advantage, and the affair remains unconcluded. Shortly after this, Sone learns that he has been chosen to succeed to the throne of Norway, but postpones his return. During the festivities after the tournament of Montargis, a minstrel arrives at court and sings a *lai* composed by Odée, and Sone at last returns to marry her. The romance ends with an account of his reign and of his decendants.

The first two insertions are both *rondets*, and are sung in the context of a description of a banquet similar to those discussed in the previous chap-

---

14. The lyric interlude is a feature of several works; in each case, songs are used in descriptive passages to contribute a celebratory mood that the audience knows, as the characters do not, is unsuited to the real state of affairs. The scene of revelry in the *Court d'amours* discussed in the previous chapter stands in sharp contrast to the battle scene that follows.

In Jehan de le Mote's fourteenth-century work (*Jean de le Mote, Le parfait du paon: édition critique,* ed. R. J. Carey [Chapel Hill: University of North Carolina Press, 1972]), a musical interlude anticipates the battle that is the principal subject of the poem. The campaign recounted in the *Parfait* begins with Alexander's ill-advised attack upon the city of Melide, where three of his peers were captured. The rival kings strike a truce, and the chiefs of both armies are lavishly entertained by the king of Melide. During the festivities, Alexander and his peers engage in a contest of poetic skill with the four daughters of Melidus, and the author includes eight *ballades* composed for the occasion.

15. Moritz Goldschmidt, ed., *Sone von Nausay,* Bibliothek des literarischen Vereins in Stuttgart, 216 (Tübingen: H. Laupp, Jr., 1899); I have made the emendations suggested by Gaston Paris, "Corrections sur Sone de Nansai," *Romania,* 31 (1902): 113–32. For a study, see K. G. D. Normand, "A Study of the Old French Romance of Sone de Nansay" (Ph.D. Diss., University of Pennsylvania, 1975).

ter. During the tournament at Châlons, Yde and Sone are seated next to each other, but "cascuns d'iaus deus se taisoit" (v. 10280; "each of them is silent"). The countess of Champagne, in an attempt to break the ice, takes each by the hand and sings:

Main se leva bielle Aëlis,
Nus ne fu plus loyalz amis
Que chilz que je tieng par le main,
Prions tout pour la bielle Ydain.
(vv. 10395–98)

[Bele Aelis raised her hand. No one was a more loyal lover than the one I hold by the hand. All pray for the beautiful Yde.]

The reference to "Ydain" in the fourth line is a clear example of adapting a song to its context.[16] Indeed, it gives the impression of an inspired improvisation. The countess's desire to reconcile the pair is evident, as she recommends Sone to his lady and enlists the good will of the audience on Yde's behalf. Sone's disinterest, as he joins the *carole* "iriés et courchiés" (v. 10406; "angry and irritated") is all the more striking and puzzling.

Somewhat later, the author uses a debate between heart and body to describe Sone's state of mind, but fails to indicate the source of his confusion. Yet what else can it be but the shift of his love from Yde to Odée? Having failed to notice Odée because of his preoccupation with Yde, Sone is unable to respond when the love he desired is within his grasp. The next day as he enters the lists, Yde hands him a lance and uses a *rondet* to declare her change of heart:

Je doins mon cuer a mon ami
Et la blanque lanche au jouster.
A mout grant tort li escondi.
Je doins mon cuer a mon ami.
(vv. 10921–24)

[I give my heart to my lover, and a white lance for jousting. Wrongly did I refuse him, I give my heart to my lover.]

16. According to Boogaard, *Les rondeaux,* p. 42, this form of the *rondeau* is not attested elsewhere; it differs significantly from the others of the "bele Aelis" type; the other versions are printed by Bec, *La lyrique française,* II, pp. 150–58.

She reiterates this regret in her speech, "M'amour trop escondi li ay" (v. 10938; "Too long did I refuse my love to him"). When she tries to explain her earlier coldness by the existence of a technical impediment to their marriage, Sone does not deign to reply, but simply rides into the lists.

The two songs in the episode stress its psychological importance for the hero. Sone's desultory affair with Yde finally comes to a crisis, and he is forced to recognize his own change of heart. Having remained faithful to Yde in the face of repeated refusals and other opportunities, Sone seems at last to realize the shabbiness of her conduct.[17] Despite his disenchantment with one lady, Sone does nothing to approach the other. The news that he has been chosen to succeed the King of Norway makes him think of Odée with regret for his indifference:

> Trechieres sui viers li,
> Che puis je bien prouver par mi.
> Et bien sai que mout bien feroie,
> Se viers li me reconnissoie.
> Si loyaus amie me fu,
> A peu n'en ot vie pierdu.
> Mais pour painne ne s'esbahi,
> Adiés trouvai confort en li . . .
> (vv. 11807–14)

[I am dear to her, this I can well prove to myself. And I know that I would do well to confess my faults to her. So loyal a lover was she to me that she almost lost her life. But she was never frightened by pain, I always found comfort in her . . .]

> Bien sai que elle mout m'amoit . . .
> (v. 11821).

[Truly do I know that she loved me.]

Nevertheless, he does not act. When Odée hears nothing from him, she

---

17. The weakness of the conclusion of the affair has been pointed out by Normand ("A Study of the Old French Romance Sone de Nansay," p. 122), who suggests that Sone's love for Yde has been transferred to a spiritual plane (p. 187). Anne Ladd ("Lyric Insertions," pp. 88–89) suggests that the love affair is to be interpreted ironically.

decides in desperation to make a public appeal and sends the minstrel Papegai to sing her *lai*.

After claiming the attention of her audience, Odée's *lai* declares her love for Sone and recalls their adventures at sea. Although they were both wounded, the companionship they enjoyed was a source of great happiness. In the last stanza she claims that Sone's absence has wounded her more gravely than the sailor's knife, and that she will die if he does not return. The purpose of the *lai* is not simply to remind Sone of her existence—that was accomplished by the news of the king's death—but to secure a judgment from the court. Odée calls upon the assembly at Montargis to act as a *court d'amours* and to render a decision on her plea. The song succeeds in its aim and wins the favor of the royal council as well as of the ladies of the court. Although the author fails to indicate Sone's reaction, he is obliged to act, and thus to resolve the affair.[18] In accordance with the judgment of the court, Sone goes to Norway to marry Odée and to found a dynasty.

In each of these works, the result of the song could well have been achieved by other means.[19] But it was not mere whim that moved the authors of these works to employ a quoted song to achieve that end, for all of the songs convey messages of love. Fresne announces her return to the man she loves, Conrad hints at his feelings for Guillaume's sister, Clarmondine sings of the impatience of love, Yde tries to indicate her change of heart to Sone, and Alexander's mistress feigns love for Aristotle. Each instance involves unintended, misconstrued, or unwanted communication—a message gone awry. Conrad is overheard and his secret exposed to an enemy; Clarmondine, too, is overheard, but reveals her vulnerability rather than her sentiments. Sone refuses to listen Yde's message of love, while Aristotle hears the message intended by the singer, not realizing until too late her malicious purpose. *Galeran de Bretagne* is an exception, for Fresne

---

18. See Normand, "Sone de Nansay," pp. 140–41. Odée's song has an unsuccessful precedent in the romance, for another lady used a *lai*, described but not quoted, to declare her love for Sone. There are other examples of lyrics which attempt, but fail, to influence a plot. In the *Roman de Cassidorus* (ed. Joseph Palermo, 2 vols. [Paris, 1963–64]) a mother and daughter in love with the same man cast their rivalry in a *débat* which they submit to his judgment in an attempt to attract his attention. The man in question (Cassidorus) is suspicious of love, and fails to respond to the ploy. In the *Roman de Kanor* (Paris, B.N. fr. 22550 and London, B. L., Harley 4903), the king of Jerusalem wishes to marry a Saracen princess, but the match is opposed by her brother. The princess sends her (positive) answer to the king in the form of a *rondeau*, but the message is intercepted, and a discouraging reply substituted.

19. This point is amply demonstrated by the contrasting practice of Adenet le Roi and Girart d'Amiens. See above, n. 12.

is able to communicate as she desires, but her song is a sort of code, intended for Galeran alone. In each case, because the form of the message symbolizes its meaning, a song is a fitting vehicle for the failure or error in communication. Conrad and Yde show themselves unworthy of the love they sing, while Aristotle is defeated by the means he scorned. Galeran and Fresne, on the other hand, are reunited by songs which recall the beginning of their love affair.

Song as Narration

The two longest works containing lyrics, the vast prose romances of *Tristan* and *Perceforest,* illustrate yet another relationship between song and narrative. Both works contain verse pieces of different types—*lais,* prayers, riddles, and inscriptions—but it is only the first that are of interest in the present context. Rather than determining the plot, the *lais* in these works recall earlier events and guide the reader (listener) through the maze of episodes. The movement is the reverse of that in *Guillaume de Dole* and similar works, for in these two romances the events of the plot are themselves cast as *lais.* These songs are more closely tied to the narrative context of their frame texts than most lyric insertions because they refer clearly to specific events. In contrast, the *refrains* and *rondeaux* quoted in other romances were conventional formulations that could be appropriated in many different contexts.

The majority of the *lais* in the *Tristan en Prose* are sung in the context of a love meditation.[20] Nevertheless, several of Tristan's songs occur in contexts which specifically allude to earlier episodes in the plot, and so summarize the main developments of the love story.[21]

Tristan's *Lai Mortel,* the first insertion in the romance, is composed in his despair at the thought that Iseut has left him for a rival. The performance of the song is preceded by a discussion (with a girl who wishes to divert him from his melancholy) of his compositions:

> "En non Dieu! fait il, vos dites verité. Voirement ne fis je onques que trois lais. Or les sonez, se Diex vos saut, demoisele, si orrai coment vos les savez." Et ele en comence maintenant un, cestui qu'il avoit fait dedenz la nacele quant il se

---

20. See above, Chapter 2.
21. See above, Chapter 2, under *"Roman de Tristan en Prose"* for a list of the *lais* and a summary of the plot.

fist metre en mer por ce qu'il ne pooit garir en Cornoaille. L'autre lai avoit il fait en la mer meïsmes, a celi point qu'il conut premierement madame Yselt par le boivre amorous, ensi com chevaliers doit conoistre dame. L'autre lai avoit il fait ou Morroiz, quant Madame Yselt demora tant avec li en la forest. Le premier lai avoit il apelé Lai de Plor, le secont le Boire Pesant, le tierz avoit il apelé Deduit d'Amor. (Curtis, vol. III, p. 168, §868)

["In God's name," he said, "you are right. Truly I have only composed three *lais*. Play them now, as God saves you, lady, then shall I hear how you know them." And she now begins one of them, the one he had composed in the boat when he put out to sea because he could not be healed in Cornwall. The other *lai* he had composed at sea, when he first knew Yseut through the love potion, as a knight ought to know a lady. The other *lai* he had composed in the Morrois when Yseut lived with him in the forest. The first *lai* he had called the "*Lai* of Weeping," the second the "Powerful Potion," the third he had named the "Pleasure of Love."]

The girl then performs each of these *lais* for Tristan, although they are not quoted here.[22] What is significant about this discussion is that while Tristan is almost at the point of death and about to compose his last song, the author recalls earlier songs, each commemorating an important event in Tristan's life. The *Lai de Plour* evokes another moment when Tristan was near death from the wound of the Morholt's poisoned sword. The beginning of the love affair, symbolized by the love philter, is recalled by the *Lai du Boire Pesant*, while the *Lai du Deduit d'Amours* suggests the happiness of the idyll in the forest. Although Tristan comments on the contrast between his former joy and his present condition, the real purpose of these allusions is to summarize the whole affair, while its end is foreshadowed by the *Lai Mortel* which is quoted here.

The author varied this pattern of allusions again near the end of the romance. Instead of merely naming the compositions, two *lais* from other periods of his life are inserted in the text. In a peaceful interlude in his journey to Cornwall to find Iseut, Tristan is entertained by a girl who sings the *Lai de Victoire*,[23] composed after the tournament at Louvezerp. The last of four tournaments described in the romance, this occasion marked the height of Tristan's knightly career. Here he defeated not only his old rival

22. The *Lai du Deduit d'Amours* seems to be a phantom *lai*; cf. Maillard, *Esthétique*, p. 83. The *Lai du Plour* is here identified as the one composed while Tristan lay in the rudderless boat dying of the poisoned wound; it too appears to be a phantom. Maillard gives the title *Lai de Plour* to the last *lai* inserted in the romance, which was composed by Tristan during a separation from Iseut.
23. No. 18. See E. S. Murrell, "The Death of Tristan from Douce Ms. 189," *PMLA*, 43 (1928): 343–83.

Palamède, but the best of Arthur's knights. In his song, Tristan attributes his success to love and calls it a recompense for his sufferings. The *lai* also evoked for Tristan what was perhaps the happiest period of his life, when he lived with Iseut in peaceful seclusion at the *Joyeuse Garde*. In response to the girl's song, Tristan sings the second *lai* of the interlude, the *Lai du Boire Pesant* (No. 19). Although Tristan says it was composed much earlier, it is performed only here. The song memorializes the beginning of his love, but stresses the ominous circumstances of that beginning. As in the earlier passage, the *lais* quoted here evoke different and contrasting stages of the love affair. Tristan's memory of success and happiness in one song is balanced by an appropriate sense of foreboding in the second; the lovers have been separated once more, and are nearing their inevitable end.

The last *lai* in the romance (No. 22) is sung on a similar occasion, during a moment of repose from Tristan's quest to find Iseut. As before, Tristan is entertained by a performance of a *lai*—Iseut's *Lai Mortel*—and responds with a song of his own. This time, however, he describes the circumstances surrounding the composition of the *lai*:

> Je chevauchoie .i. jour par la forest de haut, tout seul, sans compaignie, tant dolent et tant couroucié estrangement que je oncques en ma vie ne fui tant dolens, si conme je croy. Icy descendi adont devant une fontaine et quant je fus descendus, je m'assis delés la fontaine, et conmençay a pencer a moy meismes; si trouvay adont en celui eneer que oncques a nul jour de ce monde nul chevalier n'out autant de douleur ne de paine pour bien amer conme j'ay heu et de celle grant douleur fis un lay dont je vous vueil tout orendroit harper les vers et sachiez que oncques ne furent harpees se de moy non. (Paris, B.N., fr. 336, f. 321b–c)
>
> [I was riding through the forest one day, all alone, without company, so sad and so strangely angry that I have never in my life, so I believe, been so unhappy. Here I dismounted by a spring and when I had alighted, I sat down by the spring and began to think of myself, and so I found then in this trouble that never on any day of this world had a knight had as much sorrow and pain for loving well as I have had, and out of this great sorrow I composed a *lai* whose verses I wish to play (on the harp) for you, and know well that it has never been played but by me alone.]

The feelings he describes are similar to his present state of mind, while the invocation of Iseut's desperate *Lai Mortel* implicitly attributes similar feelings to her. It is fitting that the mood should be so melancholy, since this is the last interlude before his death.

These two incidents may be considered together, for both are interruptions in Tristan's final journey to find Iseut. The combined allusions recall the beginning of their affair and some of its happiest moments, though thoughts of pain and suffering always overshadow the memories.

Taken as a group, the songs punctuate the long separation of the lovers, but it is significant that the order of their insertion in the text is a mirror image of the plot. The first *lais* to be performed and quoted are the pair of *lais mortels*. Although the lovers do not die, it is fitting that they should be the first songs that the audience hears, for they announce the end of the story. The chronologically earlier songs are only performed near the end of the romance, and memorialize the whole affair at its conclusion. The allusions to the earlier *lais* in the context of Tristan's *Lai Mortel* achieve the same end, and the two scenes balance each other. In each case, the whole affair casts its shadow over the lovers about to die. In the first instance, the early *lais* are merely cited and death is avoided, while near the end death is inescapable and the songs are sung in full.[24] As is only fitting, Tristan is at last killed by King Mark as he sits singing to Iseut. Their love in the prose romance was inextricable from its music, and therefore this modification of the legend has a certain logic.

The *Roman de Perceforest*, written before the middle of the fourteenth century (and probably between 1330 and 1344),[25] attempts to unite in a single work the cycles of Alexander and Arthur. Throughout the work the author develops two principal themes: the exaltation of chivalry as a civilizing force and the importance of religious renewal. As it survives, the

24. Only parts of the romance have been edited: the first part by Jane H. M. Taylor, *Le Roman de Perceforest*, TLF, 279 (Geneva: Droz, 1979); the third and fourth parts by Gilles Roussineau, *Perceforest, IIIe Partie*, TLF, 365 (Geneva: Droz, 1988); *Perceforest, IVe Partie*, 2 vols., TLF, 343 (Geneva: Droz, 1987). The *lais* have been published by Jeanne Lods, *Les pièces lyriques du roman de Perceforest: édition critique,* Publications romanes et françaises, 36 (Geneva: Droz and Lille, 1953). See also the study by Jeanne Lods, *Le Roman de Perceforest: Origines, composition, caractères, valeur et influence,* Publications romanes et françaises, 32 (Geneva: Droz and Lille, 1951) and the series of articles by F.-L. Flutre, "Etudes sur le Roman de *Perceforêt*," *Romania*, 70 (1948–49): 474–522; 71 (1950): 374–92, 482–508; 74 (1953): 44–102; 88 (1967): 475–508; 89 (1968): 355–86; 90 (1969): 341–70; 91 (1970): 189–226. Flutre discussed the date in *Romania*, 70, p. 475; as did Taylor, *Perceforest*, pp. 23–29, who assigned it to the period 1330–50. More recently, D'A.J.D. Boulton, *The Knights of the Crown: The Monarchical Orders of Knighthood in Later Medieval Europe, 1325–1520* (Woodbridge, Suffolk: Boydell Press, 1987), pp. 107–8, argued for a date before 1344, as the romance influenced the form of Edward III's revived Company of the Round Table as announced in January 1344. Roussineau, *IVe Partie*, I, p. xiv agrees, placing the romance between 1337 and 1344. In the absence of a complete edition, I have also consulted MS. D (London, B.L., Royal 15.E.V), and the printed edition by N. Cousteau for Galiot Du Pré, *La Treselegante, delicieuse, melliflue et tresplaisante hystoire du tresnoble victorieux et excellentissime roy Perceforest* (Paris, 1528).

25. This *lai* is No. 18 in the list given in Chapter 2 under "*Roman de Tristan en Prose*"; subsequent numbers in parentheses also refer to this list.

romance contains sixteen insertions (twelve *lais* and four *ballades*),[26] all described as sung by characters, although no music has been preserved. There is at least one song in each of the six books of the romance; Book II has four, Book III has two, and the final book has seven. The lyrics inserted in *Perceforest* differ in type from those we have encountered thus far. The songs belong not to the repertoire of *chansons* and *rondets*, but to the later *formes fixes*, and to the genre characteristic of the prose romance, the *lai*. Unlike those in the prose *Tristan*, however, they are usually narrative in character and are attributed without dispute to the author of the romance.[27]

The story begins with the founding of Britain by Brutus after the fall of Troy. When Alexander arrives in Britain, he appoints Gadifer king of Scotland and his brother Betis (later Perceforest) king of England. Betis's kingdom is threatened by the enchanter Darnant, who is finally killed by Betis in the enchanted forest, from which his new name seems to derive. While Betis-Perceforest is absent on this quest, ten of Alexander's knights search for him in pairs and the adventures of the five pairs of knights are interlaced with stories from the Alexander cycle. A second team of searchers, this time twelve strong, sets out at the instigation of the wives of Perceforest and Gadifer. One of these is the Bossu of Suane (Suave), a deformed knight of great prowess, who recounts the story of his birth, the accusations made against his mother, and her final vindication. He ends his narrative by singing the first *lai* quoted in the romance: *La Chanson du Bossu* (Book I, ch. 80; "Ou joly mois que clercz ont figuré"). Book I ends with the coronation of Gadifer and the departure of Alexander from Britain.

Book II opens with Gadifer and Perceforest organizing parallel teams of their twelve best knights to bring peace and order to their respective kingdoms. Among the additional characters introduced in this book is Lionnel du Glat, one of Perceforest's knights, who joins in a search for the wounded Gadifer. On his way to a tournament, his shield and the trophies of his earlier adventures (a lion and the head of a giant) are stolen from him. In despair he sings the second *lai*: *Lai de Complainte* (Book II, chs. 75–84; "Plus courroucié qu'oncques hom ne nasquy"). A minstrel later sings this *lai* to Blanchette, the daughter of the queen of Scotland, whom Lionnel had

---

26. Lods, *Les pièces lyriques*, pp. 9–10, points out that some lyrics seem to have disappeared from the text in the surviving manuscripts and printed editions. Of the twenty pieces printed by Lods, the first three are described as "prières," rather than songs, and the tenth is an inscription, one of nearly a dozen in the work.

27. Lods, *Les pièces lyriques*, pp. 10–11. The chapter numbers in the summary below are taken from the modern editions for Books I, III, and IV; the rest are from the 1528 edition.

hoped to win with his exploits. She responds with an answering song, the third *lai*: *Lai de Confort* (Book II, chs. 75–84; "Au grant besoing voit son amy"), which reveals the hiding place of the trophies. The minstrel then seeks out Lionnel to sing the *lai* and bring him the information.

Meanwhile, Estonné, one of Gadifer's knights, has had a series of adventures (ch. 56), which he recounts to the Queen of England when he arrives to participate in a tournament; a lady in the audience replies to his account with the fourth *lai*, the *Lai de l'Ours* (Book II, ch. 109; "N'est tresor tant repus"). Book II ends with the inauguration of Perceforest's *Franc Palais*, which is celebrated with a tournament, and the shields of those who distinguished themselves are hung around the walls of its round tower. The feast ends with the *Lai de Pergamon*, the fifth *lai* (Book II, ch. 134; "Pergamon l'ermite, commence cy son lay"). This song relates the deeds of the knights of the twelve vows which accomplished at the coronation of the king of Scotland. It casts in lyric form the material from Book I, ch. 145, where the vows were made. Perceforest orders that this *lai* be sung henceforth at all tournaments.

Book III is devoted to twelve tournaments held at the *Chastel aux Pucelles*, each of which is won by the suitor of the girl (one of Pergamon's granddaughters) for whom it is held. These tournaments punctuate the volume, but other narrative lines are also pursued. Lionnel, imprisoned in the castle of the evil knights, is at last released by Perceforest (ch. 19), who holds a feast to celebrate the deliverance. During the revels the sixth *lai* is performed, so obscure in its allusions that only the most worthy (Lionnel, Estonné, and Le Tor) are able to understand it: the *Lai Secret* (Book III, ch. 22; "Long demourer amy changier").[28] Meanwhile the wounded Chevalier Doré is brought to an unknown country, where he is cared for by Neronés, daughter of the king of the Strange March, who falls in love with him. She is kidnapped by a rejected suitor, but escapes, disguises herself, and eventually finds the Chevalier Doré, but is afraid to reveal her identity. Finally she tells her story in a song, the seventh *lai*: the *Lai Piteux* (No. 7, Book III, ch. 42; "Pitié, qui durs cuers atendrist").

Book IV opens with the feast of the Sovereign God, a celebration of the success of Perceforest's reign, but the kingdom is invaded by Julius Caesar and all the work is undone. The book is divided into three parts: the adventures of Perceforest; the Roman invasion and the devastation of Britain; and the adventures of a new generation of knights who must

---

28. Also printed by Roussineau, *IIIe Partie*, I, pp. 275–78.

rebuild the kingdom. In part 3, Ourseau, one of the younger knights, comes to a temple dedicated to the god of desires. This god is in fact the Chevalier au Dauphin, the knight who wed the youngest of Pergamon's daughters after accomplishing a vow for each of the twelve daughters (cf. *Lai de Pergamon*, st. 35 ff.). Young ladies now come to pray before a statue of him and sing a song recalling his feats, the eighth *lai*: the *Lai des Jeunes Filles au Dieu des Desiriers* (Book IV, ch. 57; "Le confort aux pucelles").[29] Book IV ends with a tournament celebrating the reconstruction of the kingdom.

Book V is organized around twelve more tournaments established by Queen Blanche, the daughter of Gadifer and wife of Lionnel du Glat (cf. the *Lais de Complainte* and *de Confort*) for the purpose of perfecting the art of chivalry. At the last of these, which celebrates the marriage of Blanche's daughter, a minstrel tells the story of a loyal wife and then repeats the account in the ninth *lai*: the *Lai de la Rose* (Book V, ch. 42; "Il eult jadis dedens la Grant Bretaigne").[30]

Book VI is the conclusion of the romance, and is devoted to a history of Gallafar (or Gallafur), the great-grandson of both Perceforest and Gadifer, who becomes the first Christian king of Britain. Two of the knights who participate in the tournament in honor of Gallafar's coronation debate in a *jeu parti* which of them has better reason to hope—the one told to love where he pleases, or the one told he bears the name his lady loves. Together they sing the tenth *lai*: the *Parture des Chevaliers* (Book VI, chs. 32–37; "Sire tant avez fait vers vostre amee"). They then call upon their ladies to decide, but the ladies, whose affections are engaged elsewhere, can only respond with another *débat*, asking which is more guilty for having given greater false encouragement. They sing the eleventh *lai*: the *Parture des Pucelles* (Book VI, chs. 32–37; "Pucelle au cercle d'or, ma chiere amie"). The question is finally resolved by a mysterious voice singing the twelfth *lai*: the *Jugement définitif* (Book VI, chs. 32–37; "Ha chevalier de tres haulte venue").[31] In fact, neither of the ladies is guilty, and neither of the knights favored. The unlucky knights follow their more favored rivals, one of whom sings the thirteenth insertion, a *ballade* (Book VI, ch. 49; "Molt suis tenu d'amours louer sans nombre"). The song is answered by his rival with

---

29. Printed also by Roussineau, *IVe partie*, II, pp. 1100–05.

30. This *lai* and its setting were discussed by Gaston Paris, "Le conte de la rose dans le roman de *Perceforest*," *Romania*, 23 (1894): 78–140.

31. In the printed edition, but not in the manuscript, these ladies exchange *rondeaux* with the knights they love at a banquet, in the presence of the unfortunate pair.

another *ballade*, the fourteenth insertion (Book VI, ch. 49; "Vous qui avez eü ottroy d'amie"). The third *ballade*, which is the fifteenth insertion, is sung by the other happy suitor, who shares his joy with a nightingale (Book VI, ch. 49; "Rossignolet, qui chantes sur la branche"). The last knight, who sings the final insertion ("Ha! mois de pleuve et de fort yvernage"), is not so fortunate in his suit: At the end of the volume, the story of Alain le Gros, borrowed from the *Queste du Graal*, serves as a transition from the cycle of Alexander to that of the Grail.

As this brief summary of their narrative situations would suggest, most of the *lais* in *Perceforest* restate, in lyric form, earlier portions of the plot in order to enlighten other characters. At the same time, these *reprises* serve to recall episodes for the audience, and thus help one to negotiate the complex plot of the romance. Although it is clearly impossible to examine all of the quoted lyrics in detail in the present context, a fuller discussion of this work is warranted because it is so seldom studied. I have chosen three songs to exemplify the author's technique.

The *Lai de l'Ours* in the second book is composed by a lady rescued from kidnappers by a bear who is really the knight Estonné, transformed as punishment for his infidelity to his lady. The song describes Estonné's transformation and his rescue of the lady. It goes on to refer to the woman who seduced the knight, and ends with an admonition to loyalty. Once restored to his proper shape, Estonné thinks that he has dreamed the whole adventure. It is only when he returns to the court and hears the *lai* performed that he realizes that his "dream" was real. The song, moreover, reveals the meaning of the incident, and he repents of his failing. The relationship between lyric and narrative elements is demonstrated clearly here. An earlier plot sequence is crystallized in the heightened language of poetry. The new form is not merely a "history," however. It influences the behavior of at least one listener (Estonné), as well as narrating and explaining the past.

The *Lai Piteux* in Book III functions in a similar manner. After escaping from kidnappers, Neronés disguises herself as a boy (*Coeur d'Acier*) and eventually becomes the page of Nestor, the Chevalier Doré, whom she loves. She is afraid to reveal her identity to him and maintains her disguise during a long series of adventures, until they arrive at the castle of Nestor's parents. When the suspicious queen begins to question her, Neronés replies by singing a *lai*. She begins her song with a plea for pity, and then launches into her tale: "D'une pucelle non pas garce, / Du pays de l'Estrange Marche / Vous diray le ravissement" (vv. 7–9; "I will tell you of the abduction of a girl, not a trollop, from the land of the Strange March").³² Left for dead by her captors, the girl escapes and seeks shelter. She disguises herself and begins her journey home, but stops to aid a wounded knight. Although she recognizes him as her beloved, she is so ashamed of her appearance that she does not reveal herself. In the final section of the *lai* Neronés abandons the third person and addresses Nestor directly, expressing her sorrow that he has never recognized her:

> Honte me tolt le hardement
> Et mon amy l'appensement
> Dont il devroit cognoistre my,
> Pour ce nous va trop malement,
> Car l'un, qui quiert l'autre souvent,
> Dist par mots couverts: "Veez moy cy."
> (vv. 301–6)

> [Shame takes away my courage and my beloved (takes away) the reflection by which he should know me; for this reason we go on so badly, for one who often seeks the other, says with hints: "See me here."]

Nestor finally recognizes his lost love, his mother's questions are answered, and the pair are happily reunited. The song thus serves not only to explain the girl's plight and to restore her identity, but also to summarize in a new form a long series of prior adventures. In this way, one thread of the plot is isolated in a convenient form at its conclusion.

The third example I have chosen, the *Lai de Pergamon*, is quoted in the romance in the context of a feast, and like the other songs repeats an earlier plot segment. It is unique, however, in becoming a structural element in the whole romance. At the end of Book I, the author describes the coronation of Pergamon, son of Gadifer, as the king of Scotland. During the festivities, eleven knights vow to perform the tasks set by each of the eleven eldest nieces of King Pergamon, while a twelfth (the Chevalier au Dauphin) vows to perform twelve feats. The *Lai de Pergamon*,³³ performed for the first time

---

32. Lods, *Les pièces lyriques*, No. XI, pp. 57–64.
33. Lods, *Les pièces lyriques*, No. VIII, pp. 46–53.

at the end of Book II in the context of the establishment of the *Franc Palais*, is composed by Pergamon to commemorate the heroic deeds inspired by his nieces:

> Pergamon (li) l'ermite, commence cy son lay
> Des douze chevaliers, qui de coer lié et gay
> Vouërent douze voeus, dont furent en esmay
> Dames et chevaliers, mais je oy bien mon glay
>   Ens es fais achever.
> (vv. 1–5)
>
> [Pergamon the hermit begins here his *lai*, about the twelve knights who, with hearts happy and gay, made twelve vows which worried the ladies and knights, but I hear my fanfare in the feats accomplished.]

The song follows exactly the order of the narrative; the knights make their vows to the ladies in turn, until the Chevalier au Dauphin pledges himself to the youngest and then takes a task from each of her eleven sisters.

The *lai* goes on to establish the conditions set by Pergamon for his nieces' marriages: each will be won by the victor at one of a series of twelve tournaments. In this way, the *lai* announces the structure of the third book, an account of the twelve tournaments and the marriages that follow. The *Lai de Pergamon* thus recalls an earlier episode, but announces later ones at the same time. It then becomes part of the ritual of chivalry, as its performance is described (though it is not actually quoted) at each of the twelve tournaments. The significance of the lyric lies less in the event that it recalls than in its status as an emblem of chivalrous prowess. The *lai* becomes a monument to chivalry, and its invocation at successive tournaments presents an ideal to inspire the new contenders.

As this survey demonstrates, it was no simple matter to make a song constitute a unit of the diegetic sequence, unless as a speech attributed to a character. Even in *Guillaume de Dole* and *Cleomadés*—where the author explicitly attributes to the insertion a development in the plot—the particular content of the song or songs chosen does not seem essential to the context. In *Guillaume de Dole*, almost any *chanson d'amour* would have betrayed Conrad's interest in Liénor to a suspicious eavesdropper. The *refrains* sung by the cortège in *Escanor* are bolstered by other elements in the narrative which serve to assure their effect. And in *Cleomadés,* anything sung, indeed, any noise made, by Clarmondine would have attracted the magician's notice. What these works have in common is the appropriation of songs from a traditional repertory. In the cases we have examined, the authors have tried to attribute a narrative function to one or more of the songs they quoted. But because the quotations are by their nature extraneous to the narrative text, they have no inherent connection with its plot.

The songs in the *Tristan en Prose* and in *Perceforest* have a different, and indeed, opposite relation to the narrative text, because they are tied to specific episodes in the plot. The *lais* in *Tristan* are lyrical reactions to particular events. Even those *lais* not composed by the principal characters are referred to them in some way—by explicit reference, or by eavesdropping—and in most cases the sentiments expressed in the songs are entirely appropriate to the main love triangle. Several of the *lais* attributed to Tristan and Iseut serve yet another purpose; they commemorate events in the plot, and mentioning the song is a way of evoking the event.

If the *lais* in *Tristan* are responses to the plot, those in *Perceforest* are monuments to it. Most of the *lais* are narrative in nature, actually recounting stories in lyric form, but the stories they tell are taken from the narrative text. As we saw in the examples of the *Lai de l'Ours* and the *Lai Piteux,* however, the lyric forms are not simple repetitions of the text, because they invest the past with new meaning. The *lais* recall as well as explain the significance of past events.

5. The Song as Message

In the last chapter, we examined how lyrics could be anchored in the plot by attributing to them a major reversal of the action. The songs under discussion in this chapter are also woven into the plot of the narrative, but in a way that exploits their expressive potential. The "latent narrativity" of these songs, to use Zumthor's term,[1] is made explicit in the enclosing text, as the singer either performs the song in the presence of the person to whom it is addressed, or sends it as a kind of musical letter.

Although distinguishing expressive songs used as a form of monologue from those in dialogue on the basis of the number of persons involved may be artificial on strictly rhetorical grounds,[2] such a distinction is justifiable in linguistic terms.[3] A dialogue—a message spoken to another person—is essentially communicative in nature and implies the possibility of a response, whereas a monologue or soliloquy has no *destinataire*, so its function is essentially emotive or expressive.

In this chapter, we shall consider inserted songs whose function in the narrative context is primarily communicative. Rather than reflecting the inner life of the singer or arising from a social celebration, as did the songs studied in Chapters 2 and 3, these songs are meant to convey messages—usually, but not always, emotional messages—to another person. The narrative setting for such songs is correspondingly more complicated. Arrangements must be made for conveying the song-message unless it is to be sung in the presence of the other person, and even in this situation, there may be some delay between the composition of the song and its performance. In addition, there is, as we shall see, considerable variation in the placement of these songs within the narrative framework, and the placement influences the meaning as well as the function of the song. At the same

---

1. In Minette Grunmann-Gaudet and Robin F. Jones, eds., *The Nature of Medieval Narrative* (Lexington, Ky.: French Forum, 1980), pp. 39–55.
2. Muscatine, *Chaucer and the French Tradition*, p. 19.
3. Jakobson, *Essais de linguistique*, I, p. 220; see also Roger Fowler, *Literature as Social Discourse*, p. 84.

time, one must consider both the intention of the sender-singer and the interpretation of the recipient. Given the social nature of communication, the two do not always coincide. Some of these issues, as we saw in chapter 2, arose in connection with the monologue, and they will recur in the next chapter in a different way when we examine the *dit*.

Most of the lyric insertions employed as "messages" deal with love. They fall into three categories: songs used as declarations of love, songs used as correspondence by separated lovers, and songs used by lovers to celebrate their meetings. I shall consider the songs in each of these categories in turn.

Song as Declaration

Since the majority of lyric insertions deal with love, most of them, and particularly those that took the form of *chansons*, could serve as declarations of love. Relatively few of them do, however, and even some of those function primarily as expressions of the singer's emotion and only secondarily as vehicles of communication. The contrast between the lyric declarations in the *Castelain de Couci* and *Guiron le Courtois* will illustrate my point. The Châtelain de Couci, as we have seen in Chapter 2,[4] composed his first *chanson* for the express purpose of making his feelings known to the Dame de Fayel. He arranged for the song to be performed before her, she was much moved by it, and his suit was ultimately successful. Thus, the Châtelain's *chanson* was successful in communicating his message and helped to initiate the plot. Nevertheless, its insertion at the time of its composition emphasized its expressive function and, for the reader/listener, lessened its impact upon the Dame de Fayel.

In the prose romance *Guiron le Courtois*,[5] the emphasis of the inserted lyric is on its communicative function. After falling in love with the Queen of Scotland, Meliadus expresses his emotion in a *lai* whose composition is described in some detail:

> I eut en tel penser et en tel travail si mal, si morne, si pensif, que reconforter ne le puet nul, fu le roy Meliadus. . . . Tant amoit celeement la royne que il cuidoit

---

4. See above, section entitled "*Roman du Castelain de Couci et de la Dame de Fayel.*"
5. In the absence of an edition, I have used the study by Roger Lathuillère, *Guiron le courtois. Etude de la tradition manuscrite et analyse critique,* Publications romanes et françaises, 86 (Paris: Droz, 1966), and consulted the version in London, B.L. Add. 36673. According to Lathuillère (pp. 31–34), the romance was composed ca. 1235.

bien morir. Chançons trouvoit pour l'amour de li que il va chantant jour et nuit. Et ce estoit ce qui plus le reconfortoit en celuy affaire. Et qu'en diroie-je? Longuement seuffre celuy mal que il ne le fait nulli savoir. Et au dernier treuve ung dit de ses amours plus merveillant et plus subtil que nul n'avoit esté devant; et sur celuy treuve chant tel que on pouoit chanter en harpe. . . . Et celuy dit que il trouva a celuy temps par amour le reconfortoit moult. "Lay" l'apelle, en signe que il vouloit laissier tout autres chant. (London, B.L., Add. 36673, f. 149r)[6]

[King Meliadus was in such melancholy and in pain so severe, so sad and so absorbing that no one could comfort him. So much did he secretly love the queen that he thought he would die. He composed songs for the love of her that he sang day and night. And this is what gave him the most comfort in this situation. And what should I say about it? He suffers this pain for a long time and lets no one know. Finally he composes a dit about his love, more marvellous and more subtle that any other, and he composes a melody for it that could be played on the harp. . . . And this dit that he composed then for love comforted him greatly. He called it a *lai* as a sign that he wished to abandon all other songs.]

Despite the fact that Meliadus composed this song and sang it repeatedly to comfort the "pain" of his love, it is quoted not here but two folios later, when it is sung to the queen on Meliadus's behalf. This delay shifts attention away from the emotions expressed in the *lai* and highlights its effect upon the *destinataire*. The song constitutes a declaration of Meliadus's love:

Dame, a vous cestui lay mant,
Fait l'ai et sans vostre commant.
A vous trestout me recommant,
Car autre dieu je ne demant.
Pensif, ma dame, et desireux
De vous amer, et amoureux
De vos gens corps, donc eureux
Me tieng, et en sui douloureux.
(London, B.L., Add. 36673, f.151r)

[Lady, I send you this *lai*; I composed it without your command. I commend myself to you for I desire no other god. Melancholy, and desiring to love you, and loving your beautiful body, I therefore consider myself happy, even as I am sorrowful.]

---

6. See Lathuillère, *Guiron le Courtois*, § 36.

The song succeeds in its aim, which is to gain for Meliadus his lady's love: "elle dist bien que se elle devoit jamais entendre a nul amour de chevalier, elle debvroit plustost entendre a cestui que a nul autre" (f. 151v; "She said that if she were ever to listen to a knight's love, she would rather heed this one than any other"). If the queen hesitates, the song has nonetheless done its work, for he wins her at their next meeting.

The situation recounted here is that of a successful *salut d'amour*: a song composed by the lover acts as his messenger and wins the love of the lady who is its inspiration.[7] The song's underlying narrativity is made explicit and becomes subject to further narrative development.

Froissart, in the ostensibly autobiographical *Espinette Amoureuse*,[8] made a similar attempt to declare himself. His effort came to nought, but it illustrates the technique nonetheless. The work (which will be discussed more fully in the next chapter), opens with an evocation of the poet's childhood and youth. This section ends with his first encounter with Venus, who inspires his promise of unending loyalty. Shortly afterward, the poet meets a young lady reading the romance *Cleomadés*. They read together for a time, and he promptly loses his heart. When she asks him to lend her a book, he sees his opportunity: lacking the courage to approach her directly, he decides to declare himself in a letter and enclose it in the book, where she will find it. When it occurs to him that someone else may find his letter, he thinks better of the idea, and decides to compose a song, for "N'est nuls ne nulle qui mal disce / D'une cançon, se on le troeve / En un rommanch qu'on clot et oevre" (vv. 900–902; "There is no one who could say anything ill of a song if he were to find it in a romance that one closes and opens"). The poet composes a new *ballade* for the occasion, and thus declaring himself discreetly, encloses it in his book, the otherwise unknown *Baillieu d'Amours*. Froissart deals explicitly here with all of the problems of conveying a message. He considers carefully both the form of the message and the means of transmission; he even anticipates the interception of his message and alters the form to cover that contingency. Although the ploy is unsuccessful, for

---

7. Because it is meant to speak on behalf of the lover, sending a *chanson d'amour* as a declaration of love is a narrative adaptation of the *Salut d'amours* even if the song is not actually cast as a letter. At the same time, Froissart's comments in the *Espinette amoureuse* make it clear that a song is actually safer than a letter. Because it is meant to be "published," it is less personal and less revealing than a letter. Songs have a social acceptability that allows characters to send messages in code and hide them from other listeners. Other works of this type are discussed in Chapter 6.

8. *Jean Froissart: L'espinette amoureuse. Edition avec introduction, notes et glossaire*, ed. Anthime Fourrier, Bibliothèque française et romane, B, Textes et documents, 2 (Paris: Klincksieck, 1963). The date given by Fourrier (pp. 30–32) is 1365–71 (probably closer to 1370).

the lady declines to acknowledge the song when she returns the book, the passage nevertheless illustrates the importance of the messenger. A minstrel was socially acceptable as a go-between in the earlier romances, while the clerkly Froissart put a book to work for the purpose. This shift from minstrel to book as messenger illustrates a fundamental difference between thirteenth- and fourteenth-century poetics, as the written lyric displaced the performed song.[9]

The songs used by Meliadus, the Châtelain, and Froissart are all declarations, albeit indirect ones. The lovers hide behind their songs, which do not oblige a response, even if they are sometimes effective. In the interpolated version of the *Roman de Fauvel*, however, the central character takes a different approach, employing many songs in his declaration. The *Roman de Fauvel* as it survives in most manuscripts, and as it has been presented by its editor, contains no lyric insertions.[10] In the manuscript now preserved as Paris, B.N., fr. 146, however, the text is supplemented by a great number of songs of many types, both in French and Latin, and by interpolations amounting to nearly three thousand lines. The original version without insertions consists of two books, composed in 1310 and 1314 respectively. Gervais du Bus identified himself as the author of the second book, and might have been responsible for the first as well. The work was revised and expanded in 1316 by Chaillou de Pestain, and it was he who added the musical interpolations that interest us here.[11]

The *Roman de Fauvel* is a satire in which the horse Fauvel personifies all vice: the letters of his name are the initials of *Flatterie, Avarice, Vilenie,*

---

9. See Huot, *From Song to Book,* pp. 4, 105, 208.
10. Arthur Långfors, *Le Roman de Fauvel par Gervais du Bus,* SATF (Paris: Firmin Didot, 1914–19).
11. Långfors, *Roman de Fauvel,* pp. 135–38, and 142–45, discussed the author and date of the second version. The interpolated version is available in a facsimile by Pierre Aubry, *Le Roman de Fauvel, Reproduction photographique du ms. fr. 146 de la Bibliothèque Nationale de Paris avec un index des interpolations lyriques* (Paris, 1907). A new facsimile has appeared with an introduction by Edward Roesner, François Avril, and Nancy Freeman Regalado, eds., *Facsimile of B.N. ms fr. 146: Roman de Fauvel, Book I (1310) and II (1314, by Gervès du Bus),* with 2877 vv. of narrative "addicions" and 169 musical insertions compiled by Chaillou de Pestain; 8 political poems by Geoffroi de Paris; 33 love lyrics by Jehannot de l'Escurel; a *Cronique métrique* of the kingdom of France for the years 1300–1316 (New York: Broude Bros., 1990). On the musical interpolations, see Hans Spanke, "Zu den musikalischen Einlagen im Fauvelroman," *Neuphilologische Mitteilungen,* 37 (1936): 188–226; and Dom Anselm Hughes and Gerald Abraham, *Ars Nova and the Renaissance 1300–1540, The New Oxford History of Music,* III (London: Oxford University Press, 1960), pp. 5–6. The interpolated version of *Fauvel* can be read by using Långfors's edition, together with Emilie Dahnk's *L'Hérésie de Fauvel* (Leipzig, Paris, 1935). The text of Book II of *Fauvel* is as follows: Långfors vv. 1227–2892; Dahnk pp. 114–54; Långfors vv. 2893–3144; Dahnk pp. 154–70; Långfors vv. 3145–3152; Dahnk pp. 171–73; Långfors vv. 3153–3200.

Variété, Envie, and *Lacheté*, and his worldly success symbolizes the corruption of society. The first book of *Fauvel* is essentially the same in both versions, except that MS. 146 contains a great many marginal musical pieces. The second book opens with a description of Fauvel's palace: in the midst of his splendor, surrounded by his courtiers, the hero is dissatisfied with his celibate state. Recognizing that he owes his success to Fortune, and conscious of her fickleness, Fauvel decides to secure his position by marrying Fortune. She rejects his suit in a tirade of more than a thousand lines (vv. 2117–3184 of the original version). It is into this tirade that the first new passage, including a number of lyrics, is interpolated; because the new material consists of Fauvel's response to Fortune, it blends smoothly with the original text. This passage is especially interesting because its lyrics are inserted into the speeches and not simply juxtaposed to the text. The second version then rejoins the first at the end of Fortune's speech, which is followed by the account of Fauvel's marriage. The versions diverge again near the end of the earlier one, whose last sixty-odd lines are subsumed in the later version into a long passage of nearly two thousand lines, with lengthy borrowings from the *Tournoiement d'Antechrist* and the *Roman du Comte d'Anjou*.[12] This final addition, which also contains musical insertions, deals with the celebrations surrounding Fauvel's marriage to Vainglory.

The first new passage, containing some nine hundred lines and twenty-two French songs, is interpolated into the middle of Fortune's speech at line 2982 of Långfors's edition and occurs at a point which makes the change of speakers plausible. Fauvel is alarmed by Fortune's reaction to his declaration. Her references to the fall of others make him fear that he may have lost everything in seeking to consolidate his position. In an attempt to soothe her anger, he appears to retreat from his boldness in a *virelai*:[13]

> C'est merveilles a conter
> de ce qu'envayr
> l'osay. de trop haut monter
> doit l'en chaïr.
> (Dahnk, p. 115, no. 55, I)

---

12. These interpolations were printed by Långfors in the appendix to his edition, pp. 146–95.
13. The song is called *chanson* in the manuscript, where the terms *virelai* and *chanson baladée* do not occur. Its form is in fact that of a *virelai*.

[It is amazing to recount that I dared to attack her; for climbing too high, one must fall.]

But in fact, he tries to shift the blame for his audacity to Fortune herself in the refrain of the piece:

Fortune par mon desroy
   si m'a enhaï,
ne veust que soie mes roy
   Fate m'a trahi.
(Ibid.)

[Fortune, because of my impetuousness, has come to hate me; she does not wish that I be king, Fate has betrayed me.]

Fauvel continues his plea, using five *ballades*, another *virelai*, a *dit* with *refrains*, a semi-lyrical *complainte*, a motet *enté*, a *rondeau*, and a *lai*, to enhance his eloquence.[14] The list of the genres inserted in this passage is virtually a catalogue of the lyric possibilities at the beginning of the fourteenth century. Fauvel leaves no song unsung in his efforts to salvage his position. The *ballades* (two of which consist of a single stanza) and the *virelai* are fairly conventional love lyrics, courtly in tone and lacking any specific reference to the narrative. The lover in these songs pleads for mercy, praises his lady's beauty, complains of her cruelty, and claims to be on the point of expiring for love. In the *lai*, a complex piece of twelve stanzas, each metrically different, the lover adopts a different pose. He blames Love for his misfortunes and the injustice he suffers, and addresses the lady only at the end of the piece, where he promises to serve her hopefully, despite his tribulations.

The *dit* and the *complainte*, which occupy the bulk of Fauvel's speech, are hybrid compositions. Thirteen *refrains* divide the 545 lines of the *dit* into irregular sections between twenty-nine and forty-seven lines in length. Each section except the last ends with an unmatched line, whose rhyme is completed by the *refrain*. The *refrains* interrupt the flow of octosyllables metrically and logically, and yet are linked to the text in a manner reminiscent of the *Chastelaine de St Gilles*.[15] Each *refrain* rhymes with the line that

14. I have followed Dahnk's recommendation (p. 154) for inserting ff. 28bis and 28ter between ff. 27 and 28, so that Fauvel's speech comes in a single piece.
15. On the structure of this piece, see Chapter 7, "Stanzaic Works," and n. 24.

precedes it, and is echoed in the following line. The fourth *refrain* will serve to illustrate:

>   213   Et com touz iours m'a puis semblé
>   refr.4 *Son dous regart m'a mon cuer emblé.*
>   215   Emblé voire, puet ce estre voir?
>   (Dahnk, p. 122)

[And it has always seemed to me since, that *his sweet glance has stolen my heart*. Stolen indeed, can this be true?]

Not only is the form a combination of verse and music, but there is a mixture of tones as well. The sprightly rhythm and the cheerful optimism characteristic of the *refrains* tend to undermine the serious courtly lament that Fauvel has undertaken. This is even more true as some of the words of each *refrain* are repeated in the following section of the *dit*. The *refrains* are more than simple interruptions, for they require commentary, and to that extent determine the content of the *dit*. The resulting effect is of a continual shift of register, from "la bonne vie" of the *refrains* to the courtly "requête amoureuse" of the *dit*.[16]

The other long piece employed by Fauvel is a *complainte* of fifty six-line stanzas (rhyming *aabaab*), into the middle of which is inserted a motet *enté*.[17] In this piece, the eleven musical lines of the motet are interrupted by a series of six-line stanzas. The musical lines (marked ß), which are usually shorter or longer than the octosyllabic stanzas, do not rhyme with the interrupting passages, but are sometimes echoed in the following line:

>   ß1   *Han, Diex! ou pourrai ie trouver*
>   (706) Hau, diex! de tout le monde sire,
>   En quel reaume n'en quel empire,
>   En quelle contrée ne terre,
>   Qui est qui le me sache a dire

---

16. See Zumthor, *Langue et techniques poétiques,* pp. 123–78 and *Essai de poétique médiévale,* pp. 231–32, 239–42, 251 ff.; Bec, *La lyrique française,* I, pp. 32–43. See also Zumthor's "Style and Expressive Register in Medieval Poetry," in *Literary Style: A Symposium,* ed. Seymour Chatman (Oxford: Oxford University Press 1971), pp. 263–71. Cf. above, Chapter 1, under "Lyric and Narrative: Relationships Possible and Actual."

17. The stanzaic form of this section echoes an earlier passage in the work: vv. 845–1130 in the original version of Book I are stanzas rhyming aabccd.

>   Tant lointaign païs sache eslire
>   Ou pourrai ie trouver par querre:
> ß2   *Conseil*
> (712)   Le quoi trouver conseil, confort, . . .
>   (Dahnk, pp. 139–40)

[*Ah God! where shall I be able to find*—Ah God! lord of all the world, in what realm, or in what empire, in what country or land, who is it who knows how to tell me, who knows who to choose such a distant country where I shall be able to find, by searching,—*Counsel*—To find such counsel, comfort . . .]

Superficially, the motet passage resembles the *dit*: short musical phrases alternate with nonlyric stanzas, similar to the irregular passages in the *dit*. Unlike the *refrains* inserted into *dits*, however, the musical lines of the motet form a coherent whole; as a result, it is the song that is interrupted by the *dit*, and not the reverse. In fact the two forms are direct opposites: whereas the *dit* is cut by independent pieces of music, the motet *enté* is a continuous musical composition interrupted by the stanzas. The sung form is in fact "exploded" by the nonmusical stanzas of the *complainte*. Nancy Regalado rightly attributes a symbolic meaning to these hybrid forms. They show Fauvel unable to sing continuously—at the end of each musical phrase, he falls out of tune.[18] The braying of the horse reflects his moral degradation.

This motley discourse covers four full folios, and moves from one form to another with little transition. The net effect is that of a terrified character desperately trying to stave off doom with a torrent of words and notes. Clearly this was the desired effect, for the author dismisses the tirade in a single line: "Quant Fauvel ot tout favelé" (v. 970; "when Fauvel had chattered everything"), before introducing Fortune's reply.

Unimpressed by his protestations of ardor, Fortune stands on her dignity, "Et sui du tout puissant roy fille" (v. 2896; "I am the daughter of an almighty king"), spurns him haughtily, and threatens to change his luck. In

---

18. Nancy Freeman Regalado, "Grafting Verse to Music: Two Semi-Lyric Pieces in the B.N. ms. fr. 146 'Roman de Fauvel,'" read at the meeting of the Medieval Academy of America in Toronto, April 1987. See also the introduction to the facsimile: *Le Roman de Fauvel in the Edition of Mesire Chaillou de Pesstain: A Reproduction in Facsimile of the Complete Manuscript, Paris, Bibliothèque Nationale Fonds Français*, ed. Edward H. Roesner, François Avril, and Nancy Freeman Regalado, esp. pp. 21–42.

152   Chapter 5

her rejection, Fortune adopts Fauvel's musical tactics, but whereas Fauvel had sung exclusively in French, most of her songs are in Latin. The linguistic contrast enhances the imperious character of Fortune in this work. She dismisses his claims in a Latin *prosa* which begins "Vade retro sathana! tuas tolle fabulas!" (Dahnk, p. 161; "Satan, go back, take away your fables"), and in another warns him that earthly happiness is fleeting. Always changeable, Fortune at last relents, in part, and offers Fauvel her daughter Vainglory in marriage.

In the figure of its "hero" as well as its use of lyric insertions, *Fauvel* recalls *Renart le Nouvel*.[19] As in the earlier work, there is something ridiculous in this horse who brays motets, and the incongruity (visible in the miniatures of the manuscript), is likewise apparent in the awkward, excessive, and desperate way Fauvel uses songs.

Song as Letter

Using a song as a letter may seem a simple narrative elaboration of the genre of the *salut d'amour*, a genre characterized by its epistolary quality.[20] Yet of the earliest examples of letters in lyric form (those in the *Tristan en Prose*), many remain closer to the epistolary than the lyric genre. These songs, that is, are often only versified letters rather than lyrics sent as messages. In the songs employed for the same purpose by Machaut in his *Voir Dit*, composed a century later, the reverse is the case: the epistolary part of the correspondence for the most part falls to the prose letters, while the songs exchanged by the lovers are truly lyric in character. The *refrains* sent as messages by the lady in the *Roman de la Poire* and the correspondence of the lovers in the *Roman de la Dame a la Lycorne* experiment with different combinations of letters and songs, and seem to represent intermediate stages between *Tristan* and the *Voir Dit*.

The *Roman de Tristan en Prose*, like *Guiron le Courtois*, contains several letters, seven of which are in verse.[21] After spending a period of exile at

---

19. On the relationship between the two works, see Långfors, *Roman de Fauvel*, pp. lxxxvi–xcv.

20. See Paul Meyer, "Le salut d'amour dans les littératures provençale et française," *Bibliothèque de l'Ecole des Chartes* sér. 6, III (1867): 125–70. Meyer's definition of the genre has been considerably refined by Pierre Bec, *Les saluts d'amour du troubadour Arnaud de Mareuil: Textes publiés avec une introduction, une traduction, et des notes* (Toulouse, 1961), and "Pour un essai de définition du Salut d'amour," *Estudis romanics*, 9 (1961): 191–201.

21. *Guiron* contains five letters, not counting the *lai* sent by Meliadus to the Queen of Scotland. For these see G. Bertoni, "Le Lettere franco-italane di Faramon e Meliadus,"

Arthur's court, Tristan (at Arthur's insistence), is reconciled with his uncle, and returns to Cornwall. Tristan writes reassuringly to both Arthur and Lancelot, who each reply in kind, urging him to return to Logres and warning him to beware of King Mark. Mark, meanwhile, sends another verse letter of very different style to Guinevere, describing in insulting terms her affair with Lancelot. In another incident, an unknown knight arrives at Arthur's court, presents a letter to him, and sings a *lai* while the king reads. The last verse letter in the romance is written by Iseut to Tristan during a long separation.[22] In addition to these letters, referred to in the text as "brief," Iseut and Kaherdin exchange three *lais*[23] which do not open with the salutations characteristic of the letters. The romance, then, experiments with different ways of encoding messages. There are simple prose letters, verse letters (without music), *lettres en forme de lai* (accompanied by musical notation and described as sung when composed), and *lais* dispatched by means of a minstrel.

There seems to be no hierarchy among the forms: Tristan sends letters in prose and verse, but composes none of the *lettres en forme de lai*, while Mark's insulting message to Guinevere is sung despite its ignoble inspiration. One element common to all the letters is the great attention to style. The characters are aware that their compositions reflect upon them, and accordingly take pains with them. The correspondence between Arthur and Lancelot and Tristan serves several purposes: it continues the link between Tristan and the Arthurian court and so contributes to the Arthurianization of the legend; it is also in some sense a *reprise* of the earlier prose letters exchanged by Tristan and Lancelot; and the warnings it contains foreshadow Mark's next attack on his nephew. The letter and *lai* of the anonymous knight are markedly different from the Arthurian correspondence both in tone and function. Formally, the two pieces are indistinguishable: both are composed in octosyllabic quatrains and have musical accompaniment in at least one manuscript. The letter, however, is addressed to Arthur and foretells his downfall, while the *lai* is a purely personal lament. Nevertheless, both pieces have a wider resonance in the larger context of the

---

Giornale storico della letteratura italiana, 63 no. 1 (1914): 179–88; and §§ 38 and 50 of Lathuillère's analysis. On the earlier prose correspondence in the *Tristan en Prose*, see Volume III of Curtis's edition, pp. xiv–xvi, and "Some Comments on the Medieval French Art of Letter Writing (with Reference to the Tristan Romances)," in *Tristan Studies* (Munich: Fink, 1967), pp. 54–57.

22. See above, Chapter 2, under "*Roman de Tristan en Prose*" for the list of *lais* in the *Tristan en Prose*; these letters are Nos. 7–11, 14, 15, and 18.

23. Nos. 3, 4 and 5 of the list in the *Tristan* section of Chapter 2.

romance. Given that both are sung at the beginning of the Pentecost feast shortly before the proclamation of the Grail quest, they represent an ill omen for the outcome of the quest. The *lai*, in which the knight takes his leave of the world before killing himself, says nothing that will not also be true of Tristan. We see the hero, about to embark on what he thinks will be a glorious adventure, obliged to face the specter of a doomed love affair ending in death.

Iseut's letter to Tristan is particularly interesting in its form as a sung message. While Tristan is engaged in the Grail quest, Iseut composes a letter in the form of a *lai* begging Tristan to return. The composition of the letter is described in terms that clearly indicate that it is a song:

> Lors conmence .i. brief a trouver au mieulz et au plus soutillement qu'elle onques pout et moult y mettoit s'entente et avec ce elle chantoit si bien et si envoisieement que l'en ne pouist a celui point trouver nulle dame mieulz chantant de lui. (Paris, B.N., fr. 336, f. 132b)
>
> [Then she begins to compose a letter as well and as cleverly as she could, and she put much thought into it, and with it she sang so well and so joyously that one could not find a lady who sang better than she.]

The *lai* is not inserted, however, until it is delivered to Tristan. The delay deliberately stresses the communicative rather than the expressive function of her song, and the emphasis is apparent in the form. She opens with a salutation and an assurance of her love, and each stanza begins with a salutatory form. She goes on to warn Tristan that the separation is killing her, reminds him that he is everything to her, that without him life is worthless, and ends with a plea for his return:

> Amis courtois, preus et senés,
> Vostre amie pour coi penés?
> S'onques fustes d'amours penés
> Ne me demandés riens, mais venés!
> (Fotitch and Steiner, p. 111, X, 1–4)
>
> [Courteous lover, brave and wise, why do you pain your beloved? If you were ever wounded by love, ask me nothing, but come.]

Unable to interrupt his quest, Tristan replies with a letter in prose some ten folios later. The letter once again reminds the reader/listener, in the middle of a long chivalric digression, of the central love affair. We see clearly that the lovers are doomed: if separation keeps them safe from external danger, it only brings another form of death.[24]

Some ten or twenty years after the completion of the *Tristan en Prose*, Tibaut, the otherwise unknown author of the *Roman de la Poire*, used songs for the same purpose, but in a very different manner. Composed around the middle of the thirteenth century, the *Poire* is, in effect, a *salut d'amour*, for the work is sent to a lady to speak on behalf of a lover.[25] Tibaut describes his own initiation into love, and then that of his lady (for his suit is successful) in allegorical terms. Having eaten a pear given him by the lady, the lover experiences the joy and suffering of love. The dual nature of the emotion arouses the lover's resistance, and, impervious to the encouragement of *Biauté*, *Courtoisie*, *Noblesse*, and *Franchise*, he is subdued only by Love himself. Love removes the lover's heart and entrusts it to the lady, who shares his suffering. She sends six more allegorical messengers to the lover to encourage him, but he is convinced only when she sends a letter "written with sighs and tears" (v. 2757).

The nineteen *refrains* in the *Poire* are for the most part sung—either by the lover and his lady or by the allegorical characters—and, in addition to their function in the text, they serve to spell out the names of the lovers.[26] The first two *refrains*, which are not sung by a character, are quoted in the dedicatory passage, and announce the poet's grievance against love.

The lover finds himself besieged and suffers a series of attacks. Each of Love's soldiers, urging him to surrender, prefaces her message with a *chant*,

---

24. At the end of the *Castelain de Couci*, when the Châtelain has been mortally wounded in combat, he composes a song, which he sings but does not send, and dictates a letter (vv. 7646–7704). This letter balances the song he sent at the beginning of the romance. As before, it is quoted in the context of its composition, and after his death, it is sent to the Dame de Fayel with a jewel box containing his heart. This final attempt at communication is intercepted by the lady's husband, who takes revenge on his dead rival by cooking the heart and serving it to his unsuspecting wife. She sees the letter only after her husband has told her what she has eaten. The sight of the Châtelain's arms on the seal of the letter is enough to convince her, and she dies without reading it.

25. The edition by Christiane Marchello-Nizia, *Le roman de la poire par Tibaut*, SATF (Paris: Picard, 1984), replaces the older one by Friedrich Stehlich, *Messire Thibaut, Li Romanz de la Poire: Erotisch-allegorisches Gedicht aus dem 13. Jahrhundert* (Halle, 1881). On its role as "Salut" see Marchello-Nizia, *Poire*, p. xvi, and Hans Robert Jauss in *GRLMA* VI.2 (1968) p. 280. See also Marc-René Jung, *Etudes sur le poème allégorique en France au moyen âge* (Bern: Francke, 1974), pp. 310–17, who describes it as "une immense *amplificatio* d'une poésie lyrique courtoise" (p. 317). See also Sylvia Huot, "From *Roman de la Rose* to *Roman de la Poire*: The Ovidian Tradition and the Poetics of Courtly Literature," *Mediaevalia et Humanistica*, 13 (1985): 95–111; *From Song to Book*, pp. 174–93; and Doris Ruhe, *Le Dieu d'Amours avec son Paradis: Untersuchungen zur Mythenbildung um Amor in Spätantike und Mittelalter* (Munich: W. Fink, 1974), pp. 139–47.

26. See Marchello-Nizia, *Poire*, pp. xxiv–xxx, xxxiv–xxxv.

generally positive in its attitude toward love, but not particularly related to the speech recorded. *Courtoisie,* for instance, sings an implied promise of reward: "N'est il bien reison, or i pensez, / que cil qui mielz aime soit li mielz amez?" (vv. 890–91; "Isn't it right, now think of it, that he who loves best should be best loved?"), while her speech insists on the transforming power of love.

Vanquished at last, by Love, and deprived of his heart, the lover tries to convince the lady of his sincerity. She in turn, on Love's command, tries to alleviate his sufferings, but the lover is surprisingly impervious to her comfort. The lady sends six messengers, each of whom arrives singing a *refrain*. The encouraging advice of each singer is heralded by a song celebrating happy love. *Pensée*, who invites the lover to take pleasure in conversing with the lady, announces in her song: "Tant ai leal amor quise / c'or les ai a ma devise" (vv. 2414–15; "So much have I sought loyal love that now I have it according to my wish"). As before, the logical relationship between song and discourse is sometimes tangential. Occasionally, however, they are closely integrated into the speech, as in that of *Simplece*:

> "Je n'oi oncques d'Amors joie
> or croi que ge l'avré.
> Savez por quoi? Que g'é trouvé
> leal ami tot a mon gré."
> (vv. 2441–44)

[I have never had the joy of Love, now I think I shall. Do you know why? Because I have found a loyal lover who suits me.]

Nevertheless, taken as a group, these *refrains* constitute a declaration of love in the clearest terms. The lady's deputies announce:

> Bien doi endurer le mal
> puis que j'ai ami leal.
> (vv. 2484–85)

[I must indeed endure the pain for I have a loyal lover.]

> A lui m'en vois, ne m'en tendroie mie,
> Diex, ge l'aim tant.
> (vv. 2504–5)

[I go to him, I would not resist it, God! I love him so.]

Vos avroiz la seignorie,
    amis, sur moi,
ce que mes mariz n'a mie.
(vv. 2568–70)

[You shall have the mastery of me, lover, which my husband never has.]

Contenance, the last messenger, whose *refrain* implicitly accuses the lover of insincerity, wants to know why he has not responded.

At last convinced by the lady's *chartre* written "D'un soupir en sanglot de lerme" (v. 2757; "with a sign, in a tearful sob"), the lover and his lady sing the last five *refrains* to each other, spelling out the word *Amors.* The final song, sung by the lady (v. 2954; "Soutenez moi, li max d'amors m'ocit!"; "Sustain me; the pain of love kills me"), repeats the lover's lament in the dedication: "An Diez! Li maus d'amer m'ocit" (v. 284; "Ah God! the pain of love is killing me"). The *refrains* thus act out on another level the movement of the narrative. The lover, who began lamenting his pain, is consoled by his lady, who shares it, and they unite in forming Love itself.

While they echo the dynamics of the text, the *refrains* alter its meaning. The text of the *Poire* is an elaboration of themes of the courtly lyric,[27] but the *refrains* sung by its characters belong to another, more popular register. As in the interpolated *dit* in *Fauvel,* the register of the *refrains* is that of "la bonne vie," whose love is of a more cheerful, optimistic nature than the difficult *fin' amors* from which the lover suffers. This intruding register presents a lady who openly admits her love and desire. Not the aloof and inaccessible lady of *fin' amors,* this lady sends messages to declare her love to the lover. By means of the *refrains* the lady's character and role in the work have been drastically altered.

In the prologue to the *Poire,* however, the poet presents himself as wronged by love—therefore his own lady must have remained a difficult *domna.* The contrast between the *destinataire* and the fictional lady raises a question of interpretation. As the work as a whole is meant to speak on the poet's behalf (vv. 2195–2252), the transformation of courtly material by the *refrains* must be part of his strategy to persuade the lady to emulate the

---

27. Marchello-Nizia, *Poire,* pp. xvi–xix.

behavior of the image he presents in the *Poire*. As we have seen, the communicative situation in the *Roman de la Poire* is complex. Not only do we see the lover and his lady exchange sung messages, but these songs themselves spell out a message to the reader of the text,[28] and the whole composition is yet another message from the poet to his own lady.

The anonymous author of the *Roman de la Dame a la Lycorne et du Biau Chevalier au Lyon* experimented with several modes of discourse: in addition to twenty-four songs,[29] his romance contains a long letter in prose and a *dit* in verse. Like those in the *Castelain de Couci*, the lyrics included in this work are for the most part complete songs, but the *trouvère chanson* has been displaced by the *formes fixes*, particularly the *rondeau* and the *ballade*. The love affair is quickly established, and the lyrics are used exclusively as expressions of emotion. When together, the lovers sing to celebrate their love, and when separated, they exchange songs and messages. Their correspondence is made possible by the invention of a "magical" character—the *Chevalier Fée*—who acts as a messenger between the knight and his lady.

Shortly after taking leave of the lady, and just before embarking on a series of adventures in the *Val Aventureus*, the knight composes his first missive, the *dit*. Clearly the product of his melancholy, the *dit* is meant to be sent:

> Maintenant par merancolie
> Sous un arbre s'e[s]t arrestés
> Et li est prise volentés,
> Qu'a sa dame envoiera
> Un dit pour li que il fera.
> (vv. 1348–52)

---

28. See Huot, *From Song to Book*, pp. 174–84 for a discussion of the relationship of miniatures, text, and *refrains* in the *Poire*; on the miniatures, see Marchello-Nizia, pp. xlix–lvi, and Plates I–XVIII.

29. Friedrich Gennrich, ed., Gesellschaft für romanische Literatur, 18 (Dresden, Halle: Max Niemeyer, 1908). The date of the composition of this work is unclear, but it was probably written around the middle of the fourteenth century; see Philipp August Becker, "La Dame à la Licorne," *Neuphilologische Mitteilungen*, 31 (1930): 81–85. Cf. Anthime Fourrier, "La destinataire de 'La Dame à la Licorne,'" in *Mélanges . . . Le Gentil*, pp. 265–76, who reviews the dating of both Gennrich and Becker and supports the latter (pp. 274–75). For a recent study, see Alice Planche, "Les plus beaux, le plus fort, la plus belle: Les extrêmes du rêve courtois dans le *Roman de la Dame à la Licorne et du Beau Chevalier au lion* (composé vers 1350)," in *Courtly Romance: A Collection of Essays*, ed. Guy R. Mermier and Edelgard E. DuBruck, Michigan Consortium for Medieval and Early Modern Studies: Medieval and Renaissance Monograph Series, VI (1984), pp. 177–202. The romance contains fourteen *ballades*, one *ballette*, seven *rondeaux*, one *chanson*, and one *complainte*.

[Now, for melancholy, he has stopped beneath a tree and he decides to send to his lady a *dit* that he will compose for her.]

The subject of the *dit* is the bond of love, the *cheenne d'amours*, that unites their hearts, but its effect is undermined, for neither the sending nor the reception of the poem is recorded.

With the aid of the fairy knight, the lover's next attempt is more successful. He composes a long letter in prose in which he introduces the *Chevalier Fée* and invites his lady to sustain their love by corresponding:

> Mes, ma tres douce dame, je apperchoic orrendroit, que Diex vus ainme et moi encore plus; car, ma tres douce dame il li a plëu a moy avoir envoié ce message, et c'est un Chevaliers Faés, qui set les volentés et pensees des gens, liquels du tout s'est offers a faire toute la volenté de vus et de moy sans point de deffaut. Pour Dieu! ma tres douce, chiere dame, si l'ames et vus fies du tout en lui et li faites tres boine chiere et toute l'onneur que vous pores; car, ma tres douce, chiere dame, il nous peut molt valoir et aidier. . . . si vus plaise a moy fere savoir par lui vostre volenté et escrire de vo tres douce main; quar ce sera qui me donra vie et joie. (ll. 2079–2101)

> [But, my sweetest lady, I notice now, that God loves you and me even more, for my sweetest lady, he has been pleased to send me this messenger, and it is a Fairy Knight, who knows the wishes and thoughts of people, who has offered to do all our bidding, failing in nothing. By God! my sweetest, dear lady, love him and confide in him everything and welcome him and give him all the honor you can, for my sweetest dear lady, he can be very useful to us and help us. . . . May it please you to let me know your will through him, and to write with your sweet hand, for it is this which will give me life and joy.]

This passage is taken from the middle of a long letter (ll. 2038–2128), most of which the knight devotes to a description of his sorrow at his separation from the lady; he ends with a *rondeau* assuring her of his unhappiness. Unlike the letters in the *Tristan en Prose*, this one is quoted in the context of its composition rather than that of its reception. The lady sends a message in return, but her reply is oral, and very brief:

> Qui le Chevalier au Lyon
> M'ostera, mal fera li hon;
> Car je sai bien, quant avenra
> Que toute joie me faura.
> (vv. 2237–40)

[Who takes the Knight of the Lion from me does ill, for I know well when that happens that I will lack all joy.]

Given the position of the letter, and of the lady's laconic response, the former seems more effective as a kind of monologue rather than a message. Nevertheless, with the arrangements he provided for the writing and delivery of the letter, the author of the *Dame* has moved beyond the situation of the earlier verse romances. The Lady of the Unicorn is not merely evoked by the hero's recollection of her (as in *Meliacin* and the *Violette*), but appears on the scene to receive and send messages.

Later in the romance, the author interrupts his account of the knight's adventures in the service of the emperor with a description of the lady's misery. She pours out her grief and anxiety in a *complainte* that follows immediately upon the descriptive passage:

> Ha! Amours, a vus mi doi plaindre
> De male bouche, qui fait maindre
> Mon coer de moi si tres lontain.
> Helas! vi ge? pourquoi n'estain
> En moi, quant j'ai mon coer en moi?
> (vv. 2849–53)

[Ah, Love, I must complain to you of slander which makes my heart stay far from me. Alas, do I live? Why does it not die in me when I have my heart in me?]

For another sixteen lines, she dwells on the perfection of her chosen knight, and regrets his absence. In response to her distress, the *Chevalier Fée* returns to give her news of the *Beau Chevalier*, and she confides in him her most pressing problem: the unwanted attentions of the *Chevalier au Chief d'Or*:

> Tres dous amis, a li ires
> De par moy, et se li dires
> Que li Chevaliers au Chief d'Or
> D'amer me mainne grant estor,
> Nullement ne me lesse ester.
> En tous liex me prie d'amer,

> Et m'ainme tant que plus ne peut
> Palamedes onques Yseut
> N'ama si tres parfaitement.
> (vv. 2917–25)

[Sweet friend, go to him on my behalf, and tell him that the Knight of the Golden Head makes great efforts to love me. He never leaves me alone. Everywhere he begs me to love him, and loves me as much as he can. Palamède never loved Iseut so perfectly.]

These passages give some sense of the lady's existence apart from her lover—she has problems and difficulties besides loneliness. Euriaut, Celinde, and Clarmondine all had similar problems when separated from their knights, but were unable to summon any aid, since they had no way of sending messages.

The subplot of the *Chevalier au Chief d'Or* is not developed very fully, but is completed in the next exchange. The knight writes again after nearly eight hundred lines of adventures, this time sending two stanzas of a *ballade* (referred to in v. 3745 as "ces lettres"). The lady's answer, carried by the *Chevalier Fée*, supplies the third stanza of the *ballade* and completes the song. Along with her stanza, the lady includes two other *ballades*: one which was sent to her by the *Chevalier au Chief d'Or*, the other her reply. His poem is quite conventional, but hers is interesting for several reasons:

> Hons qui enprent tel folie
> Et si grande musardie
> Est con de lui assentir
> De requerre autre amie,
> Qui est unne vilenie,
> Par droit s'en doit repentir;
> Quar fins coers ne puet mentir.
> La ou a mis s'estudie,
> Si vus di par courtoisie:
> De vous amer n'ai envie;
> Mon coer est autre partie.
> (vv. 3795–3805)

[A man who undertakes such folly and such great foolishness is a "cad" to consent to seek another lady, which is base; rightly must he repent of it. For a fine heart cannot lie; where it has put its effort, so I tell you courteously: I do not wish to love you, my heart is elsewhere.]

Her emphatic response to these unwanted attentions of the villain reveals another side to the rather bland perfection she has so far displayed. Her acerbity is reminiscent of Euriaut's song to Lisiart in the *Violette,* and of Iseut's response to Kaherdin in the *lai* "Folie n'est pas vasselage." The echo is strengthened by the lady's explicit comparison of herself to Iseut hounded by Palamède. Her action in sending these songs to her lover both completes the subplot and serves as a demonstration of her loyalty.

The lady's predicament bears obvious comparison to those of the heroines of the *Violette, Cleomadés,* and *Meliacin,* but in comparing herself to Iseut, she calls attention to the influence of the *Tristan en Prose* on this work. The initial situation of the lovers is similar; in each case the lady is married and the lover is obliged to leave because of malicious gossip. The lovers in both works compose and perform songs to express their love, but the couple in the *Dame* avoid the tragic fate of their predecessors, and consequently their love affair remains unresolved. The reader is left with an impression of a great many adventures leading nowhere.

On a formal level, the experiments in meter contained in the *Dame,* though they take different forms from those of *Tristan,* are another point of resemblance between the two works, and one which announces the form of Machaut's *Voir Dit.* In addition to the insertions, the author of the *Dame* uses two meters. Its introductory section is written in decasyllabic verse, but at verse 589 (which is the beginning of the central love story) the meter becomes octosyllablic. This variety creates an impression of tentative experimentation: the inexorable flow of the narrative octosyllable, already interrupted by the songs, is broken also by a *dit* and a prose passage. But if the technical variety is impressive, the aesthetic effect is less great, since none of the experiments is exploited systematically, as they would be by Guillaume de Machaut in his slightly later *Voir Dit.*

A discussion of songs used in correspondence is perhaps the most suitable place to begin an examination of the *Voir Dit,* for the poems and letters exchanged by the poet and his lady are the core of that work. Composed by Machaut circa 1363–65,[30] near the end of his career, this work purports to be the "true account" of his love affair with the young Peronne

---

30. See Nigel Wilkins, *Guillaume de Machaut, La Louange des Dames* (Edinburgh: Scottish Academic Press, 1972, New York: Barnes and Noble, 1973), pp. 10–12 on the date.

(whom he calls "Toutebelle").³¹ The work is composite in form, consisting of more than nine thousand lines of narrative verse, forty-six letters in prose, and sixty-three lyric poems, some of which have musical notation.

Unlike the love affairs in the *Tristan en Prose* and the *Dame a la Lycorne*, which precede the sending of letters, the "affair" in the *Voir Dit* begins with an exchange of songs and is sustained almost entirely through correspondence. It is the lady, Peronne, who begins the long-distance romance, by sending to the poet a *rondel* of her own composition:

> Celle qui onques ne vous vit,
> Et qui vous aime loiaument,
> De tout son cuer vous fait present;
> Et dit qu'a son gré pas ne vit,
> Quant véoir ne vous puet souvent
> Celle qui onques ne vous vit,
> Et qui vous aime loyaument.
> Car pour les biens que de vous dit
> Tous li mondes communement,
> Conquise l'avez bonnement.
> Celle qui onques ne vous vit
> Et qui vous aime loyaument,
> De tout son cuer vous fait present.
> (Paris, p. 7, vv. 169–81)

[She who has never seen you, and who loves you loyally, makes you a gift of her whole heart; and she says that she does not see to her liking when she, who has never seen you and loves you loyally, cannot see you often. For on account of the good things that everyone commonly says of you, you have conquered her well. She who has never seen you and who loves you loyally, makes you a gift of her whole heart.]

This first poem generates the work as a whole, for it begins the relationship

---

31. In the absence of the edition by Paul Imbs, now undertaken by Jacqueline Cerquiglini, one is obliged to use that of Paulin Paris, *Le livre dou "Voir Dit" de Guillaume de Machaut* (Paris: Société des Bibliophiles françois, 1875). One of the passages omitted by Paris was printed by Anthoine Thomas, "Guillaume de Machaut et l'Ovide moralisé," *Romania*, 41 (1912): 382–400. On the shortcomings of the edition, see William Calin, *The Poet at the Fountain: Essays on the Narrative Verse of Guillaume de Machaut,* Studies in Romance Languages, 9, (Lexington: University of Kentucky Press, 1974), pp. 17–18 and Jacqueline Cerquiglini, *"Un Engin si soutil": Guillaume de Machaut et l'écriture au XIVe siècle* (Paris: Champion, 1985), p. 9.

which is the subject of the work. It also gives a clue to the peculiar characteristics of that work: the love affair begins with a declaration, but by the lady. In reversing the roles of lover and lady, Toutebelle establishes the pattern that will dominate the *Voir Dit*. This *rondel* is important thematically as well as diegetically, since it introduces a pattern of seeing/not-seeing that preoccupies the poet.

The elderly poet is pleased by the offering, and in addition to a verbal response to her messenger, writes an answering *rondel* using similar rhymes:

"Tres-belle, riens ne m'abelist
Ne donne pais, n'aligement,
Sans vous a qui suis ligement"
(Paris, p. 12, vv. 302–4)

[Most beautiful one, nothing is agreeable to me, or gives me peace or solace without you, to whom I belong absolutely]

It is significant that the affair begins in poetry and, as Toutebelle makes clear in her *rondel*, is inspired by a literary reputation. Literature is thus of essential importance in this affair, which draws its energy from the composition of the *Voir Dit* itself, as well as from the exchange of the songs inserted in it.

While the lyric exchange is soon supplemented by letters in prose,[32] the pair continue to send poems, and discussion of these compositions is a major theme of the letters. In the first letter (Paris, p. 16), Toutebelle asks Guillaume to write a *virelai* and to compose music for it and for the two *rondeaux* they have exchanged. He sends a *ballade* to her, and promises: "et y feray le chant du plus tost que je pourray aveuc vos .ii. choses que vous m'avez envoïes" (Paris, p. 42; letter IV; "and I will compose the melody for it as soon as I can, together with the two things you sent me"). In addition, he encloses a *ballade* written at an earlier, unhappy period, and asks her to learn it. Later on, she asks for his criticism of her work:

Et sur ce, je vous envoie un virelay, lequel j'ay fait; et se il y a aucune chose à

---

32. It should be noted that Paris changed the order of the first seven letters in his edition. The order in the manuscripts is as follows: I, IV, V, VI, VII, II, III; cf. Kevin Brownlee, *Poetic Identity in Guillaume de Machaut* (Madison: University of Wisconsin Press, 1984), pp. 237–38, n. 12.

amender, si le vueilliés faire, car vous le sarés mieus faire que je ne fais; j'ai trop petit engien pour bien faire une tele besognge, et aussi n'eus-je onques qui rien m'en aprenist. (Paris, p. 48, letter V)

[And in addition, I send you a *virelai* which I have written, and if there is anything to revise in it, please do it, for you will be able to do it better than I; I have too little skill to do such a task well, nor have I ever had anyone to teach me.]

She goes on to ask for copies of his works, so that she can learn from them. He answers that he has arranged for one of his books to be copied for her. As he continues, he introduces a new theme, that of his current writing:

Je vous mercy de ce que la longueur de mes escriptures ne vous anuie point; car certainement, quant je commence, je n'i say faire fin, pour la tres-grant plaisance que je pren en penser, en parler et en escrire. (Paris, p. 53, letter VI)

[I thank you that you are not bored by the length of my writing, for certainly I do not know how to end it on account of the very great pleasure I derive from thinking, speaking and writing about it.]

This "affair," inspired by his literary reputation, and developed by the exchange and discussion of poetry and music, has itself become the subject of the writing, and much of their correspondence is devoted to discussing the production of this new work, the *Voir Dit*. In Letter XXVII, for example, he reports:

Vostres livres se fait et est bien avanciés; car j'en fais tous les jours .c. vers, et par m'ame, je ne me porroie tenir du faire, tant me plaist la matere, et pour ce que je say bien que vous le verriés tres-volentiers. Mais j'ay trop à faire à querir les lettres qui respondent les unes aus autres. Si vous pri qu'en toutes les lettres que vous m'envoierés d'ores-en-avant, il y ait date, sans nommer le lieu. (Paris, pp. 202–3)

[Your book progresses and is well advanced; for I write one hundred verses of it every day, and by my soul, I could not refrain from doing it, so much does the subject please me, and for this reason I know that you would like to see it very much. But I have too much to do to seek the letters which answer each other. So I ask you that in all the letters you send me henceforth, put the date, without naming the place.]

The production of the book has thus become the object of the affair and the correspondence.

The relationship between the songs and the letters is very close, as they are (at least ostensibly) composed at the same time and are sent together.[33] Since Machaut composed the work from his own point of view, he normally quoted a letter when he wrote it and when he received its reply, and indicated his state of mind when writing, or the emotions provoked by what he read. The pattern could be varied, however, and some letters and songs are included at their composition or reception by Toutebelle. One striking example is the description (Paris, p. 55, vv. 1228–46) of Toutebelle's reaction to one of his letters. Such a change in point of view required explanation, and Machaut cites Toutebelle's maid as his source: "Et savez-vous qui le me dit? / Celle qui là presente estoit, / Et qui la chaussoit et vestoit" (Paris, p. 56, vv. 1247–49; "Do you know who told me? She who was present and who dresses her [i.e. her maid]"). As for the songs enclosed with the letters, they either precede or follow the letters they accompany.

In three places, the lovers send songs in place of letters, and these are of particular interest here. Machaut refers, in the first exchange, to the portrait of Toutebelle: "Belle vostre dous ymage, / Que j'aim amoureusement, / M'a mis en vo dous servage," (Paris, p. 73, vv. 1597–99; "Beauty, your sweet picture, which I love lovingly, has put me in your service"), and she answers: "Amis pour ce l'envoiai-ge / A vous que j'aim loyaument / De cuer, sans penser folaige" (Ibid., vv. 1610–12; "Beloved, for that reason did I send it to you, whom I love loyally with my heart without foolish thoughts"). These *rondels* are followed by another pair, also with the same rhymes and on the same theme. His worry "Se mes cuers art, et le vostres estaint, / Dame, jamais ne puis à joie ataindre" (Paris, p. 74, vv. 1623–24; "If my heart burns and yours goes out, never can I attain joy"), is calmed by her reassurance: "L'amour de vous qui en mon cuer remaint / Tres-dous amis, jamais ne puet estaindre" (Ibid., vv. 1631–32; "The love of you remains in my heart, such love can never go out"). The similarity of rhymes and meaning, the close matching of statement and response independent of explanation, constitute a vivid demonstration of the closeness attained in correspondence.

In the *Voir Dit*, Machaut has reversed the traditional relationship between love and poetry presented in the early romances. In the *Tristan en*

---

33. However, one-third of the letters are not accompanied by songs (8, 9, 16, 17, 18, 19, 22, 23, 25, 26, 30, 34, 36, 39, 40, 41, 42, 44, 45), while one-third of the songs are either sent alone or sung directly. Furthermore, some of the pieces in the *Voir Dit* were borrowed from earlier work. On this point see Brownlee, *Poetic Identity*, p. 101; Sarah J. Williams, "An Author's Role in Fourteenth-Century Book Production: Guillaume de Machaut's 'livre ou je met toutes mes choses,'" *Romania*, 90 (1969): 433–54, especially p. 453; Calin, *Poet at the Fountain*, p. 171; and Poirion, *Le Poète et le Prince*, p. 200 and n.27.

Prose, the *Castelain de Couci*, and *Meliacin*, for example, the hero's love inspires his song. In the *Voir Dit*, on the other hand, poetry inspires love. The songs and letters give rise to further creation and allow the love to exist. The "affair" is essentially literary; one song calls forth another, a letter requires an answer, and the progress of the "affair" is mirrored by the writing of the book. Given the perfection of the correspondence, the meeting of the lovers, as we shall see in the next chapter, could scarcely be other than difficult.

Froissart's *Meliador* (revised for the insertion of lyrics nearly twenty years after the *Voir Dit*) contains six lyrics (three *rondeaux* and three *ballades*),[34] which are similarly enclosed in letters as part of the message. In Froissart's romance, however, it is the letter that bears most of the communication in each case, and indeed, displays the most eloquence. The songs are appendages that add grace but little else to the missive. There are two other *rondeaux*, however, which are sent by another mode of transmission and constitute an interesting variation on the motif.

Near the end of Volume II, the secondary hero Agamanor wishes to approach Meliador's sister Phenonée without violating his incognito. He disguises himself as an artist, produces a painting of the tournament at Tarbonne where he was the winner and tries to sell it to her. As Phenonée and her friend examine the painting, they notice the figure of a lady with a scroll bearing the *rondeau*:

> Amis or gardés loyaument
> Mon coer que je vous ay donné
> En vo garde, de bon talent.
> Il est tout vostre entirement
> De tres parfaite volenté;
> Amis, etc.
> A tous jours mes certainement
> Estre en poés asseguré
> Que ja ne sera aultrement.
> Amis, etc.
> (vv. 20342–51)

[Friend, now guard loyally my heart, which I have given you, in your

---

34. Vol. I, p. 28: Camel to Hermondine; p. 63: Hermondine to Camel; p. 178: Camel to Hermondine (*ballade*); Vol. II, p. 11: Florée to Hermondine (*ballade*); Vol. III, p. 99: Melaidor to Hermondine; p. 189: Sagremor to Sebille (*ballade*).

safekeeping, willingly. It is yours entirely with perfect good will. Friend, etc. Always henceforth, you may certainly be assured that it will never be otherwise. Friend, etc.]

Like Tibaut in the *Roman de la Poire,* Agamanor has created an image of his lady and the response he would like to hear. The picture is partly a record of a real past event, partly the projection of a desired future, and the whole is used as a means of achieving the desired goal. Phenonée is given a picture of herself behaving in accord with Agamanor's desires. The ploy is not entirely successful, for Phenonée hesitates to commit herself while she is unsure of Agamanor's identity and intentions.

When Phenonée does not respond, Agamanor fears that he has lost his chance. In fact, Phenonée has guessed his intention, but is unwilling to reveal herself. When she invites him to return, Agamanor prepares another painting, a portrait of her holding a scroll with a different *rondeau*:

> En pensant a vous me conforte,
> Ma tres douce dame, tout dis.
> De ma doulour qui est trop forte
> En pensant etc.
> Ce doulz penser si me deporte
> De tout anui, et pour ce dis:
> En pensant a vous etc.
> (vv. 20802–8)

[In thinking of you I console myself, my sweet lady, always, for my sorrow which is so strong. In thinking of you, etc. with sweet thoughts I distract myself from all trouble; and for this I say: thinking of you, etc.]

This time Agamanor uses his painting in a more straightforward manner, as a vehicle for his own feelings. Pressing paintings into service as go-betweens is a stage beyond the replacement of the minstrel by the book that we observed earlier in Froissart's *Espinette Amoureuse*. The lyric is once again a written text rather than a song, but the poet here draws attention to its artistic quality in the union of poetry and painting. This combination of media, the insertion of lyric into painting, and indeed, of painting into narrative, is a phenomenon related to our subject, and one which occurs more than once.³⁵

To return to Agamanor's wooing of Phenonée, in the interview that follows his presentation of the portrait, he reverts to the indirect use of songs. He decides to speak openly, and after declaring his feelings, he recalls the occasion when he first saw Phenonée dancing the *carole* during the tournament at Tarbonne.³⁶ In describing the scene, he says that the two *rondeaux* sung by Phenonée made a great impression on him and that he remembers them still. Then, at her request, he sings them both:

Le jour de l'an, par ce bon jour,
En estrine vous voel donner
Mon coer, ma pensée, et m'amour,
Tres doulz amis, sans ja roster . . .
(vv. 21413–16)

[On New Year's day, by that good day, as a gift, I wish to give you my heart, my thought, and my love, most sweet friend, without ever withdrawing . . .]

Pour quoi avés vous nulle doubte
De moy, mon chier ami tres doulz?
J'ay mis en vous m'entente toute,
Pour quoi etc.
(vv. 21495–98)

[Why have you any doubt about me, dear sweetest friend? I have placed in you all my desire. Why etc.]

Neither of these songs, of course, was quoted in the earlier context, nor was any particular mention made of Phenonée's singing, although she presumably must have done so. Even if Agamanor's memory is correct (and

---

35. A line of Fauvel's *lai* and a *refrain* appear in two miniatures in the Paris manuscript B.N., fr. 146 of *Fauvel;* cf. Dahnk, p. 160. See Sylvia Huot, *From Song to Book,* especially Chapter 5, "The Audiovisual Poetics of Lyric Prose: *Li bestiaire d'amours* and its Reception" and Chapter 6, "Lyrical Writing and Compilation in *Le Roman de la Poire* and the *Dit de la Panthère d'Amours,*" pp. 174–208.

36. See above, Chapter 3, under "The Music of the Court," for a discussion of this episode.

Phenonée accepts it as such), her songs had no meaning for him, since she didn't even know of his existence. Agamanor attributes songs to Phenonée as fantasies of his own desires.

Song as Amorous Dialogue

Works in which songs supplement lovers' conversations are surprisingly rare in the corpus.[37] Although Tristan and Iseut are said to sing to each other, no *lais* are ever quoted in such a context. And even a poet like the Châtelain de Couci, whose *chanson* was instrumental in winning his lady, is never portrayed singing in her presence. We do see such lyric celebration of lovers' meetings in *Meliacin*, the *Dame a la Lycorne*, and the *Voir Dit*, however, and in *Guillaume de Dole* and the *Roman de la Violette*, the final reunion of the central couple is similarly celebrated in song.

In *Guillaume de Dole*, as we have seen, Conrad sang only once to Liénor, choosing a *rondet de carole* which not only asked her love, but supplied her answer.[38] The resolution of the plot of the *Roman de la Violette*, on the other hand, occurs in stages, and each of these is marked with a song. When we last saw Euriaut,[39] the heroine of the *Violette*, she had been rescued by the Duke of Metz, who had fallen in love with her. Evading his attentions was not her only difficulty, for an envious knight framed her for the murder of the duke's sister, and after some delay she was condemned to burn at the stake. Gerart, the hero of the romance, arrived just in time to act as her champion, and his victory exposed her accuser. When Euriaut was at last rescued by Gerart, she sang her relief in a *refrain*: "J'ai recouvré ma joie par bien amer" (v. 5701; "I have recovered my joy by loving well"). The words of her song express her circumstances perfectly, for she has indeed been unswervingly faithful to Gerart. The use of a *refrain* here is significant: at the beginning of the romance, Euriaut had subscribed to the most

---

37. Examples of songs in nonamorous dialogues are even more rare in the corpus. There are several in the *Violette:* Euriaut's response to Lisiart's unwelcome propositions is a *chanson de mal mariée* (vv. 441–49); Gerart's responses to Aiglente's advances before and after drinking the potion are neatly contrasting *refrains* (vv. 3331–32 and 4172–73); he answers a similar offer from a serving girl with a third *refrain* (vv. 5068–69). In Jean de Condé's *Dit du Blanc Chevalier*, the protagonist uses a *refrain* (vv. 1368–69) sung publicly to inform his wife that he is aware of her contemplated infidelity and to threaten her. The *dit* has been published by Auguste Scheler, *Dits et Contes de Baudoin de Condé et de son fils Jean de Condé*, 3 vols. (Brussels, 1866–67), II, pp. 1–48. On the career of Jean de Condé, see Jacques Ribard, *Un ménestrel du XIVe siècle: Jean de Condé*, Publications romanes et françaises, 104 (Geneva: Droz, 1969).

38. See above, Chapter 2, under *"Guillaume de Dole."*

39. Cf. above, Chapter 2, under *"Roman de la Violette."*

difficult form of love in a provençal *canso*; now, after much tribulation, she has earned the easier satisfactions of requited love. She makes the same change as Conrad, but there is no ironic intent in Gerbert de Montreuil's treatment of his heroine.

Gerart, however, though reunited with his beloved, has yet to recover his forfeited lands. Realizing this, Euriaut asks him to sing to her now that his worries are half over. He chooses a stanza by Gace Brulé that refers to her request:

> Ne mi sont pas ochoison de canter
> Pres ne vergiés, plaseïs ne buisson;
> Quant ma dame mi plaist a commander,
> N'i puis trouver plus loyal ochoison.
> (vv. 5790–93)

> [Neither meadows, orchards, gardens, nor shrubs are an occasion for me to sing; when my lady is pleased to command me, I can find no more fitting occasion.]

Having not recovered his own lands and orchards, Gerart has little reason to sing, but cannot refuse Euriaut's request. Another song marks the successful resolution of the plot. Gerart sings one last time at the feast that celebrates the victory of the lovers over their enemy:

> Qui bien aimme ne se doit esmaier
> Pour grevanche c'amors sache envoier;
> Que a chelui donne double loier
> Ki pour lui trait plus de painne et essaie;
> Ne sans amour n'a nus joie veraie.
> (vv. 6616–20)[40]

> [Whoever loves well must not be frightened by the wounds that love can send, for a double reward is given to the one who bears the most pain and trouble for it; nor can there be any true joy without love.]

This public celebration resembles the end of *Guillaume de Dole* and balances

---

40. The last line of this quotation has been identified by Boogaard, *Rondeaux et refrains* as *refrain* No. 309. The remainder of the song is unidentified, although the editor (p. xc) regarded the whole piece as a *refrain*.

the opening scene of the romance, but this song is sung to Euriaut, who agrees with its sentiments. These two pieces are important in the romance, for they mark the reunion of the lovers: Gerart, who has sung often for love of Euriaut, at last addresses her directly, and acknowledges his passion as the source of his joy. It is striking that Euriaut does not sing here, for she did so earlier in the romance. It seems that her request for a song is symbolic of her pardon of Gerart, and he, having learned much during his quest, has earned the right to sing less boastfully. In their public celebration of their joy at the end of the romance, the lovers depart from the secrecy and suffering imposed by *fin' amors*. Gerart's choice of a *refrain* signals fittingly their abandonment of that mode of love. Both have suffered in the service of the ideal and now find rewards in the register of "la bonne vie."

In *Meliacin*, Girart d'Amiens uses a duet at a much earlier stage of the love affair. The lovers sing of their love from the very beginning, and as we saw in the second chapter,[41] a pair of overheard songs helps them find each other. Each is delighted to discover the other's love, and Celinde has no qualms about eloping with Meliacin. He sings exuberantly as he carries her off on the magic horse:

> Acolés moi et baisiés doucement,
> Ma tres douce amie,
> Car je ne poroie mie
> Vivre longuement
> Sans la vostre aïe.
> En vostre douce baillie
> Mon fin cuer present.
> Maugré felons plains d'envie
> Vous servirai de cuer entirement,
> Car li maus d'amer me tient joliement.
> (vv. 4392–4401).

[Embrace me and kiss me sweetly, my sweet love, for I could never live for long without your aid. Into your sweet power I offer my fine heart; in spite of envious traitors, I will serve you wholeheartedly, for the pain of love holds me charmingly.]

He suits his actions to his words and is happily unaware that he will soon

---

41. See section entitled *"Conte du Cheval de Fust,* or *Meliacin."*

have the opportunity to prove his loyal service against the envious magician. Equally apt is the refrain of the *rondeau* he sings as they arrive at his father's castle: "Einsi doit entrer en vile / Qui Amours maine" (vv. 4425–26; "So should he enter the city, he whom Love leads"). The marriage of the lovers is considerably delayed when the bride is kidnapped by the magician. When Meliacin finds Celinde at last, she is in the custody of the Duke of Galice, who wishes to marry her, and who sings a complete *chanson* of his own composition to show his great love.[42] Meliacin and Celinde seize their opportunity to escape, and as they fly away on the magic horse, Meliacin sings a stanza by Gace Brulé:

> Li plusour ont d'Amor chanté
> Par esfors et desloiaument,
> Mais de tant me doit savoir gré
> C'onques ne chantai faussement.
> (vv. 16823–26)
>
> [Most have sung of love impetuously and disloyally, but for so much I must be grateful, that I never sang falsely.]

Here is a bald reply to the duke: he is merely one of those who sang falsely of love. Once reunited, the pair exchange lyrics in a scene reminiscent of their earlier flight. Each one begins with an evocation of spring and continues with a declaration of love. Just as their affair began with a pair of songs overheard, so they reach their happy ending with a lyric exchange.

The love affair of the *Dame à la Lycorne* and the *Beau Chevalier au Lyon* begins with such a scene. We actually see the lovers meeting, and overhear their conversations. In the first scene, the knight and lady solemnly swear oaths of loyalty and secrecy, and they elaborate upon their promised love in a series of songs that replace any spoken dialogue. To his declaration "Se je sui pris de dame a pris, / Dont doi ge bien avoir coer gai" (vv. 858–59; "If I am smitten with a worthy lady, then I should indeed be gay of heart"), she replies with the *ballade*:

> Tres bel et bon sur toute creature,
> As vus me renc, sans james departir;

---

42. Vv. 16634–89. On this song, see Antoinette Saly, "La Chanson du duc de Galice (Meliacin)," *TLL*, 10 (1972): 7–16.

> Car en vous maint sens, loiauté, mesure
> N'en vus loant ne poroie mentir,
> Si con m'est vis, et pour ce assentir
> Me voel a vous; car je me senc ciertainne,
> Que vostre beauté est sur toute[s] souverainne.
> (vv. 872–78)
>
> [Handsomest and best of creatures, I give myself to you without ever parting, for in you abide sense, loyalty, and moderation. Nor could I lie in praising you, so I think, and for this reason I wish to consent to you, for I feel certain that your beauty reigns over all.]

In the pair of *rondeaux* that end the scene, they describe the intensity of their love by imagining the pain of separation:

> Se je [ne] vus voi souvent,
> Dous amis, que porrai faire?
> (vv. 911–12)
>
> [If I do not see you often, sweet love, what shall I do?]

> Ma dame, quant je partirai
> De vostre douce conpengnie
> Du tout mon coer je vous lairai.
> (vv. 927–29)
>
> [My lady, when I leave your sweet company I leave you all my heart.]

After coming to the aid of his lady's husband, the *Beau Chevalier* is attached to the household, and they meet, as it were, under her husband's eyes. She is able to praise her knight's courage in helping her husband, but a pair of *ballades* allow them with propriety to express their feelings more openly. When he confesses his unworthiness, "Car riens ne vail et mes coers si haut tent" (v. 1160; "For I am worth nothing and my heart aims so high"), she reassures him of her admiration:

> Par tres grant joie qu'ai senc mon coer adoucir,
> Amis, quant bien regart vo tres douce beauté.

> Certes j'ai bien raison; quar onc nul temps issir
> Ne vi de vous riens que parfaite loiauté.
> (vv. 1184–87)

[With the very great joy that I have, I feel my heart soften, love, when I consider your most sweet beauty. Certainly I am right, for I have never seen from you anything but perfect loyalty.]

The lovers are soon betrayed by gossip and the knight takes his leave in a last meeting. The lyrics here supplement their speeches. The lady's dismay is developed in her song:

> Et dist la dame: "Las! aler
> Vous en volés hors du paÿs,
> Et que feré ge, dous amis?"
> Lors la dame au coer souspire
> Et doucement li prent a dire:
>   Se je ne vous voi briement,
>   M'amour, douce creature,
>   De mort sui en aventure.
> (vv. 1276–83)

[And the lady said: "Alas, you wish to leave the country, and what shall I do, sweet love?" Then the lady sighs deeply and begins to say sweetly: "If I do not see you shortly, my love, sweet creature, I am at risk of death."]

Her *rondeau* restates more forcefully the sentiments she expressed in their first meeting. In turn, the knight assures her of his own misery:

> Tant ai de doleur, que de chi
> Ne m'est avis que ja me part.
> Helas! vostre tres dous regart
> Si m'occit ne ne sai que dire.
> (vv. 1293–96)

[Such sorrow have I, that I do not think I shall leave here; alas, your sweet glance kills me, so that I do not know what to say.]

He answers her *rondeau* with a *ballade* echoing the sentiments of his speech:

> Mon tres dous coer savoureus,
> De vus partir me couvient,
> Dont j'ai le coer dolereus
> Toutes fois qu'il m'en souvient;
> Quar qui va ne set quant vient.
> Mes bien sai je n'avrai joie,
> Fins coers dous, tant que vous voie.
> (vv. 1304–10)

[My sweetest, agreeable heart, I must leave you, which makes me sad at heart every time I think of it. For whoever goes knows not when he comes. But I know well that I shall have no joy, sweet fine heart, until I see you.]

After a long separation, the lovers encounter one another at the court of the King of Frisia. During the dancing, the lady sings a *ballade,* directed to the knight, whom she has not yet been able to greet:

> Ch'est mon ami au cors vaillant
> Ou nature a tous ses bien mis,
> Si croi qu'en tout le remanant
> Du mont n'a honme de tel pris.
> (vv. 5279–82)

[It is my lover of valiant heart where nature has put all its blessings; I think that there is no man of such worth in all the rest of the world.]

Here again, a song allows the lady to express herself and to speak to her lover, without betraying herself in public. When they manage to meet privately, they once more resort to songs. The brief meeting seems to intensify the pain of their separation, which is the subject of her *ballade*:

> Diex d'Amours, trop fort s'ont blecié
> Mon coer et sueffre mainte painne,
> Quant en moi ai bien maginé
> Sa tres grant beauté souverainne
> Et voi que souvent sui lontaingne

De li qui riens n'ainme fors mi,
Et par ma foi, si fa ge li.
(vv. 5417–23)

[God of Love, too badly my heart is wounded and suffers many pains. When I have imagined to myself his supreme beauty, and I see often that I am away from him who loves nothing but me and, by my faith, so I love him.]

Near the end of the romance, the *Beau Chevalier* rescues his lady from an abductor, and they have a brief reunion, which recalls the beginning of the affair. She declares in a *ballade*:

Toute beauté est trouvee
En mon ami debonnaire;
Se li ai m'amour donnee,
Nul autre ne mi peut plaire.
(vv. 7447–50)

[All beauty is found in my gracious lover, so have I given him my love, no other can please me.]

His admiration for her is equally great:

Je me puis bien de ce vanter
Que j'ain plus belle creature
C'onques fourmast Dieu ne Nature.
(vv. 7474–76)

[I can indeed boast that I love the most beautiful creature that God or Nature ever formed.]

In a sense, this romance elaborates what is left out in the others. The author concentrates on the love affair itself, which encounters few obstacles. There is no real resolution of the story, but the songs give the principal characters something to say to each other. The character of the lady in the *Dame a la Lycorne* is a development of that of the thirteenth-century heroines, for she is the first, aside from Iseut, to compose her own songs.

In the *Voir Dit*, the last narrative to include songs used to accompany

178   Chapter 5

amorous dialogue, the two poets continue their established form of communication and exchange songs during their meetings. The prospect of direct meeting seems difficult for Guillaume, who has put off the moment as long as possible. He prepares for (and postpones describing) this long-delayed meeting with an account of an imagined meeting, where he disguises himself and presents someone else to Toutebelle in order to see whether she will guess his identity. Their actual meetings are simpler and pass in conversation, replaced on the second occasion by song.

On this occasion, Toutebelle encourages her timid lover by singing a *refrain*: "Amis, amés de cuer d'amie, / Amés comme loiaus amis" (Paris, p. 92, vv. 2162–63; "Love, beloved by the heart of a mistress, love like a loyal lover"). Thus encouraged, the poet explains his fear in a *rondeau*:

> Douce dame, quant je vous voy,
> Mes cuers ne scet que devenir;
> Ne je ne say que faire doy,
> Douce dame quant je vous voy.
> Car Honte et Paour sont en moy,
> Qui me font trembler et fremir.
> (Paris, p. 92, vv. 2166–71)

[Sweet lady, when I see you, my heart does not know what to feel, nor do I know what I should do, sweet lady, when I see you. For my shame and fear make me tremble and shake.]

She responds with reassurance cast in a *rondeau* with matching rhymes, and also tells him what he ought to feel:

> Tres-dous amis, quant je vous voy
> Vous faites mon cuer resjoïr,
> Nulle doleur ne maint en moy,
> Tres-dous amis, quant je vous voy.
> (Paris, p.93, vv. 2176–79)

[Sweetest love, when I see you, you make my heart rejoice, no sorrow remains in me, sweet love, when I see you.]

At her request, he sings another *rondeau,* which shows the effect of her encouragement: "Le bien de vous qui en biauté florist, / Dame, me fait amer de fine amour" (Ibid., vv. 2188–89; "The good of you which flowers in beauty, Lady, makes me love with a fine love").

This pattern is similar to that of their written exchanges: she sings first and he answers, then a pair of matched lyric pieces follows, and finally he composes a song at her request. As in the letters, the poetry is their surest means of communication, but the pairing of lyrics creates an impression of harmony which is only an illusion. The matching rhymes of the *rondeaux* disguise the fact that their attitudes—his, uncertain and fearful; hers, happy and confident—are strongly opposed. The differences between the two lovers emerge more clearly when not masked by song. When Guillaume composes a *ballade* (Paris, p. 100, vv. 2373–96) on the joys of complaining, Toutebelle eagerly offers to console him. But the very enthusiasm of her answer provides another source of dissatisfaction:

> Mais une chose trop m'argue,
> Qu'entre gent, partout, et en rue,
> Quant vous dites: "Venés à mi,"
> Vous m'appellez vo dous ami,
> Et volez bien que chascuns sache
> Que vous m'amez; dont je me cache,
> Quant ensement parler vous voy,
> Que de vo voie me desvoy.
> Uns biens d'amours couvertement
> Donnés, vault .c. ouvertement.
> (Paris, pp. 104–5, vv. 2517–26)

> [But one thing bothers me too much, that among people, everywhere, and in the street, when you say: "Come to me," you call on your sweet love, and you wish that everyone knew that you love me; therefore I hide when I see you speak like that, and avoid your path. A love token given secretly is worth a hundred given openly.]

This passage seems carping in its irritation, yet it expresses accurately the narrator's feeling that he and his lady are living in different poetic genres. Their different views of love can be reconciled, at least temporarily, in writing, but in person their fundamental conflict emerges clearly.

We may conclude this chapter on the song used as message with a few general observations on the development of this aspect of the device. If

Conrad was the first hero to sing to his beloved, the change of genre that signals the denouement of the romance implies the author's ironic attitude toward the *chansons* that Conrad sang earlier. Gerbert de Montreuil and Girart d'Amiens imitated the idea of direct singing, but modified it by allowing their heroines a singing voice as well. When both lover and lady use the same types of songs, a comparison is set up between them. In the *Violette,* the hero emerges less than creditably, but is reconciled to his lady in the end. Meliacin and Celinde, by contrast, are shown to be equals in love in the somewhat later *Meliacin*. In the *Dame a la Lycorne,* the lovers exchange songs in every phase of their affair. Since the affair itself undergoes so little modification or development, the poetic exchange is of prime importance in embodying the love theme. The conversion of songs into messages illustrates the importance of the lyrics as written texts in this romance. Although the lovers in the *Voir Dit* exchange songs in conversation, thus conserving the older performative quality of lyric poetry, by far the greatest part of their communication is in writing. Their writing takes the form of songs as well as letters, and as we shall see in the next chapter, the act of writing becomes a major theme of the work.

6. The Song and the *Dit*: The Poet as Hero

In our examination of the *Tristan en Prose* and the *Castelain de Couci*, we have seen how songs came to be associated with the love affair of a poet-hero. In the case of the *Tristan*, the insertion of *lais* amplifies the hero's traditional reputation as a singer and musician, even though the songs serve primarily to commemorate past stages of the affair. In the *Castelain*, on the other hand, Jakemés uses a romance plot to explain the creation of songs attributed to an historical *trouvère*. If the *Tristan en Prose* makes a poet of the lover-hero, the *Castelain de Couci* makes a hero of the poet-lover, and represents an attempt to make explicit the story latent in the *chanson*—an attempt, in other words, to cast the poet as the hero of his own story. The romance form provides "historical" contexts for the composition and performance of the poet's songs, which are merely "reported" by Jakemés as narrator. There are thus two voices in this text, the Châtelain's and the narrator's. While the speeches are addressed to other characters (and tied in this way to the narrative), the Châtelain's songs, except for the first, have no audience *in* the narrative and thus seem to address the audience.

The tendencies of the *Tristan* and the *Castelain de Couci* are taken further in the twelve *dits* of the thirteenth and fourteenth centuries containing lyric insertions. These works are first-person narratives in the tradition of Guillaume de Lorris's *Roman de la Rose* and claim to explain the poets' own lyric compositions.[1] The poet-lover becomes in these works the hero

---

1. The best discussion of the genre is by Jacqueline Cerquiglini, "Le Clerc et l'écriture: le *Voit Dit* de Guillaume de Machaut et la définition du *dit*," *Literatur in der Gesellschaft des Spätmittelalters*, ed. Hans Ulrich Gumbrecht, Begleitreihe zum *GRLMA*, 1, (Heidelberg: Winter, 1980), pp. 151–68. James Wimsatt, *Chaucer and the French Love Poets: The Literary Background of the Book of the Duchess* (Chapel Hill: University of North Carolina Press, 1968), pp. 2, 30–69, used the term *dit amoureux* to refer to these works. The discussion by Zumthor, *Essai de poétique médiévale*, pp. 406–20, is still useful. On the transition to poet-lover-hero, see G. B. Gybbon-Monypenny, "Guillaume de Machaut's erotic 'autobiography': Precedents for the Form of the *Voir Dit*," *Studies in Medieval Literature and Language in Memory of Frederick Whitehead* (Manchester: University of Manchester Press, 1973), pp. 133–52; esp. p. 150. On the *Roman de la Rose*, see P.-Y. Badel, *Le Roman de la Rose au XIVe siècle. Etude de la réception de l'oeuvre*, Publ. romanes et françaises, 153 (Geneva: Droz, 1980), esp. pp. 82–94, 154–56.

of the story he narrates. Even as it continues trends of the thirteenth-century romance, however, the *dit* differs significantly from earlier works—in its hero, its lyrics, and its obsession with writing the story. The knightly singer of the romance is displaced by a clerkly writer-narrator.[2] The lyric poetry of the fourteenth century is increasingly divorced from music; the *chanson* and the dance songs give way to the *formes fixes* which, despite their musical origins, are essentially written forms. We see another change in the function of lyricism in the fourteenth century: the "songs" are frequently addressed to someone who responds. The lyric poetry of this period is thus communicative as well as expressive. And since the author of both the poems and the narrative is the hero of the story, the profession of poet is glorified, and the act of writing often becomes a subject of narration.

In most of the *dits amoureux* containing inserted songs, the poet both speaks and sings on his own behalf; there is but a single voice, so the tension between the songs and the story is in theory resolved.[3] Despite the concentration of the different roles (narrator, poet, lover, hero) into a single persona, the *dit* itself is characterized by discontinuity. The narrative line is interrupted by lyrics, by dreams, sometimes by letters and occasionally by other *dits*. The diverse parts of a single composition are not always in accord and create an effect reminiscent of the layered voices in a polyphonic song.

Guillaume de Lorris's *Roman de la Rose* is the inspiration for many of the *dits* with lyric insertions. The dream sequence, the allegorization of psychological traits (the lover's as well as the lady's), the themes taken from the courtly *chanson*, even the "unfinished" quality of the *Rose* are elements that are borrowed and recombined by Nicole de Margival, Guillaume de Machaut, Jean Froissart, and Oton de Grandson. The quest for technical innovation characteristic of the troubadour and *trouvère* lyric seems in the fourteenth century to have been channeled into experiments in the formal structure of the *dit*. Thus we see the combination of narrative verse and lyric embellished with prose and additional forms of versification. In the latter part of the century, even the basic formula of "poet telling his own story" was subject to change. Machaut and Froissart, in the *Fonteinne Amoureuse* and the *Prison Amoureuse* use the autobiographical framework to recount

---

2. Cf. Hult, *Self-Fulfilling Prophecies*, p. 201; and Karl D. Uitti, "From *Clerc to Poète:* The Relevance of the *Romance of the Rose* to Machaut's World," in *Machaut's World*, pp. 209–16.

3. On the "je" in these works, see Paul Zumthor, *Essai de poétique médiévale*, pp. 411ff; "Autobiographie au moyen âge?" in *Langue, texte, énigme*, pp. 165–80; and "Le *je* de la chanson et le moi du poète," in ibid., pp. 181–96. See also Kevin Brownlee, "Transformations of the Lyric 'Je': The Example of Guillaume de Machaut," *Esprit Createur* 18, no. 1 (1978): 5–18; and Marchello-Nizia, "'Je' universel ou 'je' autobiographique," in *Poire*, pp. xxx–xxxi.

someone else's story, while Machaut in the *Voir Dit* admits the voice of the lady, who opposes his own. In the *Livre Messire Ode*, the narrative dissolves at the end into lyric in a series of poems. Christine de Pizan, on the other hand, adopts personas that are not her own. In one work she takes on the guise of a shepherdess, but more radically, in the *Duc des Vrais Amants*, she speaks in the voice of the lover.

Nicole de Margival

Although the *Roman de la Poire* (ca. 1250) is perhaps the earliest first-person narrative to use lyric insertions, its use of songs is still that of the romances: the songs are for the most part attributed to different characters rather than sung by the poet-narrator, and they are not presented as his own compositions. They are all, in fact, borrowed from the body of *refrains* of *rondets de carole*. It is perhaps significant that the title of this work is "roman" and not "dit." The second first-person narrative to include songs is Nicole de Margival's *Dit de la Panthere d'Amors*, composed between 1290 and 1328. This work is a much more developed but still hybrid form of the first-person account.[4] The *dit* falls neatly into two parts: the first and longer section is a dream sequence, while the second part is a sort of "personal epilogue."[5] Incorporated into this narrative are sixteen lyric quotations (nine borrowed from Adam de la Halle, seven others composed by Nicole himself) and three lesser *dits* composed in three different meters.

In the dream section, the poet, overwhelmed by the sight of a beautiful panther, has the vision explained to him by *Amors*, the god of Love. On Love's advice, he attempts to follow the panther, but is defeated by the dense undergrowth of the valley she inhabits. Love sends *Penser*, *Souvenir*, and *Esperance* to aid the lover, who explains his desire in a *dit*. The goddess Venus intervenes at this point to encourage the lover to act boldly, but the lover objects, citing Adam de la Halle to the effect that: "Trop font cil amant a haïr / Qui requierent hardiement" (vv. 1073–74; "They make themselves hated, those lovers who petition too boldly"). He goes on to invoke Adam twice more to the same effect, quoting two more of his

---

4. Henry A. Todd, ed., *Le dit de la Panthere d'amours par Nicole de Margival*, SATF (Paris: Firmin Didot, 1883); see p. xxvii on the date. See also Ruhe, *Le Dieu d'Amours*, pp. 160–63. For an excellent discussion of the *Panthere* and its relation to the *Roman de la Rose*, see Huot, *From Song to Book*, pp. 194–201.

5. The term is borrowed from Ernst Hoepffner, "Poésies lyriques du Dit de la Panthère de Nicole de Margival," *Romania*, 46 (1920): 203–30; esp. p. 215.

songs.⁶ Although the poet does not actually sing these quoted stanzas and is clearly interested only in their content—"la sentence du ver" (vv. 1098–99; "the sense of the verse")—the authority of the quotations is nevertheless derived from their status as songs: "En son chant ainsi le chanta / Ce scet bien cil qui le chant a" (vv. 1071–72; "He sang it this way in his song, he knows this well who has the song"). Venus next tries to strengthen his resolve, giving him a *dit* and a ring to give to his lady. At this point, there is a dream within the dream, and the poet attempts to follow Venus's instructions, but his lady refuses to accept his offering.

When the poet awakens from this inset dream, he resumes his argument with Venus, who urges persistence and hope, basing her case on four other stanzas by Adam that are quoted to him. As before, the quotations support emphatically the position put forth. The poet answers that he intends to persist, quoting Adam's "Grant deduit a et savoureuse vie" in its entirety in order to "describe his state of mind" (v. 1589). When the poet is unable to make use of a *dit* given him by Love, the god tells him that he must then rely on Fortune. This lady finally smiles on the poet and allows *Bone Volenté*, *Eür*, *Pitié*, and *Grace* to escort him to the panther, who grants "moi et Merci" (v. 2172; "myself and mercy") when she sees him in such company.

The poet finally awakens from his double dream (v. 2190), and then reflects upon it in the second and shorter part of the work, which is "personal" or pseudo-autobiographical. In this section most of the lyric insertions are ascribed to Nicole himself, and only two are borrowed from Adam. Upon awakening, the poet finds that his dream has renewed his determination to persevere, and his love inspires him to compose a new song: "Pour ennuy ne por contraire / Ne pour mal souffrir / Ne me puis d'amer tenir" (vv. 2226–28; "Neither for trouble, nor resistance nor for suffering evil can I keep from loving"). The reason for his devotion, of course, is to be found in his lady's perfection, which he sums up in a *ballade*:

---

6. Songs—especially *refrains*—are cited as evidence in several other works, e.g., "D'amors et de Jalousie," "La Flours d'Amours," and the translation of Ovid's *Ars Amatoria* preserved in Paris, B.N., fr. 881 and three other manuscripts. For the first two works, see the editions by Edmond Faral, "D'amour et de Jalousie: Complainte d'Amour du XIIIe siècle," *Romania*, 59 (1933): 330–50; and Joseph Morawski, "La Flours d'Amours," *Romania*, 53 (1927): 187–97. For the last work, see Bruno Roy, *L'art d'Amours: Traduction et commentaire de l' "Ars amatoria" d'Ovide, édition critique* (Leiden: Brill, 1974). For the date of this work, see also Nico H. J. van den Boogaard, "L'*Art d'aimer* en prose," in *Etudes de civilisation médiévale (IXe–XIIe siècles): Mélanges offerts à Edmond-René Labande* (Poitiers: CÉSCM, 1974), pp. 687–98.

> Biautez, bontez, douce chiere,
> Sens et avenans maniere,
> Et grace m'ont si conquis
> En monstrant dame de pris
> > Soudainement
> > Qu'a li servir me rent
> > Outreement.
>
> (vv. 2259–65)

[Beauty, goodness, sweet face, intelligence and elegant manner, and grace have so conquered me, showing a lady of merit suddenly, that I give myself to serve her absolutely.]

Having asserted both the fact of his love and the reason for it, the poet goes on to recall the progress of his affair. He began, he declares, by admiring her beauty and virtue, and for a time found sufficient delight in contemplating her. Eventually, however, he began to hope for requited love, but—like the lover in the dream—he lacked the courage to approach her. To typify the change in himself, he uses first a *rondeau*:

> Anuis meslez a contraire
> M'a si mué mon afaire
> Qu'il m'a fait longuement taire
> De chanter et de chant faire.
>
> (vv. 2341–44)

[Pain mixed with resistance has so changed my situation that it made me silent for a long time from singing and composing songs.]

and then a *chanson à refrains:*

> J'ai esté chantans, jolis
> Et gays, mais venue est l'eure
> Dont j'oÿ dire jadis:
> Tels rit au main qu'au soir pleure;
> Si n'a en moy jeu ne ris
> Car je ne puis estre oÿs
> De cele qui a m'amour,

> Por qui je sui sans sejour
> En pensee nuit et jour.
> (vv. 2385–93)
>
> [I was singing, charming and gay, but the hour came that I had heard of before: he who laughs in the morning weeps in the evening; there is in me neither game nor laughter, for I cannot be heard by her who has my love, for whom I am without rest, in meditation night and day.]

His account having rejoined the present, the lover (once more invoking Adam) summons the courage to address his lady directly. He inserts into his plea two *rondeaux*—one which he would like to hear her sing ("Soiez liez et menez joie, Amis" [vv. 2515–16; "Be happy and joyful, lover"]), and the other his answer, should she so encourage him:

> J'ai eü commandement
> D'estre liez, si le serai
> En chant de loial cuer gay.
> (vv. 2528–30)
>
> [I have been commanded to be happy, and so I shall be in song with a heart loyal and gay.]

In this way, the poet echoes the dream-adventure and attempts not only to give his affair a happy end, but to complete his narrative. But once again, the ending he supplies is only imaginary.

The outcome is desired and projected, but not achieved. This is made clear in the final passage of the work, where the poet assures his lady that his joy lies only in pleasing her, and he resorts to a final emphatic plea in the form of a *chanson royale* ("Mercy, Amour, de la douce dolour") by Adam de la Halle, quoted in its entirety. Nicole brings his *Dit de la Panthere* to a close with a plea for his lady's help in ending it:

> En ceste oeuvre veil metre fin.
> Pour ce pri merci au finer,
> Dont je ne poy onques finer,
> Que je veil que ceste oevre fine,

Merci priant a dame fine.
(vv. 2599–2603)

[I wish to put an end to this work. For this reason, I beg mercy finally which I can never finish, and I wish that this work may end, begging mercy of a fine lady.]

His poem is intended to win her favor, but without her cooperation, he cannot even finish it.

Whereas most pseudo-autobiographies purport to account for the composition of lyrics—that is, the narrative describes the circumstances that provided the creative impulse—the case of the *Panthere* is different. While the dream sequences present the story allegorically but in chronological order, the poet's own account begins in the middle (the present), relates the past, returns to the present, and pleads for the future. Nicole's own lyrics, which represent different stages of his love affair—the sight of the beautiful lady, the transformation love effected in him, his frustrated present, and the imagined happy future—are an alternative way of telling his story. They reflect the shape of the narrative, which in turn echoes the story of the dream and the dream within the dream. All three narratives (or four, counting the series of Nicole's songs) contain flashes to the future, but if most of these are optimistic, one of them is not, and the outcome is thus left open.

Nicole's *Panthere* is similar to the *dits* of the next century in allowing the poet to tell both his dream and his own story. Its use of borrowed lyrics marks the work as transitional. As in the romances, the quotation of songs by a celebrated *trouvère* (in this instance Adam de la Halle), proclaims the hero's adherence to the courtly ideals of the *chanson*. But if the borrowing is a constant, both the hero and his relationship to the songs he quotes are altered. Adam's *chansons* are not sung in the *Panthere*; his songs have become texts to be cited. The invocation of Adam's songs by Venus and by the narrator invests them with authority in the field of love. There are thus two lyric voices in the *Panthere*, and the narrator's attitude toward Adam's songs is that of disciple to master. Adam's lyrics provide an ideal against which the poet measures both himself and the progress of his affair. Nevertheless, Nicole's lover is not unquestioning in his imitation of Adam, and in the end he finds himself obliged to rely on his own poetic skill to win his lady.

Guillaume de Machaut

Guillaume de Machaut, in his *Remede de Fortune*, transformed the pseudo-autobiographical strain of the *Panthere d'Amors*. While Nicole de Margival portrayed the changing phases of his love in a song composed at each period, Machaut's narrative is more circumstantial and explains the creation or performance of each song.[7]

Composed between 1342 and 1357,[8] the *Remede* contains seven songs set to music. Not coincidentally, these include an example of each of the six genres then current: a *lai,* a *complainte,* a *chanson royale,* two *ballades,* a *virelai,* and a *rondeau*.[9] The songs occur in order of decreasing poetic complexity, while the music that accompanies them generally progresses from the monophonic *lai, complainte,* and *chanson* to the polyphony of the remaining *ballades* and *rondeau;* the monophonic *virelai* is an exception.[10]

After a prologue recommending practice of any art one wishes to learn, the *Remede* recalls Guillaume's initiation to love and describes its effect on the timid and inexperienced young man who is his youthful self. Taking his lady as his "miroir et exemplaire" (v. 171), he emulates her virtues, and spends his time praising her in songs. Afraid to address her, he hopes that she may find them and know that she is loved. One such song is the *lai,* the first of the insertions. Its twelve stanzas restate much of the preceding passages: Guillaume proclaims the efficacy of the consolation offered by thought and the sight of the lady, before repeating his wish that she may discover his love; in the end, however, he quails at the risk of refusal and decides to hide his love. If the *lai* restates the opening section, it also advances the plot, for it is the *lai* that exposes him. When she finds the

---

7. Brownlee, *Poetic Identity,* pp. 176–77, discusses the possible influence of the *Panthere* on Machaut's narrative poetry.
8. Ibid., p. 195, n. 5. For Machaut's career, see Armand Machabey, *Guillaume de Machaut 130?–1377: La Vie et l'oeuvre musicale,* 2 vols. (Paris: Richard Masse, 1955). See also Gilbert Reaney, *Guillaume de Machaut* (Oxford: Oxford University Press, 1971); "Guillaume de Machut: Lyric Poet," *Music and Letters,* 39 (1958): 38–51; and "A Chronology of the Ballades, Rondeaux and Virelais Set to Music by Guillaume de Machaut," *Musica Disciplina,* 6 (1952): 33–38.
9. Ernest Hoepffner, ed., *Oeuvres de Guillaume de Machaut,* 3 vols., SATF (Paris: Firmin Didot, 1908, 1911, 1921), II, pp. 1–157. For studies of the *Remède,* see Brownlee, *Poetic Identity,* pp. 37–63; Calin, *Poet,* pp. 55–74; Kelly, *Medieval Imagination,* pp. 130–37 and 149–50; and Lawrence M. Earp, "Scribal Practice: Manuscript Production and the Transmission of Music in Late Medieval France. The Manuscripts of Guillaume de Machaut" (Ph.D. Diss., Princeton University, 1983), pp. 276–83.
10. Cf. Friedrich Ludwig, "La Musique des intermèdes lyriques dans le *Remede de Fortune,*" in Hoepffner's edition, II, pp. 405–14, plus twenty-seven pages of transcriptions and facsimiles.

lai, the lady has him read it to her, and then asks who wrote it. Unable either to lie or to declare himself by claiming his composition, Guillaume is reduced to speechlessness:

> Je n'eüsse dit un seul mot
> Pour toute l'empire de Romme;
> Car nuls cuers ne penseroit comme
> Je perdi maniere et vigour;
> Car honte, amour, biauté paour,
> Et ce que celer li voloie
> L'amoureus mal que je sentoie,
> Me tollirent si le memoire
> Et les cinq sens.
> (vv. 704–12)

[I would not have uttered a single word for all the empire of Rome, for no one would imagine how manners and strength failed me, on account of shame, love, beauty, and what I wished to hide from her, the loving pain that I felt, took away my memory and my five senses.]

Composing the *lai* (and allowing its discovery) is Guillaume's first action in the narrative, as in the affair, but he is unable to continue this active role. His behavior repeats the ambivalence of the *lai*, both desiring and fearing change. Unable to act (speak) again, he retreats in disarray to a garden. In a lyric setting, near a spring surrounded by trees, grass, and briar roses, Guillaume begins to "penser durement" (v. 841; "think painfully"), blaming himself for his clumsiness. He decides at last to make a *complainte* out of his sorrow, his tears, and Fortune. The sheer size of this poem—thirty-six sixteen-line stanzas—bears witness to his profound distress. Fully half of the *complainte* is devoted to Fortune: her influence, her character, her appearance.[11] The portrait of this baleful figure, to whom he attributes all his trouble, is derived principally from Boethius, and balances the long, flattering description of his lady at the beginning. This capricious female is surely a substitute for his lady, one that he can revile in good conscience. The act of composing this tirade seems to assuage him, for in the second half of the poem he turns to his own situation and reproaches Love. In the final section, he invokes Hope, but in negative terms:

---

11. See Cerquiglini, *Engin*, pp. 63–72.

> Se pour ce que j'ay povre espoir
> De ma douce dame vëoir
> Et qu'Amours m'a en nonchaloir,
>   Qu'il me fera?
> M'ocira il? Il ne porra,
> Car ma loiauté m'aidera.
> Qu'ai je dit? Einsois me sera
>   Contraire, espoir.
> Car puisqu'Amours me grevera
> Et Fortune qui honni m'a,
> Ma grant loiauté m'ocira,
>   Si com j'espoir.
> (vv. 1421–32)

[If, because I have small hope of seeing my sweet lady, Love does not care about me, what will he do to me? Will he kill me? He cannot, for my loyalty will help me. What have I said? Thus Hope will be against me, for since Love wounds me and Fortune has shamed me, my great loyalty will kill me, so I hope.]

In answer to his indirect appeal, Hope or *Esperance* appears to help him. She consoles him, encourages him, criticizes his behavior, gives him reason to hope, and finally sings a *chanson royale* to cheer him up. Her song continues the work of her speech, and reveals in love itself the source of comfort:

> Car vraie Amour en cuer d'amant figure
> Trés dous Espoir et gracieus Penser:
> Espoirs attrait Joie et bonne Aventure;
> Dous Pensers fait Plaisance en cuer entrer.
> (vv. 1994–97)

[For true love creates sweet hope and gracious thought in the heart of a lover. Hope attracts Joy and Good Fortune; Sweet Thought causes Pleasure to enter the heart.]

The kind, gracious, laughing *Esperance* seems a benevolent representative of the lady and he notes the resemblance (vv. 2035–36).[12] Guillaume thanks

---

12. Cf. Calin, *Poet*, pp. 64–66.

Esperance for her instruction (and indeed, repeats her teaching), but asks how he is to defend himself from the whim of Fortune. In a passage of nearly 490 lines (vv. 2403–2892), *Esperance* considers the nature of Fortune, proves to the poet that he has no cause to blame her, and recommends *soufisance* (independence) as the source of happiness. Her last gift to the poet is a *ballade*, which he is to sing to make himself happy. The three stanzas of the song recommend love, which, despite its sufferings, is the source of joy: "C'est dous maus a soustenir, / Qu'esjoïr / Fait cuer d'ami et d'amie" (vv. 2866–68; "It is a sweet pain to bear, for it makes the heart of lover and beloved rejoice"). The poet sets himself to learn the *ballade*. In so doing he frees himself from his earlier paralysis and regains his five senses.

While he is engrossed in the song, *Esperance* disappears. Discovery of her departure makes him pensive again, but he occupies himself in recording (in his memory) all that has happened. Then, thinking to see his lady again, he composes and sings another *ballade* that expresses his sentiments clearly:

> Dame, de qui toute ma joie vient,
> Je ne vous puis trop amer, ne chierir,
> N'assés loër, si com il apartient,
> Servir, doubter, honnourer, n'obeïr;
>   Car le gracieus espoir,
> Douce dame, que j'ay de vous vëoir,
> Me fait cent fois plus de bien et de joie,
> Qu'en cent mille ans desservir ne porroie.
> (vv. 3013–20)
>
> [Lady from whom comes all my joy, I cannot love you, nor cherish you too much, nor praise you enough, as is fitting, nor serve, fear, honor, nor obey. For the gracious hope, sweet lady, that I have of seeing you gives me a hundred times more good and joy than I could deserve in a hundred thousand years.]

The contrast between this song and the *lai* could scarcely be more complete. In the first piece, the words, accompanied by a straightforward melody, seem to stumble over themselves, and the syntax is perforce simplified by the complex and frequent rhymes. The calmer, more coherently expressive *ballade*, with its four voices of music, shows that the poet has learned the lessons of *Esperance*.

As he leaves the garden, the poet is assailed by fear, but when he calls upon *Esperance*, she again comes to his aid. He continues on his way, thanking Love in a stanzaic prayer. When he rejoins his lady, he finds her singing and dancing with friends, and is invited to join them. At her request he sings a *virelai* (*chanson balladée*), an elegant declaration which repeats that of the *ballade*:

> Dame a vous sans retollir
> Dong cuer, pensée, desir,
>   Corps et amour,
> Comme a toute la millour
>   Qu'on puist choisir,
> Ne qui vivre ne morir
>   Puist a ce jour.
> (vv. 3451–57)

[Lady, I give to you without taking back, heart, thought, desire, body, and love, as to the very best that one could choose, whether he lives or dies this day.]

In return, the lady sings a *refrain*: "Dieus quant venra li temps et l'eure / Que je voie ce que j'aim si?" (vv. 3502–3; "God, when will come the time and the hour that I may see the one I love?").[13] After the poet explains his behavior in a way flattering to her, the pair exchange rings. When he leaves her, he composes a *rondelet*, the last song in the *Remede*. In the final passage, he thanks Love for his happy state and hopes that his lady will soon see the *dit* that he has just finished.

The *Remede de Fortune*, then, describes the transformation of an awkward young man into an accepted lover, at the same time that it demonstrates the role of poetry in that transformation. In keeping with his prologue, which gives advice to any who would learn an art, Machaut has written an art of love that is also an art of poetry, for the two—as we shall see again and again in his work—are really one.

In the *Fonteinne Amoureuse*, composed between 1360 and 1362, Machaut combined the traditional motifs in a new form.[14] The title acknowledges his debt to Guillaume de Lorris, whose fountain of Narcissus is its model. Though narrated in the first person, Guillaume's account concerns

---

13. This *refrain* is too late to be listed in Boogaard, *Rondeaux et refrains*, but is an interesting survival of the earlier technique.
14. Hoepffner, *Oeuvres*, III, pp. 143–244. For studies see Calin, *Poet*, pp. 146–66; and Brownlee, *Poetic Identity*, pp. 188–207.

another lover, identified in an anagram in the prologue as his patron Jean de France, Duke of Berry. The work contains three lyric insertions, and as in the *Remede* the plot springs from the first of these.

Guillaume begins by describing a night at an inn, where his sleep was disturbed by the laments of the occupant of the next room. He gives a long and comic description of the fright caused him by the noise, but pulls himself together when the unseen voice says: "Adieu, ma dame, je m'en vois" (v. 200; "Farewell, my lady, I go away"), and announces its intention of composing a *complainte*. The interest of the professional poet is aroused, and Guillaume's feelings change as he prepares to transcribe:

> Lors fui je tantost hors d'esmay,
> Si me vesti et acesmay
> Et alumay de la chandeille,
> Mais j'avoie toudis l'oreille
> Devers la cheminee a destre
> Ou il avoit une fenestre
> Par ou sa parole escoutoie,
> Car pres de la fenestre estoie.
> Si que je pris mon escriptoire,
> Qui est entaillie d'ivoire,
> Et tous mes outils pour escrire
> La complainte qu'il voloit dire.
> Si commença piteusement
> Et je l'escri joieusement.
> (vv. 221–34)

[Then I was soon out of fear, so I got dressed and equipped myself and lighted my candle, but the whole time I kept my ear close to the chimney on the right, where there was a window through which I listened to his words, for I was close to the window. As I took up my writing desk (which is inlaid with ivory), and all my tools to write down the *complainte* he wished to make, he began piteously, and I wrote it down joyfully.]

The emotional pattern of the opening passage resembles that of the *Remede*, where the poet's amorous dismay is first made into poetry and then comforted. Here his fear is given a circumstantial explanation, while the joy that replaces it is that of a poet in the presence of a rival.

In the eight-hundred-line *complainte* which follows, the lover praises his lady for all she has given him and describes the comfort of *dous regart*. Now that he is obliged to leave, however, he has lost this comfort, and he torments himself with the fear that she may forget him. In another set of stanzas he describes his bondage to love, which now seems so hopeless. He calls upon Love, thinks of writing to his lady, and then imagines the possibility of a message conveyed by a dream. This idea leads him to invoke Morpheus, the god of sleep, and he retells Ovid's story of Ceyx and Alceone as an example of the god's power. This tale of the grief-stricken wife who sees her dead husband in a dream anticipates the lover's own dream later in the work. In the final stanzas, after assuring his lady that his love is imprinted on his memory, he relates the length of his composition to her beauty:

> Ne vous anuit, dame, se plus ne rime,
> Qu'on porroit bien espuisier un abisme.
> Cent rimes ay mis dedens ceste rime,
>   Qui bien les conte.
> Prises les ay en vostre biauté qui me
> Tient sans dormir dou soir jusques a prime
> Mais en mil ans n'en diroie la disme.
> (vv. 1019–25)

[May it not annoy you, lady, if I rhyme no more, for one could as well exhaust an abyss. I have put one hundred rhymes into this poem, whoever wishes may count them. I have taken them from your beauty, which keeps me without sleep from evening until dawn, but in a thousand years, I would not describe a tenth of it.]

The *complainte* is presented here at a double remove: it is "overheard" not only by the reader, but also by the narrator. If this device distances us from the lyric, it also stresses the mediating function of the poet-narrator. However inspired the lover's lyric impulse, there would be no poem, no "written text," without the poet who transcribes. We have in this passage a vivid dramatization of the preference for written lyric over mere performance that is typical of the fourteenth century.

Like the *lai* in the *Remede*, the *complainte* is central to the plot of this *dit*. Not only does it convey to the reader essential details of the lover's situation, but it also gives rise to the rest of the plot. The quality of this apparently spontaneous poem so impresses Guillaume that he seeks to discover the identity of its author.

When they meet, Guillaume offers advice and consolation to his lovelorn companion while they walk in a garden. Guillaume here plays the role of *Esperance* in his earlier work. He and the lover come upon a beautiful fountain, decorated with mythological scenes, but neither has any inclination to drink from it: Guillaume because the fountain could not possibly make him any more loving than he is already, and the other because he has already drunk from it and been disappointed. Instead, they fall asleep and share a dream in which they are visited by two ladies. The first, Venus, explains to Guillaume the story of the inscription "A la plus belle" on the apple she carries, and then introduces her companion, the lover's own lady, who composes a *confort* in answer to his *complainte*. The *confort*, although shorter and composed in seven- rather than ten-syllable lines, uses the stanzaic form and rhyme scheme of the first insertion. The lady's answer is all the lover could wish for:

Amis, je te vieng conforter
Et joie et solas aporter
Et de ces tenebres oster
   Ou je te voy;
(vv. 2207–10)

[Lover, I come to comfort you and to bring you joy and solace and to take away the shadows in which I see you.]

Et je te promés, par ma foy,
Que m'amour et le cuer de moy
Aras toudis aveques toy,
   Et sans fausser
Seray tienne, faire le doy;
(vv. 2215–19)

[And I promise you, by my faith, that you shall have love, and my heart with you always, without falseness shall I be yours, I must do it.]

Not only does she take pity on his distress, but she shares it equally, for she loves him in return: "Car tu es miens et je suis toie" (v. 2225; "For you are mine and I am yours"). The address to the lover at the beginning echoes the opening stanza of the *complainte*. The lady goes on to use a series of mythological examples to make her point. In the last two stanzas of the *confort*, the narrative resumes:

> Adonq la dame s'abaissa,
> Qu'onques pour moy ne le laissa
> Et plus de cent fois le baisa
>   En son dormant;
> Et puis elle le resgarda
> Et de son droit braz l'embrassa
> Et li dist: "Amis, trai te sa!"
>   En sousriant.
> (vv. 2495–2502)

[Then the lady bowed, and never left him because of me, and kissed him more than a hundred times while he slept. And then she looked at him, and embraced him with her right arm and said, smiling: "Lover, get up!"]

Though the lover sleeps through all of this, she exchanges rings with him before leaving with Venus. Only then do the dreamers awaken. Just as the line between lyric and narrative is blurred, the division between dream and reality is also undermined. Although the lover has slept throughout, he nevertheless wears a different ring at the end—a sign perhaps of the truth of the dream. The dream sequence is a mirror-image of the story of Ceyx evoked in the *complainte*; there it was the lover who appeared to his wife. The lyric, then, not only gives the impulse for the unfolding of the plot, but contains the elements of that plot.

Like Guillaume in the *Remede*, the lover is transformed by his dream and sets off on his journey invigorated by hope. As before, a song signifies the change in him:

> Quant montez fu, il m'est avis
> Qu'il tourna par deça son vis,
> Et d'une vois bele et jolie,
> Pleinne de tres grant melodie
> Et d'un amoureus sentement
> Prist a chanter joliement:
>   En païs ou ma dame maint
>   Pri Dieu qu'a joie m'i remaint.
> (vv. 2819–26)

[When he got up, it seems to me that he turned his face and with a beautiful, charming voice full of melody and loving feeling, he began to sing sweetly: "In the country where my lady dwells, I beg God that I may remain in joy."]

The *Fonteinne* is structurally similar to the *Remede*, but the pattern of the transformation of the lover is complicated by the split between narrator and lover. Because there are two dreamers, there are two ladies, and the *confort* is balanced by the mythological story Venus recounts to Guillaume. The multiple frames—the poet's night at the inn, the lover's tale, and the dream—demonstrate the discontinuity of the *dit* at the same time that they imply a comparison between the two narrators. Although Guillaume projects a comic persona at the beginning, the narrative shows him completely confident in his role as poet. At the end of the work, when the comforted lover rides away, it is Guillaume who has the last word: "Je pris congié. / Dites moy, fu ce bien songié?" (vv. 2847–48; "I took my leave. Tell me, wasn't it well dreamed?"). The poet thus claims credit for the structure of the *dit* as a whole, even though he attributed a large portion of its composition to another poet-lover.

In fact, this shift of authorship is consistent with the preoccupation with writing characteristic of the *dit*. This theme is dramatized in the relation between poet and patron. In the dream, the relative status of lover and narrator are changed. While the lover dreams of his lady, Guillaume is visited by Venus herself. Thus Guillaume's account of the lovers' meeting is given the status of a specific example of a general principle. Guillaume, however comic a persona he may project, remains the *maistre*, while his patron, the lover, is only an *exemplum*. The poet-patron relationship is also reversed at another point in the *dit:* when the lover asks for a poem, Guillaume gives him his own *complainte*, transcribed during the night.

In the last of his *dits*—the *Voir Dit*—Machaut took the structure of the pseudo-autobiographical narrative and altered it more radically still. To begin with, the first-person narrative is interrupted not only by sixty-three lyrics, but also by forty-six letters in prose. Yet even this triple form fails adequately to represent the formal complexity of the work. While one normally speaks of "prose letters," and most of the letters in the work are in fact written in prose, letter XXIII is written in a highly structured verse, complete with refrain, and the beginning of letter IV (printed as II in Paris's edition)[15] is cast as a *rondeau*. Similarly, some of the verse passages of the narrative itself have a stanzaic structure (e.g. the Prayer to Venus, pp.

---

15. Cf. Chapter 5, n. 32, on the reordering of some letters by the editor.

155–57, the description of Fortune, pp. 333–39, and the songs of Fortune's virgins).

As we have seen in the preceding chapter, the *Voir Dit* is presented as the "collected correspondence" of the poet and his lady, and this fact introduces another complication—a second voice—into the narrative. While the *Fonteinne Amoureuse* had earlier introduced a second character into the first-person account, the lover was seen entirely through the eyes of the narrator, who even reported his companion's dream. In the *Voir Dit*, on the other hand, the voice of Toutebelle speaks directly; her letters and songs are recorded, rather than reported. And where the lover of the *Fonteinne* was in many ways a kindred spirit to the narrator, the lady Toutebelle is altogether more independent and frequently contradicts him.[16]

On a structural level, Machaut in this work reversed the *complainte-confort* pattern of the *Remede* and the *Fonteinne*. In the earlier works, the timid, unsure lover who complains of his treatment by Love or Fortune finally receives encouragement from his lady. The *Voir Dit*, in contrast, begins with Toutebelle declaring her admiration to the elderly poet, who tries unsuccessfully to return to his role in his earlier works.[17] In his fourth letter (VIII), for example, Guillaume reacts to a report that his lady is displeased with him:

> Et comment que je ne soie mie dignes de vous regarder ne de vous loer, se vous aviez ymagination contre moi, je seroie perdus et mors; car je aroie perdu m'esperance et mon confort, et legierement m'ariés oublié et guerpi. Mais ce seroit à tort: car, par m'ame, se toutes les dames du monde estoient en une place, je vous ameroie plus toute seule que toutes les autres. . . . Et s'aim mieulz languir pour vous que de nul autre joïr. (Paris, p. 60)
>
> [And although I am not worthy to look at you, or to praise you, if you have a prejudice against me, I should be lost and dead; for I should have lost my hope and my comfort and you will have forgotten and abandoned me easily. But it would be wrong: for, by my soul, if all the ladies in the world were in one place, I would love you alone more than all the others. . . . And so I prefer to languish for you than to enjoy any other.]

Toutebelle does not allow him the luxury of such a pose:

---

16. See Sarah J. Williams, "The Lady, the Lyrics, and the Letters," *Early Music*, 5 (1977): 462–68; and Noël Musso, "Comparaison statistique des Lettres de Guillaume de Machaut et de Perrone d'Armentière dans le *Voir Dit*," in *Guillaume de Machaut: Poète et compositeur* (Paris: Klincksieck, 1982), pp. 175–93.

17. On the narrator figure in Machaut's *dits*, see Calin, "Machaut as Narrative Poet," in *Machaut's World*, pp. 177–87; and Cerquiglini, *Engin*, pp. 107–38.

Et, mon dous cuer, je vous pri sur toute l'amour que vous avez à mi, et si acertes comme je puis, que vous ne vueilliez pas mettre vostre cuer à meschief, ne croire les paroles que vous m'avez escriptes; car en l'ame de mi, je ne le pensay onques, ne que vous me vosissiés ne daignissiés faire ce que je ne vorroie faire à vous, que j'aim plus que moi, n'autruy. (Paris, p. 62, Letter IX)

[And, my sweet heart, I pray you on all the love that you have for me, and so urge you as I can, so that you may not wish to injure your heart, not to believe the words that you have written to me; for in my soul, I never thought that you would wish or deign to do to me what I would not want to do to you, for I love you more than myself, or others.]

She attempts to comfort the poet, but her reassurance constitutes a reproach of his own weakness, which she compares to her own constancy. During one of their few meetings, he composes a *ballade* for her in the same vein:

Le plus grant bien qui me viengne d'amer,
Et qui plus fait aligier mon martire,
C'est de mes maus complaindre et doulouser,
Et de mon cuer qui pour les siens souspire.
(Paris, p. 100, vv. 2374–77)

[The greatest good that comes to me from loving, and which best alleviates my torment, is to complain and bewail my pain and my heart which sighs for its own.]

Toutebelle responds in person just as she did in her letters:

Dont doucement me reprenoit
Toutes les fois qu'il m'avenoit,
Et disoit: "Vous vous estes plains,
Dous amis; dont viennent cils plains?
Par ma foi je vous gariroie
Tout maintenant, se je savoie."
(Paris, pp. 100–101, vv. 2399–2404)

[For that, she reproached me sweetly each time it happened, and said: "You have complained, sweet love; where does this complaint come from? By my faith, I would cure you now, if I knew how."]

The opposition continues in the songs the lovers compose. When he complains in a *rondel*:

> Puis que languir sera ma destinée,
> Mes cuers ne puet si doucement languir,
> Com par vous, belle où sont tuit mi desir,
> Ce m'iert honneur et bonne renommée,
> Puis que languir sera ma destinée.
> (Paris, p. 117, vv. 2783–87)

[Since languishing will be my fate, my heart can languish no more sweetly than for you, beauty of all my desires. It is my honor and my renown, since languishing will be my fate.]

she answers him:

> Vostre langueur sera par moy sanée,
> Tres-dous amis, que j'aim sans repentir,
> Se moy laissiez et Amours couvenir.
> (Paris, p. 119, 2804–06)

[Your languor will be healed by me, sweet love, whom I love without regret, if you let me and it suits Love.]

Such immediate and positive answers to his complaints make it difficult for the poet to maintain his languishing air, and the relationship between the lovers shown in these exchanges is maintained in the rest of the work.[18] The poet's languishing pose is systematically ironized in this work. The love affair is marked by its literary quality. Since Toutebelle loves him through his poetry, it is the conventions of this lyric tradition that dictate the roles of the protagonists in the story. The poet cannot abandon those conventions because they are the only ones permitted by the controlling lyric mode. By subverting the lyric relationship between lover and lady, however, the narrative casts the lyric poetry of the work in an ironic light.

Toutebelle's transformation of the role of the lady is the chief manifestation of the structural reversal in the *Voir Dit*. While the earlier works

---

18. Cf. Calin, *Poet,* p. 187; Cerquiglini, *Engin,* pp. 143–50, discusses the role reversals of poet and lady at some length.

end on a note of encouragement for the lover, the lady in this work actually admits the poet to her bed,[19] but surprisingly, only after the affair has reached this stage does *Esperance* make her appearance. The ambiguity of the bedroom scene emphasizes the poet's real interest. Although the description of Venus's scented cloud is filled with erotic suggestion, the only action portrayed in the scene is the poet's composition of a *virelai*. In this central episode, the act of love itself is displaced by lyric poetry.

In the passages quoted above, it is obvious that all three elements—the narrative verse, the lyrics, and the letters—deal with essentially the same issues. The similarity is of crucial importance in considering the function of the lyrics in the work and their relationship to the narrative. On the literal level, the poems, like the letters, serve as authenticating pieces; they are meant to prove the veracity of the *Voir Dit*.[20] Within the narrative frame, the poems are often presented as expressions of emotion and reflections of states of mind, but such effusions are not always placed in the appropriate context. The *ballade* "Dès qu'on porroit les estoiles nombrer," for instance, was composed in a fit of melancholy "parce que je estoie un po bleciez en l'esperit, pour aucunes paroles que on m'avoit dites," (Paris, p. 69, Letter X; "because I was a little wounded in spirit on account of some words that were said to me"), and indeed the third stanza in particular reflects his mood:

Car il me fait complaindre et dolouser
Et regreter vostre viaire gent,
Et vo biauté souveraine et sans per,
Et la tres-grant douceur qui en descent;
Ainsi me fait languir piteusement,
Mon cuer esprent, et estaint mon espoir,
Le grant desir que j'ay de vous véoir.
(Paris, p. 67, vv. 1496–1502)

[For it makes me complain and grieve and regret your gentle face and your peerless sovereign beauty and the very great sweetness that comes from it; thus it makes me languish piteously, it ignites my heart and extinguishes my spirit, the great desire I have to see you.]

---

19. Calin, *Poet*, pp. 189–91.
20. Calin, *Poet*, p. 176.

The accompanying letter goes on to explain that since receiving her portrait, his mood has changed completely and he is cured of melancholy. The reception of the gift and the transformation it brought about were described earlier (Paris, p. 65, vv. 1419–42). The *ballade*, then, which represents his sadness, is quoted (and sent) in the context of a new and joyous mood. Although the poem is presented as the expression of his emotion, it is clear in the narrative that that emotion no longer exists.

While it reflects realistically the chronological difficulty of maintaining a long-distance affair, this awkwardness of insertion points to another feature of the work. As we have seen, the letters explain to Toutebelle the emotions inspiring his poems, while the narrative verse explains both parts to the reader. But both levels of explanation constitute narratives. The songs exchanged by Guillaume and Toutebelle, ostensibly representative of their emotions, reflect the development of the love affair sufficiently to reveal its outline.[21] The collection of letters is almost self-explanatory, while the verse portion of the work is overtly narrative. Machaut has thus told his tale three times, in three different styles.

In considering how the various parts of the *Voir Dit* fit together, Bakhtin's concept of dialogism is extremely helpful. On a literal level, the work is a lively dialogue between Guillaume and Toutebelle, who converse in a variety of modes. On a structural level, Machaut has overtly constructed his work as a dialogue among its parts: the letters supply commentary on the lyric pieces, and the connecting narrative verse explains the compilation of the work. Beyond this level however, the three modes of language and the three different narratives convey different attitudes toward the love affair and its lyric conventions, and these, too, are in dialogue with each other.

Jean Froissart

We have already considered Froissart's conservative manner of using the poems of his patron, Wenceslas of Brabant, in the neo-Arthurian *Meliador*, and must now turn to his *dits* in which he employs the insertion device rather more adventurously.[22] In the period of just over a decade after Machaut

---

21. For an analysis of the poems as generators of narrative, see Cerquiglini, *Engin*, pp. 33–37.

22. On Froissart's literary career, see B. J. Whiting, "Froissart as Poet," *Medieval Studies*, 8 (1946) 198–216; and Peter Dembowski, "La Position de Froissart-poète dans l'histoire littéraire: bilan provisoire," *TLL*, 16 (1978) 131–47.

began the *Voir Dit*, Froissart composed five pseudo-autobiographical *dits* or *treittées*: the *Paradis d'Amours* (ca. 1361–62), the *Joli Mois de May*, the *Espinette Amoureuse* (ca. 1370), the *Prison Amoureuse* (late 1372–early 1373), and the *Joli Buisson de Jonece* (ca. 1373).[23] All of these works are strongly marked by the influence of Machaut,[24] yet Froissart managed to combine the same elements of poetry, autobiography, allegory, and love in several different arrangements.

The *Paradis d'Amours*[25] contains a selection of lyrics similar both in number and genre to those in Machaut's *Remede*: a *complainte*, two *rondels*, a *lai*, a *virelai*, and a *ballade*; the series lacks only a *chanson royale*. Like its model, the *Paradis* exhibits the structure of *complainte-confort*, and indeed, the poet begins by describing the melancholy thoughts of love which torment him and deprive him of sleep. After an appeal to Morpheus, he promptly falls asleep to dream. Unfortunately, the beginning of his dream is as painful as his wakeful state. Recalling his youth and the joy and torment of his love, he falls into despair and begins a *complainte* reproaching Love (in the terms of "bastard feudalism") for failing to reward his faithful service:

> Amours, je te fis ja hommage
> Pour la plus belle et la plus sage,
> La mieuls adrechie en corage,
>   A mon samblant,
> Qu'onques veïsse en mon eage
> Et mon coer en presis pour gage
> Et me desis par tel langage:
>   "Pour mon servant
>   Je te retieng d'or en avant,
> Siers loyaument, je t'en di tant,
> Merchi aras, je ne sçai quant.
>   Las! quel rendage!
> J'ai ja servi un temps moult grant.
> (vv. 75–87)

23. For a discussion of the dating of Froissart's works, see Anthime Fourrier's edition of the *Espinette Amoureuse*, pp. 30–32.
24. Cf. Jakob Geiselhardt, "Machaut und Froissart: Ihre literarische Beziehungen" (Inaugural Diss., Universität Jena, 1914).
25. The edition by Peter F. Dembowski, *Jean Froissart, Le Paradis d'Amour, L'Orloge Amoureus*, TLF 339 (Geneva: Droz, 1986), replaces the older one by Auguste Scheler, *Oeuvres de Froissart: Poésies*, 3 vols. (Brussels: V. DeVaux, 1870–72), I, 1–52. For an analysis, see A. C. Spearing, *Medieval Dream Poetry* (Cambridge: Cambridge University Press, 1976), pp. 43–47.

[Love, I once did homage to you for the most beautiful and wise lady, the most sensible, in my view, that I ever saw in my life, and you took my heart as a pledge and said to me in such terms: "I retain you as my servant henceforth; serve loyally. I tell you this much, you shall have mercy, I know not when." Alas, what a return! I have already served for a great while.]

Had he known at the beginning that he would serve in vain, he would not have entered the service of Love, and at the end of the *complainte*, he turns away from love in despair:

> Ja te soel
> Honnourer, löer et cherir,
> Mais je te maudis par aïr.
> Mors, preng moi tost, el ne desire
>   Ne el ne voel.
> (vv. 198–202)

[I used to honor, praise, and cherish you, but I curse you with hate. Death take me soon, she neither desires nor wants me.]

As in the *Remede*, the poet's distress is comforted by *Esperance*, here accompanied by *Plaisance*. The two ladies manage to console him with an offer to escort him to the court of Love, and as a sign of his renewed spirits, he composes a *rondeau* which they join in singing:

> Puis que Plaisance l'accorde
> Et Esperance autressi
> A moi oster de soussi,
> C'est drois que je le recorde,
> Puis que Plaisance l'acorde etc.
> Car mon coer tire la corde
> De joie, onques ne fist si.
> Bien me plaist a vivre ensi,
> Puisque Plaisance etc.
> (vv. 851–59)

[Since Pleasure consents and Hope as well, to take me out of worry, it is right that I should record it, since Pleasure consents etc. For my heart tugs the cord of joy, never has it done so. It pleases me indeed to live like this, since Pleasure etc.]

Having acknowledged his rescue by the two ladies in one *rondeau*, he composes a second, which stands as an apology for his complaints:

> On se doit souffrir et taire
> Et tout en gré rechevoir
> Quanq qu'Amours ordonne, voir.
> Et s'on sent grieté ne haire,
> On se doit souffrir et taire.
> (vv. 888–92)

[One must suffer and be silent, and take everything willingly, whatever Love commands indeed; and if one feels grief or hate, one must suffer and be silent.]

The two ladies escort the poet to the court of Love and advise him to present his case in the form of a *lai*. Unable to compose quickly, the poet takes out one he has already written, and *Plaisance* recites it to the god of Love. The *lai* opens with a reference to the beginning of the poet's love affair, but goes on to doubt the power of poetry—or at least of his own. He thinks of Orpheus:

> Je ne sui pas Orpheüs
> Qui par ses cançons
> Et ses douls melodïeus sons
> Endormi les dieus de la jus,
> Mais sui li las Tantalus . . .
> (vv. 1139–43)

[I am not Orpheus who with his songs and sweet melodies put the gods to sleep down there, rather am I the miserable Tantalus . . .]

Consumed with desire, the poet is nevertheless unable to win his lady through his art alone. He asks the god to intercede on his behalf, to tell the lady that the poet:

> Si parfaitement s'est mis
>   En vostre amour
>   Qu'il li est vis
>   Que nuit et jour
>   Voie l'atour
>   De vo cler vis,
> Et appelle un paradis
>   Garni d'ounour . . .
> (vv. 1239–46)

[. . . has put himself so perfectly in your love that he thinks that he sees night and day, the ornament of your clear face, and calls it a paradise bedecked with honor . . .]

Love does not reply directly to this request, but promises that the lover will eventually receive his reward. As they leave, *Plaisance* suggests singing a *virelai*, and the poet agrees. His song expresses his gratitude to Love:

> Au besoing m'as secouru,
> J'en ai bien la congnissance,
> Et ricement pourveü
> De confort et d'esperance,
> Dont j'en dirai et s'en di,
>   Garnis d'espoir,
> Que je puis moult bien avoir
>   Joie par ti.
> (vv. 1436–43)

[You have sustained me in my need, I am well aware of it, and you have richly provided me with comfort and hope, therefore I shall say, and do say, arrayed in hope, that I can very well have joy from you.]

Upon his return, the poet meets his lady, and she offers encouragement. She asks him for a lyric and offers to make him a *chapelet de flouretes* in return. He sings a *ballade*, which is also a flower chain:

> Sus toutes flours tient on la rose a belle,
> Et en apriés, je croi, la violette.

> La flour de lys est bielle, et la perselle,
> La flour de glai est plaisans et parfette.
> Et li pluiseur aimment moult l'anquelie,
> Le pyone, le muguet, le soussie.
> Cascune flours a par lui son merite,
> Mais je vous di, tant que pour ma partie,
> Sur toutes flours j'aimme la margerite.
> (vv. 1627–35)

[Above all flowers, the rose is considered beautiful, and after that, I think, the violet. The lily is beautiful, and the bluebell; the gladiola is pleasant and perfect, and many like the columbine, the peony, the lily of the valley, the heliotrope. Each flower has its own merit, but I tell you that, for my part, I love above all flowers the daisy.]

Pleased with his offering, she kisses her garland as she gives it to him, and "touched" by pleasure, the poet awakens. He declares his restored faith in poetry and thanks Orpheus, who instructed him in the art of song. Nor does he neglect to thank Morpheus for the comfort of the dream, but it is in fact his own poetry that has created the *amoureus paradys* and transported him into it.

Despite its similarities to the *Remede*, the *Paradis* exhibits major structural differences. The poet's *complainte* is arguably the source of the narrative, since his reproaches call for some sort of answer from Love. Yet the poem lacks the dramatic impact of Machaut's *lai*, which embarrassed him by declaring his love at a moment when he was unable to face the declaration. In Machaut's poem, the comforting dream is set in a frame of "real-life" narrative, so the contrast in his behavior from beginning to end demonstrates the efficacy of the dream. This waking (if hardly realistic) context is missing from the *Paradis*. Although when we meet the poet he complains of wakefulness, he shortly falls asleep, and nothing happens before he does so. Similarly, the love idyll at the end of the dream, where he exchanges flower garlands with his lady, takes place before he wakes. As a result, virtually everything—the *complainte* as much as the *confort*—is reduced to the status of a dream. While dreams are not necessarily either false or meaningless,[26] Froissart does not, as Machaut did, situate his dream in

---

26. Cf. Spearing, *Dream Poetry,* pp. 8–11.

reality, and therefore we cannot judge its prophetic value. Consequently, the whole composition resembles a chart of the poet's changing moods, with the poems as signs of those moods.

The *Trettié Amourous à la Loenge dou Joli Mois de May* recalls the *Paradis* in its mirroring of shifting emotions.[27] Probably composed shortly after the *Paradis*, the work is nothing so much as a *dit enté*, a *dit*, that is, divided into sections by insertions. Its form—it begins and ends with twelve-line stanzas of octosyllables alternating with four-syllable lines, while the stanzas of the middle section are octosyllabic—resembles that of Machaut's *complaintes*,[28] yet incorporated within it are two *ballades* and a *virelai*.

The *dit* opens with an evocation of a garden in the tradition of the *Roman de la Rose*: there are roses, violets, and nightingales surrounded by a hedge, and the enclosure is filled with the song of birds. What is different about this garden is that it appears to be imaginary. Although the narrator says "Entrai l'autre jour en un clos" (v. 16; "the other day I entered a closed garden"), the place exists in his mind. He "imagines" the hedge (v. 37), and "remembers" (v. 49) that the sun shone over it. Having created the setting, he remembers his lady's beauty, and the thought makes him burst into speech. The tone of his monologue is less troubled than the beginning of the *Paradis*, because he lives in hope and will serve love loyally. The voice of the nightingale encourages him, and he takes up the song himself in a *ballade*:

> Contre le temps qui nous presente joie
> Et le douls may qui fait coers esjoïr,
> Esce bien drois que mon coer se resjoie
> Et que pres soit d'un espoir conjoïr
>   Qui me donne souvenir
> De vivre ensi et ma dame servant;
> S'en lo Amours, qui par son douls plaisir
> Si doucement conforte son servant.
> (vv. 169–76)

[Near the time that presents us with joy and the sweet May that makes hearts rejoice, it is right that my heart should rejoice, and that it should

---

27. Ed. Anthime Fourrier, *Jean Froissart. Dits et Debats: Introduction, édition, notes, glossaire. Avec en appendice quelques poèmes de Guillaume de Machaut* (Geneva: Droz, 1979), pp. 129–46; and Scheler, *Oeuvres*, II, pp. 194–208.
28. On the similarity between the *dit* and the *complainte*, see Poirion, *Poète*, p. 406.

nearly enjoy a hope that makes me remember living thus and serving my lady; and I praise Love for it, who with his sweet pleasure comforts his servant.]

The lyric, then, is a logical continuation of the preceding speech. It is fitting that he should praise Love, having enjoyed the beauty of his garden.

The verse form changes after the *ballade* and this alteration corresponds to a shift in tone. References to the rose and the lily lead him to a description of his lady, whose beauty he goes on to praise in the second *ballade*: "Dame d'onneur, au cler jour comparee" (v. 323; "Lady of honor, compared to the bright day"). As a result of this song, his joy intensifies, but he is obliged to leave when he sees that the sun has moved. The final lyric, a *virelai*, reveals the purpose of the poem: it is a gift for his lady.

> Ma dame, je vous presente
>   De coer gai
> En lieu de joie et de mai,
> Mon coer, m'amour et m'entente.
> (vv. 439–42)

[My lady, I present to you with a gay heart, in a place of joy and May, my heart, my love, and my thoughts.]

The poem, a mental elaboration of the lyric themes of spring and love, assimilates the poet to his material and makes him a part of the scene he has imagined.

If the autobiographical-narrative element virtually disappeared from the *Paradis* and the *Mois de May*, that strand constitutes the charm of the *Espinette Amoureuse*.[29] The idyllic evocation of the poet's childhood and a description of a dream vision of Venus introduce the story of his first love affair. The resemblance to Machaut's *Remede* is again strong, but Froissart's narrative is both more complicated and more firmly rooted in an ostensible "real life." As we saw in the preceding chapter, the poet in the *Espinette* fell in love while reading *Cleomadés* with a beautiful lady, and used a *ballade* (in preference to a letter) to declare his passion.[30] The remaining lyrics—four

---

29. For studies, see William W. Kibler, "Self-Delusion in Froissart's *Espinette Amoureuse*," *Romania*, 97 (1976): 80–96; and Huot, *From Song to Book*, pp. 305–11.
30. See above, Chapter 5, under "The Song as Declaration."

more *ballades*, three *virelais*, three *rondeaux*, a *complainte*, and a *lai*—serve either to give expression to the poet's varying emotions, or else are used by him to gain his lady's love.

When his first ploy is unsuccessful, the poet gives the lady a rose. Overjoyed at her acceptance of this token, he withdraws to compose a *virelai*. Its refrain reflects an exuberance tempered by the uncertainty expressed in the verses:

>Mes en larmes font,
>Car, quant j'ai a tout pensé,
>Ne sçai se li oseroie
>Dire que ma vie est soie;
>Et s'elle n'en a pité,
>N'est drois que plus dire doie:
>Coers qui rechoit [en bon gré
>Che que li temps li envoie
>En bien, en plaisance, en joie,
>Sen eage use en santé
>Par tout dire l'oseroie.]
>(vv. 1039–45; abbreviated refrain expanded)

[But I dissolve in tears, for when I thought about it all, I do not know if I would dare to tell her that my life is hers. And if she has no pity, it is not right that I should say any more: A heart that receives willingly what time sends it, in goodness, pleasure and love, spends its life in health, I would say it everywhere.]

Having gained her favor, the poet is accepted as one of her friends, but is not distinguished from the others. On the advice of one of her companions, he once more sends a *ballade* to declare himself. This effort is at least read, but the response it elicits is not encouraging: "Ce qu'il demande, c'est grant cose!" (v. 1296; "What he asks is a great thing"). He persists in his suit, but when he discovers that she is to be married, he despairs and then falls ill. The two lyrics he composes during his illness, a *ballade* and a *complainte*, both express his misery. In the refrain of the *ballade*, he unhesitatingly announces his end: "Je finerai ensi que fist Tristans, / Car je morrai pour amer par amours" (vv. 1476–77; "I shall end like Tristan, for I shall die for loving"). The fifty-stanza *complainte* is strikingly different in tone[31]:

> A boire! A boire! Li coers m'art,
> Car ferus est d'un ardant dart.
> Pour ce desire tempre et tart
>   Boire a fuison,
> Car la flame par tout s'espart:
> Ja est bruïs plus que d'un quart,
> Et se n'i sçai voie ne art
>   De garison,
> Ne medecine ne puison,
> Car touchiés est dou droit tison
> Dont Cupido une saison,
>   Se Diex me gart,
> Feri Phebus en l'oquison
> De Dane a la clere façon.
> (vv. 1556–69)

[To drink! to drink! My heart burns, for it has been stuck with a burning dart. For this reason I desire soon and late, to drink in quantity, for the flame spreads everywhere: It is already more than a quarter grilled, and so I do not know any way or art of cure, or medicine or draft, for it has been touched by the very shaft with which Cupid, as God keeps me, struck Phoebus in pursuit of bright-faced Daphne.]

This opening stanza plays on the actual symptoms of the poet's illness and the metaphor of the lovesickness. The strength of the imagery in fact changes our opinion of the poet's love, which up until now has seemed agreeable, even in its failure to progress. Froissart cannot sustain this inspiration, however, and the next twelve stanzas constitute a sort of *dit*, a narrative of the love of Apollo for Daphne. Although he sees in the legend a metaphor for his own sufferings, Froissart fails to examine the implications of the god's aggression and Daphne's desperate flight. Instead he compares her determined refusal to his lady's behavior and not only judges Daphne's

---

31. On this remarkable piece, see Poirion, *Poète,* pp. 416–18.

fate as just, but wishes it also on his own lady (vv. 1780–84). In the next five stanzas, however, he regrets this malicious wish, blaming Fortune for his rashness. But the thought of his lady recalls her beauty, and the wound caused by her *dous regart*, and leads him back to his grievance. Eventually, he takes up again the opening metaphor:

> Or ai je demandé a boire;
> Et que ma demande soit voire
> On m'en puet loyaument bien croire,
>   Que grant soif j'ai;
> Mais ce n'est pas de vin d'Auçoirre,
> De Saint Poursain ne de Saussoirre,
> Tant soit clers ne frians en voirre
>   Ne de goust gai,
> Ains est d'un simple parler vrai
> Qui viengne dou coer.
> (vv. 2020–29)

[Now I have asked for drink, and that my request may be true, one may truly believe me that I have a great thirst. But it is not for the wine of Auxerre, of Saint Poursain, or of Sancerre however clear, delicious, or delightful of taste they may truly be, but it is for a simple true speech that comes from the heart.]

Seeing in her his cure, the poet addresses his lady directly in the final section of the *complainte*, but loses confidence in his eloquence at the end:

> Dame, cent clauses desparelles,
> Pour vostre amour,—n'est pas mervelles—,
> Ai mis en rime. Or crieng moult celles
>   A mal dittees.
>   S'ensi est, encoupés les belles . . .
> (vv. 2340–44)

[Lady, a hundred different stanzas for your love—it is not a marvel—have I rhymed. Now I greatly fear those badly said. If it is so, cut out the beautiful ones.]

Thus, in his doubt, he tries to turn his lady into an editor! Although he addresses the lady, there is no evidence that he actually sends the *complainte* to her. After his illness, he decides to regain his strength by traveling, and takes his leave in a *virelai*. To console him during the separation, his lady's companion, who is his ally, gives him a mirror in which he sees "l'ombre de la belle" (vv. 2430–31; "the shadow of the beauty"). The three *rondeaux* he composes during his journey reflect the ambivalent state of his feelings: the references to dying for love and to the loss of his heart are tempered by the sprightly form of the *rondeau*. The "joyeuse merancolie" (v. 2532) he describes in the third *rondeau* may be the best characterization of his mood.

During his exile, the poet sleeps with the mirror under his pillow, and consequently sees his lady in a dream. She consoles him with a *reconfort*, which answers his *complainte* and assures him of her love. She explains her apparent indifference as caution in the face of gossipers. Her *reconfort* returns to the images and allusions of his *complainte*, and then she pledges her love:

> Confortes toi en ce que te dirai:
> Secretement tous les jours amé t'ai,
> Mes onques mes de ce ne te parlai.
> D'or en avant je le te monsterai.
> (vv. 2965–68)

> [Be comforted in what I shall tell you: I have always loved you secretly, but I have never spoken of it to you. Henceforth I shall show it to you.]

Encouraged by the dream, the poet decides to return. He casts his joy at the prospect of seeing his lady in the form of a *virelai*, which he sends to the lady of the court he is visiting, and uses it to win permission to leave.

The dream was not false. His lady welcomes him happily, and at her request he composes a *ballade* to celebrate their reunion:

> D'uns douls regart amoureusement tret
> Se doit amans en coer moult resjoïr,
> Car, quant il voit dame ou desirs l'atret,
> Qui bellement le daigne conjoïr . . .
> (vv. 3538–41)

> [With a sweet glance lovingly given must a lover greatly rejoice at

heart, for, when he sees a lady where desire brings him, who prettily deigns to rejoice with him . . .]

His happiness is short-lived, however, for when he next sees her, she is cold to him. The poet is stunned by this change; he complains in a monologue and composes a *ballade* in an attempt to console himself. He then confronts his lady once more and appeals for mercy. The *Espinette Amoureuse* is thus another variation on the *complainte-confort* structure used in the *Paradis*. The *complainte* is the most important structural element in the work. It occurs at the midpoint of the composition, summarizes the movement of the first section, and implicitly demands a response. Although the poem is not actually sent to the lady, her *reconfort* is clearly a reply to it. As before, the comfort is given only in the context of a dream-vision, whereas the rest of the poem is rooted in the poet's "autobiography." The wish-fulfillment dream of the *Espinette* is nevertheless validated by the lady's reception of him on his return. Once again, however, Froissart puts the optimistic conclusion in question when the lady suddenly and without explanation alters her behavior. As a result, the final *lai*, which might have been a celebration of requited love, remains a *requête d'amour*, similar in intent to the *ballades*.

Froissart's next *dit*, the *Prison Amoureuse*, shows the influence of Machaut's *Fonteinne Amoureuse* in its interest in the love affair of another, of the *Remede de Fortune* in its didacticism, and of the *Voir Dit* in its use of multiple forms.[32] The *Prison* incorporates twelve prose letters and sixteen lyrics (eight *virelais*, six *ballades*, a *lai*, and a *complainte*) as well as two lesser *dits* into a narrative frame. Like the poems in the *Voir Dit*, these lyrics are enclosed with the letters, but they are not presented as expressions of emotion. On the contrary, they reflect the interests of a professional poet, Flos (Froissart) and his patron (Rose), a literary amateur.

While the formal elements of the *Prison* may have been based on Machaut's works, Froissart altered the relationship among those elements. As we have seen, the verse, the poems and the letters in the *Voir Dit* reinforce each other and to some extent tell the same story. The verse recounts (among other things) the composition of the work and the early

32. Anthime Fourrier, ed., *Jean Froissart: La Prison amoureuse*, Bibliothèque française et romane, 13 (Paris: Klincksieck, 1974). For studies, see Kelly, *Imagination*, pp. 160–70; and William W. Kibler, "Poet and Patron: Froissart's *Prison Amoureuse*," *Esprit Créateur*, 18, no. 1 (1978): 32–46; Henrik Heger, *Die Melancholie bei den französischen Lyrikern des Spätmittelalters*, Romanistische Versuche und Vorarbeiten, 21 (Bonn: Universität, romanisches Seminar, 1967), pp. 111–23, and Huot, *From Song to Book*, pp. 311–16.

stages of its "publication," when sections of it are shown to Machaut's patrons. In the opening and closing sections of the *Prison*, Flos declares that he writes to please his own lady and his patron. As the work unfolds, however, we see the poet and patron engaged in correspondence, each reporting (Flos in the narrative verse, Rose in his letters) the progress of his own love affair. Machaut's lady had a considerable voice in the *Voir Dit*, but the ladies of Flos and Rose appear only through their lovers' eyes and speak scarcely at all. Flos shows the work not to his patron, who participates in it, but to his lady. In this way, Flos tries to return the *dit* to the status of the courtly *chanson*, where the poet sang to please his lady. Although Flos's position as poet clearly depends on patronage, just as did Machaut's, both he and Rose claim to be writing for a lady.

As in the *Fonteinne Amoureuse*, the roles of poet and patron are reversed: it is the poet, Flos, who dispenses advice and is called "maistre," while the patron, Rose, requests

> "que vous me retenés a compagnon. Si me poés escrire et mander comme a vostre disciple, car tout ce que d'ore en avant je pourfiterai, je le tenrai de vous. Chiers maistres et grans amis . . ." (Letter III, ll. 5–8)
>
> [that you retain me as a companion. So you can write to me and command me as your disciple, for I shall hold from you everything that will be of use to me henceforth. Dear master and great friend . . .]

Rose thus makes himself the client or vassal of his client, using the language of a lover in the service of *Amours*. In this way, Froissart carries further the role reversal implicit in the *Fonteinne* and elevates correspondingly the status of the poet.

If the *Espinette* recounts the poet's initiation into love against the background of autobiographical recollections of his childhood, the *Prison* continues the pattern. The poet betrays few details of his current circumstances, but alludes to his service in England. In this respect, Froissart's work contrasts with the "autobiographical" strain of Machaut's *dits*, most of which contain homely details of his situation at the time of writing. Froissart's suppression of this sort of detail is related to his conception of the role of the poet. Where Machaut seemed interested in the act of composition, Froissart stresses the poet's role in the structure of the work. The narrator in Froissart's *Prison* stands out, not simply as a chronicler of events, or a reporter of dreams, but as the compiler of the *dit*: it is he who arranges and interweaves the reflections on the nature of love, the memories, the lyrics, the letters, the mythological *dittié*, and the dream, to form a harmonious whole. His preoccupation in the text with the physical makeup of the book emphasizes his role in organizing the diverse materials into a work of art.

In the *Prison Amoureuse* Froissart is playing a complicated game of insertion, first indicated by his allusions to Tristan and Iseut, the Châtelaine de Vergi, the Châtelain de Couci, and the Dame de Fayel (vv. 217–35). Froissart cites all of these as exemplary lovers, but their stories all occur, as we have seen, in forms with lyric insertions. The insertion of lyrics and prose letters into the narrative verse of the *Prison* is immediately apparent, and closer examination reveals less obvious forms of insertion that dramatize the formation of the book itself. The opening section contains a passage of recollection of nearly two hundred lines into which is inserted a *virelai* recalled from several years earlier. When the correspondence begins, most of the letters are accompanied by lyrics, but Froissart fills a gap in the exchange with three *ballades*. The *lai* begun at this point is interrupted by the next three letters and the *dittié* enclosed with the first of these. The *dittié* itself, in which Rose recounts a dream provoked by Flos's *dit*, contains three other lyric insertions—a *complainte* and two *virelais*. With its insertions within insertions, the *Prison Amoureuse* recalls the complexity of the *Dit de la Panthere d'Amors*.

The inserted lyrics in the *Prison* reflect the diversity of the composition as a whole. Some of Flos's songs are written for his patron and seem to reflect the latter's interests. The *virelai* enclosed with Flos's second letter (vv. 1011–42), for example, opens with the refrain:

> Heure de bonne heure nee
>   M'aheura le jour
> Quant premiers vous vi, m'amour,
>   Car, celle journee,
> Heure me fu ajournee
>   De bien et d'onnour.
> (vv. 1011–16)

[Hour born of happiness, made happy for me the day when I first saw you, my love, for on that day, the hour dawned of goodness and honor.]

Presumably referring to Flos's own lady, the song is equally applicable to Rose, who had described meeting his lady for the first time in the preceding letter. When Rose's fifth letter (VIII) asks for a *lai*, Flos completes one begun earlier during a lull in the correspondence. The new series of stanzas begins with a series of questions:

> Las, ou me trairai?
>   Que dirai?
>   Que ferai?
> Ne de qui arai
> Consel des mauls que j'endure?
>   Qui compagnerai?
>   Je ne sçai.
> (vv. 3515–21)

[Alas, where shall I go? What shall I say? What shall I do? And from whom shall I have advice for the pains I endure? Whom shall I accompany? I do not know.]

This uncertainty reflects the situation of Rose, who is unsure and seeks advice, rather than of Flos, who though melancholy knows what he is about.

While Flos composes two *virelais* for his own lady (vv. 295–326; 1215–43), he also quotes another, supposedly composed by someone else (vv. 429–60), and describes his pangs of jealousy when his lady sings it. Still other poems— three *ballades* (vv. 2036–2113) and the first part of the *lai*— are written to fill a hiatus in the correspondence and are kept until the poet "les voloie / Envoiier, donner ou proumettre" (vv. 2119–20; "wanted to send, give, or promise them"). Rose, on the other hand, composes his first *ballade* under the inspiration of his passion, but his second effort is simply a *virelai* sung at the request of two other ladies, and his remaining poems (a *complainte* and two *virelais*) are inserted into the *dit* he wrote to report a dream.

The act of writing—one of the major themes of Machaut's *Voir Dit*— remains of central concern in Froissart's *Prison*. Where Machaut discussed the emotions that inspired his poetry, however, and attributed his productivity to his lady, Froissart seems more concerned with the physical dimensions of his book, with the writing of his letters, and with the preservation of copies of his poems. Rose is worried by the uncertainty of correspondence: both men adopt pseudonyms and seal their letters with a signet, "Car se celles estoient perdues et mon nom avoec ma devise ens cogneüs, il me tourroit a grant contraire" (Letter I, ll. 51–53; "For if they were lost, and my name were recognized with my badge, it would turn against me badly"). Flos follows his instructions precisely:

> La lettre, et la balade ossi,
> Tout en un volume escripsi,
> Puis le ploiai et saielai.
> (vv. 786–88)

[The letter, and the *ballade* as well, I wrote into a gathering, then folded it and sealed it.]

> Sitos que la lettre cloï,
> Le virelai ens encloï;
> Puis arestai sus mon signet.
> (vv. 1042–44)

[As soon as I closed the letter, I enclosed the *virelai* inside; then I placed my signet on it.]

Flos carries Rose's first two letters and poems in an "aloiiere" attached to his belt. The *dits* are bound and placed in boxes; Flos puts his in cloth, "Pour mieuls garantir de le plueve / Je l'encloï en toille noeve, / Bien ciree et bien aournee" (vv. 2006–8; "In order to secure it better against the rain, I enclosed it in new cloth, well waxed and prepared"), while Rose's is "envolepé de kamoukas" (v. 2222; "wrapped in satin").

The actual compilation of the work only becomes a theme near the end, when Rose, at the request of his lady, asks the poet to assemble it:

> et ossi ma tres souverainne y prent grant esbatement et, quant elle s'est mise au lire, elle ne s'en poet partir. Et encor par l'information et requeste de li, je vous pri chierement que toutes lettres, trettiés, balades, virelais que nous avons envoiiet l'un l'autre, vous voelliés rassembler et mettre en .I. volume par maniere de livret et cheli donner nom par quoy on le congnoisse. (Letter X, ll. 8–15)

[And also my sovereign lady finds great diversion in it, and when she began to read it, she could not stop; and again at her request, I beg you dearly that you collect all the letters, *trettiés*, *ballades*, and *virelais* that we have sent each other, and put them into a volume in the manner of a small book, and give it a name one can know it by.]

The lady who instigates the compilation likewise begins the copying; having read some of the letters in Rose's possession, she has them copied before returning them.

The *Prison Amoureuse*, then, transforms the *complainte-confort* pattern by superimposing it on the relationship of poet and patron. Because the subjects of the correspondence are love and poetry, this relationship, too, is reversed, and the poet becomes the *maistre*. His authority allows him to stand in place of the allegorical figures who comforted Guillaume in his *dits*. The poet thus replaces *Esperance*, for example, in consoling and instructing the patron, the apprentice lover.

The last of Froissart's *dits* with lyric insertions, the *Joli Buisson de Jonece*, was composed in 1373[33] and provides a sequel to the *Espinette Amoureuse*. The *Buisson* contains twenty-eight songs—ten sung by the poet, the remainder by the allegorical characters he encounters during his dream.

After a passage announcing its subject, the poem opens with a dialogue between the poet, who thinks of renouncing his career, and Philosophy, who urges him to produce another book. She suggests that he draw his material from the past, if the present offers him no subject. The poet takes out a ten-year-old portrait of his lady and is moved to compose a *virelai*:

Vémechi ressuscité
Et hors de peril jetté
   Puis que je voi
Le reconfort ou je doi
Prendre lieche et santé.
(vv. 563–67)

[Here I am revived and thrown out of danger because I see the comfort whence I must find happiness and health.]

The song is the sign of the resurrection it announces, for once he has returned to his muse, the poet continues to pursue it. Yet the situation is not that of the *Espinette*: the inspiration is not his lady, but her portrait. The young lady no longer exists, and Art has replaced Love as the source of poetry.

33. Anthime Fourrier, ed., *Jean Froissart: Le Joli buisson de jonece,* TLF 222 (Geneva: Droz, 1975). For studies, see Fourrier's "Aspects de l'oeuvre," pp. 21–36 of his edition; Michelle A. Freeman, "Froissart's *Le Joli Buisson de Jonece:* A Farewell to Poetry?" in *Machaut's World*, pp. 235–47; and Huot, *From Song to Book*, pp. 316–23.

The poet falls asleep, and though he dreams of Venus, the month is November, not May. When he reminds the goddess that his love has not gone well (as she had promised in the *Espinette*), she reproaches his lack of trust and offers to take him to the "Buisson de Jonece" or Bush of Youth. As they set out, he experiences such joy that he is unable to proceed without singing:

> Deduit, solas et plaisance
> Et tout joieus sentement
> Sont en moi presentement
> Et m'ont en leur gouvrenance.
> S'en lo Amours qui me paie
> D'un si plaisant guerredon.
> (vv. 1138–43)

[Delight, solace, and pleasure and all joyous feeling are in me now and have me in their dominion. So I praise Love who pays me such a pleasant reward.]

Venus's shortcomings forgotten, he gives himself up to the delight of spring and completes the scene by declaring his devotion in a third *virelai*. He recalls his reaction to the first sight of his lady and renews his pledge to remain hers always. When they arrive at the bush, Venus commits the poet to the care of Youth, who explains the structure and allegorical significance of the place. Much of this is lost on the poet, who is distracted by the charm of his surroundings. The poet, at the request of Youth, then sings a *virelai* addressed to his lady:

> De tout mon coer vous fai don
>   Entirement,
> Ma douce dame au corps gent,
>   Et le vous don
> Pour tous jours en abandon
>   Tres liement.
> (vv. 1768–73)

[I bestow my heart on you entirely, my lady with the fine figure, and give it to you forever most happily.]

Although he restates his pledge of loyalty, we must remember that the poet is addressing a lady of the past, who now exists only in the portrait and in his memory. Thus it is significant that Youth replaces Venus as his guide. After the song, he comments:

> Moult grandement nous rafresci
> Li virelais que j'ai dit chi,
> Car matere lie et nouvelle
> Toute joie en coer renouvelle.
> (vv. 1800–1803)

[Greatly were we refreshed by the *virelai* I recited, for happy new material renews in my heart every joy.]

Here speaks the poet—happy to have rediscovered "matere"—rather than the lover. No longer are the songs expressions of ardent emotion; nostalgic love is cultivated expressly to inspire the poetry.

Youth takes the poet to another part of the garden, where his lady (who has not changed) appears surrounded by allegorical companions. He ignores the threat of *Refus*, *Dangier*, and *Escondit*, to take his place beside her in the *carole*. Unable to address her, he withdraws to watch and composes a *ballade*. He specifies the impulse for the song: "Car sa douche phizonomie / Me fait bonne matere avoir / Pour dire une balade, voir" (vv. 2988–90; "For her sweet features give me material to compose a *ballade*, truly"). As before, the poet is less overwhelmed by love than interested in a good subject.

Goaded by Desire, and afraid to approach his lady, the poet's suffering increases until Desire offers to take her a message. The poet then sends a poem (not quoted here) and composes a *lai* while awaiting her response. In the *lai* he describes the torment of his love, and pours out his *sentement* (v. 3776):

> Ardanment me voi espris
>   Et sans confort
> De feu d'amours qui me mort,
> Si que tous fris.
> (vv. 3552–55)

[I see myself smitten ardently and without comfort by the fire of love that kills me, so that everything trembles.]

Meanwhile, Desire and Youth both intercede with the lady on the poet's behalf; at their request, she opens his letter and reads the *ballade*, which describes his feelings by restating some of the themes of the *lai*: "D'ardant desir pris et atains, / Tains sui, et ceste ardeurs m'afine" (3996–97; "Taken and touched by ardent desire, I blush, and this ardor kills me"). The delay in quoting the *ballade* stresses the different functions of the two lyrics: the *lai* gives free rein to his feelings, while the *ballade* communicates those feelings in a more restrained form. To encourage the lady, Youth and Desire warn her of the danger of refusal, citing the example of another lady who, twenty years earlier, expressed regret for her decision in a *virelai*. The poet, meanwhile, still waiting for her answer, composes another *virelai* declaring his constancy:

> Je ne cesse nullment
>   Que de penser
> A ma dame entirement
>   Et liement.
> Chils pensers me vient souvent
>   Amonnester.
> (vv. 4383–88)

[I do not cease at all thinking of my lady, entirely and happily. This thought comes often to warm me.]

In this way, he indirectly calms her doubts. Desire returns at last and brings the poet to join the others in a game of *roi qui ne ment*, which gives him the opportunity of speaking to his lady. As always, she responds evasively, and gives him little satisfaction. A poetic contest then claims their attention: each of the lady's companions composes a *souhet*[34] to be written down by the poet. Although each personnage wishes good fortune to the lovers, the affair remains inconclusive; before the competition can be judged, the poet awakens and the scene dissolves.

The return to reality is abrupt: "On me boute, et lors je m'esvelle" (v.

---

34. These poems consist of four eight-line stanzas, monorhymed and equal in length, except for the last line of each stanza, which is short and has a different rhyme.

5081; "Someone bumps me and then I wake up"). Despite the intensity of the dream, reality imposes itself on him with the chill of winter (vv. 5088–89), and he finds himself inclined to turn his back on earthly distractions. The work ends with a *lai* in honor of the Blessed Virgin.

From this survey of the *Buisson*, it is clear that Froissart has again treated the theme of writing that ran through the *Prison*. But instead of the physical act of writing, it is the creative impulse itself that concerns him now. The dream sequence demonstrates the inspiration that love and the lady are still capable of providing. But the old inspiration can overcome only temporarily the poet's reluctance to continue in that vein.

The final *lai* and the first *virelai* are the only insertions that do not belong to the dream sequence. Therefore, the bulk of the lyricism in the *Buisson* is relegated to the realm of unreality. The opening *virelai* stands in opposition to the *lai* that answers it, just as the *Buisson* itself answers the *Espinette*. The *virelai*, inspired by an image, belongs to the realm of the illusory, as do the other lyrics and love itself.[35] At the end of the work, Froissart is ready to abandon "teles wiseuses" (v. 5160; "such idle distractions"), and find his inspiration in a new, charitable, love. He gives voice to this new love in the final *lai*, thus demonstrating less the abandonment than the transformation of his career. In like manner, the *Buisson*, which represented youth and was explained as a figure of the structure of the firmament, becomes in the final *lai* the burning bush of Moses. Earthly inspiration is replaced by religious, and the poet begins to reinterpret his past.

Oton de Grandson

Froissart in his *dits* continually undermined the idea of happy love and doubted the power of poetry to achieve it. The lady's encouragement was most evident in dreams; when she gave it in the waking world, her sincerity was called into question by subsequent indifference. Oton de Grandson in the *Livre Messire Ode*[36] turned this less than optimistic view of love into outright pessimism, and the change in attitude is reflected in a series of

---

35. Cf. Fourrier, *Buisson*, pp. 28–29.
36. Arthur Piaget, ed., *Oton de Grandson, sa vie et ses poésies*, Mémoires et documents pub. par la Société d'Histoire de la Suisse romande, 3e série, no. 1 (Lausanne: Payot, 1941), pp. 383–478; see also "Oton de Grandson et ses poésies," *Romania*, 19 (1890): 237–59, 403–48; "Notice sur le manuscrit 1727 du fonds français de la Bibliothèque Nationale," *Romania*, 23 (1894): 192–208; and Normand R. Cartier, "Oton de Grandson et sa princesse," *Romania*, 85 (1964): 1–16. For a brief discussion of Oton, see Kelly, *Imagination*, pp. 179–83.

structural alterations. The formal elements used by Oton are familiar: the *Livre* consists of narrative verse interrupted by seventeen lyrics (with thirteen more added at the end), a prose letter, and a letter in verse. In addition, one section (vv. 1190–1510) constitutes a *dit*, although it is not separated from the rest of the text. Rather less familiar is the way Oton combines these elements.

In contrast to the *dits* of Machaut and Froissart, which recounted either a past love or the earlier stages of a current one, Oton begins his *Livre* in the present, and gives only enough history to account for his melancholy state. He is miserable because his bold address to his lady has been met by refusal. The theme of the compilation of the book is introduced at the same time. The *Livre* is a sort of diary begun to keep a promise to his lady (vv. 2–3). The work is to contain all his compositions, but although he intends to send it to her, we never actually learn its fate.

Oton begins in the middle of his affair, and his book is the record of his current distress, rather than the history of the love affair. As in the earlier *dits*, there are dream sequences in the *Livre*: two dreams (vv. 192–1715; 1865–1974), separated by a brief period of wakefulness, occupy the greater part of the book. These dreams, however, differ in tone from the earlier ones. The dreaming poet enters a beautiful garden (vv. 195–207), whose only effect is to remind him of his sorrow. Feminine figures are completely absent from the work; the only inhabitants of the poet's dream are other young men. A male *Espoir* replaces the feminine *Esperance* of Machaut and Froissart. The lady herself scarcely appears in the work. When the poet encounters her after composing the *Lay de Plour*, he only describes her as "environnee de Reffuz" (v. 835). On the one occasion when the poet addresses her directly (1016–35), she will accept no more than a piece of the heart he offers her.

Given the lady's resolute indifference, these sequences, unlike Froissart's wish fulfillment in the *Espinette*, provide the lover no comfort in his distress. At the end of the first segment, the lover exclaims:

> Amours, Amours, tant travaillier
> M'avez fait qu'a ce resveiller
> Me fault faire de vous complaincte.
> Mon dormir n'est quë une estraincte.
> Quant on cuide que je repose
> Pour ce qu'on voit ma veue close,

Lors est ce que croist mon travail,
Qu'oncques maiz ne viz le pareil.
(vv. 1720–27)

[Love, Love, you have so tormented me that in waking I must complain to you. My sleep is nothing but constraint; when you think that I rest, because you see my eyes closed, it is then that my torment increases, for never have I seen the like.]

Machaut received instruction from *Esperance* and Venus in his dreams, and Froissart, like Nicole de Margival, was able to imagine happiness; but Oton is so desperate that these traditional remedies fail him. While Machaut complained of Love's torment and Froissart wrote of dying for love, Oton's despair is such that he contemplates suicide when his lady repeats her refusal. Only fear of being thought a coward restrains him, and instead he seeks escape in a chivalrous death: he writes to an English knight challenging him to combat.

The lack of contrast between dream and waking is reflected in the way Oton blurs the boundaries between the different modes. He begins his work as a diary and thereafter carefully records all his compositions (and those of others) even while dreaming:

Alors que j'euz mon lay finé
Et en mon livre enregistré,
En mon dormant m'estoit advis
Qu'aprochoie prés du pays . . .
(vv. 825–28)

[When I had finished my *lai* and written it in my book, it seemed to me in sleeping that I was approaching the country . . .]

Quant j'euz toutes mes lectres dictes
Et dedans mon livrë escriptes,
Mon songe se print a changier . . .
(vv. 1118–20)

[When I had dictated my letter and written it in my book, my dream began to change.]

The book exists, even though the composing and transcribing are all part of the dream. Just as waking and dreaming are colored by a single emotional tone, the activities of one state continue in the other.

The line between the narrative and lyricism is further obscured after the intervention of Hope. Oton converses with a young man who seems even more miserable than himself. In answer to Oton's questions, the young man begins a *ballade* with a distinct narrative line: the first stanza describes his youthful happiness, interrupted in the second by the sight of a hawk, while the third stanza comments on how this incident changed him. He continues his account without a pause in the passage following the poem. Oton and the young man then discuss his tale in alternate stanzas of a *ballade*. The last stanza of this *jeu parti* falls to Oton, who advises the young man to think of more serious things than hawks. Their dialogue spills over into the verse, where Oton explains his own problems in a speech that includes a *chançon* (*rondeau*).

Alone again, Oton begins a *complainte* whose lyricism is more dramatic. The poem consists of a dialogue between Body, who complains of love's sufferings, and Heart, who proclaims its loyalty to the ideal of love. Body sings two *rondeaux* in the course of the *complainte*, but the pair finally reach agreement, and join in singing the *rondeau* that ends the poem:

> Mectez nous en droit souvenir
> Du parfont de vostre pensee,
> Nostre princesse desiree.
> Faictes nous devers vous venir.
> (vv. 1699–1702)

[Keep us in true memory in the depths of your thoughts, desired princess; have us come close to you.]

In this *complainte* Oton attempts to resolve his ambivalent feelings about love, to reconcile the ideal with the actual misery he experiences. The agreement at the end of the poem demonstrates the triumph of Heart, and thus of love. But the resolution is illusory, for the poet resumes his reproaches to Love immediately upon awakening. He compares himself to Palamède (v. 1743) hopelessly in love with Iseut, and refers to his lady as "tel dame murtriere" (v. 1741; "such a murderous lady").

This brief period of wakefulness introduces another dream, which consists exclusively of lyrics. Catching sight of *Dangier*, the poet composes another *complainte*. The last line of this *complainte*—"cela m'avint le jour saint Valentin," (v. 1974; "That happened to me on St. Valentine's day")— seems to conclude the narrative part of the *dit*. The next thirteen lyrics follow each other without narrative commentary. In a general way, these poems reflect the movement of the *Livre* as a whole. In the first *ballade* (vv. 1975–2011), he takes leave of the lady after her refusal, and in the first *rondeau* (vv. 2012–28), he bids her farewell. The *complainte* that follows is not addressed to her, but is a meditation on his own folly and misfortune:

> Maiz j'ay empris une trop grant folie
> D'amer celle qui d'amer n'a vouloir.
> Je pers le sens, la force et le pouoir.
> Mal eust sur moy Amours tant de puissance
> De m'asservir a la non per de France.
> Serf demourray, sans jamais afranchir.
> (vv. 2061–66)

> [But I undertook too great a folly in loving one who has no wish to love; I lose my senses, strength, and power. Unfortunately, love had enough power over me to put me in service to the Unequalled of France. I shall remain a serf without every being free.]

These lines sum up his predicament: he loves even though he realizes that his lady does not wish his love, and he cannot (or will not) free himself of her thrall. The next series of lyrics—five *ballades* and a *complainte*—are all addressed to her. Despite the lucidity shown in the lines of the *complainte* just quoted, he tries in these poems to touch at least her compassion. In the final *complainte*, he tries to explain his constancy:

> Et puisqu'elle a tant de beaulté,
> D'onneur, de gracieuseté,
> Que de biens c'est la non pareille,
> Ne doy je estre reconforté,
> Se je seuffre mal et durté?
> (vv. 2368–72)

> [And because she has as much honor and graciousness as wealth, she is the Unequalled; must I not be comforted for suffering pain and hardship?]

The last three *rondeaux* develop this idea by celebrating her beauty, the source of his constant devotion.

Because the poet cannot achieve a satisfactory conclusion to his love, even in dream or imagination, the sense of narrative progression in the work is minimal. The lover's situation remains essentially unchanged, and the lyrics reflect his lack of progress. Oton realizes that he has little chance of touching his lady, but having chosen "Belle des bonnes non pareille," he can only continue to love her. Choosing another would inevitably mean accepting less than perfection. The lover's predicament effectively limits the poet to three related poses: in the lighter moments, he can sing her praises, and find some consolation in her perfection. Such thoughts inevitably lead him to plead, and when she refuses, there is nothing left but the *complainte*. Oton's *Livre* presents several narrative variations on this pattern, and then repeats it in the closing series of lyrics. The absence of a narrative conclusion and the essential circularity we observe in the *Livre Messire Ode* reflect the impossibility of narrative progression when the narrative is dominated by lyric. Oton seems to have renounced even the progression of the *complainte-confort* structure in favor of the stasis inherent in the lyric *complainte* that shapes his book.

Christine de Pizan

In her *Dit de la Pastoure* and *Livre du Duc des Vrais Amants*, Christine de Pizan uses the techniques we have been examining—first-person narration and lyric insertions—in ways that differ significantly from the precedents established by Machaut and Froissart. Her principal deviation from the convention is to tell in the first person a tale that makes no pretense to autobiography. In the two works in question, Christine adopts in turn the voice of a shepherdess and that of a young man.

The *Dit de la Pastoure*,[37] composed in 1403, is a narrative elaboration of the lyric *pastourelle*.[38] Christine allows the shepherdess to tell her own story,

---

37. Ed. Maurice Roy, *Oeuvres poétiques de Christine de Pisan*, II, SATF (Paris: Firmin Didot, 1891), pp. 223–94. For considerations of Christine's career, see Charity Cannon Willard, *Christine de Pizan, Her Life and Works* (New York: Persea Books, 1984); S. Solente, "Christine de Pizan," in *HLF,* 40 (1974): 305–422; and Daniel Poirion, *Poète,* pp. 237–54. On the *Pastoure,* see Joël Blanchard, *La pastorale en France aux XIVe et XVe siècles: Recherches sur les structures de l'imaginaire médiévale,* Bibliothèque du XVe siècle, 45 (Paris: Champion, 1983), pp. 93–118. See above, Chapter 3, for a discussion of the two *refrains* in this work.

38. On the *pastourelle,* see Bec, *Lyrique française,* pp. 119–36; Michel Zink, *La Pastourelle: Poésie et folklore au moyen âge* (Paris: Bordas and Montreal, 1972). For the texts, see Karl

in contrast to most lyric versions of the genre, where the encounter between the shepherdess and the knight is told from the man's point of view.[39] She does this by using the techniques of the pseudo-autobiographical *dit* as developed by Machaut and Froissart.

The work begins with a double prologue: after explaining that she wrote to soothe her own sorrow, but at the request of a patron, Christine gives voice to the shepherdess, Marotele, who introduces her tale as an *exemplaire* for ladies of the power of love. Her story includes variants of the characteristic structures of the lyric *pastourelle*: the encounter, the love debate, and the lament.[40] The idyllic evocation of the pastoral life shows the shepherdess, too proud to accept the love of her fellow shepherds, already partially isolated from her companions. Singing, music, and dancing are the principal diversions of the shepherds, but Marotele also sings when alone:

Mes berbietes gardant,
La seoie en regardant
Les floretes que cueilloye,
Qu'en la fontaine mouilloie,
Et de haulte voix serie
Chantoye si que l'orie
Du boys en retentissoit.
(vv. 469–75)

[Guarding my sheep, I sat there looking at the flowers that I was gathering, which were wet from the spring, and in a high, clear voice I sang so that the edge of the woods resounded with it.]

In a lyric context, by a spring, Marotele's song attracts the attention of a group of noblemen riding through the forest, and their leader prevails upon her to sing. She overcomes her fear and sings two *bergierettes*. The first celebrates the pastoral life:

Bartsch, *Romances et Pastourelles françaises des XIIe et XIIIe siècles: Altfranzösische Romanzen und Pastourellen* (Leipzig: F. C. W. Vogel, 1870; repr. Darmstadt: Wissenschaftliche Buchgesellschaft, 1967); and Jean Claude Rivière, *Pastourelles*, 3 vols., TLF, 213, 220, 232 (Geneva: Droz, 1974–76).

39. Jean Bodel anticipated this alteration of the traditional situation in one of his lyric *pastourelles*; cf. Charity Cannon Willard, "Jean Bodel and Christine de Pizan, Pastoral Poets," in *Mélanges . . . Foulon*, II (Liège: Marche Romane, 1980), pp. 293–300.

40. Cf. Bec, *Lyrique française*, p. 120.

> Il n'est si jolis mestier
> Com de mener en pasture
> Ces aigneaulx sus la verdure,
> Jamais faire aultre ne quier.
> (vv. 627–30).

[There is not prettier trade than that of leading these lambs into pasture on the verdure, never do I seek another.]

The second song alludes to her surroundings:

> Au joly bousquet
> Vont ces pastoureles
> Cueillir du muguet.
> Chappellet de flours
> Font a leurs amis,
> Par fines amours
> Ou chief leur ont mis.
> (vv. 667–73)

[To the pretty wood go these shepherdesses to gather lilies of the valley. They make flower garlands for their lovers, with fine love they put them on their heads.]

These songs, which celebrate her simple life, are performed at a meeting of two worlds, the pastoral and the courtly. While she sings the happiness of her life, the shepherdess also demonstrates her alienation from her world. Both songs refer to the love between shepherds and shepherdesses, but Marotele, "d'amours rebelle" (v. 458; "rebelling against love"), has withdrawn from the others. She has made flower garlands, but not "par fines amours." These two songs, apparently so typical of the pastoral life, seem to mark the end of it for Marotele.

The initial meetings of the knight and the shepherdess are not private. He is accompanied by several other knights, and on the second occasion she brings her friend Lorete, in an attempt to gain her approval. Their two worlds thus overlap briefly, but neither approves of the lovers. His friends mock him: "Bien vous siet estre bergier; / Oncques si jolis pastour / Ne repaira cy entour" (vv. 709–11; "It suits you well to be a shepherd; never did such a handsome shepherd live in this place"). In a different vein, Lorete warns Marotele of disaster. Thereafter, the two worlds separate, and the lovers meet alone.

After this second encounter, Marotele sings another *bergierette*, but its tone differs markedly from the earlier ones:

> Dont me vient telle aventure
> Qu'amer me fault maugré mien?
> Je ne cuidasse pour rien
> Qu'amours fust de tel nature.
>   Simple sans amer estoye
> Ne pensée sossieuse,
> Je me jouoye et chantoye,
> De plus n'estoye envieuse.
>   Or n'ay fors de penser cure
> Ne je n'ay nul aultre bien
> Fors veoir cil qui le mien
> Cuer a tout, je le lui jure,
> Dont me vient telle aventure?
> (vv. 1218–30)

[Whence comes to me this chance that makes me love in spite of myself? I would not have believed for anything that love was of such a nature. I was simple without loving, unworried by thoughts, I rejoiced and sang, and desired no more. Now I care for nothing but thinking, nor do I have any other benefit than seeing the one who has all my heart, I swear to him. Whence comes to me this chance?]

She has clearly lost her heart and realizes that love is not within her control. The song also acknowledges how she has been transformed from her earlier, carefree self. The form of the song harks back to this earlier period, while its uncharacteristic subject matter announces the later songs.

The second stage of the lyric *pastourelle* is a debate between the knight and the shepherdess, who tries with varying success to evade his advances. Christine transposes the debate to another level; in Marotele's discussion with Lorete, the question at issue is the wisdom of such a love. The first *ballade* represents Marotele's internal debate. She complains to Love, who answers[41]:

> —Tort as quant de ce te complaings.
> —Non ay voir, car ma joye estains.
> —Joye en aras s'en toy ne tient.
> —Trop crain le grant mal qui en vient.
> —Pense au bien, non pas au domage.
> (vv. 1555–59)

[You are wrong when you complain of this.—No, I am right, for my joy has gone.—You shall have joy of it, if you do not hold to yourself.—I fear too much the great misfortune that comes of it.—Think of the good, not of the harm.]

Her fears have come to the surface, and though a nagging worry underlies her love, she is nevertheless unable to abandon it. This anxiety for the future distinguishes the shepherdess's *dit* from those of Machaut, Froissart, and Grandson. What they sought was to overcome the lady's indifference, to provoke a response other than refusal. Marotele is far from indifferent:

> Vostre douleur voirement antamé
> A le mien cuer qui jamais ne pensast
> Estre en ce point, mais si l'a enflammé
> Ardent desir qu'en vie ne durast
> Se doulz penser ne le reconfortast,
> Mais souvenir vient avec lui gesir.
> (vv. 1767–72)

[Your sorrow has truly touched my heart which never thought to be in this state, but ardent desire has so inflamed it that it would not remain in life, if sweet thoughts did not comfort it, but remembrance comes to lie with it.]

Not only does she express a desire as ardent as that of the male poet-lovers, she does so in the same language when she describes the comfort of "doulz

---

41. On this type of *ballade*, see Omer Jodogne, "La ballade dialoguée dans la littérature française médiévale," in *Fin du Moyen Age et Renaissance: Mélages de Philologie française offerts à Robert Guiette* (Anvers: Nederlandsche Boekhandel, 1961), pp. 71–85.

penser" and "souvenir." Unlike her male predecessors, her worry is not for the present, but the future: "Trés bel et bon, qui mon cuer vient saisir, / Ne m'oubliez, ce vous vueil je requerre" (vv. 1785–86; "Most handsome and good, who come to seize my heart, don't forget me, this I ask of you"). If her worry seems unreasonable, it has its equivalent in the almost permanent lack of satisfaction expressed in the earlier *dits*, where any encouragement was always insufficient.

When Marotele senses a change in her lover, she composes a *ballade* to warn him of the power he has to hurt her:

> Tart venroye au repentir,
> Mais oncques perte ou domage
> Ne me fist tel dueil sentir
> Com j'aray trestout mon age
> Se de moy vous voy retrait
> Et que m'aiez fait tel trait,
> Pour tant se j'é me donné
> A vous et abandonné.
> (vv. 1938–45)

[I would come late to repentence, but never would loss or harm make me feel such sorrow as I shall have for my whole life if I see you retreat from me, and were you to serve me such a turn, for so much have I given and abandoned myself to you.]

Although he soothes her fear, it is justified, for he is obliged to leave for a time. The *rondel* she composes in his absence asks why he has gone; he would not have done so if he had known her suffering.

The *complainte* proper—the third stage of the *pastourelle*—begins at this point. Marotele describes her grief and continues her lament in the final *ballade* whose three stanzas reflect the shape of her affair. The sight of happy lovers breaks her heart, for she remembers her own lover, who has left:

> Ainsi sera langoreux,
> Mon cuer en ce grief contraire
> Plein de souspirs doulereux
> Jusques par deça repaire
> Cil qu'Amours me fait tant plaire;

>   Mais du mal qui me confont
>   A pou que mon cuer ne font!
>   (vv. 2026–32)
>
> [So my heart will be languishing in this contrary grief full of sorrowful sighs until the one returns whom Love makes so pleasing to me; but with the pain that confounds me, my heart almost breaks.]

The reunion hoped for in this stanza comes to pass, for the knight returns, but only to leave again. The *dit* ends, leaving the shepherdess's fate undecided.

Like other narrators of *dits*, Marotele is clearly a poet-lover. She uses her songs to express her emotions, and exchanges the carefree *bergierettes* for the more serious *ballades* when she falls in love. Her singing brought on the affair, not because it was a particularly effective declaration, but because it attracted the knight's attention. Unlike the sophisticated court poets (however naïve a persona they chose to project), Marotele is not concerned with the production of poetry. She seems to compose effortlessly in response to the demands of her emotions, and never mentions writing, copying, or preserving her poems. Thus Christine's choice of a shepherdess for her heroine may reflect nostalgia for an earlier, oral lyricism. The author herself was not a composer, and her lyrics are not accompanied by music in the manuscripts, but her heroine is nevertheless a singer, not a writer, of lyrics. Marotele differs from male poet-lovers in another respect. She does not intend her *dit* to move her lover. Having announced it as a lesson, she draws no moral from her tale, but simply asks her audience of *fins amans* (v. 2271) to pray for him. The shepherdess's audience is identical with Christine's and she tells her story as an *exemplum*. Author and narrator share the same concern for the fate of faithful lovers.

Like the *Pastoure*, the *Livre du Duc des Vrais Amants* was composed by Christine at the request of a patron.[42] At first glance, the formal structure of the *Livre* resembles that of the *Voir Dit* or the *Prison Amoureuse*, for the duke's account of his love is punctuated by nineteen lyrics (sixteen *ballades*, two *rondels*, and a *virelai*) and eight prose letters. In the *Livre du Duc des Vrais Amants*, Christine combines the familiar elements in a new configuration.

---

42. Ed. Roy, *Oeuvres poétiques*, III, pp. 59–208; on the date (end of the fourteenth or beginning of the fifteenth century), see pp. xiv–xvi. For a recent study, see Liliane Dulac, "Christine de Pisan et la malheur des *Vrais amants*," in *Mélanges . . . Le Gentil*, pp. 223–33.

The work can be divided into four sections: the first and longest is the duke's account of falling in love which ends (v. 2328) when he writes to declare his love to the lady. The second part deals with the development of this love affair, for the lady responds compassionately to the duke's misery. This section ends (v. 3166) when she receives a long and severe letter from Dame Sebille de la Tour, to whom she turned for assistance. The third section deals with the later stages of the affair, when the lovers are increasingly separated. The book concludes with a series of lyrics, the "Balades de pluseurs façons," including a *complainte*, four *rondels*, and three *virelais* as well as nine *ballades*.

The first section is a conventional *dit*: the duke presents himself as a poet-lover—like those of the *Remede de Fortune* or the *Espinette Amoureuse*—who describes his first love. He composes *ballades* and *rondels* to reflect his shifting emotions,[43] which are otherwise given only the briefest of descriptions. In contrast to his predecessors, the duke exerts some practical effort to advance his cause. He arranges a tournament and makes sure that his beloved is invited in order to create an opportunity of conversing with her. In this early stage, he enjoys her company, but keeps his feelings to himself: he is content to dream of her beauty and to imagine speeches to her in private, while he dances with her in public. Only when the idyll is broken and the lady is summoned home by her jealous husband does desire torment him:

> Amours, jamais ne cuidasse
> Qu'a ton servant procurer
> Deusses tel doleur qui passe
> Toutes, car ne puis durer.
> Si te puis sur sains jurer
> Qu'a la mort m'en vois le cours
> Se de toy n'ay brief secours.
> (vv. 1403–09)

[Love, I would never have thought that you should obtain for your servant such sorrow that surpasses all others, for I cannot endure it. So I can assure you without swearing that I follow the path to death if I do not have help from you quickly.]

---

43. Cf. Dulac, "Christine," pp. 227.

This first, pleasant stage of love lasted only for a day in the *Espinette* and was not described at all in the *Remede* or the *Livre Messire Ode*. The effect of this gradual development is to give some background to the expressions of desire and to root the duke's passion in a companionable friendship. Even here, his sorrow is more directly attributable to the lady's departure than to frustrated desire:

> Or est du tout ma joye aneantie
> Et mon soulas tourné en amertume,
> Trés doulce flour, puis que la departie
> Je voy de vous, et la doulce coustume,
>   Las! que j'avoye
> De tous les jours vous veoir, qui en joye
> Me soustenoit, sera tourné[e] en yre.
> (vv. 1474–80)

[Now is all my joy annihilated, and my solace turned to bitterness, sweet flower, because I see your departure, and the sweet custom, alas, that I have had of seeing you every day, which maintained me in joy, will be turned to anger.]

Despite the similarity of expression of these *ballades* to those of Froissart or Oton, there is nevertheless a difference. The duke complains of the cruel necessity which deprives him of his lady's company, rather than of her cruelty. Although she appears only vaguely through his eyes, there is no hint of hardness or caprice in the reflection.

When the duke falls ill from his suffering, only outside intervention can help. But instead of Venus, or *Esperance*, it is a cousin who seeks to comfort the young duke. His advice is practical; he urges the duke to declare himself, sensibly pointing out that the lady can hardly take the initiative. This well-wisher even visits her to explain the situation. With the way prepared, the duke finally writes to the lady. He requests in the letter that she:

> vueillez en pitié ouïr et recepvoir la douleureuse complainte de vostre servant, lequel, comme contraint, ainsi comme cellui qui est a mort et prent remede perilleux pour estre a fin ou de mort ou de vie, trés doulce dame, a vous qui par vostre escondit me pouez paroccire et par le doulz reconfort de vostre ottroy

remettre en vie, je viens requerir ou mort hastive ou garison prochaine (Roy, vol. III, p. 128)

[please hear and receive in pity the sorrowful complaint of your servant, who, under constraint, like one who is dying and takes a dangerous remedy to be finally either dead or alive, sweet lady, to you who could kill me with your refusal and could bring me back to life with the sweet comfort of your agreement, I come to seek either a hasty death or a quick cure.]

He repeats his request in the two *ballades* enclosed with it. These *ballades* may be conventional, but the lady's reply is unprecedented. Her answering letter changes the work, for she at last appears clearly and speaks in her own voice. If she is careful of her honor, she is certainly not *sans merci*. She is touched by his suffering:

Sy sachiez que s'il est ainsi que pour cause de moy aiez tant de mal, il m'en poyse de tout mon cuer; car ne vouldroye estre achoison de grevance a nulluy, et plus de vous me peseroit, en tant que vous congois, que d'autre quelconques. (Roy, vol. III, p. 133)

[Know that if it is so because of me that you have such pain, it grieves my heart; for I would not wish to be the occasion of pain to anyone, and for you especially it would grieve me, as much as I know you, than for any other.]

As for love, she exhibits none of the evasiveness of Froissart's *amie*:

Mais, se ainsi estoit qu'amour de dame donnée honnourablement et sans villain penser vous peust souffire, sachiez que je suis celle qu'Amours a ad ce menée qui vous vueil asmer trés or et trés ja. . . . Si vueil que vous chaciez de vous toute malencolie et tristece, et soiez liez, jolis et joyeux, mais sur toutes riens je vous charge et enjoing que secret soiez. (Roy, vol. III, pp. 133–34)

[But if it were so that a lady's love, given honorably and without evil thoughts, might be sufficient for you, know that I am one whom Love has brought to this, who wishes to esteem you now and forever. . . . So I wish that you would chase away your melancholy and sadness and be happy, charming and joyful, but above all, I charge and enjoin that you be secretive.]

If she is not Froissart's coy beauty, neither is she Machaut's bold Toutebelle; she is prudent, yet compassionate and honest.

When the duke writes again, the enclosed *ballade* marks the change in him:

---

44. The opening line is perhaps modeled on Machaut's "Je maudi leure et le temps et le jour," *Poésies lyriques,* ed. V. Chichmaref, 2 vols. (Paris: Champion, 1909), I, ccxiii.

> Plaisant et belle,
> Ou se repose
> Mon cuer, et celle
> En qui enclose
> Est toute et close
> Bonté et grace,
> Prenez m'en grace.
> (vv. 2415–21)

[Pleasant and beautiful, where my heart rests and she in whom is enclosed all goodness and grace, take me in grace.]

A dangerous idyll of clandestine meetings follows this exchange, but their happiness is celebrated in the duke's songs. On one occasion, his declaration of love is answered by her *ballade*:

> Benoite soit la journée,
> Le lieu, la place et demeure,
> Doulx amis, qu'ad ce menee
> Fus, trop y os fait demeure
> Que vous donnay
> Toute m'amour, amis, meilleur don n'ay,
> J'en lo Amours qui la commence a faite,
> Car j'en reçoy joye toute parfaite.
> (vv. 3097–3104)[44]

[Blessed be the day, the place, the location, and the house, sweet love, that has brought me to this, too long did I wait before I gave you all my love; love, a better gift I have not. I praise Love who made the beginning, for I have received perfect joy from it.]

This is the only poem composed by the lady within the narrative, but its inclusion prepares the way for the series of poems attributed to her at the end of the text.

The lady unintentionally destroys the idyll when she writes to the Dame Sebille de la Tour to enlist her aid: that lady exposes the inconsistencies of courtly ideology and directs a cold blast of common sense on the lovers' passion. The danger, especially for the lady, is real:

ne vous y decevez ne laissiez decevoir, et prenez exemple a de teles grans maistresses, avez vous veu en vostre temps, qui, pour seulement estre souspeçonnées de tele amour, sanz ce que la verité en fust oncques attainte, en perdoient l'onneur et la vie, de teles y ot. (Roy, vol. III, pp. 164–65).

[Do not deceive yourself or let yourself be deceived, and take an example from such great mistresses that you have seen in your time, who, for being only suspected of such a love, without the truth being ascertained, lost honor and life on account of it; there were such.]

Dame Sebille goes on to examine and criticize the clichés of courtly love:

Et a dire: je feray un homme vaillant, certes je dis que c'est trop grant folie de soy destruire pour acroistre un autre, poson que vaillant en deust devenir, et celle bien se destruit qui pour reffaire un aultre se deshonnoure. Et quant a dire: j'aray acquis un vray ami et serviteur, Dieux! et de quoy pourroit servir si fait ami ou serviteur a la dame? car si elle avoit aucun affaire il n'oseroit porter en nul cas pour elle pour paour de sa deshonneur; doncques de quoy lui pourra servir si fait serviteur qui ne s'osera employer pour le bien d'elle? Et mès ilz sont aucuns qui dient qu'ilz servent leurs dames quant ilz font beaucoup de choses soit en armes ou autres fais, mais je di que ilz servent eulx mesmes quant l'onneur et le preu leur en demeure et non mie a la dame." (Roy, vol. III, p. 167)

[And to say "I will make him a valiant man," indeed, I say that it is too great a folly to destroy oneself in order to increase another, supposing that he should become valiant, and she does indeed destroy herself who dishonors herself in order to make over another. And when they say: "I shall have acquired a true friend and servant," God! and how can such a friend or servant serve the lady? For if she has some affair, he would not dare to undertake it in any case for her, for fear of her dishonor. Then how can such a servant serve her who dares not employ himself for her good? And yet there are some who say that they serve their ladies when they do many things in arms or in other deeds, but I say that they serve themselves when the honor and the prowess remain with them and not with the lady.]

The letter ends with a warning of the moral dangers of love outside of marriage. Rather suprisingly, the lady Sebille encloses a *ballade*, but the poem simply restates some of the arguments of the letter.

Sobered by these strictures, the lady tries to break off her affair and sends Sebille's letter to explain what has happened. Although the duke respects her decision, he gives full rein to his misery in a *ballade* enclosed with his letter: "Ha! Mort, Mort, Mort viens a moy je t'appelle" (v. 3249; "Alas Death, Death, Death, come to me, I call you"). She is moved by his distress and relents, but they cannot recapture their idyll. When he is obliged to enhance his reputation by seeking adventures, they are reduced to exchanging poetry:

> Si fu mainte chançon faitte,
> Puis de dueil, puis de repos,
> De nostre fait; a prepos
> De divers cas je disoie
> Balades que je faisoie,
> Lais complaintes, autres diz,
> Dont un joyeux entre dix
> Doloreux avoit: C'est guise
> De fol cuer qu'Amours desguise,
> Ma dame m'en renvoioit
> A son tour quant lui seoit.
> (vv. 3504–14)

[Thus were many songs composed, some in sorrow, some in peace, about our situation; in various cases I recited *ballades* that I composed, *lais*, *complaintes*, other poems, where there was one happy one for ten sorrowful. It is the guise of a foolish heart that love transforms. My lady sent me some back in her turn when it suited her.]

The series of lyrics appended to the *Duc* are, in effect, explained by these lines. As the lovers seem not to meet again, there is nothing to report, and the poems explain themselves as they continue the development of the plot. The first two *ballades*—dialogues between lover and lady—set the pattern and show them parting. The remaining *ballades* and the three *virelais* are spoken alternately. These poems show the difficulties of maintaining the affair in this way. When she wonders if he has found another lady, he reassures her. He tries to visit her, but it is too dangerous. There follow four of his *rondeaux*, with nothing from her, when he is obliged once more to depart. In contrast to the rest of the work, the lady speaks last, in a long *complainte* in which she expresses her growing conviction that he has abandoned her:

> Il clamera
> Autre dame et reclamera
> Et en elle s'affermera,

Dont mon las cuer en semera,
   Ha! larme mainte
Mais ja ne s'en differmera,
Ainçois toudis s'affermera
Jusques mort l'en deffermera
   Qui m'a ratteinte.
(Roy, vol. III, p. 208, vv. 152–60)

[He will name and implore another lady and will confirm himself in her, then will my poor heart shed many tears; but never will it disengage itself, but affirm itself always until death releases it from what has trapped me.]

As we have seen throughout this chapter, it is unprecedented for a woman to give voice to a *complainte*. The concluding lyrics and the one inserted *ballade* attributed to the lady, as well as her letter, allow her more of a voice in the *dit*, and consequently present her as a more developed character, rather than merely the projection of the lover's desire. The lady, like the duke, turns to poetry in response to the vicissitudes of love.

Christine's innovations in the traditional *dit amoureux* clearly emerge from this survey of the *Duc*. First of all, this work has a longer plot line than those of Margivol, Machaut, Froissart, and Grandson. While the earlier works ended with the encouragement—real or imagined—or the refusal of the lady, Christine developed the love affair along lines reminiscent of the romance. Instead of a narrative elaboration of the lyric situation, we see here a courtly love affair maintained over time. From another point of view, the scope of the *Duc* widens in each stage of the narrative. The first section, which is the closest to the earlier *dits*, is restricted to the emotional life of the young duke. In the second section, the lady is admitted to this closed world, while the last sections show the impact of the outside world on the lovers.

Christine's purpose in writing the *Duc* was different from that of her predecessors. Most of these poets, however pessimistic they might have been about their own success, reaffirmed the values of courtly love. Guillaume de Machaut's *Voir Dit*, in exposing the contradictions inherent in the ideology, is an exception, but where Machaut revealed the problems of the courtly poet, Christine was interested in the effect of this ideology on the woman who is the poet's inspiration. Her conclusions were, as we have seen, discouraging. She portrayed a young man's idealistic love, generously returned by his lady, and showed how it inevitably led her to risk social and moral disaster. Such love, even for the high-minded lovers of the *Duc*, brings happiness to no one. Christine was thus more radical than Machaut in her intentions. She used the conventions of the *dit amoureux* for the purpose of undermining its ideology.

The pseudo-autobiographical *dits amoureux* that we have examined do not simply explain the composition of songs or poems. The lyrics are indeed given more or less plausible contexts and inspiration, but the works deal also with greater issues than the writing of individual poems. Nicole showed a poet-lover coping with the burden of tradition in trying to model his behavior on an earlier poet's poetry, at the same time as he dealt with the contrast between the ideal (dream) and reality. Transcribing this contrast was yet another attempt to abolish it, for his work was meant, like the individual songs, to gain his lady's favor. The narrative which chronicles his writing thus serves to validate the poet's sincerity.

Machaut, and then Froissart and Grandson, recombined these elements—narrative and lyrics, dream and waking, love and poetry—into new configurations, of which the *Voir Dit* is the most complex. Following Machaut's innovation in the *Voir Dit*, Christine not only allowed her heroines to speak, but also reexamined the whole cluster of conventions to discover its effect on the lady involved.

One feature common to all of these *dits* is an explicit relationship between the songs and the story. In each work we have examined, the narrative explains the composition of the inserted lyrics. In the group of texts to be discussed in the next chapter, however, this bond is abandoned, and the two elements are juxtaposed without explanation. The lyrics in these *dits* interrupt the narrative line and divide it into segments.

7. The Song as Refrain: Lyrics as Elements of Form

In the previous five chapters, all of the lyric insertions we have examined have had a fairly close relationship to the diegetic structure of the narrative. Even the songs quoted as part of the description of a festival came increasingly to be subjected to the demands of the plot, while in the case of the first-person narratives, it has been argued that the songs are actually the source of the narrative.[1] On the other hand, the insertions always remained somehow separate from their context, and their status *qua* songs was not only recognized, but one of the essential reasons for their quotation. In Jakobson's terminology, even when the songs were used expressively or connotatively, their poetic function was never lost. That it is possible for the poetic function of songs to overwhelm, if not exclude their diegetic function, will become clear in this chapter.

There is a body of works in which songs, at first *refrains*, but later whole poems, are used like the *refrains* in the *chanson avec des refrains*, each of whose stanzas is followed by a different *refrain*. Such *refrains*, even though not repeated elements, can be recognized by their placement at regular intervals, and fill some of the functions of the repeated refrain.

Since the lyric insertions in these works were employed like refrains, it is necessary to consider first the nature and function of the refrain. The term in English is defined as "a phrase or verse recurring at intervals, especially at the end of a stanza of a song or poem."[2] In French, the same word is used both in this sense and, by extension, to designate short lyric pieces which occur either independently or inserted into other works, even though they are not repeated. Thus, the *Dictionnaire des Lettres Françaises* defines *refrain* in the latter sense as "une citation de paroles et musique insérée dans un

---

1. Cf. Cerquiglini, "Typologie," p. 9, and "Le montage des formes: l'Exemple de Guillaume de Machaut," *Perspectives médiévales*, 3 (1977): 23–26.
2. *Oxford English Dictionary: Compact Edition* (Oxford: Clarendon Press, 1972), II, p. 2466.

texte différent, que celui-ci soit lui-même chanté ou non."[3] Most of the lyrics "cited" were doubtless recurring in their original context, but their increasing use out of context led to their being assigned the status of a separate genre. As a result, new *refrains* were composed in imitation of the others, and even though they were never employed as a recurring element, they were still considered to be *refrains*, because they were so conceived of by their authors.[4]

In considering the relationship of the refrain to its surrounding text, Nico van den Boogaard commented that it seems always to occur in symbiosis with another literary genre.[5] Michel Zink, seeking to refine the definition of the relationship between the two parts, turned to the etymology of the word.[6] "Refrain" comes from *refractum*, the past participle of *refringere*, which usually means "to break."[7] The refrain, then, is something that "breaks," or perhaps, interrupts the poem. As Zink points out, the refrain is set off by meter, rhyme, and melody from the stanza and usually introduces some change in the sense as well. It seems a foreign element, even though it fits well into its setting, and creates the impression of an apt quotation.[8] While it may interrupt the sense of the stanza, the refrain also determines its structure. Nigel Wilkins has clearly demonstrated the role of the refrain in structuring the fixed forms of the fourteenth and fifteenth centuries—the *ballade*, the *rondeau*, and the *virelai*.[9]

Nonrecurring *refrains* fill essentially the same functions of interrupting and structuring in three stanzaic narrative works composed in the second half of the thirteenth century: the *Confrere d'Amours*, a *Salut d'Amours*, and the *Chastelaine de Saint Gille*. A *complainte* of the same period uses not only

---

3. Vol. I, *Le Moyen Age* (Paris: Fayard, 1964), p. 630. See also Richard H. Hoppin, *Medieval Music*, Norton Introduction to Music History (New York: Norton, 1978), pp. 293–96.

4. See Boogaard, *Rondeaux et refrains*, p. 16.

5. Ibid., p. 17. Cf. Eglal Doss-Quinby, *Les Refrains*, p. 140.

6. Zink, "Lyrisme en rond: Esthétique et séduction des poèmes à forme fixe au moyen âge," *Cahiers de l'Association internationale des études françaises*, 32 (1980): 71–90; pp. 74–75. Cf. Zumthor, *Essai*, p. 246 and Bec, *La Lyrique française*, I, p. 43.

7. *Oxford Latin Dictionary* (Oxford: Clarendon Press, 1982), p. 1597.

8. Zink, "Lyrisme," pp. 75–76. See also Zumthor, *Essai*, pp. 246 ff.

9. "The Structure of Ballades, Rondeaux and Virelais in Froissart and in Christine de Pisan," *French Studies*, 23 (1969): 337–48. See also Doss-Quinby, *Les Refrains*, pp. 62–84; and Gustav Thurau, *Der Refrain in der französischen Chanson. Beiträge zur Geschichte und Charakteristik des französischen Kehrreims* (Berlin: E. Felber, 1901). On repeated refrains, see also Pierre Jonin, "Le refrain dans les chansons de toile," *Romania*, 96 (1975): 209–44; and Susan M. Johnson, "The Role of the Refrain in the Pastourelle *à refrain*," in *Literary and Historical Perspectives of the Middle Ages* (Proceedings of the 1981 SEMA Meeting), ed. Patricia W. Cummins, Patrick W. Conner, and Charles W. Connell (Morgantown: West Virginia University Press, 1982), pp. 78–82.

refrains but complete *rondeaux* in the same fashion. In the *dits entés* of Jehan de Lescurel, composed in the early fourteenth century, the use of *refrains* harks back to the technique of the *Confrere d'Amours*.

From the end of the thirteenth century, these techniques were extended to nonstanzaic narrative works, which were divided into more or less equal sections by *chanson* stanzas (the *Complainte Douteuse*), by *refrains* (the *Prison d'Amours*), by complete songs (the *Amoureuse Prise*), and finally by song cycles (the *Tresor Amoureux*). In spite of the fact that these works lack a strophic structure, the lyrics they include perform essentially the same functions as a lyric at the end of a stanza.

Stanzaic Works

Multiple, unrepeated *refrains* fulfill the functions of structuring and interruption in several nonlyric stanzaic works. One group of these works—a total of four in number—is preserved in a single Paris manuscript, B.N., fr. 837, produced toward the end of the thirteenth century.[10]

The *Confrere d'Amours* is a miniature *dit amoureux*: the lover announces his membership in Love's confraternity, and proclaims his love and his loyalty, before declaring himself to his lady and asking her favor.[11] The work consists of twelve quatrains of monorhymed alexandrines, each followed by a two-line *refrain*. Although its narrative content is slight, the *Confrere* illustrates neatly the technique of linking a *refrain* to its context. The second line of each *refrain* rhymes with the preceding stanza, and there is sometimes a semantic link with the following stanza. Each *refrain* sums up or repeats the idea of the preceding stanza and simultaneously generates the first line of the following one, which responds to it. This second type of linking, anadiplosis in modern terminology, is called *coblas capfinidas* in the *Leys d'Amors*.[12] Stanzas five to seven will serve to illustrate this linking. The

---

10. Henri Omont, *Fabliaux, dits et contes en vers français du XIIIe siècle: Facsimile du manuscrit 837* (Paris: E. Leroux, 1932). This manuscript also contains two *complaintes* (published by Paul Meyer as *saluts d'amour* [see below n. 13]) and three *saluts d'amour* which use *refrains,* in addition to the *Confrere d'Amours,* the *Chastelaine de Saint Gille,* and the two *complaintes* discussed in this chapter. On the date, see Paul Zumthor, *Histoire littéraire de la France médiévale (VIe–XIVe siècles),* (Paris: Presses Universitaires de France, 1954), p. 297.

11. Arthur Långfors, ed., "Li Confrere d'amours: poème avec des refrains," *Romania,* 36 (1907): 29–35.

12. G. Molinier, *Las Flors del gay saber estier dichas las Leys d'Amors,* ed. A. Gatien Arnoult; 4 vols. (Toulouse, 1841–43; repr. Geneva: Slatkine, 1977), I, p. 280. See also Hilka, *Direkte Rede,* pp. 104–5, 139–40.

fifth stanza, which describes the lover's sufferings, ends with the announcement "Je li demanderoie porqoi au cuer me touche" ("I will ask her why she touches my heart"). Its *refrain* goes on to make a direct appeal: "Je sent le mal d'amer por vous. / Et vous? Por moi sentez le vous, ma douce?" ("I feel the pain of love for you. And you? Do you feel it for me my sweet?"). The sixth stanza continues the lover's declaration with protestations of sincerity, an idea summed up in its *refrain* "Icel jor me faille Diex / Que je trahirai m'amie!" ("May God fail me the day I betray my love"). The opening line of stanza VII is semantically linked to the previous *refrain*: "Diex, comment trahiroie ce que plus amer vueil" ("God! How should I betray what I wish to love?"). The repetition is not exact, for a different tense is used, but the whole stanza denies the idea of betrayal.

The structural and logical linking of the *refrain* to its stanza, while it announces the theme of the next stanza, is worked out more perfectly in some of the *saluts* preserved in the same manuscript, and particularly in the *Chastelaine de Saint Gille*. The *Confrere* seems to represent a more primitive, or perhaps simply a less polished version of the technique.

An anonymous *complainte d'amours* from the same manuscript—"Celui qu'Amors conduit et maine"—is constructed on the same principles as the *Confrere*, but its longer stanzas are usually separated by longer lyric pieces, and more of the stanza is generated by the interrupting lyrics.[13] The lover begins by greeting his lady, but then goes on to say that she is *not* his lady, for she does not love him. He pleads with her and describes how love has wounded him. After asking the help of *Amors*, who must surely help such a faithful lover, he ends by asking once more for her *guerredon*.

The poem consists of fourteen eleven-line stanzas, each followed by a lyric—ten by *rondeaux*, and four by *refrains*. As before, each song is linked to both of the surrounding stanzas, whose unmatched final line rhymes with the first line of the song. There is again a logical connection between each stanza and its song. This can be fairly loose, but usually the relationship between the two elements is close. In the first stanza, for instance, a reference to the lady's mouth elicits a *rondeau* beginning: "A la bouche ma dame ja vilains n'i touche" ("The mouth of my lady no *vilains* shall ever touch"). In three other stanzas (II, IV, XIV) the lover says he will sing the song.

The second, third, and fourth stanzas of the *complainte* illustrate how

---

13. It was published as a *salut d'amours* by Paul Meyer, "Le Salut d'amour dans les littératures provençale et française," *Bibliothèque de l'Ecole des Chartes*, sér. VI, 3 (1867): 125–70, esp. pp. 154–62.

The Song as Refrain 247

the lyrics are linked to the following context. The lover says he will never cease singing the second *rondeau*, which ends: "Fins cuers ne se doit repentir / Quar de ma mort puet bien garir / et repasser" ("A fine heart must not repent for it can indeed recover from my death and be cured"). The third stanza comments on the song:

>   Se c'est voirs que la chançon dite
>   Que bien amer la mort respite,
>   Se Dieu plest, je n'i morrai pas,
>   Ains aurai de mes maus respas
>   Dont s'amor ades me torment;
>   Mes le sien secors trop m'alente
>   A doner moi le don d'amie;
>   Si me dout la chançon ne die
>   Trestout' autre chose que voir.
>   Mes à ma dame faz savoir
>   En chantant de cuer angoissex:
>   "Se je sui en lointain païs
>   Plus sont mi penssé amorous!"
>   (Meyer, p. 156)

[If what the song says is true, that loving well gives respite from death, if God pleases, I shall not die, but I shall have a cure for my pain with which her love continually torments me; but her aid holds me back from giving me the gift of a mistress. So I suspect that the song says something other than the truth. But I let my lady know in singing with anguished heart: "If I am in a far away country, my thoughts are all the more loving."]

The lover finds hope in his song, but when he considers his lady's behavior, he begins to doubt its message. He then sings his anguish and comments on that song in the fourth stanza:

>   Veritez est, ma douce dame,
>   Par cele foi que je doi m'ame
>   Ce que ceste chançon a dit,
>   Et sachiez je sui cil qui vit
>   A si tres angoisseuse vie
>   Que durer ne porroie mie

> Se Diex tel grace ne m'envoie
> Que par tens de vostre amor j'oie.
> (Meyer, p. 156)

[It is true, my sweet lady, by the faith I have in my soul, what this song said, and know that I am the one who lives an anguished life that I should not endure if God did not send me such grace as I sometimes have in your love.]

He refers to the song, but adds the motif of his torment from the line introducing it. On the basis of these ideas, the lover adds the new theme of the stanza—that he cannot endure without her love.

These examples show how the poet has used the structure of the *coblas capfinidas* to organize his poem, and that his technique is different from that of the *Confrere* poet. Instead of a single verse responding to a *refrain*, the poet of "Celui qu'Amors conduit" may use most of a stanza to comment on a *rondeau*. But despite the strengthening of the logical connection between the lyrics and the following stanzas, an exact semantic repetition is rare.[14] The direct commentary of the framing *complainte* on its lyric insertions is a vivid dramatization of Bakhtin's dialogism. While many of the stanzas grow out of the songs that precede them, those same stanzas often take issue with the songs. Thus we see the poet-narrator weighing the message of the song, first believing it, then doubting it—always measuring the lyric against his own experience.

The third work in B.N., fr. 837, the *Chastelaine de Saint Gille*, is a sort of *fabliau*, and as a result has a much stronger narrative line that the *dits* and *complaintes*.[15] It consists of thirty-five seven-line stanzas, each followed by a different *refrain*. As in the "Celui qu'Amors conduit," the rhyme is in couplets, but here the odd line is completed by the second line of the *refrain*. The last words of the *refrain* are then repeated in the opening line of the next stanza.[16] The semantic repetition in this work only rarely involves the kind of discussion of the lyric that we have noted in "Celui qu'Amors conduit." The Châtelaine's reluctant acquiescence to the marriage of convenience is a good example:

---

14. There is one between stanzas IV and V.
15. Oscar Schultz-Gora, ed., *Zwei altfranzösische Dichtungen: La Chastelaine de Saint Gille; Du Chevalier au Barisel*, 4th ed. (Halle: M. Niemeyer, 1899). The date of the text is given as 1250–70 (p. 3). Zumthor, *Histoire*, p. 297 calls it "une sort de fabliau-pantomine," but it is not included by Per Nykrog in his list of *fabliaux*, in *Les fabliaux: Etude d'histoire littéraire et de stylistique médiévale* (Copenhagen: Ejnar Munksgaard, 1957), pp. 311–24.
16. Cf. Hilka, *Direkte Rede*, pp. 104–5, 139–40.

Peres, je ferai vo voloir,
mes trop me fet le cuer doloir
ceste chançons et me tormente:
   nus ne se marïe
   qui ne s'en repente.
Repente? ce vueil je bien croire,
peres, que la chançon soit voire:
Cil se repent qui se marïe;
quar je me sui ja repentïe
d'avoir mari, ainz que je l'aie.
(vv. 50–59)

[Father, I shall do your will, but this song makes my heart sorrow too much and torments me: No one marries who does not repent. Repent? This I can well believe, father, that the song is true: he repents who marries, for I have already repented having a husband before I have him.]

The *refrain* here sums up the Châtelaine's doubts at the same time that it serves as a basis for further reflections. The passage illustrates another characteristic of the text, the lack of congruence between the narrative and the stanzaic structure. Only two *refrains* constitute an entire speech, while nine begin and three others end one. The vast majority of the *refrains* in this work occur somewhere in the middle of a speech.

The plot of the *Chastelaine* is that of "Lochinvar": the beautiful Châtelaine, forced to marry a rich *vilain*, is snatched from the church by her noble *ami*. The *refrains* used by the characters—especially those of the Châtelaine and the *vilain*—reflect the reversal worked out in the plot. As she argues with her father, the Châtelaine says: "Se je sui joliëte / nus ne m'en doit blasmer" (vv. 44–45; "If I am pretty, no one can blame me"), but she greets her marriage in a different vein: "Je n'ai pas amoretes / a mon voloir, si en sui mains jolie" (vv. 134–35; "I do not have love according to my wishes, therfore am I less pretty"). When order is restored, her *refrain* changes as well: "J'ai amoretes a mon gre / s'en sui plus joliëte assez" (vv. 298–99; "I have love according to my wishes, and am prettier for it"). Likewise, the *vilain*'s bold declaration at the beginning: "L'avoirs done au vilain / fille a chastelaine" (vv. 71–72; "Money gives to the *vilain* the Châtelaine's daughter") is balanced by the jeering of the onlookers at the end: "Vilains, lessiez vostre plorer, / si vous prenez au laborer" (vv. 261–62; "*Vilain*, stop your weeping; take yourself off to work"). Another pair of *refrains* marks the *vilain*'s downfall. Anticipating his wedding, he sings: "Je prendrai l'oiselet / tout en volant" (vv. 80–81; "I shall catch the bird in flight"), but when the girl escapes, he laments: "J'ai trové le ni de pïe, / mais li piot n'i sont mïe; / il s'en sont trestuit volé" (vv. 279–81; "I have found the magpie's nest, but there aren't any magpies, they have all flown away"). The Châtelaine's three *refrains* are attested elsewhere, and seem to belong to the repertoire, but all of the *vilain*'s are *unica*. Their very aptness makes it probable that they were composed for the context.

The *refrains* in the *Chastelaine* are integrated into the verse structure with great skill and are logically appropriate, but this careful incorporation seems to undermine their interrupting function. Because they are carefully woven into the dialogue, only their meter distinguishes them from the stanzas. Given the rapid movement of the plot and the tendency of the speeches to overflow the limits of the stanza, the *refrains* seem less effective as structural markers than those in the *Confrere*.[17]

A fourth poem in this manuscript—the *salut d'amour* "Amors qui m'a en sa justise"—is structured as a *complainte* followed by a *confort*.[18] The lover addresses his lady, whose sad fate was actually that so narrowly escaped by the Châtelaine. He describes his joy in loving "une dame de valor" (v. 14; "a worthy lady"), then describes the suffering of love and begs for mercy. These themes are repeated three times, ending with the question of the final *refrain*: "Fins cuers douz, / avrez vous merci de moi?" (vv. 201–2; "Sweet fine heart, will you have mercy on me?"). The lady's initial reaction in the second part is cynical: "Je ne cuit pas que vous soiez / si destroiz por moi com vous dites" (vv. 2–3; "I do not think that you are as afflicted for me as you say"), but when the lover protests his sincerity in the second stanza, she accepts him with alacrity.

The *salut* thus has two parts, the *complainte* (twenty-seven stanzas), roughly twice as long as the answer (thirteen stanzas). The stanzas are identical in form to those of the *Chastelaine de Saint Gille,* and the anadiplosis fails in only two places. The pattern of complaint and response is similar but not identical to that of the fourteenth-century *dits amoureux* discussed in the preceeding chapter. Although the lover is accepted, the lady is moved less by his suffering and devotion than by her own *mauvais mariage*. If his *complainte* lies firmly in the courtly tradition, the generic

17. Unless, of course, they were sung; but the manuscript gives no notation, nor does it leave any space for it. In the manuscript, the *refrains* are distinguished from the stanzas by paraph marks in the margin.
18. Oscar Schultz-Gora, ed., "Ein ungedruckter *Salut d'amors,* nebst Antwort," *ZRP,* 24 (1900): 358–69. The first part (202 verses) is found on pp. 359–64; the second part (92 verses) is found on pp. 364–66.

model for her response is the *chanson de mal mariée*. The contrast between the two parts is highlighted by the choice of *refrains*. He refers to love, its joy and misery, his beautiful lady, and requests mercy. The *refrains* in her response include declarations of love, but the references to her *vilain* husband are more numerous. In contrast to the first part, there is a distinct progression in the lady's reaction. Once assured of the lover's sincerity, she declares her love, and then thinks (cheerfully) of her husband's dismay: "La jolivete de moi / fera vilain le cuer doloir" (vv. 27–28; "My prettiness will make the *vilain*'s heart sorrow"). She goes on to say she does not love her husband and is better off with a lover, and she exclaims, in common with the Châtelaine: "Ostez le moi cel vilain la! / se plus le voi, je morrai ja" (vv. 56–57; "Take that *vilain* away from me; if I see him anymore I shall die"). In this context, her declarations seem more expressive of defiance than of love: "Vous le m'i deffendez, l'amer, / mes par Dieu je l'amerai" (vv. 70–71; "You forbid me to love, but by God, I shall love him"). The final *refrain* is spoken by the lover: "Douce dame, granz merciz! / et je plus ne demant" (vv. 91–92; "Sweet lady, great mercy, I ask no more"). His acknowledgment of her favor concludes the poem in a fashion that imitates, while it answers, the end of his *complainte*.

In the early fourteenth century, not long after the preparation of B.N., fr. 837, Jehan de Lescurel composed two *dits amoureux* similar in form to the *Chastelaine*.[19] Both of these *dits* are composed of nine-line stanzas of rhyming couplets, with the last couplet completed by a *refrain*, but anadiplosis is not a feature of composition. Where the stanzas of the earlier works were isometric, the third and sixth lines of Jehan's stanzas have four syllables, the remainder being octosyllables. The length of the *refrains* varies: some single-line *refrains* are octosyllabic and one has four syllables; these blend with the metrical pattern of the stanza. In contrast, others are two or more lines long. Even the brief *refrains* constitute a considerable break at the end of the stanza, however, for all are accompanied by musical notation in the manuscript, and hence were presumably meant to be sung. In general each *refrain* sums up or reinforces the main idea of the stanza it follows. Because they repeat the central idea in such a striking way without announcing the next theme, the *refrains* bring each stanza to a conclusion.

The first of the two *dits* in question, "Gracieuse, faitisse et sage," is a

---

19. The old edition by A. de Montaiglon, *Chansons, ballades et rondeaux de Jehannot de l'Escurel*, Bibliothèque Elzévirienne (Paris: P. Jannet, 1855), pp. 49–56 and 57–66, has been replaced by Nigel Wilkins, *The Works of Jehan de l'Escurel: Edited from the ms. Paris, B.N.f. fr. 146*, Corpus Mensurabilis Musicae, 30 (Rome: American Institute of Musicology, 1966), pp. 21–27 and 28–36.

double *complainte*, for its twenty-four stanzas are divided between lover and lady. The lover, who has been happy, is obliged (like the duke in Machaut's *Fonteinne Amoureuse*) to travel to "terre estrange": his joy is changed to sorrow, and spring becomes winter. When he describes his distress and his joy in remembering her beauty, his one fear is that she may forget him. Hence in the last two stanzas he addresses the lady, prays to be remembered, and promises to return.

The second part of the *dit* is the lady's complaint. She has no comfort to offer, for she shares his misery and, like him, is tormented by fear of losing him. The formal structure of this section is identical, but its movement is the reverse of the first part. She addresses him for most of the poem and turns away to pray to *Amors* only at the end. The lovers are separated in their misery, and their protestations of love and loyalty bring comfort to neither.

Since the *refrains* reinforce the central idea of the stanzas, they reveal the outline of the *dit*. The songs and the *dit* are juxtaposed and tell the same story. In this way, Lescurel anticipated on a miniature scale Machaut's technique of juxtaposing narratives in different media in the *Voir Dit*. At the same time Lescurel has juxtaposed two voices, but there is no dialogue: lady and lover are reacting to the same event, and illustrate the misunderstanding that seems the inevitable result of separation. In its structure, the *dit* is perhaps closer to the ending of Christine de Pizan's *Duc des Vrais Amants*, where the separated lovers end by singing in isolation.

The second of Lescurel's *dits*, "Gracieus temps est quant rosier," consists of twenty-eight nine-line stanzas, each completed by a different *refrain* which rhymes with the final line of the stanza and is thematically related to it. A rather conventional dream sequence opens the work, after which the plot is developed in dialogue. The narrator enters a garden in spring and falls asleep. He dreams of another garden where he is accompanied by his lady and other pairs of lovers. These stanzas recall the beginning of Guillaume de Lorris's *Roman de la Rose*, but the musical *refrains* that mark the ends of the stanzas add a suggestion of a different register, that of "la bonne vie" typical of the dance songs. When the narrator awakens, he feels the loss of his dreamed idyll and seeks to replace it with a real love. He meets a lady, whose beauty he describes at some length, and declares himself to her. With the lady's answer, the *dit* ceases to be conventional:

"Beau sire, puisque vous m'amez,
Mon sen devroit estre blasmez
   Se vous héoie,

Je vous aim; qui voudra si l'oie."
(Wilkins, Stanza 17)

[Handsome sir, since you love me, my sense should be blamed if I hated you. I love you; whoever wishes to may hear it.]

Her frank response anticipates the attitude of Machaut's Toutebelle, and effectively shifts the work to the register of its *refrains*. The lady proves herself inconstant, however, for when the young man sees her alone a fortnight later and repeats his declaration, she rejects him out of hand: she has married, and desires no other love. When he pleads with her, she denounces him:

E[h]! plus estes plains de mensonges
Vous hommes, que ne soit uns songes,
   Et vous plaigniez.
Et si bien mal avoir faigniez,
Face Dex tiex gens mahagniez.
   Car il deceuvent,
Les jeunes fames, et deceuvent
Leurs vouloirs quant il s'aparçoivent
Que nice sont. Pour tel pensée,
Fausse Amour, Je vous doins congié.
(Wilkins, Stanza 26, p. 65)

[Ah! You men are more full of lies than a dream, and you complain, and if you have pretended well to be ill, may God harm such people, for they deceive young women and deceive their wishes when they notice that they are naïve. For such a thought, *false love, I send you away.*]

This response is reminiscent of the Châtelaine de Saint Gille's, although the situation of the two women is reversed. Where the Châtelaine tried to reject a repugnant marriage, this lady repulses a would-be *fin' amant*. The lady's speech continues for two more stanzas, and ends the *dit*, so her denunciation of love is not answered. Lescurel has thus used the conventions of the *dit amoureux* to subvert those same conventions. The lady exposes the dream as false and shows the courtly lover "courtois au commencement" ("courteous at the beginning"), but loving falsely. The *refrains* prepare for the lady's otherwise unexpected reactions, which are as foreign to the register of "la bonne vie" as they are to the repertoire of courtly behavior and undermine the lover's pretensions to *fin' amors*. The form of the *dit* suggests that if his rhetoric is courtly, his desires are less so. In her rejection of the conventions of courtly love, the lady stands as a precursor of Christine de Pizan's Dame Sebille and also of the Belle Dame Sans Merci. "Gracieus temps est" belongs to a tradition of works critical of the courtly lyric, and uses lyric insertions to express that criticism. The work juxtaposes contrasting registers, but it is the register of the *refrains* that gives the lady her freedom of expression. In the courtly tradition the lady is inaccessible and silent, but in the *refrains* she is able to speak in surprising ways. At the end of the *dit*, the lover makes no response to her diatribe, and the audience is left amidst the debris of exploded conventions.[20]

Non-Stanzaic Works

Among the non-stanzaic works in which inserted lyrics serve as elements of structure, the one closest in form to the stanzaic works just discussed is another piece from the Paris manuscript B.N., fr. 837, the *Complainte Douteuse*.[21] This poem is a lover's lament about the pains of love and contains two *chansons*. The first is inserted stanza by stanza throughout the poem, dividing it into five sixty-five-line sections, and the second is added at the end. With its five main sections, each ending with a half-line followed by a stanza of the *chanson*, the structure of the *Complainte Douteuse* is clearly modeled on that of a *chanson*. Even the *envoi* of the *chanson* has its equivalent in the final eleven-line section of the *dit*.

The narrative of the *Complainte*, like the two *chansons* it incorporates, deals with the problem of how, and indeed whether, to address a lady. The lover begins by asking where he can seek advice, and turning to *Amors*, he concludes that, since he is unable to speak in her presence, he must rely on a song. In the first stanza he explains that it is love's torment that prompts his

---

20. The motet *enté* in the *Roman de Fauvel* presents a variation on this technique. See above, Chapter 5, under "Song as Declaration" for a discussion of this piece.
21. A. Jubinal, ed., *Nouveau recueil de contes, dits, fabliaux, et autres pièces inédites des 13e, 14e, et 15e siècles*, 2 vols. (Paris: E. Pannier, 1842), II, pp. 242–56. The preceding group of works used a recognizable stanzaic structure—monorhymed quatrains or strophes of seven, nine, or eleven lines, with complex rhyme schemes repeated in each; the works in this group do not display such stanzas, even if their lyric insertions divide them (as in the *Complainte Douteuse* and the *Tresor Amoureux*) into regular sections. Passages of 65 or 800 octosyllabic couplets, however regularly repeated, do not qualify as stanzas.

song, but acknowledges that only through *Amors* can he succeed. The second section, echoing the song, says that he can not keep silent, so great is his suffering. He pleads with *Amors* for mercy and describes his pain; but he lacks the courage to speak of it to his lady. The second stanza of the song asks for advice: should he hide his passion or speak? But fear of rejection enjoins silence. The third part of the *dit*, again echoing the preceding stanza, also seeks advice, and continues the portrait of his malady with a description of his symptoms. It concludes that there is no cure but *fin' amors*, which promised mercy. The fourth stanza makes an exception to his vow of silence—he can delight in song, hoping for the promised mercy. This hope confirms his silence, for if she rejected him, he would lose it. The narrative passage develops these themes and ends with a catalogue of the lady's virtues. In the fifth stanza he declares that he has loved her since he saw her, and that he is sustained by *douz pensser*. As before, he prefers to live in hope rather than to risk what he has by asking for more. The final short passage of the *dit* repeats these ideas, and the *envoi* pledges his perseverance in love.

From this summary, it should be apparent that the principle of *coblas capfinidas* governs the structure of the *dit*: each section begins with the last theme of the preceding section—the theme, that is, of the *chanson* stanza. Only the first stanza is introduced by the narrative; the remaining ones mark a shift in the thought which is then developed in the next passage.

The complete *chanson* at the end of the *dit* is not introduced either, but is related thematically to the rest of the work. It begins with the idea that the lover can request in song what he cannot ask for in speech. He has served his lady, and whatever his pain, he will accept her wish, even if she wishes to refuse him. Nevertheless, he so fears her rejection that he prefers to languish; he lacks the courage to tell her of his pain except in song. He dares not ask for her mercy, because he cannot speak in her presence. In the last stanza, he thinks of her merit, and prefers to remain in torment rather than risk being sent away. The *envoi* sends his song to intercede for him.

This *chanson*, like the *dit* itself with its interpolated song, presents the predicament of the poet, who is prompted to seek solace for his pain, but who chooses to do nothing lest he worsen his position. The only possible remedy is the *chanson* that will express what cannot be spoken. We have already encountered the song in this role in the *dits* of Machaut and Froissart, particularly the *Remede de Fortune* and the *Espinette Amoureuse*. In both cases, poems gave the lover a means of declaring himself, while affording him some protection. The *Complainte Douteuse* anticipates the later works, for the poet has woven two songs into a *dit* on the same themes, and used the whole both to speak for him and to explain his silence. Unlike the fourteenth-century works discussed in the preceding chapter, however, the *Complainte Douteuse* gives no circumstantial detail about composition and reception. On the contrary, the *dit* is virtually assimilated by the songs which dominate its form as well as its themes. One of the striking features of this *dit* is its lack of linear progress. Each time the poet seems about to take some action to advance his cause, his fearful (*douteuse*) reasoning forestalls him. Here again, one is reminded of the circular movement of the *chanson*.[22] The *chanson* stanzas that divide the *Complainte* into sections also introduce the themes of those sections. Consequently, the insertions determine the logic of the poem as well as its structure.

Roughly contemporary with the *Complainte Douteuse*, Baudoin de Condé's *Prison d'Amours* alters the combination of *dit* and lyric insertion.[23] Forty-nine *refrains* divide this work into sections, varying from 31 to 171 lines. In each section, the poet compares the progress of his own affair to the movement of the lover through the prison of Love. Each *refrain* rhymes with the last line of its passage and clearly separates it from the next. Only three *refrains* at the beginning are linked by anadiplosis, while fully half of the sections open a new subject, announced by expressions like "or," and "a celui revieng et retour." Although they are not connected to the following passage, the *refrains* are closely related to the preceding one: more than a third of them are either introduced by, or complete the sense of, the final sentence. Although some are treated as songs, more often the *refrains* complete the thought of the passage:

> Et saciés bien, ma douce dame,
> Sor Dieu le vos jur et sor m'ame
> Et sor l'amor, dont je vous proi:
>   Je ne vous oblierai jà,
>   Pour Diu aiiés merchi de moi.
> (vv. 1186–90)
>
> [And know well, my sweet lady, I swear to you by God and by my soul,

---

22. Paul Zumthor, "De la circularité du chant," *Poétique*, 2 (1970): 129–40.

23. "Li Prisons d'amours que Bauduins de Condé fist," in *Dits et Contes de Baudoin de Condé et de son fils Jean de Condé*, ed. Auguste Scheler, 3 vols. (Brussels: V. DeVaux, 1866–67) I, pp. 267–377. Scheler gives the dates 1240–80 for Baudoin's career; Wimsatt, *Chaucer*, pp. 32–36 finds the first date rather early. See also Ruhe, *Le Dieu d'Amours*, pp. 126–28.

and by the love for which I ask you: I shall never forget you; by God, have mercy on me.]

In many instances, the *refrain* supplies a conclusion to the section or restates one of its main ideas. The tenth section (vv. 585–637), for example, where the lover describes how he was brought to the prison by his eyes and ears, concludes with the *refrain:* "Entrés m'est li maus d'amer / Ou cuer par l'uel" (vv. 636–37; "The pain of love entered my heart through my eye"). Elsewhere the lover describes how some men seek consolation elsewhere when their lady proves cruel, while he himself concentrates on one slow to reward him. The *refrain* "Çou que jou aim ne puis avoir, / Et çou que j'ai ne m'a talent" (vv. 2173–74; "What I love I cannot have, and what I have does not want me") encapsulates his predicament.

When the *refrains* are referred to as songs in the text, they are usually cited as authorities. Near the beginning of the *dit,* Baudoin uses a *refrain* to justify the extended metaphor that is his subject:

Quant je di k'amors a prizon
Et il dient, par mesprizon,
Que jou me faing et je le songe,
Mais n'i a faintisse ne songe,
Ains lor di fine verité,
Si le proeve d'auctorité
D'un rondet dont c'est ci li dis:
 Sa biele boucete, par un très douc ris
 A mon cuer en sa prizon mis.
Ceste prizons dont ci parolle
Iceste cançon de carolle,
C'est la prizons d'amors sans doute
Et mult set poi que de çou doute.
(vv. 119–31)

[When I say that love has a prison, and they say, mistakenly, that I make it up and dream it, but there is no pretense or dream, rather I tell them a fine truth, and prove it by the authority of a rondet which says: "Her beautiful little mouth, with a very sweet laugh, has put my heart in her prison." This prison that the carole song speaks of, it is without doubt the prison of love and he knows very little who doubts this.]

At another point, the lover hopes to be able to sing a particular song, but he can only do so, of course, if his lady were to see fit to reward him:

> Ha! blance flor, belle sur l'ente,
> De tout çou qui me destalente
> Et que mes cuers va redoutant,
> M'aurés gari, se vous de tant
> Vostre consel i volés metre
> De nient payer et de promettre,
> Si que ceste cançons soit moie:
>   Elle m'a dit que m'amera
>   La belle à cui mes cuers s'otroie.
> (vv. 2370–78)

[Ah! white flower, lovely on the branch, of all that discouraged me and made my heart fearful, you will cure me, if you wish to put your counsel to it, to pay nothing and to promise that this song may be mine: "She has said that she will love me, the beauty to whom my heart is given."]

These examples are typical of Baudoin's technique. Taken as a group, the *refrains* reflect, rather than determine, the development of the *dit*. They conclude each section in epigrammatic form, but do not introduce new themes.

Unlike the fearful lover of the *Complainte Douteuse*, who dared address his pleas only to *Amors*, the narrator's position in the *Prison d'Amours* is more complex. The narrator-lover plays two roles and addresses himself to two audiences. His declared purpose (vv. 15–20) is to describe the joy and pain of love within the framework of the allegorical prison, but he also intends "c'a ma dame plaize / Mes traitiés" (vv. 96–97; "that my treatise may please my lady"). His work is thus both a general reflection on the nature of love and an examination of his own passion. The wider audience, addressed frequently as *vous/vos*, occasionally responds, asking questions to encourage the narrator: "Or nos di dont, si feras bien, / Ou en puet issir et comment" (vv. 1496–97; "Now tell us, do it well, how and where one can escape"). Accounts of the actions of "hom plains de savoir" (v. 682), "on" (v. 716), "qui bien amer acoustume" (v. 813), "cil qui amours maistroie" (v. 1065), "Cil de cui s'amie n'a cure" (v. 1130), for example, alternate with more personal comments: "Mais je sui si lonc tans amere" (v. 821; "but I have been bitter for a long time"); "Hé las! ensi quidai monter" (v. 1077; "alas, I thought to ascend"); "Dire le puis, car bien le sai" (v. 1215; "I can say it, for I know it well").

The *dit*, as Baudoin makes clear, is meant not only to please, but to influence his lady. The composition is meant to secure his reward:

> Mais se Dieu plaist de cest afaire
> Et Amors, qui bien le puet faire,
> Ma dame m'en desmentira,
> Si que tout autrement ira.
> Car bien sai, tout cil qui liront
> Cest lai et tout cil qui l'oront,
> Quant il l'aront parleü tout,
> Diront que trop a cuer estout
> Ma dame, et trop est sans pité
> Et trop sans debonnaireté
> S'ele n'ot de celui merci
> Qui pour li fist cest traitié chi.
> (vv. 1619–30)

[But if God is pleased with this affair, and Love, who may well be, my lady will make a liar of me, so that it will happen otherwise. For I know well, all those who will read this *lai* and all those who will hear it, when they have read it to the end, will say that my lady's heart is too hard and too pitiless, and too graceless, if she does not have mercy on him who composed this treatise.]

In contrast to the poet of the *Complainte Douteuse*, who professes himself willing to accept even his lady's indifference, Baudoin relies on public opinion to oblige his lady to accept him. He says that he hopes that hearing her behavior denounced by others will cause her to see the justice of his complaints and reward him. His appeal to the public is, of course, veiled, for he has concealed the identity of his lady, but he expects nonetheless to be vindicated by the merits of his arguments and the elegance of his composition.

Paradoxically, the poem that is to effect the change in his fortunes cannot be completed without the lady's aid. He therefore calls on her to command him to finish it, but she declines to do so. Finally despairing of her help, the poet turns to Fortune and resigns himself to ending the work before winning his lady's love. At the end, he repeats more forcibly his threat of exposing her to censure:

> Pour çou, douce dame, retrai
> A vous pour consel et secours,
> Car mult serés en toutes cours
> Blasmée, et apriès vo mort,
> Se francisse ne vous remort
> Ke la paine soit desiervie
> De celui qui vous a siervie
> Et tant pour vous a travellié
> Et tant pensé et tant vellié,
> Com il pert et c'om puet savoir
> Par cest lai, ù tant a savoir . . .
> (3052–62)

[On this account, sweet lady, I return to you for counsel and aid for you will be much blamed in all courts, and after your death, if frankness does not cause you remorse. That his pain may be rewarded, who served you and suffered for you so much, and thought and lay awake so much that he lost; and this can be known by this *lai*, where there is such knowledge.]

The *Prison d'Amours* is therefore unfinished. Like the troubadour *canzo*, it points to a love affair outside itself; and because the work is the chronicle of the love affair, it cannot be completed while the affair continues. In this respect, the poem resembles the *Panthere d'Amors*: since both works are intended to remedy the lover's unhappiness, neither poet can complete his story within the limits of his poem. Where Nicole de Margival imagined a happy ending, Baudoin contents himself with simply taking leave.[24]

The *Amoureuse Prise*[25] by Jehan Acart is similar in form and intent to the *Prison d'Amour*. Composed in 1322, the work describes, in terms of an

---

24. A *dit* inserted into Fauvel's speech to Fortune in the *Roman de Fauvel* makes use of *refrains* in a manner similar to the works discussed in this section. See above, Chapter 5, under "Song as Declaration," for a discussion of this piece.

25. This title occurs in the text (vv. 6, 54) and is to be preferred to the designation in the rubric; cf. Antoine Thomas, "Frère Jean Acart, Poète français," in *HLF*, 37 (1938): 412–18. The edition by Ernst Hoepffner, *La Prise Amoureuse von Jehan Acart de Hesdin, allegorische Dichtung aus dem XIV. Jahrhundert* (Dresden: Gesellschaft für romanische Literatur, 22, 1910), was based on Paris, B.N., fr. 24391; he corrected it with the aid of additional manuscripts in an article, "Zur 'Prise Amoureuse' von Jehan Acart de Hesdin," *ZRP*, 38 (1917): 513–27.

allegorical hunt, the beginning of the poet's love affair, and pleads for the lady's mercy. *Amors*, the hunter, pursues his quarry, the lover, down the paths of the forest of youth, and his hounds attack each of the lover's senses in turn. The work is divided by nine *ballades* and nine *rondeaux* into seventeen unequal sections. These vary in length from 36 to 198 lines, and *ballades* alternate with *rondeaux* in defining the sections.[26]

The songs function not only as structural divisions, but provide a temporal framework for the narrative; one *ballade* announces the hunt, and in another the lover acknowledges his capture by the lady. In contrast to the lyric insertions in the other works in this chapter, the *ballades* and *rondeaux* are independent of the rhyme of the narrative passages. Although a third of the lyrics[27] are spoken or sung by characters, most have no syntactic link with the narrative verse. Furthermore, the thematic relationship between the lyrics and the passages they follow is not close; despite a general appropriateness of theme, the lyrics neither summarize passages nor announce new subjects.

The formal discontinuity of the inserted lyrics is reinforced by their disruptive effect on the narrative. There is a tension between the chronology of the narrative and that of the lyrics that is apparent from the beginning of the poem. In the opening *ballade*, the poet describes himself as caught, "Si plaisamment m'avés pris" (vv. 1–2), before he has even begun to relate the hunt. At the end of his descriptions of the spring day on which he was caught, the poet sings another *ballade* (II), in which he refers to his encounter with Love in the past tense. Later in this same lyric, he addresses his lady (whom, at this point, he has not yet seen) and begs her mercy.

In the fourth section of the work, the poet catches sight of *Amors* and his hounds. Having seen others caught by the hunter, he realizes that his own downfall is near. In the *ballade* that ends this section, the poet claims that his love is greater than that of others, as is only fitting, for his lady is superior to all others. Once again, the time implicit in the song is considerably in advance of the narrative context in which it occurs.

During the remainder of the poem, the poet is under attack from different sides, as Love besieges one after another of his senses. In the narrative, the poet is not actually taken until the end of his poem. Nevertheless, in the fourth *rondeau* the poet describes himself as caught: "Puis que de vous est espris, / Eureusement est pris" (vv. 781–82; "Since he [the lover] is

---

26. *Rondeaux* VII and VIII follow each other to maintain the symmetry of a *ballade* at the beginning and the end.
27. *Ballades* II, IV, V, VI, VII; *Rondeaux* VII, VIII.

smitten by you, he is happily caught"). Similarly, in the sixth *ballade*, the poet surrenders to his lady and gives up his flight:

> Bele et boinne entierement,
> Tresors de joie et d'amour,
> Or ne puis je longuement
> Fuïr contre vostre amour
> . . . .
> Si me renc pris et vaincus
> En vo dous commandement.
> Vostres sui, je ne sai plus.
> (vv. 1098–1104 [*sic* in edition])

> [Wholly beautiful and good, treasure of joy and love, I cannot for long fly away from your love, . . . so I render myself captured, vanquished in your sweet command. I am yours, I know nothing more.]

In the narrative, however, he continues his resistance for another six hundred lines. We have already remarked that the poet asks for mercy in the second *ballade*. Near the middle of the poem, before his capture is complete, he repeats his request, making it clear that he considers the reward to have been promised. The seventh *ballade* and *rondeau* both betray this confidence:

> Fins cuers dous, quant paieront
> Vostre oel ce qu'il m'ont pramis?
> (vv. 1338–39)

> [Sweet noble neart, when will your eyes pay what they have promised?]

> Vos dous samblans asseüre,
> Et se puis le dechaciés,
> N'est ce traïsons obscure?
> S'en vostre douce figure,
> Dame, est escondis muciés,
> C'est decevans couverture.
> (vv. 1449–54)

[Your sweet appearance assures, and if I could chase it away, is it not a dark treason? If in your sweet figure, Lady, refusal is hidden, it is a deceptive cover.]

It is clear from these examples that the lyrics in the *Amoureuse Prise* do not arise from the context in which they are inserted. The narrative describes the beginning of the love affair, while the lyrics assume its existence, and the composition as a whole is intended to bring it to a successful conclusion. The lyrics are the result of the poet's capture, while it is the hunt, the process of being caught, that is the subject of the narrative. If the lover in the narrative is just awakening to love, the lover in the lyrics is wholly engaged in the service of his lady and appears to have been so for some time. By beginning the work with a *ballade* and sprinkling lyrics throughout, Jehan Acart assures his audience at once of the lover's fate; escape is not even a possibility. At the same time, the lyrics reveal that the lover has not yet achieved his reward, and the work ends with another plea for mercy in the final *ballade*. The disruption of the narrative by the lyric insertions and the temporal discontinuity of the composition both result from the paradoxical position of the first-person narrator, whose narrative voice is located simultaneously in the past (the time of the story) and in the present (the time of the actual telling). This same paradox had already been exploited by Guillaume de Lorris in his manipulation of the dream sequence in the first part of the *Roman de la Rose*.[28] Jehan Acart represents the shift from one to the other generically, as the narrator periodically abandons his recital of past events to sing in his present voice. The alternation between narrative description of the past and lyrics expressing current sentiments is thus a reworking of the lyrico-narrative poetics of the *Roman de la Rose*.

Writing around 1339, Jehan de le Mote used *ballades* as formal divisions in his *Regret Guillaume*.[29] This poem is a eulogy of Guillaume, late count of Hainaut, dedicated to his daughter, Philippa, Queen of England, and is cast in the form of a love allegory.

The poet falls asleep to dream of a forest in full flower, filled with

---

28. Cf. Hult, *Self-Fulfilling Prophecies*, pp. 140 ff.; and Huot, *From Song to Book*, pp. 83–99.

29. Auguste Scheler, ed., *Li Regret Guillaume Comte de Hainaut: Poème inédit du XIVe siècle* (Louvain: Impr. J. Lefever, 1882). On the poems, see Ernst Hoepffner, "Die Baladen des Dichters Jehan de la Mote," *ZRP*, 35 (1911): 153–66. See also Wimsatt, *Chaucer*, pp. 147–49.

singing birds. The opening description is typical of the love dream, but when the poet arrives at the castle the mood changes abruptly:

> Que quant je sui priès aprociés
> De ce castiel, j'oÿ crier,
> Plaindre, gemir et souspirer,
> Plorer si dolereusement
> Et si tres esragiement . . .
> (vv. 180–84)

[From this castle, I heard crying, lamenting, moaning, sighing, weeping, so sorrowful and so deranged . . .]

Upon entering the castle, the poet meets its ladies, who, unlike most allegorical personnages, are dressed and behave in an uncourtly fashion:

> Si tres horriblement crioient,
> Li une estoit eskievelée,
> L'autre ou visage esgratinnée,
> Li autre tordoit poins et bras,
> Li autre deskiroit ses dras.
> (vv. 318–22)

[They shouted horribly, some were disheveled, others had scratched their faces, some were wringing their hands, others rent their clothes.]

The contrast between the sweetness of the season and the bitter emotions of the characters is shocking, but nevertheless consistent with a type of courtly *chanson*.[30] The poet is introduced to fully thirty allegorical ladies. In addition to the courtly virtues (*Debonaireté, Courtoisie, Plaisance*, and so on) inherited from the *Roman de la Rose*, Jehan includes personifications of aristocratic qualities (*Largece, Proece, Hardemens, Justice*, etc.), as well as specifically Christian virtues (*Humelité, Carité*). The last speaker, *Perfection*, sums up the qualities of the count. Each lady laments the loss of the count, lists his virtues, and ends her speech with a *ballade*. The work thus contains thirty lyrics whose function appears to be purely formal—to mark the change of speakers.

30. Cf., for example, by Gace Brulé, "Au renoviau de la douçor d'esté."

None of the lyrics in the *Regret Guillaume* is linked to the verse by rhyme, although each is introduced as a song: "Dolentement en canterai" (v. 1148; "Sorrowfully shall I sing of it"); "S'en voel celle balade faire" (v. 1339; "I wish to compose this *ballade*"), for example. Each *ballade* concludes a long speech praising Guillaume and regretting his death, and serves as a final expression of the speaker's grief. As a result, the themes treated in the lyrics are variations on death, loss, and sorrow. In spite of this concentration upon mourning, there are also frequent references to love. Guillaume (although also referred to as *père, fils,* and *frère*) is frequently called *ami*, and thus each lady mourns not only a paragon of virtue, but a lost lover. *Loiauté*, for instance, declares: "Je moru avoec mon ami, / Mon sierf, mon mestre, mon mari" (vv. 1702–3; "I died with my lover, my serf, my master, my husband"); and *Raison* regrets: "Ha! ciers amis, vrais sire de tous, / Vostre amour trop tost definna" (vv. 2551–52; "Ah, dear friend, true lord of all, your love died too soon"). In her ballade, *Humelité* warns lovers that all has changed with Guillaume's death, an idea repeated in *Loiauté*'s song. *Largece* invites all lovers to join in her lament:

Entre vous qui avés apris
Les dons d'amours à recevoir,
Gens nobles, grans et de haut pris,
Vous devés bien dolour avoir.
(vv. 923–26)

[Among you who have learned to receive the gifts of love, noble people, and of great merit, you must indeed be sorrowful.]

Three *ballades*—those of the ladies *Estableté, Misericorde,* and *Puissance*—resemble love lyrics more than dirges, and represent the author's most direct attempt to associate his subject with that of love. *Estableté*'s lyric opens with an evocation of spring (vv. 3442–50), with all the elements of a typical "nature introduction." The beauty of nature is explicitly associated with the joy of love and contrasts with the singer's state of mind, but it is not until the second stanza that it becomes clear that the lover is dead. *Misericorde* begins her *ballade* by asserting the dual nature of love, source of joy and pain. Unlike a love lyric, however, it is not the beloved's cruelty, but rather his death, that causes the singer's sorrow. *Puissance* borrows another theme, the consolation of song (v. 4418), but rejects it because comfort is no longer possible.

These examples illustrate how Jehan de le Mote took the form of the *dit amoureux* and adapted it to suit his commemorative purpose. All the characteristics of the genre—the dream, the springtime setting, the characters, and the lyrics—are present, yet transformed. The dream is a continuation of the poet's melancholy, the season reinforces the gloom of mourning by contrast, and the cast is supplemented by characters unfamiliar to his model. Jehan's clever adaptation of the *dit amoureux* to eulogy demonstrates not only the versatility of the form, but its prestige in the fourteenth century. Lyric insertions in a lyrico-narrative context were significant vehicles for the expression not only of emotion but also of important cultural values. The use of this format, extremely popular in aristocratic circles, was a means of flattering not only the subject of the work, but its patroness as well.

The anonymous author of the *Tresor Amoureux*, a contemporary of Froissart, used lyrics to mark the divisions of his work in an unprecedented way. The four eight-hundred-line segments of this dream poem are separated by *ballade* cycles of 44, 40, and 44 poems respectively, including a dozen in each group that begin with, and incorporate, a *rondeau*.[31] The lyric cycles do indeed divide the work, but because they are so long, they add a substantial amount of new material. As a result they go beyond the refrain-function of the lyrics in the other works we have discussed.

The unusual form of the *Tresor* is prescribed in extraordinary detail by *Amours*:

> Parmi ce que tu en as fait,
> Seize cens coupplettes feras
> Et en quatre pars le mettras;
> Ce sont quatre cens en chascune
> Partie de rytme commune.
> Entre les quatre pars espasses
> Ara trois, se tu les compasses
> Justement; et en ta premiere
> Espasse, par bonne maniere,
> Des balades y veuil avoir

---

31. Auguste Scheler, ed., *Oeuvres de Froissart: Poésies,* III, pp. 52–281. For a study of this work, see Kelly, *Imagination,* pp. 114–20. On its doubtful attribution of Froissart, see Karl Nuss, "Ueber die Echtheit der Cour de May und des Tresor Amoureux" (Inaugural Diss., Universität Jena, 1914).

Quarante quatre au dire voir;
Et en l'espasse du milieu,
Que pour quarante n'i ait lieu;
Et en l'espasse derreniere
Autel nombre qu'en la premiere.
Des rondeaulz y veuil trente six,
Justement entez et assis,
Douze en chascun nombre des trois,
Afin qu'il ne soit trop estrois.
Douze balades esliras,
Où les douze rondeaulz liras.
Quant tu les y aras entez.
(vv. 734–55)

[Among what you have composed, you will write sixteen hundred couplets[32] and put them in four sections, these of four hundred each, separated by meter. Between the four parts there will be three spaces, if you arrange it right; in the first space, in good form, I wish to have forty-four *ballades*, to speak truly; and in the middle space may there be place for forty; and in the last space a number equal to the first. I wish there to be thirty-six *rondeaux*, properly inserted, twelve in each number of the three, so that they are not too close. You shall choose twelve *ballades* where the *rondeaux* will be read when you have inserted them.]

Despite the god's vagueness about content, his formal requirements are most precise. The interruptions provided by the lyrics are the more pronounced because they are preceded by lists of first lines and refrains. These catalogues (omitted in Scheler's edition) are part of the specifications and not mere embellishments by the rubricator. On the other hand, however marked the pause, the structure of the work is not reinforced by the shape of the narrative. The first few *ballades* restate several of the themes of the first section and seem to serve as a prologue to the rest of the work. The young man who will debate with the lover arrives and is described in *ballades* VII and VIII, and they agree to debate in *ballade* X. Thereafter, they speak in turn. The lover and the young man alternate stanzas or whole *ballades* and continue their exchange without pause in speeches in the

---

32. "Coupelette" here has the modern sense of a rhyming pair of verses; cf. vv. 97–98: "couplets/En fourme de lignes doubletes."

second and third sections of the work. In *ballade* XXVII of the third cycle, the young man suggests that they submit their dispute to *Cognoissance*. He then leaves and the lover receives instruction from the allegorical lady. Her first speech covers several *ballades*, and her second, in answer to the lover's questions, spills over into the couplets of the fourth section. The lover finally submits his work, the record of his debate, to *Amours*. When the god criticizes the book, *Cognoissance* intervenes, and the debate is renewed. Neither the stages of the debate nor the arrival and departure of characters is related to the metrical divisions of the work. Thus although the lyrics mark clear divisions on the structural level, they tend to be absorbed into the narrative in a manner reminiscent of the *refrains* in the *Chastelaine de Saint Gille*, and of the inserted lyrics in the *Livre Messire Ode*.

During his long debate, the poet is also concerned with the composition of his work. The book began as a means of preserving the dream (v. 88 ff), but it also expresses his desire:

> Et disoie: Je fay cy vers,
> Lesquels ne sont pas trop divers,
> Car ilz ne sont que de couppletes
> En fourme de lignes doubletes,
> Et les fay faisant mencion
> De l'amoureuse intention
> Que j'avoie quant me levay . . .
> (vv. 95–101)

[And I said, I write this poem, which is not too diverse because there are only couplets in the form of double lines, and I make them mention the amorous intention I had when I got up. . .]

> De tout ce qu'il m'est advenu
> Puis lors dont il m'est souvenu,
> Et qu'il m'advient et advenra,
> Bien m'en souvient et souvenra
> Se je puis, et selon mon sens
> Et que j'en ay senty et sens
> Et sentiray, versifier
> En veuil vers, et verifier
> A mon povoir.
> (vv. 105–13)

[Everything that happened to me since I have remembered, and I remember well what is happening, and will remember what will happen, if I can, and according to the sentiments that I have felt, do feel, and shall feel, I wish to write verses, and check them according to my power.]

The dream and its record are thus bound up with his own love affair. When the lover presents to *Amours* the beginning of his book, the offering wins the god's approval, and his service is to complete the work. In serving Love, he also serves "la guardienne du Tresor" (v. 697), that is, his lady. The book is to serve another purpose at the same time, however:

Mettre te fault ton estudie
A faire un livre bel et gent
Pour conforter toute no gent
Et esjoïr quant ilz aront
Aucun ennoi et qu'ilz seront
En tristesce et en desconfort
Par Dangier et par son effort.
(vv. 712–18)

[You must put your effort to make a beautiful and noble book to comfort all our people, and to make them joyful when they have any trouble or discomfort from *Dangier*, or on account of his efforts.]

The *Tresor Amoureux*, then, is both personal and general in scope. The account of the dream is intended to please the lady as a form of love service, but also, and perhaps more importantly, to be of use to a wider public of lovers. It is to this wider audience that the author addresses his reflections on the nature of love and its place in society.

To an even greater extent than similar works, the *Tresor* mediates between dream and reality. The work exists in the real world, but it was both conceived and executed within the framework of the dream. The reception of the work is similarly dramatized within the dream, for the book is read twice. *Cognoissance*, the first reader, tries to reconcile the opposing positions held by the lover and his interlocutor. Near the end, *Amours* reads it carefully, but takes exception to some of the opinions expressed. The lover is saved by the intervention of *Cognoissance*, who adds a series of questions for the consideration of the wider audience. The book that was the record of a dream becomes itself the subject of discussion.

The *Tresor* dramatizes the role of inspiration and the tension between form and content, while it discusses the nature and role of love. But the lady, who never figured clearly in the work, is lost from sight by the end. The poet is caught up in his book and his general, rather than his particular, audience.

In all of the works containing lyrics inserted for structural purposes, the interrupting and structuring functions of the refrains in a fixed-form poem are achieved in a variety of ways. As we have seen, the inserted lyrics interrupt the flow of the narrative verse not only metrically, but probably musically as well. The insertions are often linked to the text by their rhyme, but they nevertheless disturb the normal pattern of couplets. On the logical level, however closely the insertions may be tied to the thought of the text, they also interrupt that thought. Sometimes they summarize it in epigrammatic form, while in other instances they introduce a new topic. In the *Amoureuse Prise* the insertions interrupt more abruptly, since they are rarely linked more than tangentially to the text, and often break the chronology of the narrative. The interruptions caused by the lyric cycles in the *Tresor Amoureux*, on the other hand, are so great that the narrative line eventually continues despite the different metrical structure of the cycles. The *Tresor Amoureux* and the *Complainte Douteuse* thus seem to represent different poles in the tension inherent in lyrico-narrative poetics: in the first case the narrative element seems to override the lyric form, while in the other, the lyric dominates and blocks the narrative development.

We have already observed in discussing the *Amoureuse Prise* that the lyric insertion device lends itself to the exploration of the paradox of the narrative voice, simultaneously speaking of past events and expressing emotions in the present. The technique in the *Tresor* explores another paradox (one exposed also by Machaut), namely the double audience of the *dit amoureux*. At the same time that the poet composes the story of his own painful love affair in order to win favor with his lady, he is also compiling a book which he hopes will win him sympathy and literary admiration from a wider audience of courtly readers and lovers.

Given the complex temporal situation of the speaking voice, the tension between past and present is not always held in balance. Sometimes the stasis of the lyric voice predominates and blocks the narrative development, as in the *Complainte Douteuse*. In other works, the narrative impulse is strong enough to make itself heard even in the lyric forms. Thus at points in the *Livre Messire Ode* and in the *Tresor Amoureux*, the narrative line spills over the bounds of the narrative verse and continues in the lyric verse forms of the *ballade* and the *rondeau*. In this context, as in the others we have examined in this study, the lyric insertion device thus proved extremely flexible.

8. Conclusion

With its introduction by Jean Renart in his *Roman de la Rose* or *Guillaume de Dole*, the lyric insertion device appeared as a new element in the narrative repertoire at the beginning of the thirteenth century. Despite its novelty, however, the device was thoroughly consistent with the literary tradition inherited from the romances of the twelfth century. The previous generation of romance writers, and Chrétien de Troyes in particular, had already wrestled with the problems caused by incorporating the ideology of *fin' amors*, borrowed from the lyric works of the earlier troubadours, into the narrative structure of the romance. What the writers of the thirteenth century did was to explore other aspects of the relationship between the lyrical *chanson* that continued to embody *fin' amors* and the longer narrative works that put that ideology to the test. Jean Renart, by quoting *chanson* texts in his romance, confronted directly the prestige of the lyric *chanson*, and his *Roman de la Rose* is in some sense a response to the *chanson*. A little later than Renart, Guillaume de Lorris explored in his more famous *Roman de la Rose* the ambiguities of narrative voice. He assumed the voice of the lyric "I" and elaborated the themes of the *chanson* in an allegorical narrative. Later users of lyric insertions came under the influence of the models presented in the two *Romans de la Rose*.[1] Jean Renart and his successors dealt directly with the prestige of the lyric by incorporating lyric forms into their works. Thus they confronted not only the ideology of the *chanson* or the ambiguities of its speaking voice, but also the formal existence of the songs, with their poetic as well as communicative or referential functions. These writers formed new configurations from the double tradition inherited from the romances and lyric poetry of the previous century. In so doing, they were obliged to grapple with problems arising from the confrontation of two distinct genres, one of which was their different dynamic: where the movement of the lyric is circular, a narrative is characterized by a

---

1. Cf. D. Poirion, ed., *Précis de la littérature français du moyen âge* (Paris: Presses Universitaires de France, 1983), p. 97 for a suggestion that the identity of title was not merely fortuitous.

forward, linear movement. Another problem arose from the ambiguity inherent in lyric poetry: the songs were both private and social; the love affair was to be secret, but was celebrated in public song. Writers using lyric insertions recognized this ambiguity and exploited it in various ways in their works.

The use of lyric insertions had important implications for the formal and stylistic aspects of thirteenth- and fourteenth-century narrative works. As we have noted in the preceding chapters, the metrical combinations and hybrid forms created by Jean Renart and his successors were more diverse than the single term "lyric insertion" suggests. Not only were the incorporating narratives diverse in form and nature, but the insertions themselves varied considerably in length, genre, and register. The contrasting effects that were created by inserting lyrics into narratives were thus multiplied, and in discussing them we must speak of a "poetics of contrast" as well as a "poetics of allusion." In this final chapter, I shall discuss the lyric insertion device first as part of the continuing effort by medieval French writers to reconcile the lyric and narrative traditions. I shall then examine it as a type of formal experiment and try to consider its implications for the literary history of the thirteenth and fourteenth centuries.

Lyric and Narrative

Chrétien de Troyes's *Chevalier de la Charette* has been interpreted as an attempt to cast the ecstatic lover of courtly lyric poetry as the hero of a romance.[2] The authors who used lyric insertions worked in the same tradition and articulated repeatedly the tension between lyric conventions and narrative form.[3] There is, of course, no absolute division between lyric and narrative elements in the literature of the period, for the narrative

---

2. Jean Frappier, *Chrétien de Troyes: L'Homme et l'oeuvre* (Paris: Hatier, 1957), p. 126. See also F. Douglas Kelly, *Sens and Conjointure in the Chevalier de la Charette* (The Hague: Mouton, 1966); A. H. Diverres, "Some Thoughts on the *Sens of Le Chevalier de la Charette*," *Forum for Modern Language Studies*, 6 (1970): 24–36; and Stephen F. Noreiko, "Le *Chevalier de la charette:* Prise de conscience d'un fin' amant," *Romania*, 94 (1973): 463–83.

3. See Joan Ferrante, "The Conflict of Lyric Conventions and Romance Form," in *In Pursuit of Perfection: Courtly Love in Medieval Literature*, ed. J. M. Ferrante, G. D. Economou, and Frederick Goldin (Port Washington, N.Y.: Kennikat Press, 1975), pp. 135–78; and Lowanne E. Jones, "Narrative Transformations of the Twelfth Century Troubadour Lyric," in *The Expansion and Transformation of Courtly Literature*, ed. Nathaniel B. Smith and Joseph Snow (Athens: University of Georgia Press, 1980), pp. 117–27. Helen Solterer, "*Acorder li chans au dit:* The Lyric Voice in Medieval Narrative, 1220–1320" (Ph.D. Diss., University of Toronto, 1986), speaks of "renegotiating" the lyric.

works always include non-narrative elements, especially of description and soliloquy. Similarly, some lyric genres, including the *chanson de toile* and the *pastourelle,* are overtly narrative, and even the most circular *chanson d'amour* has a latent narrativity, or an implicit story.[4] Nevertheless, the *chanson*, at least, is essentially static, while the characteristic movement of a story is linear. This fundamental contrast between movement and stasis was manifested in the romances of Chrétien as a tension between love and adventure. In the thirteenth century, this same tension took different forms, first in the romances, where the authors reacted to (or in Bakhtin's term, entered a dialogical relationship with) the lyric ideal of *fin' amors,* and later in the *dits amoureux,* which translated the themes of courtly love into narrative situations.

In romances like Jean Renart's *Guillaume de Dole,* Gerbert de Montreuil's *Roman de la Violette,* Girart d'Amiens's *Meliacin,* and Jakemés's *Castelain de Couci,* the *chanson d'amour* was treated as the language of love, and therefore the best expression of it. The characters, through their choice of songs, declared adherence to a particular type of love—that of *fin' amors.* By inserting lyrics into their romances, the authors of these works posited another language, different from the rest of their work, and were then obliged to enter into some sort of relationship with it. We have seen how Jean Renart and Gerbert de Montreuil exploited (in slightly different ways) the ironic possibilities of the situation, presenting heroes who were deceived by envious slanderers and who thus failed to live up to their ideal. Gerbert went further in this direction and contrasted his heroine with his hero very neatly by giving each of them a "son poitevin." While Euriaut's song demonstrated her loyalty, Gerart—albeit under the influence of a magic potion—sang for another lady and betrayed Euriaut. In both romances, the ideal represented by troubadour and *trouvère chansons* was undercut by the narrative, and Jean Renart dramatized the abandonment of the ideal with a shift of genre in the final scene. In addition to the contrast between *chanson* and story, the *chansons* exist, perhaps as anachronisms, in the context of other songs, especially *rondets de carole* and *refrains,* which are usually more direct and less idealized in their expressions of love and desire.

The attitude of Girart d'Amiens and Jakemés toward the songs they quoted was markedly different. Both authors still believed in the ideal of *fin' amors* and treated their heroes without irony. Meliacin and Renaut became

---

4. Paul Zumthor, "Les Narrativités latentes dans le discours lyrique médiévale," in *The Nature of Medieval Narrative,* ed. Minette Grunmann-Gaudet and Robin F. Jones (Lexington, Ky.: French Forum Monographs, 22, 1980), pp. 39–45.

singers and composers under the inspiration of their love; their poetic "careers" depended upon their role as lover. As a result, the narrative in each romance supported and validated the songs that were the emblems of their love. *Meliacin* and the *Castelain de Couci*, together with the *Panthere d'Amors* (which will be treated in more detail below), are interesting because they illustrate the transition from the romance to the pseudo-autobiographical *dit*. Girart's Meliacin began as a borrower of songs, but as his love matured under trial, he became a composer as well. Jakemés, on the other hand, took the historical figure of a known poet, the Châtelain de Couci, and attempted to provide him with a romance "biography" that would explain the composition of his songs. Events in the hero's story were thus shown to be the inspiration for his poetry, and the sincerity of the songs was authenticated by those events. The narrator of Nicole de Margival's *Panthere d'Amors*, like Meliacin, began by quoting songs composed by Adam de la Halle before he turned to writing his own. But this work differed from the earlier romances, for the poet-hero of the work was also its narrator, and the *dit* was at least ostensibly "autobiographical." Of the authors of the fourteenth-century *dits*, only Froissart used lyric poetry borrowed from another poet, and even he did so only to please the patron who had written them.

The issue of quotation—of using borrowed songs in a new context—brings out another feature common to these works, namely their nostalgic attitude toward the literary past. In justifying the inclusion of songs, Jean Renart adduced his desire to insure the preservation of the lyric corpus as one of his motives. His precaution seems to have been warranted, given the fact that more than a quarter of the songs he quoted are unattested elsewhere. Nostalgia may also explain the respect with which quoted songs were treated by authors. Even when the actions of the characters contradict the ideals of the songs they sing, this discrepancy arises at least as much from the inadequacies of the characters as from the inappropriateness of the model. In Jean Renart's *Roman de la Rose*, we saw two competing lyric ideologies, and it was the tradition of the anonymous, uncomplicated, and perhaps older genres—the *rondets de carole*, *chansons de toile*, and *pastourelles*—which were reaffirmed by the action.

The authors who borrowed all or most of their songs—Jean Renart, Gerbert de Montreuil, Girart d'Amiens, and Jakemés in particular—were using material in some sense traditional, and their narratives responded to it in various ways, either accepting its assumptions, or undermining its pretensions. Most of the authors of *dits amoureux*, on the other hand, quoted their own poetry and claimed that it had been composed for the occasion.

Nicole de Margival was a transitional figure between the earlier and the later practices, as he used borrowed work alongside his own. The songs of the "maistre" Adam de la Halle, quoted by Nicole in his *Panthere d'Amors*, balance those of the narrator-poet. The advice of the master was contradictory at best, so the poet was obliged to rely on luck (*Fortune*) and his own poetry. But his success—within the limits of the work, at any rate—was confined to dreams and wishes. The ability of the younger generation to attain the ideal was thus left in doubt when measured against the lyric tradition. In his equivocal attitude toward the work of the master, Nicole dramatized the predicament of the courtly poet who worked in a traditional medium and yet had to redefine the tradition in his own terms.

Nicole's successors—Machaut, Froissart, Oton de Grandson, and Christine de Pizan—all addressed the same problem. Machaut's *dits* were characterized by an increasing preoccupation with the power of poetry. His works attempted to articulate a new relationship between love and song. Although the poetry and its inspiration remained interdependent, the craft of the poet became increasingly obvious. Machaut never portrayed his songs as spontaneous outbursts, but insisted on the work of composition, both of words and of music. However carefully constructed were the *chansons* of the *trouvère* in the *Castelain de Couci*, his literary effort itself was not portrayed. In that romance, the poet-lover was shown singing in direct response to emotional inspiration. In the *Voir Dit*, on the other hand, the narrator carefully juggled the responsibilities of his various roles—as lover of Toutebelle, poet, composer, courtier, and member of society. If Machaut invented a comical persona and portrayed himself as an incompetent lover scarcely ever successful, he remained superbly confident of his poetic skill. Machaut's simultaneous appearance as skillful poet and bumbling lover may in fact be a narrative representation of his awareness of the impending separation of poetry and music.[5] Poetry, in cutting itself off from music, could be seen as leaving behind the roots of its emotional inspiration.

Froissart, who inherited these roles from Machaut, combined them in new patterns, and we have seen him assume the role of master and guide to his illustrious patron, Wenceslas of Brabant. By Froissart's day, however, the relationship between poetry and inspiration was less sure; Froissart seems even less confident than Machaut of the efficacy of his poetry, of its power to advance the cause of his love. If Machaut showed himself incom-

---

5. It is a cliché of literary history to identify Machaut as the last poet-composer, but see Nigel Wilkins, "The Post-Machaut Generation of Poet-Musicians," *Nottingham Medieval Studies*, 12 (1968): 40–84.

petent as a lover, it was nevertheless his poetry that attracted Toutebelle in the *Voir Dit*. His poetry was capable of inspiring love, even if the poet could not live up to his own ideal. The doubtful quality of the poet's success was a theme common to much of Froissart's work. The most optimistic of his *dits*—the *Joli Mois de May*—allowed the lover to attain happiness, but only within the context of a dream. The happy dream of the *Espinette Amoureuse*, on the other hand, was first confirmed and then contradicted by the lady's behavior. As a result, the poet-lover's fate at the end of the poem was problematic.

If Froissart was uncertain of the power of his poetry, his contemporary Oton de Grandson lost heart altogether; not only were his poems despairing, but the narrative was unable to reach a conclusion, and finally dissolved into a series of songs. Christine de Pizan, on the other hand, writing mainly for the next generation, used the traditional form conservatively while rejecting its assumptions. She produced works that combined elements of both the romance and the *dit* traditions. She worked in the narrative voice of the *dit amoureux*, but created new personas for it. Consequently, even when speaking in the first person, she did not tell her own story, but someone else's. Unlike the early romances, Christine's works presented no tension between song and story. Nor did she treat the ideals of her lovers ironically. For Christine, the problem of *fin' amors* lay in its own unsuitability to social context rather than in the shortcomings of the lovers. The shepherdess, as well as the knight, was perfectly sincere in her love. Christine allowed the spectacle of the girl's misery—caused by the demands of social responsibility rather than by infidelity or betrayal—to preach the dangers of love. In the *Duc des Vrais Amants*, she treated the lovers with sympathy, and turned to prose to expose the flaws of the lyric ideal enacted by the narrative. She was thus more radical than any of her predecessors, for she worked within the tradition, but used its conventions to undermine its very foundations.

The attitude of thirteenth- and fourteenth-century authors toward the ideology of courtly poetry, and toward the power of that poetry, was reflected on the level of the individual song in the way it was invested with meaning. The sincerity of the songs of the troubadours and *trouvères* was always ambiguous and inevitably remained in question when the songs were quoted in later works. On the one hand, the lyric poets proclaimed their sincerity of feeling in their songs, and this claim was certainly given credence by the authors of the biographical *vidas*. This tradition of attributing biographical sources to the poems continued in the *Castelain de Couci*, as well as in the erotic pseudo-autobiographies, where the feeling expressed in the inserted lyrics was often meant to be taken at face value. On the other hand, the *chansons d'amour* were extremely conventional in nature, and most of the poets' skill was directed toward formal invention. Moreover, these songs were intended for public performance, and were sung by minstrels in contexts devoid of emotional content. The sincerity of the feelings they expressed was thus highly suspect.

Jean Renart, Gerbert de Montreuil, and Girart d'Amiens all exploited the ambiguity inherent in the songs they borrowed. These songs were treated by the characters in their romances as sincere expressions of love, and when the characters appropriated them, they invested them with their own personal meaning. Still other romance characters—including Tristan, Iseut, and many secondary characters in that romance, the Châtelain de Couci, the Lady of the Unicorn, and her knight—were shown composing songs under the influence of their love. Even the philosopher Aristotle in the *Lai d'Aristote* believed the deceptive meaning of the girl's songs. Furthermore, in the *dits amoureux*, and especially the pseudo-autobiographical ones, the songs formed part of the authenticating material; they served, as in the *Voir Dit*, to prove the truth of the narrative.

At the same time, because the songs were theoretically impersonal, characters could sing them in social contexts and invest them with hidden meanings. Fresne's sung declaration of her unhappiness in *Galeran de Bretagne,* and Marthe's *lais* in *Ysaÿe le Triste*, functioned in this way. For Fresne and Marthe, their songs were part of their disguise: as professional entertainers, no one would suspect them of singing their personal misery. Similarly, in a reversal of this situation, real minstrels could serve as messengers, singing declarations of love to ladies on behalf of King Meliadus and the Châtelain de Couci. When songs were written out, rather than sung by minstrels, they could be left in strategic places, for the meaning would be correctly interpreted only by the intended lady. Guillaume de Machaut's *lai* in the *Remede de Fortune* was found by his lady, and obliged him to declare himself, and Froissart hoped for the same result from his *ballade* in the *Espinette Amoureuse*. Amateur singers also profited from the supposed impersonality of social songs to say more than would otherwise have been possible in public. Sometimes the meaning was transparent, as in Conrad's final song declaring his satisfaction when he finally met Liénor and asked her to marry him. In other cases, the significance of the song was obscure to all but those equipped with the knowledge needed to interpret it. The meaning of the Dame de Fayel's song during the *carole* was meant to be secret, but was correctly interpreted by her rival. The *Blanc Chevalier*, whose song seemed to be a sign of conviviality, nevertheless managed to threaten his wife with it. And Fresne, by singing the *lai* taught to her by Galeran, was able to convey a message to him. Jacquemart Gielée subjected this feature of public singing to parody when he allowed the animals of *Renart le Nouvel* to dramatize the words of their songs. As they did so, the impersonal quality of their *refrains* disappeared, and the meaning of the words was taken literally. The songs ceased to be ambiguous, and as a result it was impossible to sing them in public without comic effect.

In all of these instances, the use of a song allowed the meaning to be both revealed and hidden. Lyric form enabled the characters to express themselves publicly while observing the requirements of polite behavior. Yet this very capacity of a song to convey a secret message implied the danger that its message might be surprised, intercepted, or misinterpreted. Hence Conrad's overheard song in *Guillaume de Dole* revealed his plans to an enemy, and one of Gerart's in the *Violette* led a scheming lady to think him in love with her. Girart d'Amiens exploited this possibility for its sentimental value, when he had one of Celinde's songs make Meliacin think she loved someone else. His song in reaction was also overheard, but Celinde was bolder than he and quickly sorted out the misunderstanding. If the significance of some songs was intercepted, unintended meanings were inferred from others. In *Cleomadés*, it was Clarmondine's presence, rather than her sentiments, that interested the evil magician, while Gifflet read a message of extravagant pride in the songs of Escanor's cortege. Many of the *lais* in the *Tristan en Prose* were sung by minor characters, but overheard by the members of the central triangle; by virtue of their eavesdropping, these extraneous songs were given an extra resonance in the text and related to the principal love affair.

If a supposedly impersonal song could be invested with personal meaning, this new meaning might well alter the normal interpretation of the genre of the song. In the *Roman de la Violette*, Euriaut appropriated a *chanson de mal mariée* to express her unambiguous rejection of the villain's lecherous advances, and the words of the song are admirably apt for her purpose. But while the genre itself declared impatience with the bonds of marriage and announced the singer's intended infidelity, Euriaut recast it as a declaration of fidelity to her first love. In the *Lai d'Aristote*, however, the philosopher either assumed such a reinterpretation of the genre or else failed to recognize the genre for what it was, for he took the girl's *chanson de toile* as a declaration of love. Consequently, he did not recognize himself as the jealous old man from whom the lovers would be free.

The notion of the song as a privileged mode of expression, and the idea that one could *sing* more than one could possible *say*, were both explored by *Coeur d'Acier* in *Perceforest*. Called upon to explain herself, she was unable to begin without the safety offered by a *lai*. Behind its screen of relative anonymity, she was able to recount her painful history, and in so doing gained the courage she needed to reveal her identity. This power of poetic form, as we have already noted, was a central theme of the *dits amoureux*, but the *Complainte Douteuse* presented it as a paradox. The poet could indeed sing more than he would dare utter, but the power of the song made it too dangerous to use. Having brought himself to a standstill, the poet was finally forced to rely on his poem as intercessor, but seemed to expect the worst from his attempt.

The tension between lyric and narrative was not confined to the ideology of the *chanson* and its emotional sincerity, but had formal implications as well. We have observed some uncertainty over which type of discourse should dominate in the hybrid forms we have examined. Some authors made considerable efforts to bring the insertions under the influence of the plot, and in the *Chastelaine de Saint Gille* the *refrains* were so well integrated into the storyline as to be unnoticeable except for their metrical contrast. In the *Amoureuse Prise*, on the other hand, the songs emphatically interrupted the temporal structure of the narrative, and were unrelated to the development of the plot, even if they ultimately resulted from it. The *Voir Dit* demonstrated another approach to the problem, for Machaut used three different modes of discourse to recount essentially the same story. At the end of our period, however, it is the lyric poetry that overcomes the narrative. The *Livre Messire Ode* and the *Duc des Vrais Amants*, for example, both end in a series of lyric poems that continue to advance the plot line. These works represented graphically the breakdown of the courtly narrative, for the plot failed to reach a successful conclusion, but ended without producing any change in the situation of the lovers.

Such diegetic arrangements of lyrics heralded Christine de Pizan's *Cent Balades de l'Amant et de la Dame*, which would rehearse, without benefit of connecting narrative, a plot similar to that of the *Duc*. The alternating *ballades* of the lover and the lady would convey their story in dialogue. The form of Christine's work in turn would anticipate the otherwise quite different *Belle Dame Sans Merci* of Alain Chartier. The alternating stanzas of this poem—not lyrics in themselves—would resemble the stanzas of a *complainte*, itself a form closely allied to the *dit*.⁶ Thus in the fifteenth century, the constituent elements of the lyric insertion device were separated into lyric and nonlyric poetry, both of which might convey narrative development, but which were no longer joined in a hybrid form.

Formal Experimentation

The appearance of Jean Renart's *Guillaume de Dole* coincided with the beginning of a period of intense formal experimentation in French literature. Though important both for its incidence and its influence, the idea of inserting lyrics into a narrative (introduced, perhaps, in *Galeran de Bretagne*, but certainly popularized by *Guillaume de Dole*) was but a single manifestation of the "stylistic heterogeneity" characteristic of the literature of the thirteenth and fourteenth centuries.⁷ It will be useful at this point to consider briefly the nature of some of the more clearly related forms. Perhaps the best known example of a "heterogeneity" comparable to that created by lyric insertions is to be found in the *chantefable, Aucassin et Nicolette*.⁸ Composed before the middle of the thirteenth century, this work consists of forty-one passages of alternating prose and verse. The latter, though sung (they are completely notated in the manuscript), do not belong to any of the standard lyric genres. They are composed in assonanced octosyllabic meter, and vary in length from ten to forty lines. Despite this difference in form, the prose and verse passages cannot be distinguished by their function. Certainly the sung passages cannot be treated as lyric interludes or embellishments inessential to the plot. On the

---

6. Cf. Poirion, *Le Poète et le prince*, p. 407: "ce genre la frontière du lyrisme et de la narration."
7. The term is borrowed from Jeanette M. A. Beer, "Stylistic Heterogeneity in the Middle Ages: An Examination of the Evidence of *Li Fet des Romains*," in *Jean Misrahi Memorial Volume: Studies in Medieval Literature*, ed. Hans R. Runte, Henri Niedzielski, and William L. Hendrickson (Columbia, S.C.: French Literature Publication Co., 1977) pp. 100–114.
8. *Aucassin et Nicolette, chantefable du XIIIe siècle*, ed. Mario Roques, 2e édition (Paris: Champion, 1967); however B. Blakey, "Aucassin and Nicolette XXIX, 4," *French Studies*, 22 (1968): 97–98 suggested the date 1270. Among the many studies of this work, see especially J. Trotin, "Vers et prose dans *Aucassin et Nicolette*," *Romania*, 97 (1976): 481–508; Tony Hunt, "Precursors and Progenitors of *Aucassin et Nicolette*," *Studies in Philology*, 74 (1977): 1–19; Eugene Vance, "The Word at Heart: *Aucassin et Nicolette* as a Medieval Comedy of Language," *Yale French Studies*, 45 (1970): 33–51, and *Aucassin et Nicolette* as a Medieval Comedy of Signification and Exchange," in *The Nature of Medieval Narrative*, pp. 57–76; and Michel Zink, "Le premier type: De l'alternance à l'insertion," *Perspectives médiévales*, 3 (1977): 15–21.

contrary, most of them are partly narrative in character, while five of them (I, IX, XIX, XXI, and XLI) are wholly so. Furthermore, this verse narration adds elements not contained in the prose passages. Hence neither the prose nor the verse can be considered dispensable "insertions." Both portions of the text contain direct discourse ascribed to the characters, and only two sung passages (XXV and XXXIII) consist exclusively of a character's speech. The verse of *Aucassin et Nicolette* differs, therefore, both in form and function, from the lyric insertions in the romances contemporary with it. It seems to anticipate some of the late *dits amoureux*, such as the *Livre Messire Ode* and the *Tresor Amoureux*, where the narrative continued without respect for metrical form.

The use of sung passages in *Aucassin et Nicolette* seems to have been peculiar to that work, but several comparable ways of combining genres became widespread in the thirteenth century, giving rise to new hybrid genres. One of these was the *chanson avec des refrains*. The practice of using *refrains* in *chansons*, first attested in the later twelfth century, became much more common in the thirteenth. Both repeated refrains and nonrecurring "*refrain-citations*" occur frequently in *chansons* composed after 1200. The latter type of *refrain*, as found in the *chansons avec des refrains*, is of particular interest to us, because it provides an example in a lyric context of the insertion technique we have examined in narratives. As in the case of some of the *dits* we have looked at, the body of the *chanson* and its *refrains* belong to different registers, and the contrast between them could vary considerably.[9]

Another hybrid genre of the thirteenth century, the motet, combined texts of various types in an entirely different manner. There is no question here of "insertion," for the genre was defined by the juxtaposition—or rather the layering—of two, three, or four different voices. These "voices" consisted of different texts sung to different melodies. There were usually linguistic as well as musical and registral contrasts, for the *tenor* or first voice of most motets was a fragment of Latin liturgical chant, while the *motetus, triplum,* and *quadruplum* could be in French.[10] The genre thus depended for its effects on a simultaneous unfolding of texts and was essentially "intertextual" in nature. Although the precise quality of the textual relation-

9. See Zumthor, *Essai,* pp. 247–49, for a discussion of some of the effects. Pierre Bec goes even farther, and sees in these refrains the manifestation of a traditional oral literature coexisting with the "grant chant courtois" (*La Lyrique française,* I, p. 43).

10. On the motet, see Bec, *La Lyrique française,* I, pp. 214–20; Zumthor, *Essai,* pp. 261–63; and Dom Anselm Hughes, "The Motet and Allied Forms," in *Early Medieval Music Up to 1300: The New Oxford History of Music* II (Oxford: Oxford University Press, 1955; repr. 1969).

ships has yet to be defined,[11] most motets relied on effects of contrasting registers similar to those of the *chansons avec des refrains*, if more complex.[12]

Although the motet as a genre was constructed on the principle of juxtaposition rather than that of insertion, the motets *entés* of the *Roman de Fauvel* are exceptions. In these examples, one voice of a motet was removed from its context, and its individual verses were interrupted by passages of nonmusical narrative verse. On the page, the appearance of the motet *enté* resembles that of narrative verse punctuated by *refrains*. The cases are different, however, because the individual musical lines of the motet *enté* fit together to form a coherent stanza, while *refrains* are always independent.

As this suggests, the device of inserting passages in a different genre lent itself to many different forms of heterogeneity. In addition to the lyric insertions that have been the subject of this study, we have encountered many other types of insertion during the course of our survey: verse inscriptions and prayers in the prose romances; verse letters in both prose and verse romances; prose letters in the verse romances and *dits*; and *dits* inserted into romances and other *dits*—to say nothing of the hybrid forms found in *Fauvel*: the motet *enté*, the *dit enté*, and semi-lyric compositions. The lyric insertions themselves are also very diverse. In length they range from the short *refrain* fragment, through *chansons* of five stanzas and *lais* of twelve or more stanzas, to *complaintes* of up to eight hundred lines. Their genres include dance songs (*rondets de carole*), *chansons d'amour*, motet fragments, and the *formes fixes* (*rondeau, ballade*, and *virelai*), as well as *chansons royales, pastourelles, chansons de toile*, and *bergierettes*. In some works, heterogeneity is produced by the insertion of lyrics of only a single genre, but in others the effect is made richer by the insertion of several, and in a few, the lyrics are joined by other types of insertion and juxtaposition.

The variety in the form of the inserted material is paralleled by the diversity in the nature of the incorporating texts. Although our attention has concentrated on romances in prose and verse and on verse *dits*, we have seen that these categories disguise a more complex reality. In addition to the full-length works of these types, many shorter pieces—including *fabliaux* (like the *Chastelaine de Saint-Gille* or the *Trois Dames de Paris*), *lais* (such as

---

11. Motet texts have received less attention than the music; among recent exceptions to this observation are the following papers: Beverly Evans, "Chanson and Motet: Textual Content and Musical Structure," and Sylvia Huot, "The Poetics of Simultaneity: Critical Approaches to the Motet," both read at the Twenty-second International Congress on Medieval Studies, Kalamazoo, Michigan, 1987.

12. See Zumthor, *Langue et technique*, p. 173. He goes on to identify similar contrasts in monodic genres, pp. 174–76.

the *Lai d'Aristote* or the *Blanc Chevalier*), *saluts d'amour* ("Celui qu'Amours conduit et maine," and "Amours qui m'a en sa justise"), and short *dits* (like those of Jean de Lescurel, the *Complainte Douteuse*, and the *Confrere d'Amours*) contain inserted lyrics. Even a verse romance like the *Dame a la Lycorne* used decasyllabic as well octosyllabic verse for its narrative, and the *Roman de la Poire* and the *Voir Dit* both vary octosyllabic couplets with nonlyric stanzas.

In some works, heterogenous effects are multiplied by the introduction of variety into the containing narrative itself. The narrative verse of the *Dame a la Lycorne* begins in decasyllabic meter before shifting to octosyllabic couplets. The metric contrast corresponds to the narrative break between an introductory plot sequence and the beginning of the main love story. In both the *Roman de la Poire* and the *Voir Dit* the predominant octosyllabic couplets of the narrative verse are occasionally broken by nonlyric stanzas. Here again, their authors exploited these metrical shifts to enhance structural effects.

Whatever the precise genres involved, the inserted song stands out from its narrative context in meter, register, and temporal reference.[13] We have noted in many places the metrical disruption caused by lyric insertions. Usually the contrast is quite obvious, as in the *lais* set into prose in *Tristan en Prose* and *Perceforest*, or the *chanson* stanzas set into octosyllabic couplets in *Guillaume de Dole*, the *Roman de la Violette*, and *Meliacin*. But even in the rare cases when the quoted songs *are* in the meter of their context, as in the *Chastelaine de Saint Gille* and the *dits* of Jehan de Lescurel, they interrupt the pattern of rhyming couplets. Although for the purposes of the rhyme a *refrain* is usually treated as a single line, most of them actually exceed this length, and many are accompanied by musical notation.

The contrast in register between a lyric insertion and its context may be more or less pronounced, according to the case. Sometimes this contrast is confined to a difference of language and style. In *Guillaume de Dole* and the *Violette*, there are *sons poitevins*, which are written in Occitan in contrast to the Francien of the narrative and the other insertions. Since Occitan was almost an icon for the concept of *fin' amors*, however, these insertions coincide closely in register with the other *chansons* quoted in each romance. Both in these romances and in the *Castelain de Couci*, there is also a functional separation between the lyrics and the narrative, since the songs

---

13. See especially, Dragonetti, *La technique poétique;* pp. 15–139; Zumthor, *Essai*, pp. 225–43, on the linguistic characteristics of the *chanson d'amour*. Similar contrasts are possible even within the *chanson* when one or more *refrains* is incorporated; cf. Zumthor, *Essai*, pp. 246 ff.

largely replace any other discussion of love. This contrast is less marked in works like the *Tristan en Prose* and *Meliacin*, where the narrative sets the scene for each song in terms which are derived from the lyric tradition. The contrast between the two elements is minimized in another way in *Perceforest*, where many of the *lais* restate the narrative in lyric form. Another type of song, like the *refrains* in the *Chastelaine de Saint-Gille*, fits easily into a narrative context that is at least as cynical. Finally, in allegorical *dits* such as the *Amoureuse Prise* and the *Panthere d'Amors*, where the narrative is an elaboration of the themes of the poetry, there is little stylistic contrast between the two sections. But even when the registral contrast between narrative and insertion is minimized, the lyric always exhibits a heightened form of language that is more intense than that of the narrative.

Such contrasts are more acute when the narrative and the lyrics, or different groups of lyrics, belong to different registers. If the *rondets de carole* in *Guillaume de Dole* harmonize well with the ease and gaiety of the imperial court, Conrad's songs of painful, languishing love are pointedly out of place. Although one would expect the aristocratic ideal elaborated by the troubadours and *trouvères* to be appropriate in a court setting, it is the *rondet de carole* rather than the *chanson* that serves as the hallmark of Conrad's courtiers. The court itself, it would seem, has departed from the courtly ideal, and Conrad's attempt to attain it appears old-fashioned and impractical as well as impossible. In the same way, the *refrains* in Baudoin de Condé's *Prison d'Amours*, in the *Roman de la Poire*, and in Jehan de Lescurel's *dits*, stand out strongly from their contexts in style and tone. Such juxtapositions of register have a great impact on the meaning of a work, and will be discussed again in the next section.

Even more disconcerting are the temporal dislocations caused by lyric insertions. Although the song is clearly rooted in the present of the narrative performance, it nonetheless echoes the past. This historic reference is clear in the case of songs borrowed from the existing repertoire, where the poet is obviously using a predecessor's work. We have seen how Jean Renart and Nicole de Margival acknowledged their debt to the past at the same time they took issue with it. The romance *Guillaume de Dole* confronts the pretensions of *fin' amors* with the poses of a would-be *fin' amant*, and the result is a cheerful modification of the aspirations of the *chansons*. If the hero fails to achieve the height of refinement of *fin' amors*, he settles happily for the less difficult love of the *rondet de carole* and the *refrain*. In the *dit* by Nicole, on the other hand, the poet-lover is reduced to paralysis by his fear of rejection. While he emulates the example of "maistre Adam" by loving, suffering, and composing, he is unable to act on the master's advice, and is thus obliged to cast his fate to Fortune. In each work, the poetic inspiration of the past ultimately proves ineffective in its new context. Froissart, in the *Buisson de Jonece*, reversed the chronological *écart* of the two earlier works: while the lyrics derive from the present of the narrative, the love inspiration itself is from his past. But even here, the poet seems to have summoned up his muse only to take leave of her, and at the end of the poem, he turns to other inspirations.

Chronological disruption takes a different form in most of the *dits amoureux*, where the narrator recounts earlier stages of his love affair, but seems to draw his poetic inspiration from his present state. The *rondeaux* and *ballades* in Jehan Acart's *Amoureuse Prise* seem always to anticipate the end, rather than to grow out of the narrative setting. In one of the letters in the *Voir Dit*, the narrator draws attention to the lapse in time between the composition and the quotation of a song. He also mentions that the sentiments that inspired the song had been transformed and replaced by different feelings by the time he sent it to Toutebelle.

In other works, the song's allusion to the past is more restricted, but no less important. We have seen how the *lais* in the *Tristan en Prose* were used to evoke earlier stages of the love affair, while in several of the *dits amoureux* songs were used to mark the stages of the lover's entanglement in a narrative recounting how he came to love. In the *dits amoureux*, however, the authors were not content simply to recall the past; their object was to use it to influence the future. The lover's account of his enslavement to love was meant to move the beloved and bring the affair to a satisfactory conclusion. Consequently, works like the *Panthere d'Amors*, the *Complainte Douteuse*, the *Amoureuse Prise*, and the *Prison d'Amours* end with an apparent lack of closure. The final resolution of the problem they presented lay outside the limits of the narrative. The poet seems to require an answer that was not forthcoming before he could conclude. The absence of closure clearly reflects the lyric influence on the works containing them. The open ending remains true to the lyric quality of these works.[14] Since the lyrics in the *dits* are rooted in the future as well as in the past and the present, the temporal framework of the work becomes particularly dense at the points where insertions occur.

---

14. See Hult, *Self-Fulfilling Prophecies*, pp. 175, 293, and Huot, *From Song to Book*, pp. 86–90, on the "lyric" open-endedness of the *Roman de la Rose*, a model for these *dits*.

Coherence from Disruption: The Poetics of Contrast

The disruptive quality of a lyric insertion is one of its most obvious features. By virtue of the shift from reading to singing, it brings the narrative to a halt and creates the most emphatic kind of "lyric pause." The lyric insertion interrupts the action even more decisively than a passage of psychological analysis, for it needs to be made plausible. A context must be created for it, and this necessity has narrative consequences.

The metrical shift between text and insertion underscores the change in register between the song and its context. In the romances—*Guillaume de Dole, Roman de la Violette, Castelain de Couci, Tristan en Prose, Dame a la Lycorne*—a difference in function is frequently associated with the metrical and registral contrast. While the verse or prose of these narratives sets the scene and recounts the adventures, the emotional resonances of the plot are largely confined to the lyric elements, which tend to replace other forms of psychological analysis. If this is less true in *Meliacin*, it is primarily because Girart d'Amiens created such elaborate contexts for his insertions, setting the psychological as well as the physical stage for the songs. In all of these instances, the basic contrast is between love and adventure, between the *chanson* of *fin' amors* and the episodic account of the narrative, but other effects are possible.

The contrasts of register between *refrains* and courtly *dit* echo the irony used by some of the romance writers. In the *Roman de la Poire*, the inserted *refrains* introduced the register of "la bonne vie" into a narrative derived from the courtly register.[15] Although the author began by evoking the tradition of the *complainte*, the narrator's pose was undercut by the *refrains*, in which the lady clearly acceded to his wishes. Indeed, Tibaut used the *refrains* to spell out an anagram announcing the happiness of the couple.[16] In the *dit* "Amors qui m'a en sa justise" a similar contrast of register between text and *refrain* was arranged differently. Here it is the two sections of the work—the *complainte* and the *confort*—that contrast. Both sections contain *refrains*, but while those of the lover harmonize fairly well with the narrative, the lady's *refrains* clearly belong to the register of the *chanson de mal mariée*. Here again, the lover's pining received a favorable

---

15. Cf. Zumthor, *Essai*, p. 251.
16. The initials of the *refrains* spell out Annes, Tibaut, and Amors; cf. above, Chapter 5, note 26. The game is hinted at by the opening line of the work: "Amors, qui par A se commence."

answer, but one from a different tradition. The juxtaposition of the two registers had an effect similar to that in *Guillaume de Dole*: the posture of the *fin' amant* was shown to be exaggerated, or perhaps misplaced, for the lady was not an inaccessible *domna*. Jehan de Lescurel's *dit*, "Gracieus temps est," provided a variation on this contrast. While the stanzas of the lover's *complainte* protested loyal love, the *refrains* suggested the less than elevated nature of his love, and the lady's final response exposed the poet's declarations for the deceitful propositions that they really were. *Refrains* were used to represent the same type of love in the *Lai d'Aristote*, and also in the *Blanc Chevalier*. In the former, there was no attempt to hide the blatant seduction, but in the latter, the knight pulled away the mask of courtliness by using a genre (the *refrain*) that opposed it.

In all of these works, it is clear that the presence of the lyrics has greatly altered the meaning of the narrative. In some cases, the two strands are in harmony and serve to reinforce each other. But rather more often the relationship of lyric and narrative is more complex, and each element brings the other into question. In this context, Bakhtin's principle of dialogism appears particularly illuminating.[17] The lyric insertions belong to a different register and constitute an image of language different from that of the narrative. The writers of romances and *dits* articulated the relationship between the two "languages," as we have seen, in most of the possible ways.

Eugène Vinaver, in discussing the *Chanson de Roland*, observed a paradox similar to the one that confronts us here: "La discontinuité tout en s'opposant au principe de la cohérence, n'exclut pas, ici la cohésion: elle semble même l'appeler, soucieuse de s'imposer une contrainte indispensable."[18] Likewise, however marked a disruption the lyric insertions cause, they nevertheless form part of a greater whole. If they alter the meaning of a work, they also help to create that meaning. Songs inserted into a narrative not only contrast stylistically with it, but enlarge the frame of reference of the narrative. They add a series of implications that are distinct from, if not in conflict with, the meaning of the narrative.

These various genres and techniques attest to a taste for what Curtius called "play and variegated color."[19] Paul Zumthor, in a more positive vein, considered the "jeu de contrastes" one of the constants of medieval poetics,[20] and one firmly established by the first quarter of the thirteenth

---

17. Cf. above, Chapter 1, under "The Song in the Story."
18. E. Vinaver, *A la recherche d'une poétique médiévale* (Paris: Nizet, 1970), p. 54.
19. Curtius, *European Literature*, p. 152.
20. Zumthor, *Langue et technique*, p. 177.

century. We have seen the developments and variations of these contrasts in the works surveyed here and have noted increased formal experimentation in the course of the fourteenth century. The evolution of the "game of contrasts" can be traced in part to changes in the modes of performance of literary works. In the twelfth century, the literary work was almost always "performed" in a social context: lyric and epic poetry was sung to an audience, while verse romances were read aloud to small groups. Given this context, the insertion of lyrics into narratives bridged the not very great gap between the two modes.[21] Jeannette Beer has analyzed the role of stylistic diversity in engaging the audience's attention.[22] In his prologue to *Guillaume de Dole,* Jean Renart referred explicitly to this advantage of his technique: "Ja nuls n'iert de l'oïr lassez, / car, s'en vieult, l'en i chante et lit" (vv. 18–19; "Never will anyone tire of hearing it, for, if you wish, you can sing and read in it"). Because of the variety of discourse in his romance, his audience, including his many successors in the use of lyric insertions, did not tire of it.

Lest it appear that poetic diversity became an absolute literary value in the thirteenth and fourteenth centuries, it should be stressed that the lyric insertions of most of the works we have discussed actually contribute to the coherence of the works containing them. The lyric insertions in a narrative work, particularly those of the *dits,* often mirror the movement of the framing narrative, despite some chronological tampering.[23]

The Poetics of Allusion

The chief effect of lyric insertions on the incorporating narrative is paradoxically both to disrupt and to unify it. While the inserted songs are often disruptive—adding stylistic traits and ideologies foreign to the narrative world of the characters, or upsetting the chronological sequence of the narrative—they nevertheless contribute to the meaning and thus to the unity of the whole work. When the phenomenon is considered from the point of view of literary history, we see the same two forces at work, for most genres came to be disrupted by the insertion of elements of other

---

21. Faral, *Les Jongleurs,* pp. 234–35, attributes the form of *Guillaume de Dole* and similar works to the influence of the mode of performance on composition.
22. Beer, "Stylistic Heterogeneity."
23. See, for example, *Voir dit, Fontaine amoureuse, Tristan en Prose.*

genres during the course of our period, and these interruptive elements were employed in a similar way to bond together the interrupted text.

As early as the late twelfth century, several lyric genres—the *chanson d'amour,* the *pastourelle,* and the *chanson de toile*—were interrupted, first by repeated refrains, and then by borrowed "*refrains.*"[24] Then the *chanson d'amour* itself was dismembered and quoted in new, usually narrative contexts. In the *Complainte Douteuse,* the different stanzas of a *chanson,* including the *envoi,* interrupted the flow of couplets in the manner of a refrain, so that the whole composition seems to take on a lyric form. From the middle of the thirteenth century, an increasing variety of elements—*dits,* verse letters, prose letters, and verse inscriptions and riddles—broke into the narrative line, while in the fourteenth century, the *Roman de Fauvel* presented forms like the motet *enté,* where the musical line of a single song was interrupted by narrative passages. Froissart's *Prison Amoureuse* may exhibit the greatest variety of insertion: one of its inserted *dits* was interrupted by a *complainte* and a *virelai,* and another by an "*oraison*"; both the narrative verse and the prose letters contained lyric insertions; and its *lai* was interrupted by both verse passages and prose letters.

Despite the fragmented appearance of these works, however, a strong unifying principle seems to underlie them. A *refrain* that interrupts the longer text in which it occurs can also be said to bind together the texts on either side of it. This is true of lyric insertions in other kinds of works, including the narratives I have studied in this book.[25] The lyric insertion device is thus a means of incorporating one text within another, of linking two texts that would otherwise be separate.

It is instructive in this context to consider both the encyclopedic tendency of the prose romances—which attempted to include as many heroes and adventures as possible within their bounds—and Jean de Meun's influential continuation of the *Roman de la Rose.* With these examples before us, the inclusiveness of the authors who used lyric insertions emerges more clearly and is more easily understood. What else did Jean Renart do, if not confront and appropriate most of the lyric genres available to him? In addition to the *rondets* and the *chansons d'amour* that have attracted our attention, he also made use of *chansons de toile, pastourelles, chansons d'histoire,* and even an epic *laisse.* Gerbert de Montreuil used a similar range of genres, once again including an epic *laisse.* Both authors

---

24. See above, Chapter 7, n. 9 for bibliography on the function of refrains.
25. Doss-Quinby, *Les refrains,* p. 241; cf. Boogaard, *Rondeaux et refrains,* p. 17, who pointed out the symbiosis between the *refrains* and other genres.

tried to embrace and surpass the entire range of the literary tradition known to them. Nicole de Margival, always a transitional figure, restricted his quotations to *chansons d'amour* by Adam de la Halle, but composed his own poems in all the new genres known as the *formes fixes*. Here again, old and new in the literary tradition were combined into a single whole. Toward the end of our period, Guillaume de Machaut presented his *Remede de Fortune* as a double art of love and poetry, and included an example of each of the six genres then current, with complete musical accompaniment. Rather than reaching into the past, Machaut embraced the full range of contemporary poetry in this work, but it was no less inclusive than either *Guillaume de Dole* or the *Panthere d'Amors*.

So far we have spoken of a kind of "generic" allusion, whereby the romance and the *dit* try to incorporate other genres within their limits; but there is another kind of unifying tendency operating within the corpus of works containing lyric insertions, and that is textual allusion. The quotation within a narrative work of part or all of a work by another author is an allusion of the most obvious sort. Certainly the authors who quoted from the songs of the troubadours and the *trouvères* were alluding not only to the work in question, but as we have seen, to the whole tradition of which those songs were a part. Thus when Conrad in *Guillaume de Dole* sings a stanza by Gace Brulé, he is not only using borrowed words to express his emotions, but is associating himself with the tradition of the poet-lover. The same is true of Gerart in the *Violette*, Meliacin, and the knight in the *Chastelaine de Vergi*, whose author explicitly compared him to the Châtelain de Couci.

The exact extent of the allusions in our corpus raises interesting questions. It has been assumed that in a work with borrowed insertions, all of the songs were in fact "borrowed" from the repertoire. Although Jean Renart, Nicole de Margival, Jakemés, and the author of the *Chastelaine de Vergi* were the only authors to credit the poets from whom they borrowed, many of the longer lyric insertions have since been attributed by scholars. Some of Jakemés's attributions are definitely wrong, however, and others are dubious. Still other insertions remain anonymous, and when they are unattested elsewhere, it always is possible that the author of the narrative composed his own "insertion." We have already noticed several probable examples of this procedure: in the *Violette* the *chanson de toile* that mentions Euriaut's name seems so apt that it might have been composed by Gerbert de Montreuil. In contrast, the song of the Duke of Galice in *Meliacin*, and the *virelai* sung by the dying Renaut in the *Castelain de Couci* (which have been tentatively ascribed to the writers of the romances) are much less suitable in their contexts than the borrowed songs. It is more difficult to establish the authorship of a *refrain*, but of the forty agreed on by most of the manuscripts of *Renart le Nouvel*, twenty-two are unique to the romance, and Boogaard has suggested that they were composed by Jacquemart.[26] Of the thirty-five *refrains* in the *Chastelaine de Saint Gille*, twenty-one are *unica*, and here too, it seems likely that at least some were composed for the occasion, especially since they cause so little disruption to the narrative line. Given such results and the lack of any clear pattern of borrowing, it appears that the authors were in general more likely to be guided by the genre of the insertion and its general appropriateness for the context, than by a desire to quote particular poets.

There is also a small number of overt allusions to narratives within the the corpus. Tristan is the most popular reference,[27] but not perhaps the most significant, since he became legendary as a lover very early and was certainly seen in that light within the prose romance itself. Another love icon is the Châtelaine de Vergi, referred to in the *Regret Guillaume*, the *Paradis d'Amours*, the *Voir Dit*, and the anonymous *Pastoralet*. A more interesting allusion of this type is Froissart's use of the *Cleomadés* as a pretext to become acquainted with his lady, although he did not comment on its use of *rondeaux*.

The most interesting examples of intertextuality in our corpus are not to be found in direct allusion, however, but in imitation. The *Roman de la Violette* has long been recognized as an allusion to the *Roman de la Rose*, as *Guillaume de Dole* was called by its author. The influence is apparent in the title and in the slander of the heroine, as well as in the way lyric insertions are used. Nevertheless, while the authors of the works in the corpus seem to have been aware of working in a tradition that they were free to modify, only Froissart's dependence on Machaut parallels the closeness of the first two romances.

The real allusions made by lyric insertions are intergeneric. As we have seen, the traditional verse romance used quotations from the twelfth-century courtly poets to embrace that poetic and erotic tradition. In the *Tristan en Prose*, the author or authors turned to another type of lyric poetry to celebrate a different sort of love. Quoting songs by Adam de la Halle

---

26. Boogaard, "Jacquemart Giélée," p. 350.
27. There are allusions in the *Roman de la Poire*, the *Castelain de Couci*, the *Paradis d'Amour*, and the *Prison Amoureuse*. Iseut is mentioned in the *Dame a la Lycorne*, and Palamède in the *Livre Messire Ode*.

similarly allowed Nicole to incorporate the courtly tradition into the allegorical *dit,* and to measure himself against that tradition. This courtly ethos is in turn confronted and opposed by the "popularizing" strain of the dance songs, the *rondets* and the *refrains*, found in the verse romances and the allegorical *Roman de la Poire*. In the fourteenth century the relationship between love, poetry, and narrative changed. No longer was it necessary to quote the twelfth- and thirteenth-century *chanson d'amour* in order to evoke the poet-lover. Instead, the authors of the *dits amoureux* quoted their own poetry in order to establish their credentials as lovers, and made themselves the heroes of their own adventures. Here again, although the elements had changed, the resulting compositions were based on principles of intergeneric allusion.

Appendix 1: List of Narrative Works Containing Lyric Insertions

Renaut, *Galeran de Bretagne*, XIII (first decade): 1 *refrain* (or fragment of a *pastourelle*).

Jean Renart, *Guillaume de Dole*, 1215–28 (after *Galeran*, before *Violette*): stanzas from 16 *chansons*, including 3 in Occitan; from 4 *chansons de toile* (or *chansons d'histoire*); from 2 *chansons dramatiques*; from 2 *pastourelles*; from 1 *chanson d'éloge*; 17 *rondets de carole*; 3 *refrains*; 1 *tournoi de dames*; 1 *laisse* of a *chanson de geste*.

Art d'Amours (translation of Ovid), 1215–40 (Books I and II); 1268–1300 (Book III): 67 *refrains*.

Gerbert de Montreuil, *Roman de la Violette*, 1227–29 (after *Guillaume de Dole*): 25 *refrains*; stanzas from 12 *chansons*; from 1 *chanson de toile*; from 1 *chanson de mal mariée*; 1 *laisse* of a *chanson de geste*.

Henri d'Andeli, *Lai d'Aristote*, c. 1230: 2 *rondets*; stanza from 1 *chanson de toile*.

Guiron le Courtois, c. 1235: 4 *lais*; 7 *lettres en vers* (some mss. have fewer insertions; there is no critical edition).

Tristan en Prose, c. 1240 (extant versions): 15 *lais*; 7 *lettres en forme de lais*.

Thibaut, *Roman de la Poire*, XIII (middle): 19 *refrains*.

Mariage des Sept Arts, XIII: 4 *refrains*; 1 complete *chanson*.

Richart de Fournival, *Bestiaire d'Amours*, XIII (second quarter, before 1260): 1 *refrain* (not included in critical edition).

Richart de Fournival, *Commens d'Amours*, XIII (second quarter, before 1260): 1 *refrain*; stanza from 1 *chanson*.

D'Amors et de Jalousie, XIII (second third): 20 *refrains* (other estimates are 18 and 21).

Robert de Blois, *Castoiement des Dames*, XIII (second third): 1 complete *chanson*.

Baudoin de Condé, *Conte de la Rose*, 1240–80: 1 *refrain*.

Baudoin de Condé, *Prison d'Amours*, 1240–80: 51 *refrains*.

Chastelaine de Saint Gille, c. 1250–70: 35 *refrains*.

Confrere d'Amours, XIII (second half): 12 *refrains*.

"Amors qui m'a en sa justise," XIII (second half): 40 *refrains*.

"Celui qu'Amours conduit et maine," XIII (second half): 10 *rondeaux*; 4 *refrains*.

Complainte Douteuse, XIII (second half): 2 complete *chansons* (the first inserted stanza by stanza in the *complainte*).

Flours d'Amours, XIII (middle; before 1285): 2 *refrains*.

Chastelaine de Vergi, 1250–88: stanza from 1 *chanson*.

La Court de Paradis, XIII (second half): 18 *refrains*.

Amiot Nevelon, *Dit d'Amours*, 1270–80: 2 *refrains*.
Continuations of the *Roman des Sept Sages*:
 Laurin, 1250–70: 3 *rondeaux*.
 Cassidorus, ca. 1270: 1 *débat*.
 Peliarmenus, XIII (second third, before 1292): 1 *refrain*; 1 *rondeau*.
 Kanor, 1278–92: 1 *refrain*; 2 *rondeaux*.
Girart d'Amiens, *Escanor*, c. 1281 (1277–82): 2 *refrains*.
Adenet le Roi, *Cleomadés*, before 1285: 7 *rondeaux*.
Jacques Bretel, *Tournoi de Chauvenci*, 1285: 35 *refrains*.
Ludus Anti-Claudien before 1286: 2 *rondeaux*.
Jacquemart Gielée, *Renart le Nouvel*, c. 1289: (as edited) 65 *refrains*, including 3 three repeats; 2 liturgical pieces in Latin.
Girart d'Amiens, *Meliacin*, c. 1290: 2 *rondeaux*; 1 *refrain*; 7 motets; stanzas from 13 *chansons*; 1 complete *chanson*.
Mahieu le Poirier, *Court d'Amours* (Suite), 1275–1322: 33 *refrains*.
Mahieu le Poirier, *Ju de le Capete Martinet*, 1275–1322: 1 *refrain*.
Branque, *Sone de Nansay*, XIII (end): 2 *rondets*; 1 *lai*.
Jakemés, *Roman du Castelain de Couci et de la Dame de Fayel*, c. 1300: 3 *rondeaux*; 6 complete *chansons*; 1 *virelai*.
Nicole de Margival, *Dit de la Panthere d'Amors*, 1290–1328: 2 complete *chansons*; stanzas from 7 other *chansons*; 3 *rondeaux*; 4 *refrains*.
Abeïe dou chastel amoureus, XIII/XIV: 15 *refrains*.
Jehan de Lescurel, "Gracieus temps est," XIV (early): 28 *refrains*.
Jehan de Lescurel, "Gracieuse faitisse et sage," XIV (early): 24 *refrains*.
Chaillou de Pestain, *Roman de Fauvel* (interpolated version), 1316: in French: 3 complete *ballades*; stanzas from 2 other *ballades*; 2 *virelais*; a *dit* with 13 *refrains*; 1 *complainte*; 1 motet *enté*; 1 *refrain*. In Latin: 4 versets; 3 prosas; 2 motets; 1 *rondeau*. Many pieces in both French and Latin in the margins of the manuscript.
Watriquet de Couvin, *Trois Dames de Paris*, 1320: 2 *refrains*.
Jean le Court, dit Brisebare, *Restor du Paon*, XIV (first quarter): 1 *rondeau*.
Jehan Acart, *Amoureuse Prise*, 1322: 9 *ballades*; 9 *rondeaux*.
Jean de Condé, *Le Dit du Blanc Chevalier*, 1300–1345: 1 *refrain*.
Roman de Perceforest, 1330–44: 12 *lais*; 4 *ballades*.
Roman de la Dame a la Lycorne et du Biau Chevalier au Lyon, XIV (middle): 7 *rondeaux*; 15 *ballades*; 1 *ballette*; 1 *chanson*; 1 *complainte*.
Jehan de le Mote, *Li Regret Guillaume*, c. 1339: 30 *ballades*.
Jehan de le Mote, *Parfait du Paon*, 1340: 8 *ballades*.
Guillaume de Machaut, *Remede de Fortune*, 1342–57: 7 complete songs: *lai*, *complainte*, *rondeau*, 2 *ballades*, *virelai*, *chanson roial*.
Guillaume de Deguilleville, *Pelerinage de l'ame*, 1355: 4 *chansons*; 1 *complainte*, all in the same meter as the narrative.
Guillaume de Machaut, *Fonteinne Amoureuse*, 1360–62: 1 *complainte*; 1 *confort*; 1 *rondel*.
La Cour de Mai, 1361: 1 *rondel*.
Jean Froissart, *Paradis d'Amours*, 1362: 1 *complainte*; 2 *rondels*; 1 *lai*; 1 *virelai*; 1 *ballade*.

Jean Froissart, *Joli Mois de May*, c. 1363: 2 *ballades*; 1 *virelai*.
Guillaume de Machaut, *Le Livre dou Voir Dit*, 1363–65: 30 *rondels*; 19 *ballades*; 9 *chansons balladées*; 3 *complaintes*; 1 *lai*; 1 *lettre en vers*; 1 *chanson*; 1 *refrain*.
Jean Froissart, *Espinette Amoureuse*, c. 1370: 5 *ballades*; 3 *virelais*; 3 *rondeaux*; 1 *complainte*; 1 *confort*; 1 *lai*.
Jean Froissart, *Prison Amoureuse*, late 1372–early 1373: 8 *virelais*; 6 *ballades*; 1 *lai*; 1 *complainte*.
Jean Froissart, *Joli Buisson de Jonece*, 1373: 12 *virelais*; 3 *rondeaux*; 2 *lais*; 2 *ballades*; 8 *souhaits*.
Oton de Grandson, *Livre Messire Ode*, 1350–97: 6 *chansons* (*rondeaux*); 9 *ballades*; 3 *complaintes*. A series of lyrics is added at the end: 4 *rondeaux*; 6 *ballades*; 3 *complaintes*.
Débat du Clerc et de la Demoiselle, XIV (end; after 1370): 2 *refrains*.
Jean Froissart, *Meliador* (revised version with lyrics), 1382–83: 11 *ballades*; 16 *virelais*; 52 *rondels*, all by Wenceslas of Bohemia.
Tresor Amoureux, c. 1396: 128 *ballades*, 36 of which incorporate *rondeaux*.
Ysaÿe le Triste, XIV (second half): 18 *rondeaux*; 7 *lais*.
Christine de Pizan, *Dit de la Rose*, 1402: 2 *ballades*; 1 *rondeau*.
Christine de Pizan, *Dit de la Pastoure*, 1403: 2 *refrains*; 3 *bergeriettes*; 4 *ballades*; 1 *rondeau*.
Christine de Pizan, *Livre du Duc des Vrais Amants*, 1403–5: 16 *ballades*; 2 *rondels*; 1 *virelai*. A series of lyrics added at the end: 1 *complainte*; 4 *rondels*; 3 *virelais*; 9 *ballades*.
Pastoralet, 1422–25: 5 *rondeaux*, 1 *ballade*, 3 *lais*, 12 motets *marlés* (tercets); 5 sixains and quatrains; 1 *neuvain*, 1 douzain, 1 *vingtain*, 1 *chansonnette*.

Note: In ten of these works (*D'Amors et de Jalousie*, *Abeïe dou Chastel Amoureus*, Amiot Nevelon's *Dit d'Amours*, the *Flours d'Amours*, the *Debat du Clerc et de la Demoiselle*, the *Art d'Amours*, Robert de Blois's *Castoiement des Dames*, Baudouin de Condé's *Conte de la Rose*, Richard de Fournival's *Bestiaire d'Amours*, and Mahieu le Poirier's *Je de la Capete Martinet*) the inserted lyrics (normally only one or two) are employed exclusively to replace proverbs; like proverbs, they are quoted as authorities, and are often used either to open or to close the work. Since this use ignores completely their lyrical and musical qualities, and avoids most of the problems of integrating lyrics into a narrative, I have omitted the works in question from the present study. They are, however, discussed in a chapter of my thesis: "Lyric Insertions in French Narrative Fiction in the Thirteenth and Fourteenth Centuries" (M.Litt. thesis, Oxford University, 1980), pp. 265–85.

Appendix 2: Music in the Manuscripts

There does not appear to be a single work of which every manuscript contains music for all of the lyric insertions. Manuscripts of several works, however, contain at least some music:

Tristan en Prose: Vienna, Ö.N.B., 2524, for seventeen *lais*; Paris, B.N., fr. 776, for the first stanza of three *lais*.
Roman de Fauvel: Paris, B.N., fr. 146, for all insertions and marginal pieces.
"Gracieuse faitisse et sage" and "Gracieus temps est": Paris, B.N., fr.146, for all the *refrains*.
Restor du Paon: Oxford, Bodleian Libr., Bodl. 264, music for the *rondeau*; Paris, B.N., fr. 12565, space left for music.
Court de Paradis: Paris, B.N., fr. 25532, music for all refrains.
Renart le Nouvel: Paris, B.N., fr. 372, fr. 1593, and fr. 15566 have music for all the *refrains*, but do not always agree.
Roman de la Poire: Paris, B.N., fr. 24431, for three *refrains*.
Prison d'Amours: Vienna, Ö.N.B., 2621, staves for all the *refrains*, music for three of them.
Voir Dit: Only eight of the pieces were set to music.
Remede de Fortune: Paris, B.N., fr. 25524, for all insertions.

There are in addition manuscripts of several other works in which there are blank staves or spaces left for music:

Dame a la Lycorne: Paris, B.N. fr. 12562.
Court d'Amours: Paris, B.N., n. a. fr. 1731.
Cleomadés: Paris, B.N., fr. 24404, 24405, 24430.
Laurin: Paris, B.N., fr. 17000.
Cassidorus: Paris, B.N., fr. 22549; London, B.L., Harley 4903.
Peliarmenus, Paris, B.N., fr. 22550; London, B.L., Harley 4903.
Kanor: Paris, B.N., fr. 22550; London, B.L., Harley 4903.
Amoureuse Prise: Paris, B.N., fr. 24432; fr. 24391, each lyric is preceded by a rubric "Balade" or "Rondel."
Meliacin: Paris, B.N., fr. 1589, fr. 1633.
Escanor: Paris, B.N., fr. 24374.
Commens d'Amours: Dijon, Bibl. mun., 526.

Roman de la Poire: Paris, B.N., fr. 2186, six blank staves, space left for the others.
Renart le Nouvel: Paris, B.N., fr. 1581.

In the manuscripts of five further works, the lyrics are distinguished in some way from the text, although there is no music, nor any space left for it:

Art d'Amours (translation of Ovid): Paris, Arsenal 2741, "Chancon" is written in the margin.
Roman de la Violette: Paris, B.N., fr. 1374, the lyric insertions are written in red.
Li Regret Guillaume: Paris, B.N., n.a.fr. 7415, the insertions are preceded by the rubrics "cancon" or "balade."
Restor du Paon: Paris, B.N., fr. 1554, words of the *rondeau* are underlined in red.
Remede de Fortune, Voir Dit: Paris, B.N., fr. 22545, the songs are labeled in the rubrics.

This survey is by no means complete, but it is nonetheless suggestive. From the evidence of the manuscripts I have examined, it would seem almost certain that the lyric insertions were intended to be sung in those works where they were set to music, or where there are spaces clearly intended for music.

Bibliography

Texts

Abeïe dou chastel amoureus. Unpublished manuscript. Angers, Bibliothèque municipale, Ms. 403.
Acart, Jehan. *L'Amoureuse Prise*. Ed. Ernst Hoepffner. *La Prise Amoureuse von Jehan Acart de Hesdin, allegorische Dichtung aus dem XIV. Jahrhundert*. Gesellschaft für romanische Literatur, 22. Dresden, Halle a. S.: Niemeyer, 1910.
Adenet le Roi. *Cleomadés*. Ed. Albert Henry. *Les oeuvres d'Adenet le Roi*, V *Cleomadés*. 2 vols. Travaux de la Faculté de Philosophie et Lettres, 26. Brussels: Ed. de l'Univiversité de Bruxelles, 1971.
"Amors qui m'a en sa justise." Ed. Oscar Schultz-Gora. In "Ein ungedruckter *Salu d'Amors* nebst Antwort," *ZRP*, 24 (1900): 358–69.
L'Art d'Amours: Traduction et commentaire de l' "Ars amatoria" d'Ovide. Edition critique. Ed. Bruno Roy. Leiden: Brill, 1974.
Aucassin et Nicolette. Chantefable du XIIIe siècle. Ed. Mario Roques. 2nd edition. CFMA, 41. Paris: Champion, 1967.
Baudoin de Condé. "Li Prisons d'amours que Bauduins de Condé fist." Ed. Auguste Scheler. In *Dits et Contes de Baudoin de Condé et de son fils Jean de Condé: Publiés d'après les mss. de Bruxelles, Turin, Rome, Paris et Vienne, et accompagnés de variantes et de notes explicatives*. 3 vols. Brussels: DeVaux, 1866–67. I (1866), pp. 267–377.
Branque. *Sone de Nansay*. Ed. Moritz Goldschmidt. *Sone von Nausay*. Bibliothek des Literarischen Vereins in Stuttgart, 216. Tübingen: Laupp, 1899.
Bretel, Jacques. *Le Tournoi de Chauvency: édition complète*. Ed. Maurice Delbouille. Paris: E. Droz & Liège: Vaillant-Carmanne, 1932.
Roman de Cassidorus. Ed. Joseph Palermo. 2 vols. SATF. Paris: Picard, 1963–64.
"Celui qu'Amors conduit et maine." Ed. Paul Meyer. In "Le Salut d'amour dans les littératures provençale et française," *Bibliothèque de l'Ecole des Chartes* sér. VI, 3 (1867): 154–62.
Chaillou de Pestain. *Roman de Fauvel* (interpolated version). Pub. Pierre Aubry, *Le Roman de Fauvel, Reproduction photographique du ms. fr. 146 de la Bibliothèque Nationale de Paris avec un index des interpolations lyriques*. Paris: Geuthner, 1907.
———. *Roman de Fauvel in the Edition of Mesire Chaillou de Pesstain: A Reproduction in Facsimile of the Complete Manuscript, Paris, Bibliothèque Nationale, Fonds Français 146*. Ed. Edward Roesner, François Avril, and Nancy Freeman Regalado. New York: Broude Bros., 1990.

Chastelain de Couci. *Chansons attribuées au Chastelain de Couci (fin du XIIe–début du XIIIe siècle)*. Ed. Alain Lerond. Paris: Presses Universitaires de France, 1964.
La Chastelaine de Saint Gille. Ed. Oscar Schultz-Gora. *Zwei altfranzösische Dichtungen: La Chastelaine de Saint Gille. Du Chevalier au Barisel*. 4th ed. Halle: Niemeyer, 1899.
La Chastelaine de Vergi. Poème du XIIIe siècle. Ed. Gaston Raynaud. 3e éd. revue et corrigée par Lucien Foulet. CFMA. Paris: Champion, 1921.
La Châtelaine de Vergi. Ed. Frederick Whitehead. Manchester: Manchester University Press, 1944; 2nd ed., 1951.
La Chastelaine de Vergi. Edition critique du ms. B.N. f. fr. 375 avec Introduction, Notes, Glossaire et Index, suivie de l'édition diplomatique de tous les manuscrits connus du XIIIe et du XIVe siècles. Ed. René Ernst Victor Stuip. The Hague: Mouton, 1970.
Christine de Pizan. *Dit de la Pastoure*. Ed. Maurice Roy. *Oeuvres poétiques de Christine de Pisan*, 3 vols. SATF. Paris: Firmin Didot, 1891–96. II (1891), pp. 223–94.
———. *Dit de la Rose*. Ed. Maurice Roy. *Oeuvres poétiques de Christine de Pisan*, II (1891), pp. 29–48.
———. *Livre du Duc des Vrais Amants*. Ed. Maurice Roy. *Oeuvres poétiques de Christine de Pisan*, III (1896), pp. 59–208.
Complainte Douteuse. Ed. A. Jubinal. *Nouveau recueil de contes, dits, fabliaux et autres pièces inédites des 13e, 14e, et 15e siècles*, 2 vols. Paris: Pannier, 1839–42. II (1842), pp. 242–56.
Li Confrere d'Amours. Ed. Arthur Långfors. In "*Li Confrere d'amours*: poème avec refrains (Bibl. Nat. fr. 837)," *Romania*, 36 (1907): 29–35.
La Cour de Mai. Ed. A. Scheler. *Oeuvres de Froissart: Poésies*. 3 vols. Brussels: DeVaux, 1870–72; repr. Geneva: Slatkine, 1977. III (1872), pp. 1–51.
La Court de Paradis. Ed. E. Vilamo-Pentti. Annales Academiae Scientiarum Fennicae, B. 79, 1. Helsinki: Société de Littérature Finnoise, 1953.
Le Romans de la Dame a la Lycorne et du Beau Chevalier au Lyon: Ein Abenteuerroman aus dem ersten Drittel des XIV. Jahrhunderts. Ed. Friedrich Gennrich. Gesellschaft für romanischen Literatur, 18. Dresden, Halle a.S.: Max Niemeyer, 1908.
"D'Amors et de Jalousie." Ed. Edmond Faral. In "D'Amour et de Jalousie. Complainte d'amour du XIIIe siècle," *Romania*, 59 (1933): 333–50.
"La *Flours d'Amours*." Ed. Joseph Morawski. *Romania*, 53 (1927): 187–97.
Froissart, Jean. *Dits et Débats: Introduction, édition, notes, glossaire. Avec en appendice quelques poèmes de Guillaume de Machaut*. Ed. Anthime Fourrier. TLF, 274. Geneva: Droz, 1979.
———. *Espinette amoureuse: Edition avec introduction, notes et glossaire*. Ed. Anthime Fourrier. Bibliothèque française et romane, 2. Paris: Klincksieck, 1963.
———. *Le joli buisson de jonece: Edition avec introduction, notes et glossaire*. Ed. Anthime Fourrier. TLF, 222. Geneva: Droz, 1975.
———. *Meliador. Meliador par Jean Froissart: Roman comprenant les poésies lyriques de*

Wenceslas de Bohème duc de Luxembourg et de Brabant. Ed. Auguste Longnon. 3 vols. SATF. Paris: Firmin Didot, 1895–99.
———. *Paradis d'Amours*. Ed. Auguste Scheler. *Oeuvres de Froissart: Poésies*. 3 vols. Brussels: DeVaux, 1870–72; repr. Geneva: Slatkine, 1977. I (1870), pp. 1–52.
———. *Le Paradis d'Amour. L'Orloge Amoureus. Edition avec notes, introduction et glossaire*. Ed. Peter F. Dembowski. TLF, 339. Geneva: Droz, 1986.
———. *La Prison amoureuse. Edition avec introduction, notes et glossaire*. Ed. Anthime Fourrier. Bibliothèque française et romane, B: Edition critiques de textes, 13. Paris: Klincksieck, 1974.
———. *Trettié Amourous à la Loenge dou Joli Mois de May*. Ed. Auguste Scheler. *Oeuvres de Froissart: Poésies*. 3 vols. Brussels: DeVaux, 1870–72; repr. Geneva: Slatkine, 1977. II (1871), pp. 194–208.
———. *Trettié Amourous à la Loenge dou Joli Mois de Mai*. Ed. Anthime Fourrier. *Dits et Débats: Introduction, édition, notes, glossaire. Avec en appendice quelques poèmes de Guillaume de Machaut*. TLF, 274. Geneva: Droz, 1979, pp. 129–46.
Geoffroi de Vinsauf, *Poetria Nova*. Trans. Margaret F. Nims, *Poetria Nova of Geoffrey of Vinsauf*. Toronto: Pontifical Institute of Medieval Studies, 1967.
Gerbert de Montreuil. *Le Roman de la violette ou de Gerart de Nevers par Gerbert de Montreuil*. Ed. Douglas Labaree Buffum. SATF. Paris: Champion, 1928.
Gervais du Bus. *Le Roman de Fauvel par Gervais du Bus*. Ed. Arthur Långfors. SATF. Paris: Firmin Didot, 1914–19.
Gielée, Jacquemart. *Renart le nouvel par Jacquemart Gielée*. Ed. Henri Roussel. SATF. Paris: Picard, 1961.
Girart d'Amiens. *Le Cheval de fust* or *Meliacin*. Ed. Paul Aebischer. *Girard d'Amiens: Le Roman du cheval de fust ou de Meliacin: Extraits publiés d'après le texte du ms. dans la Biblioteca Riccardiana de Florence avec une introduction et un glossaire réduit*. TLF, 222. Geneva: Droz, 1974.
———. *Girart d'Amiens, Meliacin, ou le Cheval de fust. Edition critique*. Ed. Antoinette Saly. *Senefiance*, 27. Aix-en-Provence, 1990.
———. *Escanor*. Ed. H. Michelant. *Der Roman von Escanor von Gerard von Amiens*. Bibliothek des Literarischen Vereins in Stuttgart, 178. Tubingen: Laupp, 1886.
Guillaume de Deguileville. *Pèlerinage de l'âme*. Ed. J. J. Stürzinger. Printed for the Roxburghe Club. London: Nichols & Sons, 1895.
Guillaume de Machaut. *La fonteinne amoureuse*. Ed. Ernest Hoepffner, *Oeuvres de Guillaume de Machaut*. 3 vols. SATF. Paris: Firmin Didot, 1908–21. III (1921), pp. 143–244.
———. *Le livre dou 'Voir Dit' de Guillaume de Machaut. Où sont contées les amours de Messire Guillaume de Machaut et de Peronnelle Dame d'Armentieres avec les lettres et les réponses, les ballades, lais et rondeaux dudit Guillaume et de ladite Peronnelle. Publié sur trois manuscrits du XIVe siècle*. Ed. Paulin Paris. Paris: La Société des Bibliophiles François, 1875.
———. *La Louange des Dames*. Ed. Nigel Wilkins. Edinburgh: Clark, 1972.; New York: Barnes and Noble, 1973.
———. *Poésies lyriques*. Ed. Vladimir Chichmaref. 2 vols. Paris: Champion, [1909].

———. *Le Remede de Fortune*. Ed. Ernest Hoepffner, *Oeuvres de Guillaume de Machaut*. 3 vols. SATF. Paris: Firmin Didot, 1908–21. II (1911), pp. 1–157.
Guiron le Courtois. Unpublished manuscripts. London, British Library, Add. MS. 36673. Paris, Bibliothèque Nationale, fr. 338.
Henri d'Andeli. *Le lai d'Aristote de Henri d'Andeli publié d'après tous les mss*. Ed. Maurice Delbouille. Paris: Société d'édition "Les Belles Lettres," 1951.
Jakemés. *Le Roman du Castelain de Couci et de la Dame de Fayel*. Ed. Maurice Delbouille and John E. Matzke. SATF. Paris: Paillart, 1936.
Jean de Condé. *Le dit du Blanc Chevalier*. Ed. Auguste Scheler. *Dits et Contes de Baudoin de Condé et de son fils Jean de Condé*. 3 vols. Brussels: DeVaux, 1866–67. II (1866), pp. 1–48.
Jean le Court, dit Brisebare. *Le restor du paon: édition critique*. Ed. Richard J. Carey. TLF, 119. Geneva: Droz, 1966.
Jehan de le Mote. *Le parfait du paon par Jean de Le Mote: Edition critique*. Ed. Richard. J. Carey. Studies in Romance Languages and Literatures, 119. Chapel Hill, N.C.: University of North Carolina Press, 1972.
———. *Li Regret Guillaume Comte de Hainaut: Poème inédit du XIVe siècle par Jehan de la Mote, pub. d'après le ms. unique de Lord Ashburnham*. Ed. Auguste Scheler. Louvain: Imprimerie de J. Lefever, 1882.
Jehan de l'Escurel. "Gracieuse, faitisse et sage." "Gracieus temps est." Ed. A. de Montaiglon. In *Chansons, ballades et rondeaux de Jehannot de l'Escurel, publié pour la première fois, d'après un manuscript de la Bibliothèque impériale*. Bibliothèque Elzévirienne. Paris: Jannet, 1855, pp. 49–56 and 57–66.
———. "Gracieuse, faitisse et sage." "Gracieus temps est." Ed. Nigel Wilkins. In *Balades, rondeaux et diz entez sus refroiz de rondeaux. The Works of Jehan de l'Escurel. Edited from the ms. Paris, B.N. f. fr. 146*. Corpus Mensurabilis Musicae, 30. Rome: American Institute of Musicology, 1966, pp. 21–27, 28–36.
Roman de Kanor. Unpublished manuscript. London, British Library, Harley Ms. 4903. Ed. in preparation by Meradith McMunn.
Roman de Laurin, fils de Marques le Seneschal. Text of Ms. B.N. f.fr. 22548. Ed. Lewis Thorpe. University of Nottingham Research Publications, 2. Cambridge: Heffer, 1960.
Ludus-Anticlaudien. "'Ludus-Anticlaudien': A Thirteenth Century Translation of the *Ludus Super Anticlaudianum* of Adam de la Bassee by 'A Monk from Cysoin.'" Ed. Paul Henry Rastatter. Ph.D. Diss., University of Oregon, 1966.
Ludus super Anticlaudianum, d'après le manuscrit original conservé à la Bibliothèque municipale de Lille, publié avec une introduction et des notes. Ed. Paul Bayart. Tourcoing: Frères, 1930.
Mahieu le Poirier. *La Court d'Amours, La Suite, Le Ju de le Capete Martinet*. Ed. Terence Scully. *Le Court d'Amours de Mahieu le Poirier et la Suite anonyme de la "Court d'Amours."* Waterloo, Ont., Canada: Wilfrid Laurier University Press, 1976.
———. "*Le Ju de le Capete Martinet*." Ed. Gaston Raynaud. *Romania*, 10 (1881): 521–32.
Le Mariage des Sept Arts (anonymous version). Ed. Arthur Långfors. *Le Mariage des*

sept arts par Jehan le Teinturier d'Arras suivi d'une version anonyme: Poèmes français du XIIIe siècle. CFMA, 31. Paris: Champion, 1923.
Mathieu de Vendôme. *Ars Versificatoria*. Trans. Aubrey E. Galyon. *Matthew of Vendôme. The Art of Versification*. Ames: Iowa State University Press, 1980.
Molinier, G. *Las Flors del gay saber estier dichas las Leys d'Amors*. Ed. A. F. Gatien-Arnoult. *Monuments de la littérature romane*, 4 vols. Toulouse, 1841–43; repr. Geneva: Slatkine, 1977.
Nevelon, Amiot. "Le Dit d'Amour." Ed. Alfred Jeanroy. "Trois Dits d'amour du XIIIe siècle," *Romania*, 22 (1893): 45–70, esp. pp. 54–58.
Nicole de Margival. *Le dit de la Panthère d'amours par Nicole de Margival: Poème du XIIIe siècle*. Ed. Henry A. Todd. SATF. Paris: Firmin Didot, 1883.
Oton de Grandson. *Livre Messire Ode*. Ed. Arthur Piaget. *Oton de Grandson, sa vie et ses poésies*. Mémoires et documents pub. par la Société d'histoire de la Suisse romande, 3e sér., 1. Lausanne: Librairie Payot, 1941, pp. 383–478.
Le Pastoralet. Edité avec introduction notes et glossaire. Ed. Joël Blanchard. Publications de l'Université de Rouen. Paris: Presses Universitaires de France, 1983.
Roman de Pelyarmanus. Unpublished manuscripts. London, British Library, Harley MS. 4903; Paris, Bibliothèque Nationale, fr. 22550.
Le Roman de Perceforest: 1ère Partie. Ed. Jane H. M. Taylor. TLF, 279. Geneva: Droz, 1979. *IIIe Partie*. Ed. Gilles Roussineau. TLF, 365. Geneva: Droz, 1988. *4e Partie*. Ed. Gilles Roussineau. 2 vols. TLF, 343. Geneva: Droz, 1987.
Perceforest. Les Pièces lyriques du roman de Perceforest: édition critique. Ed. Jeanne Lods. Publications romanes et françaises, 36. Geneva: Droz, and Lille: Girard, 1953.
Perceforest. Unpublished manuscript. London, British Library, Royal Ms. 15.E.V.
Perceforest. La Treselegante, delicieuse, melliflue et tresplaisante hystoire du tresnoble victorieux et excellentissime roy Perceforest. Pub. N. Cousteau for Galiot Du Pré. Paris, 1528.
Renaut. *Galeran de Bretagne. Jean Renart (sic): Galeran de Bretagne. Roman du XIIIe siècle*. Ed. Lucien Foulet. CFMA, 37. Paris: Champion, 1925.
Renart, Jean. *Le roman de la rose ou de Guillaume de Dole. Publié d'après le manuscrit du Vatican*. Ed. G. Servois. SATF. Paris: Firmin Didot, 1893.
———. *Le roman de la rose ou de Guillaume de Dole*. Ed. Rita Lejeune-Dehousse. Paris: Droz, 1936.
———. *Jean Renart: Le roman de la rose ou de Guillaume de Dole*. Ed. Félix Lecoy. CFMA, 91. Paris: Champion, 1970.
Tibaut. *Le roman de la poire par Tibaut*. Ed. Christiane Marchello-Nizia. SATF. Paris: Picard, 1984.
———. *Messire Thibaut, Li Romanz de la Poire: Erotisch-allegrisches Gedicht aus dem 13. Jahrhundert*. Ed. Friedrich Stehlich. Halle: Niemeyer, 1881.
Le Tresor Amoureux. Ed. Auguste Scheler, in *Oeuvres de Froissart: Poésies*. 3 vols. Brussels: DeVaux, 1870–72; repr. Geneva: Slatkine, 1977. III (1872), pp. 52–281.
Le Roman de Tristan en prose. Ed. Renée L. Curtis. 3 vols. Arthurian Studies, 12–14. Cambridge: D.S. Brewer, 1985; vol. 1 first publ. Munich: Fink, 1963; vol. 2 first published Leiden: Brill, 1976.

Le Roman de Tristan en prose. Gen. ed. Philippe Ménard. Vol. I. *Des aventures de Lancelot à la fin de la "Folie Tristan."* Ed. Philippe Ménard. TLF, 353. Geneva: Droz, 1987. Vol. II. *Du bannissement de Tristan du royaume de Cornouailles à la fin du tournoi du Château des Pucelles.* Ed. Marie-Luce Chênerie and Thierry Delcourt. TLF, 387, Geneva: Droz, 1990.

Le Roman de Tristan en prose. Le "Roman de Tristan en prose," Les deux captivités de Tristan. Ed. Joël Blanchard. Bibliothèque française et romane, B: Editions critique de textes, 15. Paris: Klincksieck, 1976.

Le Roman de Tristan en prose. Unpublished manuscripts. Paris, Bibliothèque Nationale, fr. 335–36, 757, 24400.

Le Roman de Tristan en prose. Les lais du roman de Tristan en prose d'après le manuscrit Vienne 2542. Ed. Tatiana Fotitch and Ruth Steiner. Münchener romanistische Arbeiten, 38. Munich: Fink, 1974.

Watriquet de Couvin. *Les Trois dames de Paris.* Ed. A. Scheler, in *Dits de Watriquet de Couvin.* Brussels: De Vaux, 1863, pp. 381–90.

Ysaÿe le triste: Roman arthurian du moyen âge tardif. Ed. André Giachetti. Publications de l'Université de Rouen, 142. Rouen: Presse Universitaire de Rouen, 1990.

Studies

Accarie, M. "La fonction des chansons du Guillaume de Dole." In *Mélanges Jean Larmat. Regards sur le Moyen Age et la Renaissance (Histoire, langue, et littérature).* Annales de la Faculté des Lettres et Sciences Humaines de Nice, 39, 1982. Paris: Les Belles Lettres, 1983, pp. 13–29.

Alain de Lille, Gautier de Châtillon, Jakemart Giélée et leur temps. Ed. H. Roussel and F. Suard. Actes du Colloque de Lille (Oct., 1978). Lille: Presse Universitaire de Lille, 1980.

Auerbach, Erich. *Literary Language and Its Public.* Trans. Ralph Manheim. New York: Pantheon Books, 1965.

———. *Mimesis: The Representation of Reality in Western Literature.* Trans. Willard Trask. Princeton: Princeton University Press, 1953, 1968; first published Bern: Francke, 1946.

Badel, Pierre-Yves. "Rhétorique et polémique dans les prologues de romans au moyen âge." *Littérature,* 20 (1975): 81–94.

———. *Le Roman de la Rose au XIVe siècle: Etude de la réception de l'oeuvre.* Publications romanes et françaises, 153. Geneva: Droz: 1980.

Bakhtin, Mikhail. *The Dialogical Imagination: Four Essays by M. M. Bakhtin.* Ed. Michael Holquist. Trans. Caryl Emerson and Michael Holquist. Austin: University of Texas Press, 1981.

———. *Problems of Dostoevsky's Poetics.* Trans. R. W. Rotsel. Ann Arbor, Mich.: Ardis, 1973.

———. *Problems of Dostoevsky's Poetics.* Ed. and trans. Caryl Emerson. Minneapolis: University of Minnesota Press, 1984.

Bartsch, Karl Friedrich. *Romances et Pastourelles françaises des XIIe et XIIIe siècles:*

Altfranzösische Romanzen und Pastourellen. Leipzig: Vogel, 1870; repr. Darmstadt: Wissenschaftliche Buchgesellschaft, 1967.

———. "Zum Roman de la Poire." *ZRP,* 5 (1881): 571–75.

Baumgartner, Emmanuèle. "Les citations lyriques dans le *Roman de la Rose* de Jean Renart." *Romance Philology,* 35 (1981–82): 260–66.

———. *La Harpe et l'épée.* Paris: SEDES, 1990.

———. *Le "Tristan en prose": Essai d'interprétation d'un roman médiéval.* Publications romanes et françaises, 133. Geneva: Droz, 1975.

———. "Sur les pièces lyriques du Tristan en prose." In *Etudes de langue et de littérature du moyen âge offerts à Félix Lecoy.* Paris: Champion, 1973, pp. 19–25.

Beardsmore, Barry. "Les Enfances Auberon dans *Ysaïe le Triste* et leur importance dans la structure du roman." In *Mélanges de langue et littérature françaises du moyenâge offerts à Pierre Jonin. Senefiance,* 7 (1979): 103–13.

Bec, Pierre. *La lyrique française au moyen âge (XIIe–XIIIe siècles). Contribution à une typologie des genres poétiques médiévaux. Etudes et Textes.* 2 vols. Publications du Centre d'Etudes Supérieures de Civilisation Médiévale de l'Université de Poitiers, VI. Paris: Picard, 1977–78.

———. *Les saluts d'amour du troubadour Arnaud de Mareuil. Textes publiés avec une introduction, une traduction et des notes.* Toulouse: Privat, 1961.

———. "Pour un essai de définition du Salut d'amour." *Estudis romanics,* 9 (1961): 191–201.

Becker, Philipp August. "La Dame à la Licorne." *Neuphilologische Mitteilungen,* 31 (1930): 81–85; repr. Amsterdam: Swets & Zeitlinger, 1967.

Beer, Jeanette, M. A. "Stylistic Heterogeneity in the Middle Ages: An Examination of the Evidence in *Li Fet des Romains.*" In *Jean Misrahi Memorial Volume: Studies in Medieval Literature.* Ed. Hans R. Runte, Henri Niedzielski, and William L. Hendrickson. Columbia, S.C.: French Literature Publishing Co., 1977, pp. 100–14.

Bertoni, G. "Le Lettere franco-italane di Faramon e Meliadus." *Giornale storico della letteratura italiana,* 63, no. 1 (1914): 179–88.

Blakey, B. "Aucassin and Nicolette XXIX, 4." *French Studies,* 22 (1968): 97–98.

Blanchard, Joël. *La pastorale en France aux XIVe et XVe siècles: Recherches sur les structures de l'imaginaire médiévale.* Bibliothèque du XVe siècle, 45. Paris: Champion, 1983.

Boland, Margaret Munroe. *Cleomadés: A Study in Architectonic Patterns.* Romance Monographs, 11. Jackson: University of Mississippi Press, 1974.

van den Boogaard, N. H. J. "L'Art d'aimer en prose." In *Etudes de civilisation médiévale (IXe–XIIe siècles): Mélanges offerts à Edmond-René Labande.* Poitiers: CESCM, 1974, pp. 687–98.

———. "Jacquemart Giélée et la lyrique de son temps," In *Alain de Lille, Gautier de Châtillon, Jakemart Giélée et leur temps.* Ed. H. Roussel and F. Suard. Actes du Colloque de Lille (Oct., 1978). Lille: Presse Universitaire de Lille, 1980, pp. 333–53.

———. "Les Insertions en français dans un traité de Gérard de Liège." In *Mélanges de philologie et de littérature offerts à Jeanne Wathelet-Willem.* Liège: Marche Romane, 1978, pp. 679–97.

———. *Rondeaux et refrains du XIIe siècle au début du XIVe. Collationnement, introduction et notes*. Bibliothèque française et romane, D. Initiation, Textes et Documents, 3. Paris: Klincksieck, 1969.

Bossuat, Robert. "Un débat d'amour dans le roman de Cassidorus." In *Etudes romanes dédiées à Mario Roques*. Paris: Droz, 1946, pp. 63–75.

———. "Une prétendue traduction de l'*Anticlaudien* d'Alain de Lille." In *Mélanges de linguistique et de littérature offerts à M. Alfred Jeanroy*. Paris: Droz, 1928, pp. 265–77.

———. *Le Roman de Renard*. Connaissance des Lettres, 49. Paris: Hatier, 1967.

Boulton, D'A. J. D. *The Knights of the Crown: The Monarchical Orders of Knighthood in Later Medieval Europe, 1325–1520*. Woodbridge, Suffolk: Boydell and Brewer, 1987.

Boulton, Maureen. "E. R. Curtius, the Medieval Theory of Styles, and the Rhetorical Innovations of Guillaume de Dole." *Annals of Scholarship*, 4, no. 3 (Spring 1987): 75–85.

———. "Guillaume de Machaut's *Voir Dit:* The Ideology of Form." In *Courtly Literature: Culture and Context*. Selected papers from the Fifth Triennal Congress of the International Courtly Literature Society, Dalfsen, The Netherlands, 9–16 August 1986. Ed. Keith Busby and Eric Kooper. Utrecht Publications in General and Comparative Literature, 25. Amsterdam and Philadelphia: John Benjamins, 1990, pp. 39–47.

Brault, Gerard J. "A Study of the Works of Girart d'Amiens." Ph.D. Diss., University of Pennsylvania, 1958.

———. "Arthurian Heraldry and the Date of Escanor." *Bulletin Bibliographique de la Société Internationale Arthurienne*, 11 (1959): 81–88.

———. "Les manuscrits des oeuvres de Girart d'Amiens." *Romania*, 80 (1959): 433–46.

Brownlee, Kevin. *Poetic Identity in Guillaume de Machaut*. Madison: University of Wisconsin Press, 1984.

———. "The Poetic Oeuvre of Guillaume de Machaut: The Identity of Discourse and the Discourse of Identity." In *Machaut's World: Science and Art in the Fourteenth Century*. Ed. Madeleine Pelner Cosman and Bruce Chandler. New York: Annals of the New York Academy of Sciences, 314, 1978, pp. 219–33.

———. "Transformations of the Lyric 'Je': The Example of Guillaume de Machaut." *Esprit Createur*, 18, no. 1 (1978): 5–18.

de Bruyne, Edgar. *Etudes d'esthétique médiévale*. 3 vols. Bruges: De Tempel, 1946.

Buffum, Douglas L. "The Refrains of the *Cour de Paradis* and of a *Salut d'Amour* (Jubinal, 235)." *Modern Language Notes*, 27 (1912): 5–11.

———. "The Songs of the *Roman de la Violette*." In *Studies in Honor of A. Marshall Elliott*. 2 vols. Baltimore, 1911. I, pp. 129–57.

Calin, William. "Le *Moi* chez Guillaume de Machaut." In *Guillaume de Machaut: Poète et compositeur*. Colloque de Reims, 1978. Actes et Colloques, 23. Paris: Klincksieck, 1982, pp. 241–52.

———. "Machaut as Narrative Poet." In *Machaut's World: Science and Art in the Fourteenth Century*. Ed. Madeleine Pelner Cosman and Bruce Chandler. New York: Annals of the New York Academy of Sciences, 314, 1978, pp. 177–87.

———. *The Poet at the Fountain: Essays on the Narrative Verse of Guillaume de Machaut*. Lexington: University Press of Kentucky, 1974.

Caplan, Harry, "Memoria: Treasure-House of Eloquence." In *Of Eloquence: Studies in Ancient and Medieval Rhetoric*. Ed. with an introduction by Anne King and Helen North. Ithaca: Cornell University Press, 1970, pp. 196–246.

Cartier, Normand R. "Oton de Grandson et sa princesse." *Romania*, 85 (1964): 1–16.

Cerquiglini, Jacqueline. "Le Clerc et l'écriture: le *Voir Dit* de Guillaume de Machaut et la définition du *dit*." In *Literatur in der Gesellschaft des Spätmittelalters*. Ed. Hans Ulrich Gumbrecht. Begleitreihe zum *GRLMA*, 1. Heidelberg: Winter, 1980, pp. 151–68.

———. *"Un Engin si soutil": Guillaume de Machaut et l'écriture au XIVe siècle*. Paris: Champion, 1985.

———. "Ethique de la totalisation et esthétique de la rupture dans le *Voir Dit* de Guillaume de Machaut." In *Guillaume de Machaut: Poète et compositeur*. Colloque de Reims, 1978. Actes et Colloques, 23. Paris: Klincksieck, 1982, pp. 253–62.

———. "Le montage des formes: l'Exemple de Guillaume de Machaut." *Perspectives médiévales*, 3 (1977): 23–26.

———. "Pour une typologie de l'insertion." *Perspectives médiévales*, 3 (1977): 9–14.

Chaytor, H. J. *From Script to Print: An Introduction to Medieval Vernacular Literature*. Cambridge: Cambridge University Press, 1945; repr. Heffer, 1950.

Colby, Alice M. *The Portrait in Twelfth Century French Literature: An Example of the Stylistic Originality of Chrétien de Troyes*. Geneva: Droz, 1965.

Coldwell, Maria Veder. "*Guillaume de Dole* and Medieval Romances with Musical Interpolations." *Musica Disciplina*, 35 (1981): 55–86.

Compagnon, A. *La seconde main ou le travail de la citation*. Paris: Seuil, 1979.

van Coolput, Colette-Anne. *Aventures querant et le sens du monde. Aspects de la réception productive des premiers romans du graal cycliques dans le* Tristan *en prose*. Medievalia Lovaniensia I.XIV. Leuven: Leuven University Press, 1986.

Cremonesi, Carla. "Yvain et le *Roman de la Dame à la Lycorne et du Biau Chevalier au Lyon*." In *Mélanges de langue et de littérature françaises du moyen âge et de la renaissance offerts à M. Charles Foulon*. 2 vols. I, Rennes: Institut de français de l'Université de Haute Bretagne, 1980. II, Liège: Marche romane 30, nos. 3–4, 1980. II, pp. 49–53.

Crosby, Ruth. "Oral Delivery in the Middle Ages." *Speculum*, 11 (1936): 88–110.

Curtis, Renée L. "Les deux versions du *Tristan* en prose: examen de la théorie de Löseth." *Romania*, 84 (1963): 390–98.

———. "Pour une Edition Définitive du *Tristan* en prose." *Cahiers de Civilisation Médiévale*, 24 (1981): 91–99.

———. "The Problems of the Authorship of the *Prose Tristan*." *Romania*, 79 (1958): 314–38.

———. "Tristan *Forsené*: The Episode of the Hero's Madness in the *Prose Tristan*." In *The Changing Face of Arthurian Romance: Essays on Arthurian Prose Romances in Memory of Cedric E. Pickford*. A Tribute by the Members of the British Branch of the International Arthurian Society. Ed. Alison Adams, Armel H. Diverres, Karen Stern, and Kenneth Varty. Arthurian Studies, 16. Cambridge: D.S. Brewer, 1986, pp. 10–22.

———. *Tristan Studies*. Munich: Fink, 1969; repr. Woodbridge, Suffolk: D.S. Brewer, 1986.

———. "Who Wrote the *Prose Tristan*? A New Look at an Old Problem." *Neophilologus*, 67 (1983): 35–41.

Curtius, Ernst Robert. *European Literature and the Latin Middle Ages*. First published Bern, 1948; Engl. trans. Willard R. Trask, New York: Bollingen Foundation, 1953; repr. Harper and Row, 1963.

Dahnk, Emilie. *L'Hérésie de Fauvel*. Leipzig: Vogel, 1935.

Dembowski, Peter F. "La position de Froissart-poète dans l'histoire littéraire: bilan provisoire." *TLL*, 16 (1978): 131–47.

———. *Jean Froissart and His Meliador. Context, Craft, and Sense*. Lexington, Ky.: French Forum, 1983.

Deschaux, Robert. "Le monde arthurien dans 'Meliador.'" In *Mélanges de langue et de littérature françaises du moyen âge et de la renaissance offerts à M. Charles Foulon*. 2 vols. I, Rennes: Institut de français de l'Université de Haute Bretagne, 1980. II, Liège: Marche romane 30, nos. 3–4, 1980. II, pp. 63–67.

Deyermond, Alan. "Lyric Traditions in Non-Lyrical Genres." In *Studies in Honor of Lloyd Kasten*. Ed. Theodore S. Beardsley et al. Hispanic Seminary of Medieval Studies. Madison: University of Wisconsin Press, 1975, pp. 39–52.

Dictionnaire des Lettres Françaises. Le Moyen Age. Ed. Robert Bossuat et al. Paris: Librairie Arthème Fayard, 1964.

Diverres, A. H. "Les aventures galloises dans *Meliador* de Froissart." In *Mélanges de langue et de littérature françaises du moyen âge et de la renaissance offerts à M. Charles Foulon*. 2 vols. I, Rennes: Institut de français de l'Université de Haute Bretagne, 1980. II, Liège: Marche romane 30, nos. 3–4, 1980. II, pp. 73–79.

———. "Jean Froissart's Journey to Scotland." *Forum for Modern Language Studies*, 1 (1965): 54–63.

———. "The Geography of Britain in Froissart's *Meliador*." In *Medieval Miscellany Presented to Eugène Vinaver*. Ed. Frederick Whitehead, A. H. Diverres, and A. E. Sutcliffe. Manchester: University of Manchester Press, 1965; New York: Barnes & Noble, 1965, pp. 97–112.

———. "The Irish Adventures in Froissart's *Meliador*." In *Mélanges de langue et de littérature du moyen âge et de la renaissance offerts à Jean Frappier, Professeur à la Sorbonne*. Geneva: Droz, 1970, pp. 235–51.

———. "Some Thoughts on the *Sens* of *Le Chevalier de la Charrette*." *Forum for Modern Language Studies*, 6 (1970): 24–36.

———. "The Two Versions of Froissart's *Meliador*." In *Studies in Medieval French Language and Literature Presented to Brian Woledge in Honour of His 80th birthday*. Ed. Sally Burch North. Publications romanes et françaises, 180. Geneva: Droz, 1987, pp. 37–48.

Doss-Quinby, Eglal. *Les refrains chez les trouvères du XIIe siècle au début du XIVe*. American University Studies, Series III, Romance Languages & Literature, 17. New York, Bern, Frankfurt-am-Main: Peter Lang, 1984.

Doutrepont, Georges. *La littérature française à la cour des Ducs de Bourgogne, Philippe le Hardi, Jean sans Peur, Philippe le Bon, Charles le Téméraire*. Paris: Champion, 1909.

Dragonetti, Roger. *Le mirage des sources: L'art du faux dans le roman médiéval.* Paris: Seuil, 1987.

———. *La technique poétique des trouvères dans la chanson courtoise: Contribution à l'étude de la rhétorique médiévale.* Bruges: De Tempel, 1960; repr. Geneva: Slatkine, 1979.

Dubs, Ingebord. *Galeran de Bretagne: Die Kriese im französischen höfischen Roman.* Studiorum Romanicorum Turicensis, 3. Bern: Francke, 1949.

Dufournet, Jean, ed. *Nouvelles recherches sur le Tristan en prose: Etudes recueillies.* Paris: Champion, 1990.

Dulac, Liliane. "Christine de Pisan et le malheur des *Vrais Amans.*" In *Mélanges de langue et de littérature médiévales offerts à Pierre Le Gentil par ses collègues, ses élèves, et ses amis.* Paris: SEDES, 1973, pp. 223–33.

Earp, Lawrence M. "Scribal Practice, Manuscript Production and the Transmission of Music in Late Medieval France: The Manuscripts of Guillaume de Machaut." Ph.D. Diss., Princeton University, 1983.

Faral, Edmond. *Les arts poétiques du XIIe et du XIIIe siècle: Recherches et documents sur la technique littéraire du moyen âge.* Bibliothèque de l'Ecole des Hautes Etudes, 238. Paris: Champion, 1924.

———. *Les Jongleurs en France au moyen âge.* Paris: Champion, 1910; repr. 1964.

Ferrante, Joan. "The Conflict of Lyric Conventions and Romance Form." In *In Pursuit of Perfection: Courtly Love in Medieval Literature.* Ed. Joan M. Ferrante, George D. Economou, and Frederick Goldin. Port Washington, N.Y. and London: Kennikat Press, 1975, pp. 135–78.

Flinn, John. *Le Roman de Renart dans la littérature française et dans les littératures étrangères du moyen âge.* Toronto: University of Toronto Press, 1963.

Flutre, F.-L. "Etudes sur le *Roman de Perceforêt.*" *Romania*, 70 (1948–49): 474–522; 71 (1950): 374–92, 482–508; 74 (1953): 44–102; 88 (1967): 475–508; 89 (1968): 355–86; 90 (1969): 341–70; 91 (1970): 189–226.

Foulet, Lucien. "*Galeran* et Jean Renart." *Romania*, 51 (1925): 76–104.

———. "Marie de France et les lais bretons." *ZRP*, 29 (1905): 19–56, 293–322.

———. "Marie de France et la légende de Tristan." *ZRP*, 32 (1908): 161–83, 257–89.

Fourrier, Anthime. "La destinataire de la 'Dame à la Licorne.'" In *Mélanges de langue et de littérature médiévales offerts à Pierre Le Gentil par ses collègues, ses élèves, et ses amis.* Paris: SEDES, 1973, pp. 265–76.

Fowler, Maria Veder. "Musical Interpolations in 13th- and 14th-Century French Narratives." Ph.D. Diss., Yale University, 1979.

Fowler, Roger. *Literature as Social Discourse: The Practice of Linguistic Criticism.* Bloomington: Indiana University Press, 1981.

Frank, Grace. "*Le Roman de la rose ou de Guillaume de Dole,* ll. 1330ff." *Romanic Review*, 29 (1938): 209–11.

Frappier, Jean. *Chrétien de Troyes: L'Homme et l'oeuvre.* Paris: Hatier, 1957.

Freeman, Michelle A. "Froissart's *Le Joli Buisson de Jonece*: A Farewell to Poetry?" In *Machaut's World: Science and Art in the Fourteenth Century.* Ed. Madeleine Pelner Cosman and Bruce Chandler. New York: Annals of the New York Academy of Sciences, 314, 1978, pp. 235–47.

Gallais, Pierre. "Recherches sur la mentalité des romanciers français du moyen âge." *Cahiers de Civilisation Médiévale*, 7 (1964): 479–93.
Gégou, Fabienne. "Jean Renart et la lyrique occitane," In *Mélanges de langue et de littérature médiévales offerts à Pierre Le Gentil par ses collègues, ses élèves, et ses amis*. Paris: SEDES, 1973, pp. 319–23.
Geiselhardt, Jakob. "Machaut und Froissart. Ihre literarische Beziehungen." Inaugural Diss., Universität Jena, 1914.
Gennette, Gérard. "Frontières du récit." In *Figures* II. Paris: Seuil, 1969; repr. Paris: Points, 106, 1979.
———. *Narrative Discourse: An Essay in Method*. Trans. Jane E. Lewin. Ithaca: Cornell University Press, 1980; first published Paris: Seuil, 1972.
Gennrich, Friedrich. *Das altfranzösische Rondeau und Virelai im 12. und 13. Jahrhundert*. Langen bei Frankfurt: Summa Musicae Medii Aevi X, 1963.
———. "Der Gesangswettstreit im 'Parfait du Paon.'" *Romanische Forschungen*, 58–59 (1944–47): 208–32.
———. "Die Musik als Hilfswissenschaft der romanischen Philologie." *ZRP*, 39 (1919): 330–61.
———. *Rondeaux Virelais und Balladen*. 2 vols. Gesellschaft für romanische Literatur, 43, 47. Dresden, Halle a. S.: Niemeyer 1921–27.
Gerold, Théodore. *La musique au moyen âge*. CFMA, 73. Paris: Champion, 1932.
Giachetti, André. "Une nouvelle forme du lai apparue à la fin du XIVe siècle." In *Etudes de langue et de littérature du Moyen Age. Offertes à Félix Lecoy par ses collègues, ses élèves, et ses amis*. Paris: Champion, 1973, pp. 147–55.
———. "Ysaie le Triste et l'Ecosse." *Bulletin Bibliographique de la Société Internationale Arthurienne*, 15 (1963): 109–19.
Green D. H. "Irony and Medieval Romance." *Forum for Modern Language Studies*, 6 (1970): 49–64.
———. *Irony in Medieval Romance*. Cambridge: Cambridge University Press, 1979.
Guiette, Robert. "D'une poésie formelle en France au moyen âge." *Revue des sciences humaines*, n.s. 54 (1949): 61–69; repr. Paris: Nizet, 1972.
Guillaume de Machaut. Poète et compositeur. Colloque de Reims, 1978. Actes et Colloques, 23. Paris: Klincksieck, 1982.
Gybbon-Monypenny, G. B. "Guillaume de Machaut's Erotic 'Autobiography': Precedents for the Form of the *Voir Dit*." In *Studies in Medieval Literature and Language in Memory of Frederick Whitehead*. Ed. W. Rothwell, W. R. J. Barron, David Blamires, and Lewis Thorpe. Manchester: Manchester University Press; New York: Barnes & Noble, 1973, pp. 133–52.
Hamon, Philippe. *Introduction à l'analyse du descriptif*. Paris: Hachette-Classiques, 1981.
———. "Qu'est-ce qu'une description." *Poétique*, 12 (1972): 465–85.
Hardison, O. B., Jr., Alex Preminger, Kevin Kerrane, and Leon Golden, eds. *Medieval Literary Criticism: Translations and Interpretations*. New York: Frederick Ungar, 1974.
Heger, Henrik. *Die Melancholie bei den französischen Lyrikern des Spätmittelalters*.

Romanistische Versuche und Vorarbeiten, 21. Bonn: Universität, romanisches Seminar, 1967.

d'Heur, Jean-Marie, and Michel Zink. "Pastourelle et Courtoisie: Sur un arrêt inédit de 'Le court d'amours' de Mahiu li Poirier." In *Mélanges de philologie et de littérature offerts à Jeanne Wathelet-Willem*. Liège: Marche Romane, 1978, pp. 126–42, 741–52.

Hilka, Alfons. *Die direkte Rede als stilistisches Kunstmittel in den Romanen des Kristians von Troyes*. Halle: Niemeyer, 1903.

Hoepffner, Ernst. "Die balladen des Dichters Jehan de le Mote." *ZRP*, 35 (1911): 153–66.

———. "Les lais de Marie de France dans *Galeran de Bretagne* et *Guillaume de Dole*." *Romania*, 56 (1930): 212–35.

———. "Les poésies lyriques du *Dit de la Panthère* de Nicole de Margival." *Romania*, 46 (1920): 204–30.

———. "Renart ou Renaut?" *Romania*, 62 (1936): 196–231.

———. "Zur 'Prise amoureuse' von Jehan Acart de Hesdin." *ZRP*, 38 (1917): 513–27.

Hoppin, Richard H. *Medieval Music*. Norton Introduction to Music History. New York: Norton, 1978.

Hughes, Dom Anselm, and Gerald Abraham. *Ars Nova and the Renaissance, 1300–1500*. In *The New Oxford History of Music*, vol. III. London: Oxford University Press, 1960.

Hult, David F. *Self-Fulfilling Prophecies: Readership and Authority in the First* Roman de la Rose. Cambridge: Cambridge University Press, 1986.

Hunt, Tony. "Precursors and Progenitors of *Aucassin et Nicolete*." *Studies in Philology*, 74 (1977): 1–19.

Huot, Sylvia. "From *Roman de la Rose* to *Roman de la Poire*: The Ovidian Tradition and the Poetics of Courtly Literature." *Mediaevalia et Humanistica*, 13 (1985): 95–111.

———. *From Song to Book: The Poetics of Writing in Old French Lyric and Lyrical Narrative Poetry*. Ithaca, N.Y.: Cornell University Press, 1987.

Jakobson, Roman. *Essais de linguistique générale*. Trans. Nicolas Ruwet. 2 vols. Paris: Editions de Minuit, 1963–73.

Jammers, Ewald. "Die Rolle der Musik im Rahmen der romanischen Dichtung des XII. und XIII. Jahrhunderts." *GRLMA*, I (1972): 483–537.

Jauss, Hans Robert. "Entstehung und Strukturwandel der allegorischen Dichtung." *GRLMA* VI, part 1 (1968): 146–244.

———. "La transformation de la forme allégorique entre 1180–1240: D'Alain de Lille à Guillaume de Lorris." In *L'humanisme médiéval dans les littératures romanes du XIIe au XIVe siècles*. Colloque organisé par le Centre de Philologie et de Littératures romanes de l'Université de Strasbourg du 29 janvier au 2 février, 1962. Ed. Anthime Fourrier. Actes et Colloques, 3. Paris: Klincksieck, 1964, pp. 107–44.

———. "Littérature médiévale et théorie des genres." *Poétique*, 1 (1970): 79–101.

Jeanroy, Alfred. *Les origines de la poésie lyrique en France au moyen âge: Etudes de littérature française et comparée*. First published, Paris: Hachette, 1889; 2nd ed.

with additions and bibliographical appendix, 1904; 4th ed. Paris: Champion, 1969.

———. "La *Passion Nostre dame* et *Le 'Pèlerinage de l'âme'* de Guillaume de Digulleville." *Romania*, 36 (1907): 361–66.

Johnson, Susan M. "The Role of the Refrain in the Pastourelle *à refrain*." In *Literary and Historical Perspectives of the Middle Ages* (Proceedings of the 1981 SEMA Meeting). Ed. Patricia W. Cummins, Patrick W. Conner, and Charles W. Connell. Morgantown: West Virginia University Press, 1982, pp. 78–82.

Jones, Lowanne E. "Narrative Transformations of the Twelfth Century Troubadour Lyric." In *The Expansion and Transformation of Courtly Literature*. Ed. Nathaniel B. Smith and Joseph Snow. Athens: University of Georgia Press, 1980, pp. 117–27.

Jonin, Pierre. "Le refrain dans les chansons de toile." *Romania*, 96 (1975): 209–44.

Jung, Marc-René. "L'empereur Conrad, chanteur de poésies lyriques." *Romania*, 101 (1980): 35–50.

———. *Etudes sur le poème allégorique en France au moyen âge*. Bern: Francke, 1974.

Kelly, Douglas. *Medieval Imagination: Rhetoric and the Poetry of Courtly Love*. Madison: University of Wisconsin Press, 1978.

Kelly, F. Douglas, *Sens and Conjointure in the Chevalier de la Charette*. The Hague: Mouton, 1966.

Kennedy, E. M. "Royal Broodings and Lovers' Trances in the First Part of the Prose Lancelot." In *Mélanges de philologie et de littérature offerts à Jeanne Wathelet-Willem*. Liège: Marche Romane, 1978, pp. 301–14.

Kibler, William W. "Poet and Patron: Froissart's *Prison amoureuse*." *Esprit Créateur*, 18, no. 1 (1978): 32–46.

———. "Self-Delusion in Froissart's *Espinette Amoureuse*." *Romania*, 97 (1972): 77–98.

Kittredge, G. L. "Chaucer and Froissart (with a Discussion of the Date of the *Meliador*)." *Englische Studien*, 26 (1899): 321–36.

Koenig, Vernon Frederic. "Jean Renart and the Authorship of *Galeran de Bretagne*." *Modern Language Notes*, 49 (1934): 248–55.

Kristeva, Julia. *Semiotikè: Recherches pour une sémanalyse*. Paris: Seuil, 1969; repr. Paris: Seuil, Points, 96, 1978.

Lacy, Norris J. "'Amer par oïr dire.' *Guillaume de Dole* and the Drama of Language." *The French Review*, 54 (1981): 779–87.

Ladd, Anne. "Attitude Toward Lyric in the *Lai d'Aristote* and Some Later Fictional Narratives." *Romania*, 96 (1975): 194–208.

———. "Lyric Insertions in Thirteenth-Century French Narrative." Ph.D. Diss., Yale University, 1977.

Lancner, Lawrence Harf. "La chasse au cerf blanc dans le 'Meliador': Froissart et le mythe d'Acteon." In *Mélanges de langue et de littérature françaises du moyen âge et de la renaissance offerts à M. Charles Foulon*. 2 vols. I Rennes: Institut de français de l'Université de Haute Bretagne, 1980. II Marche romane 30, 3–4, 1980. II, pp. 143–52.

Långfors, Arthur. "Mélanges de poésie lyrique française. VI. Les refrains dans le poème intitulé *D'Amors et de Jalousie*." *Romania*, 60 (1934): 204–17.

Langlois, Ch.-V. *La Vie en France au moyen âge de la fin du XIIe au début du XIVe siècle d'après les romans mondains du temps*. Paris: Hachette, 1924.
Lathuillère, Roger. *Guiron le courtois: Etude de la tradition manuscrite et analyse critique*. Publications romanes et françaises, 86. Paris: Droz, 1966.
Lavis, Georges. *L'expression de l'affectivité dans la poésie lyrique française du moyen âge (XIIe–XIIIe siècles): Etude sémantique et stylistique du réseau lexical joie-dolor*. Paris: Belles Lettres, 1972.
Lecoy, Félix. "Sur quelques passages difficiles du *Guillaume de Dole*." Romania, 82 (1961): 244–60.
———. "Sur la date du *Guillaume de Dole*." Romania, 82 (1961): 379–402.
Le Gentil, Pierre. "A propos de 'Guillaume de Dole.'" In *Mélanges de linguistique romane et de philologie médiévale offerts à M. Maurice Delbouille*. Gembloux: Duculot, 1964, pp. 381–97.
———. "Christine de Pisan, poète méconnu." In *Mélanges d'histoire littéraire offerts à Daniel Mornet*. Paris: Nizet, 1959, pp. 1–10.
Lejeune, Rita. "A propos de la structure du *Roman de la Rose* de Guillaume de Lorris." In *Etudes de langue et de littérature du moyen âge offerts à Félix Lecoy*. Paris: Champion, 1973, pp. 315–48.
———. "Le roman de *Guillaume de Dole* et la principauté de Liège." *Cahiers de Civilisation Médiévale*, 17 (1974): 1–24.
———. *L'oeuvre de Jean Renart: Contribution à l'étude du genre romanesque au moyen âge*. Paris: Droz; Liège: Faculté de Philosophie et de Lettres, 1935.
Lods, Jeanne. "Les parties lyriques du *Tristan en prose.*' *Bulletin Bibliographique de la Société Internationale Arthurienne*, 7 (1955): 73–78.
———. "Les poésies de Wenceslas et le *Meliador* de Froissart." In *Mélanges de langue et de littérature françaises du moyen âge et de la renaissance offerts à M. Charles Foulon*. 2 vols. I Rennes: Institut de français de l'Université de Haute Bretagne, 1980. II Marche romane 30, nos. 3–4, 1980. I, pp. 205–16.
———. *Le Roman de Perceforest: origines, composition, caractères, valeur et influence*. Geneva: Droz, 1951.
Löseth, E. *Le roman en prose de Tristan, le roman de Palamède et la compilation de Rusticien de Pise: Analyse critique d'après les mss. de Paris*. Bibliothèque de l'Ecole des hautes études, 82. Paris: E. Bouillon, 1890–91; repr. New York: Burt Franklin, 1970.
Lorenz, Emil. *Die altfranzösische Versnovelle von der Kastellanin von Vergi in spätern Bearbeitungen*. Halle: Kaemmerer, 1909.
Ludwig, Friedrich. "La Musique des intermèdes lyriques dans le *Remede de Fortune*." In *Oeuvres de Guillaume de Machaut*. Ed. E. Hoepffner. 3 vols. SATF. Paris: Firmin Didot, 1908–21. II (1911), pp. 405–14, plus twenty-seven pages of transcriptions and facsimiles.
———. "Die Quellen der Motetten 'ältesten Stils.'" *Archiv für Musikwissenschaft*, 5 (1923; repr. 1964): 185–222.
Lyons, Faith. *Les éléments descriptifs dans le roman d'aventure au 13e siècle (en particulier Amadas et Ydoine, Giligalois, Galeran, l'Escoufle, Guillaume de Dole, Jehan et Blonde, Le Castelain de Couci)*. Geneva: Droz, 1965.
———. "The Literary Originality of *Galeran de Bretagne*." In *Medieval Miscellany*

presented to Eugène Vinaver. Ed. Frederick Whitehead, A. H. Diverres, and A. E. Sutcliffe. Manchester: University of Manchester Press, 1965; New York: Barnes & Noble, 1965, pp. 206–19.

Machabey, Armand. *Guillaume de Machaut 130?–1377: La vie et l'oeuvre musicale.* 2 vols. Paris: Richard Masse, 1955.

Machaut's World: Science and Art in the Fourteenth Century. Ed. Madeleine Pelner Cosman and Bruce Chandler. New York: Annals of the New York Academy of Sciences, 314, 1978.

Maillard, Jean. "A vous Tristan." In *Mélanges de philologie et de littérature offerts à Jeanne Wathelet-Willem.* Liège: Marche Romane, 1978, pp. 395–402.

———. "Coutumes musicales au moyen âge d'après le *Tristan* en prose." *Cahiers de Civilisation Médiévale,* 2 (1959): 341–53.

———. *Evolution et esthétique du lai lyrique des origines à la fin du XIVe siècle.* Paris: Université de Paris, 1963.

———. "Folie n'est pas vasselage." In *Mélanges de littérature du moyen âge au XXe siècle offerts à Mlle. Jeanne Lods.* 2 vols. Collection de l'Ecole Normale Supérieure de Jeunes Filles, No. 10, Paris: Ecole Normale Supérieure de Jeunes Filles, 1978. I, pp. 414–32.

———. "Le lai lyrique et les légendes arthuriennes." *Bulletin Bibliographique de la Société International Arthurienne,* 9 (1957): 124–27.

———. "Lais avec notation dans le *Tristan* en prose." In *Mélanges offerts à Rita Lejeune, Professeur à l'Université de Liège.* 2 vols. Gembloux: J. Duclot, 1969, II, pp. 1347–64.

———. "Les refrains de caroles dans Renart le Nouvel." In *Alain de Lille, Gautier de Châtillon, Jakemart Giélée et leur temps.* Ed. H. Roussel and F. Suard. Actes du Colloque de Lille (Oct., 1978). Lille: Presse Universitaire de Lille, 1980, pp. 277–93.

Maraud, André. "Le lai de *Lanval* et la *Chastelaine de Vergi*: la structure narrative." *Romania,* 93 (1972): 433–59.

Marchello-Nizia, Christiane. "A la charnière du type I et du type II: *Le Roman du Châtelain de Coucy et de la Dame de Fayel.*" *Perspectives médiévales,* 3 (1977): 22–23.

Martin, Wallace. *Recent Theories of Narrative.* Ithaca: Cornell University Press, 1986.

Mattioli, Carmela. "Sulla datazione del *Guillaume de Dole.*" *Cultura Neolatina,* 25 (1965): 91–112.

McLeod, Enid. *The Order of the Rose: The Life and Ideas of Christine de Pizan.* London, 1976; Totowa, N. J.: Rowman & Littlefield, 1976.

Mélanges de langue et de littérature françaises du moyen âge et de la renaissance offerts à M. Charles Foulon. 2 vols. I, Rennes: Institut de français de l'Université de Haute Bretagne, 1980. II, Liège: Marche romane 30, nos. 3–4, 1980.

Mélanges de langue et de littérature médiévales offerts à Pierre Le Gentil par ses collègues, ses élèves, et ses amis. Paris: SEDES, 1973.

Mélanges de philologie et de littérature offerts à Jeanne Wathelet-Willem. Liège: Marche Romane, 1978.

Ménard, Philippe. "La composition d'Aucassin et Nicolette." In *Mélanges de phi-*

lologie et de littérature offerts à Jeanne Wathelet-Willem. Liège: Marche Romane, 1978, pp. 413–32.
Meyer, Herman. *The Poetics of Quotation in the European Novel*. Trans. Theodore and Yetta Ziolkowski. Princeton, N.J.: Princeton University Press, 1968.
Meyer, Paul. "Le Salut d'amour dans les littératures provençale et française." *Bibliothèque de l'Ecole des Chartes*, sér. VI, 3 (1867): 125–70.
Micha, Alexandre. "Meliador." In *Dictionnaire des Lettres Françaises. Le Moyen Age*. Ed. Robert Bossuat et al. Paris: Librairie Arthème Fayard, 1964, p. 506.
Morawski, Joseph. "Fragments de poèmes et refrains inédits." *Romania*, 56 (1930): 253–64.
Murphy, James J. *Rhetoric in the Middle Ages: A History of Rhetorical Theory from Saint Augustine to the Renaissance*. Berkeley: University of California Press, 1974, 1981.
Murrell, E. S. "The Death of Tristan from Douce Ms. 189." *PMLA*, 43 (1928): 343–83.
Muscatine, Charles. *Chaucer and the French Tradition*. Berkeley: University of California Press, 1957; repr. 1966.
Nolting-Hauff, Ilse. *Die Stellung der Liebeskasuistik im höfischen Roman*. Heidelberg: Winter, 1959.
Noreiko, Stephen. "Le *Chevalier de la charette*: Prise de conscience d'un *fin' amant*." *Romania*, 94 (1973): 473–83.
Normand, K. G. D. "A Study of the Old French Romance of *Sone de Nansay*." Ph.D. Diss., University of Pennsylvania, 1975.
Nuss, Karl. "Über die Echtheit des 'Cour de May' und des 'Tresor Amoureux' im III. Band der 'Poésies de Froissart ausg. Aug. Scheler.'" Inaugural Diss., Universität Jena, 1914.
Nykrog, Per. *Les Fabliaux: Etude d'histoire littéraire et de stylistique médiévale*. Copenhagen: Ejnar Munksgaard, 1957.
Omont, Henri. *Fabliaux, dits et contes en vers français du XIIIe siècle. Facsimile du manuscrit 837*. Paris: E. Leroux, 1932.
van Os, J. A. "Structures mélodiques et rythme déclamatoire dans la chanson de trouvère." In *Langue et littérature françaises du moyen âge*. Ed. R. E. V. Stuip. Assen, Amsterdam: Van Gorcum, 1978, pp. 51–62.
Paden, William D. "Old Occitan as a Lyric Language: The Insertions from Occitan in Three Thirteenth-Century French Romances." *Speculum*, 68 (1993). Forthcoming.
Page, Christopher. *Voices and Instruments of the Middle Ages: Instrumental Practice and Songs in France, 1100–1300*. Berkeley: University of California Press, 1986.
Paris, Gaston. "Chrétien Legouais et autres traducteurs ou imitateurs d'Ovide." *HLF*, 29 (1885): 455–525.
———. "Corrections sur *Sone de Nansai*." *Romania*, 31 (1902): 113–32.
———. "Girard d'Amiens." *HLF*, 31 (1893): 151–205.
———. "Le conte de la rose en vers et en prose dans le roman de *Perceforest*." *Romania*, 23 (1894): 78–104.
———. "Le cycle de la gageure." *Romania*, 32 (1903): 480–511.

———. "Les Chansons." In *Le roman de la rose ou de Guillaume de Dole*. Ed. G. Servois. SATF. Paris: Firmin Didot, 1893, pp. lxxxix–cxxi.

Payen, Jean-Charles. "Structure et sens de la 'Châtelaine de Vergi.'" *Le moyen âge*, 79 (1973): 209–30.

———. "Structure et sens de *Guillaume de Dole*." In *Etudes de langue et de littérature du moyen âge offertes à Félix Lecoy*. Paris: Champion, 1973, pp. 483–98.

Piaget, Arthur. "Notice sur le manuscrit 1727 du fonds français de la Bibliothèque Nationale." *Romania*, 23 (1894): 192–208.

———. *Oton de Grandson, sa vie et ses poésies*. Mémoires et Documents publiés par la Société d'histoire de la Suisse Romande, 3e sér., I. Lausanne: Librairie Payot, 1941.

———. "Oton de Grandson et ses poésies." *Romania*, 19 (1890): 237–59, 403–48.

Planche, Alice. "Les plus beaux, le plust fort, la plus belle. Les extrêmes du rêve courtois dans le *Roman de la dame à la licorne et du beau Chevalier au lion* (composé vers 1350)." In *Courtly Romance: A Collection of Essays*. Ed. Guy R. Mermier and Edelgard E. DuBruck. Michigan Consortium for Medieval and Early Modern Studies: Medieval and Renaissance Monograph Series, VI (1984), pp. 177–202.

———. "Sur deux dits de Jean Froissart: L'impossible mariage de lyrique et de roman." *Perspectives médiévales*, 3 (1977): 27–35.

Plasson, A. M. "L'obsession du reflet dans *Galeran de Bretagne*." In *Mélanges de langue et de littérature médiévales offerts à Pierre Le Gentil par ses collègues, ses élèves, et ses amis*. Paris: SEDES, 1973, pp. 673–89.

Poirion, Daniel. *Le poète et le prince: L'évolution du lyrisme courtois de Guillaume de Machaut à Charles d'Orléans*. Grenoble: Publications de la Faculté des Lettres et Sciences humaines, 35, 1965; repr. Geneva: Slatkine, 1978.

———, ed. *Précis de la littérature française du Moyen Age*. Paris: Presses Universitaires de France, 1983.

Reaney, Gilbert. "A Chronology of the Ballades, Rondeaux and Virelais Set to Music by Guillaume de Machaut." *Musica Disciplina*, 6 (1952): 33–38.

———. *Guillaume de Machaut*. Oxford Studies of Composers, 9. London: Oxford University Press, 1971.

———. "Guillaume de Machaut: Lyric Poet." *Music and Letters*, 39 (1958): 38–51.

Reyes, Graciela. *Polifonía Textual: La Citación en el Relato Literario*. Biblioteca romanica hispanica, II, Estudios y ensayos, 340. Madrid: Gredos, 1984.

Ribard, Jacques. *Un ménestrel du XIVe siècle: Jean de Condé*. Publications romanes et françaises, 104. Geneva: Droz, 1969.

Rivière, J.C. *Pastourelles*. 3 vols. TLF 213, 220, 232. Geneva: Droz, 1974–76.

Roberts, J. G. "*Renart le Nouvel*—Date and Successive Editions." *Speculum*, 11 (1936): 472–77.

Roussel, Henri. "Etude sur *Renart le Nouvel* du poète lillois Jacquemart Gielée." Thèse, Faculté des Lettres, Paris, 1956.

Ruhe, Doris. *Le Dieu d'Amours avec son Paradis: Untersuchungen zur Mythenbildung um Amor in Spätantike und Mittelalter*. Munich: Fink, 1974.

Ruwet, Nicolas. "Fonction de la parole de la musique vocale." *Revue belge de*

musicologie, 15 (1961): 8–28. Reprinted in *Langage, musique, poésie*. Paris: Seuil, 1972, pp. 41–67.
Sahlin, Margit. *Etude sur la carole médiévale: l'origine du mot et ses rapports avec l'église.* Uppsala: Almqvist & Wiksells Boktryckeri, 1940.
Saly, Antoinette. "La chanson dans le *Meliacin*." *TLL*, 23, no. 2 (1985): 7–23.
———. "La chanson du duc de Galice (*Meliacin*)." *TLL*, 12. no. 2 (1974): 7–16.
———. "Source d'un épisode de *Cleomadés* et de *Meliacin*." *TLL*, 10 (1972): 7–22.
Scholz, Manfred Günter. *Hören und Lesen: Studien zur primär Rezeption der Literatur im 12. und 13. Jahrhundert*. Wiesbaden: Steiner, 1980.
Schultz-Gora, Oskar. "Ein ungedruckter *Salu d'Amors* nebst Antwort." *ZRP*, 24 (1900): 358–69.
Segre, Cesare. "What Bakhtin Left Unsaid: The Case of the Medieval Romance." In *Romance: Generic Transformations from Chrétien de Troyes to Cervantes*. Ed. with an introduction by Kevin Brownlee and Marina Scordilis Brownlee. Hanover, N.H.: University Press of New England for Dartmouth College, 1985, pp. 23–46.
Silver, Isidore. "The Marriage of Poetry and Music in France: Ronsard's Predecessors and Contemporaries." In *Poetry and Poetics from Ancient Greece to the Renaissance: Studies in Honor of James Hutton*. Ed. G. M. Kirkwood. Cornell Studies in Classical Philology, 38. Ithaca: Cornell University Press, 1975, pp. 152–84.
Solente, S. "Christine de Pizan." *HLF*, 40 (1974): 305–422.
Solterer, Helen. "'Acorder li chans au dit': The Lyric Voice in French Medieval Narrative, 1220–1320." Ph.D. Dissertation, University of Toronto, 1986.
Spanke, Hans. *G. Raynauds Bibliographie des altfranzösischen Liedes neu bearbeitet und ergänzt erster teil*. Leiden: Brill, 1955.
———. "Zu den musikalischen Einlagen im Fauvelroman." *Neuphilologische Mitteilungen*, 37 (1936): 188–226.
Spearing, A. C. *Medieval Dream Poetry*. Cambridge and New York: Cambridge University Press, 1976.
Spitzer, Leo. "Note on the Poetic and the Empirical 'I' in Medieval Authors." *Traditio*, 4 (1946): 414–22. Repr. *Romanische Literaturstudien 1936–1956*. Tübingen: Max Niemeyer, 1959, pp. 100–112.
Stengel, F. "Die altfranzösischen Liedercitate aus Girardin's d'Amiens *Conte du cheval de fust*." *ZRP*, 10 (1886): 460–76.
Stevens, John. *Words and Music in the Middle Ages: Song, Narrative, Dance and Drama, 1050–1350*. Cambridge: Cambridge University Press, 1986.
Sutherland, D. R. "The Love Meditation in Courtly Literature. (A Study of the Terminology and its Development in Old Provençal and Old French)." In *Studies in Medieval French Presented to Alfred Ewert*. Oxford: Clarendon Press, 1961, pp. 165–93.
Switten, Margaret. "Remarks on Versification with Some Definitions of Poetic Styles and Forms." In *The Medieval Lyric: Commentary Volume*. Ed. Howell Chickering and Margaret Switten. 3 vols. South Hadley, Mass.: Mount Holyoke College, 1987–88, pp. 59–75.
Taylor, Jane H. M. "The Lyric Insertion: Towards a Functional Model." In *Courtly*

Literature: Culture and Context. Selected Papers of the Fifth Triennial Congress of the International Courtly Literature Society, Dalfsen, The Netherlands, 9–16 August 1986. Ed. Keith Busby and Eric Kooper. Amsterdam & Philadelphia: John Benjamins, 1990, pp. 539–48.

———. "Reason and Faith in the *Roman de Perceforest.*" In *Studies in Medieval Literature and Languages in Memory of Frederick Whitehead.* Ed. W. Rothwell, W. R. J. Barron, David Blamires, and Lewis Thorpe. Manchester: Manchester University Press; New York: Barnes & Noble, 1973, pp. 303–22.

Thomas, Antoine. "Frère Jean Acart, Poète français." *HLF,* 37 (1938): 412–18.

———. "Guillaume de Machaut et l'*Ovide moralisé.*" *Romania,* 41 (1912): 382–400.

Thurau, Gustav. *Der Refrain in der französischen Chanson: Beiträge zu Geschichte und Charakteristik des französischen Kehrreims.* Berlin: Felber, 1901.

———. *Singen und Sagen: Ein Beitrag zur Geschichte des dichterischen Ausdrucks.* Berlin: Weidmannsche Buchhandlung, 1912.

Tobler, Adolf. "*Der Roman von Escanor von Gerard von Amiens,* herausgegeben von Dr H. Michelant." *ZRP,* 11 (1887): 421–29.

Todorov, Tzvetan. *Les genres du discours.* Paris: Seuil, 1978.

———. *Mikhail Bakhtin: The Dialogical Principle.* Trans. Wlad Godzich. Theory and History of Literature, 13. Minneapolis: University of Minnesota Press, 1984.

Treitler, Leo. "Music and Language in Medieval Songs." In *The Medieval Lyric: Commentary Volume.* Ed. Howell Chickering and Margaret Switten. 3 vols. South Hadley, Mass.: Mount Holyoke College, 1987–88, pp. 12–27.

Trotin, Jean. "Vers et prose dans *Aucassin et Nicolete.*" *Romania* 97 (1976): 481–508.

Uitti, Karl D. "From *Clerc* to *Poète*: The Relevance of the *Roman de la Rose* to Machaut's World." In *Machaut's World: Science and Art in the Fourteenth Century.* Ed. Madeleine Pelner Cosman and Bruce Chandler. New York: Annals of the New York Academy of Sciences, 314, 1978, pp. 209–16.

Vance, Eugene. "The Word at Heart: *Aucassin et Nicolette* as a Medieval Comedy of Language." *Yale French Studies,* 45 (1970): 33–51.

———. "*Aucassin et Nicolette* as a Medieval Comedy of Signification and Exchange." In *The Nature of Medieval Narrative.* Ed. Minette Grunmann-Gaudet and Robin F. Jones. French Forum Monographs, 22. Lexington, Ky.: French Forum, 1980, pp. 57–76.

Vinaver, Eugène. *A la recherche d'une poétique médiévale.* Paris: Nizet, 1970.

———. *Etudes sur le Tristan en prose: Les sources, les manuscrits, bibliographie critique.* Paris: Champion, 1925.

———. *The Rise of Romance.* Oxford: Clarendon Press, 1971.

Walker, Emil. *Der monolog im höfischen Epos: Stil und Literaturgeschichtliche Untersuchungen.* Stuttgart: Kohlhammer, 1928.

van der Werf, Hendrik. *The Chansons of the Troubadours and Trouvères: A Study of the Melodies and Their Relation to the Poems.* Utrecht: A. Oosthoek's Uitgeversmaatschappij, 1972.

Whiting, B. J. "Froissart as Poet." *Medieval Studies,* 8 (1946): 198–216.

Wilkins, Nigel. *The Lyric Art of Medieval France.* 2nd revised edition. Fulbourn: New Press, 1989.

———. "Music in the Fourteenth Century 'Miracles de Nostre Dame.'" *Musica Disciplina,* 28 (1974): 39–73.
———. "The Post-Machaut Generation of Poet-Musicians." *Nottingham Medieval Studies,* 12 (1968): 40–84.
———. "The Structure of Ballades, Rondeaux and Virelais in Froissart and in Christine de Pisan." *French Studies,* 23 (1969): 337–48.
Willard, Charity Cannon. *Christine de Pizan, Her Life and Works.* New York: Persea Books, 1984.
———. "Jean Bodel and Christine de Pizan, Pastoral Poets," In *Mélanges de langue et de littérature françaises du moyen âge et de la renaissance offerts à M. Charles Foulon.* 2 vols. I, Rennes: Institut de français de l'Université de Haute Bretagne, 1980. II, Liège: Marche romane 30, nos. 3–4, 1980. II, pp. 293–300.
Williams, Sarah Jane. "An Author's Role in Fourteenth-Century Book Production: Guillaume de Machaut's 'Livre ou je met toutes mes choses.'" *Romania,* 90 (1969): 433–54.
———. "The Lady, the Lyrics and the Letters." *Early Music,* 5 (1977): 462–68.
———. "Machaut's Self Awareness as Author and Producer." In *Machaut's World: Science and Art in the Fourteenth Century.* Ed. Madeleine Pelner Cosman and Bruce Chandler. New York: Annals of the New York Academy of Sciences, 314, 1978, pp. 189–97.
Wimsatt, James. *Chaucer and the French Love Poets: The Literary Background of the Book of the Duchess.* Chapel Hill: University of North Carolina Press, 1968.
Winn, James A. *Unsuspected Eloquence: A History of the Relations between Poetry and Music.* New Haven: Yale University Press, 1981.
Wolfzettel, Friedrich. "La poésie lyrique en France comme mode d'appréhension de la réalité: remarques sur l'invention du sens visuel chez Machaut, Froissart, Deschamps et Charles d'Orléans." In *Mélanges de langue et de littérature françaises du moyen âge et de la renaissance offerts à M. Charles Foulon.* 2 vols. I, Rennes: Institut de français de l'Université de Haute Bretagne, 1980. II, Liège: Marche romane 30, nos. 3–4, 1980. I, pp. 409–19.
Zeidler, J. "Der Prosaroman Ysaye le Triste." *ZRP,* 25 (1901): 175–214, 472–89, 641–68.
Zink, Michel. *Belle: Essai sur les chansons de toile suivi d'une édition et d'une traduction.* Paris: Champion, 1978.
———. *Les Chansons de toile.* Collection Essais sur le moyen âge, 1. Paris: Champion, 1977.
———. "Froissart et la nuit du chasseur." *Poétique,* 41 (1980): 60–77.
———. "Lyrisme en rond. Esthétique et séduction des poèmes à forme fixe au moyen âge." *Cahiers de l'Association internationale des études françaises,* 32 (1980): 71–90.
———. *La Pastourelle: Poésie et folklore au moyen âge.* Paris: Bordas and Montreal, 1972.
———. "Le Premier type. De L'alternance à l'insertion." *Perspectives médiévales,* 3 (1977): 15–21.
———. "Les toiles d'Agamanor et les fresques de Lancelot." *Littérature,* 37 (Feb. 1980): 43–61.

———. "Remarques sur les conditions de l'anonymité dans la poésie lyrique française du moyen âge." In *Mélanges de langue et de littérature françaises du moyen âge et de la renaissance offerts à M. Charles Foulon.* 2 vols. I, Rennes: Institut de français de l'Université de Haute Bretagne, 1980. II, Liège: Marche romane 30, nos. 3–4, 1980. I, pp. 421–27.

———. *Roman rose et rose rouge: Le roman de la rose ou de Guillaume de Dole de Jean Renart.* Paris: Nizet, 1979.

———. *La Subjectivité littéraire.* Paris: Seuil, 1989.

Zumthor, Paul. "Autobiographie au moyen âge?" In *Langue, texte, énigme.* Paris: Seuil, 1975, pp. 165–80.

———. "De la chanson au récit: 'La Châtelaine de Vergi.'" In *Langue, texte, énigme.* Paris: Seuil, 1975, pp. 219–36.

———. "De la circularité du chant." *Poétique,* 2 (1970): 129–40.

———. *Essai de poétique médiévale.* Paris: Seuil, 1972.

———. *Histoire littéraire de la France médiévale (VIe–XIVe siècles).* Paris: Presses Universitaires de France, 1954; repr. Slatkine, 1973.

———. *Langue et techniques poétiques à l'époque romane (XIe–XIIIe siècles).* Bibliothèque française et romane, C, Etudes littéraires, 4. Paris: Klincksieck, 1963.

———. "Le *je* de la chanson et le moi du poète." In *Langue, texte, énigme.* Paris: Seuil, 1975, pp. 181–96.

———. "Les Narrativités latentes dans le discours lyrique médiévale." In *The Nature of Medieval Narrative.* Ed. Minette Grunmann-Gaudet and Robin F. Jones. French Forum Monographs, 22. Lexington, Ky.: French Forum, 1980, pp. 39–55.

———. *La poésie et la voix dans la civilisation médiévale.* Paris: Presses Universitaires de France, 1984.

———. "Un Problème d'esthétique médiévale: l'utilisation poétique du bilinguisme." *Le Moyen Age,* 66 (1960): 301–36, 561–94.

———. "Rhétorique et poétique latines et romanes." *GRLMA,* I (1972): 57–90.

———. "Style and Expressive Register in Medieval Poetry." In *Literary Style: A Symposium.* Ed. Seymour Chatman. Oxford: Oxford University Press, 1971, pp. 263–71.

Index

Abeïe dou chastel amoureus, 296
Acarie, M., 18
Acart, Jehan, *Amoureuse Prise*, 4, 245, 260–63, 270, 280, 285, 286, 296
Adam de la Halle, 6, 111–12, 183–84, 186–87, 275, 276, 285, 291, 292
Adenet le Roi, *Cleomadés*, 16, 54, 120, 126–28, 131, 141–42, 146, 162, 209, 279, 292, 296
allusion, 64, 216, 275, 289–93
D'Amors et de Jalousie, 184 n.6, 295
"Amors qui m'a en sa justise," 250–51, 284, 287–88, 295
amour lointain, 27, 30, 69, 72
Amoureuse Prise. *See* Acart, Jehan
amplificatio, 81, 118
Angicourt, Perrin, 55
Aristote, *Lai de*. *See* Henri d'Andeli
Art d'Amours, 184 n.6, 295
artes poeticae, 9
Aucassin et Nicolette, 3, 77, 281–82

Bakhtin, Mikhail, 22–23, 25, 118, 202, 248, 274, 288
ballade, 283; in *Amoureuse Prise*, 260–63; in *Dame a la Lycorne*, 158, 161–62, 173–77; in *Duc des Vrais Amants*, 234, 237–39, 240, 245, 236, 237–38, 239, 240, 241; in *Espinette Amoureuse*, 146, 209–10, 213, 214; in *Fauvel*, 149; in *Joli Buisson de Jonece*, 221, 222; in *Joli Mois de May*, 208–9; in *Livre Messire Ode*, 226, 227, 270; in *Meliador*, 69, 167; in *Panthere d'Amors*, 184–85; in *Paradis d'Amours*, 203, 206–7; in *Pastoure, Dit de la*, 232–34; in *Perceforest*, 136, 238–39; in *Prison Amoureuse*, 214, 216, 217; in *Regret Guillaume*, 263, 265; in *Remede de la Fortune*, 188, 191; in *Rose, Dit de la*, 117–18; in *Tresor Amoureux*, 266–68, 270; in *Voir Dit*, 164, 179, 199, 201–2
Baudoin de Condé, *Conte de la Rose*, 295; *Prison d'Amours*, 6, 245, 256–60, 285, 286, 295
Baumgartner, Emmanuèle, 43

Bec, Pierre, 43
Beer, Jeannette, 289
bergierette, 229–31, 234, 283
Bernart de Ventadorn, 21, 37, 41
Blanc Chevalier. *See* Jean de Condé
"bonne vie, la." *See* Register
Boogaard, Nico H. J. van den, 15, 244, 292
Branque, *Sone de Nansay*, 120, 128–31, 296
Bretel, Jacques, *Tournoi de Chauvenci*, 6–7, 92–95, 117, 296
Brisebare. *See* Jean le Court
Brulé, Gace, 26, 29, 31, 36, 38, 55, 61, 87, 171, 173, 291
Buffum, D. L., 15

carole, 21, 36, 83, 95–96, 100–102, 105, 107, 111, 129, 169
Cassidorus, Roman de, 95 n.17, 131 n.18, 296
Castelain de Couci et de la Dame de Fayel, Roman du. *See* Jakemés
"Celui qu'Amours conduit et maine," 246–48, 284
Cerquiglini, Jacqueline, 17
Chaillou de Pestain, *Roman de Fauvel*, 147–52, 283, 290, 296
chanson à refrains, 185, 282
chanson avec des refrains, 4 n.6, 243, 282, 283
chanson courtoise, 3, 5, 7, 14, 21, 54, 61, 78, 81, 85, 87–88, 144, 187, 215, 272, 280, 285; in *Castelain de Couci*, 62–66, 181; in *Complainte Douteuse*, 254–56; in *Guillaume de Dole*, 26–33, 123–24, 180, 272; in *Chastelaine de Vergi*, 51–53; in *Mariage des Sept Arts*, 116; in *Meliacin*, 55–60, 173; in *Violette, Roman de la*, 36–41. *See also* Chanson d'amour
chanson d'amour, 13–14, 24, 28, 36, 58, 87, 123, 141, 274, 278, 283, 290, 291, 293
chanson de geste, 3
chanson de mal mariée, 37, 251, 279, 287
chanson de toile, 13, 21, 28, 39, 85–86, 87, 124, 125, 274, 275, 280, 283, 290, 291
chanson royale, 186–87, 188, 190, 283

Chartier, Alain, *La Belle Dame sans Merci*, 280
Chastelaine de Saint Gille, 149, 244, 248–50, 268, 280, 283, 284, 285, 292, 295
Chastelaine de Vergi, 6, 25, 51–53, 78, 291, 295
Châtelain de Couci (Gui de Throuotte), 6, 27–28, 31, 41, 51–52, 61, 62, 275, 291
Cheval de Fust, Conte du. See Girart d'Amiens, *Meliacin*
Chrétien de Troyes, 274, *Chevalier de la Charette*, 273
Christine de Pizan, 8, 183, 228, 254, 276, 277; *Cent Balades de l'Amant et de la Dame*, 280; *Duc des Vrais Amants, Livre du*, 183, 234–42, 252, 277, 280, 297; *Pastoure, Dit de la*, 82, 112–14, 228–34, 207; *Rose, Dit de la*, 82, 114, 117–18, 207
Clarmondine. *See* Adenet le Roi, *Cleomadés*
Cleomadés. See Adenet le Roi
complainte, 228, 246, 248, 250, 252, 281, 283, 287; in *Dame a la Lycorne*, 160; in *Duc des Vrais Amants*, 235, 240–41; in *Espinette Amoureuse*, 210, 211–13, 214; in *Fauvel*, 149, 150–51; in *Fonteinne Amoureuse*, 193–94, 197; in *Livre Messire Ode*, 226, 227, 228; in *Paradis d'Amours*, 203–4, 207; in *Prison Amoureuse*, 214, 216, 290; in *Remede de Fortune*, 188, 189–90
complainte-confort, 195, 198, 203, 207, 213–14, 219, 228, 250, 287
Complainte Douteuse, 245, 254–56, 258, 259, 270, 280, 284, 286, 290, 295
Comte d'Anjou, 148
confort, in *Fonteinne Amoureuse*, 195–96, 197; in *Espinette Amoureuse*, 213–14
Confrere d'Amours, 244, 245–46, 284, 295
Conrad. *See* Renart, Jean, *Guillaume de Dole*
Cour de Mai, 296
Court d'Amour (Suite). *See* Mahieu le Poirier
Court de Paradis, 82, 103, 104–5, 111, 117, 119, 295
Curtis, Renée L., 42, 43
Curtius, E. R., 9, 288

Dame a la Lycorne et du Beau Chevalier au Lyon, Roman de la, 22, 77, 152, 170, 173–77, 278, 279, 284, 287, 296
Dante (Alighieri), 8, 13, 14; *De Vulgari Eloquentia*, 14
Débat du Clerc et de la Demoiselle, 297
decorum, 12–13

Dembowski, Peter, 67, 70
dialogism, 23, 25, 202, 248; dialogical relationship, 35
dit, 150, 181–83, 197, 208, 215, 235, 281, 283; development of, 181 n.1; inserted in *Dame a la Lycorne*, 158–59; in *Fauvel*, 149–50; in *Livre Messire Ode*, 224; in *Panthere d'Amours*, 183, 184; in *Prison Amoureuse*, 214, 215, 216, 218
Dit d'Amours. See Nevelon, Amiot
Dit de la Rose. See Christine de Pizan
Duc des Vrais Amants, Livre du. See Christine de Pizan

Escanor. See Girart d'Amiens
Espinette Amoureuse. See Froissart, Jean

fabliau, 3, 248, 283
Faral, Edmond, 9, 13
Fauvel, Roman de. See Chaillou de Pestain
fin' amors, 21, 27, 31, 37, 41, 53, 62, 63, 71, 78, 84, 85, 87, 88, 96, 157, 172, 253, 254, 272, 274, 277, 284, 285, 287
Flours d'Amours, 184 n.6, 295
Fonteinne Amoureuse. See Guillaume de Machaut
Froissart, Jean, 8, 182, 202–3, 224, 225, 228, 242, 275, 276, 277; *Espinette Amoureuse*, 146–47, 168, 203, 209–13, 219, 235, 236, 255, 278, 297; *Joli Buisson de Jonece*, 22, 203, 219–23, 286, 297; *Joli Mois de May*, 203, 208–9, 277, 297; *Meliador*, 17, 18, 25, 66–72, 77, 79, 82, 100–103, 167–70, 202, 297; *Paradis d'Amours*, 203–8, 296; *Prison Amoureuse*, 22, 67, 182, 203, 214–19, 234, 290, 292, 297

Galeran de Bretagne. See Renaut
Gennrich, Friedrich, 16
Geoffroi de Vinsauf, 12, 13
Gerardin de Boulogne, 60
Gerart de Nevers. *See* Gerbert de Montreuil, *Roman de la Violette*
Gerbert de Montreuil, 54, 275, 278, 290; *Roman de la Violette*, 5, 25, 35–42, 47, 53, 55, 61, 66, 77, 78, 81, 87–89, 95, 119, 120, 124 n.9, 162, 170–72, 180, 274, 279, 284, 287, 291, 292, 295
Gielée, Jacquemart, *Renart le Nouvel*, 82, 103, 105–9, 111, 152, 279, 292, 296
Girart d'Amiens, 66, 275, 278; *Escanor*, 54, 89–92, 100, 103, 141, 296; *Meliacin* or

Conte du Cheval de Fust, 2, 25, 54–61, 77, 78, 162, 167, 170, 172–73, 180, 274, 275, 279, 284, 285, 287, 291, 296
Gracieus temps est. *See* Jehan de Lescurel
Gracieuse faitisse et sage. *See* Jehan de Lescurel
Grandson. *See* Oton de Grandson
Gui de Throuotte. *See* Châtelain de Couci
Guiette, Robert, 34
Guillaume de Deguilleville, *Pelerinage de l'ame*, 100 n.20, 296
Guillaume de Dole. *See* Renart, Jean
Guillaume de Lorris, *Roman de la Rose*, 181, 182, 192, 208, 252, 263, 272
Guillaume de Machaut, 2, 8, 182, 224, 225, 228, 242, 270, 276; *Fonteinne Amoureuse*, 182, 192–97, 198, 214, 252, 296; *Remede de Fortune*, 188–92, 198, 203, 207, 209, 214, 235, 236, 255, 278, 291, 296; *Voir Dit, Le Livre dou*, 22, 73, 74, 79, 152, 162–67, 170, 177–79, 180, 183, 197–202, 214, 215, 234, 241, 252, 276, 277, 278, 280, 284, 286, 292, 207
Guiron le Courtois, 144–46, 152, 295

Henri d'Andeli, *Lai d'Aristote*, 16, 120, 124–25, 131–32, 278, 279, 284, 288, 295
Henry, Albert, 15, 16
Huot, Sylvia, 17

interruption, 3, 4, 14, 244, 261, 287
intertextuality, 1, 4, 292. *See also* Allusion
irony, 25, 29, 31, 35, 36, 37, 38, 77, 78, 97, 125, 200, 274–75, 287

Jacquemart. *See* Gielée, Jacquemart
Jakemés (Sakesep), 275; *Roman du Castelain de Couci et de la Dame de Fayel*, 2, 25, 61–66, 78–79, 81, 95–97, 155 n.24, 158, 167, 181, 274, 279, 284–85, 287, 291, 296
Jakobson, Roman, 18, 19, 81, 143 n.3, 243
Jean Froissart. *See* Froissart, Jean
Jean Renart. *See* Renart, Jean
Jean de Condé, *Le Dit du Blanc Chevalier*, 170 n.37, 279, 284, 288, 296
Jean de Meun, 290
Jean le Court, dit Brisebare, *Restor du Paon*, 99 n.20, 296
Jeanroy, Alfred, 15, 16
Jehan de le Mote, *Parfait du Paon*, 128 n.14, 296; *Li Regret Guillaume*, 263–66, 292, 296
Jehan de Lescurel, 245, 251, 284, 285; *Gracieus temps est*, 252–54, 288, 296; *Gracieuse faitisse et sage*, 251–52, 296
Joli Buisson de Jonece. *See* Froissart, Jean
Joli Mois de May. *See* Froissart, Jean
Ju de le Capete Martinet. *See* Mahieu le Poirier

Kanor, Roman de, 95 n.17, 131 n.18
Kelly, Douglas, 17

Långfors, Arthur, 116, 148
lai, 43, 72, 132, 283; in *Espinette Amoureuse*, 210, 214; in *Fauvel*, 149; in *Guiron le Courtois*, 144–46; in *Joli Buisson de Jonece*, 221–22, 223; in *Livre Messire Ode*, 224; in *Paradis d'Amours*, 203, 205; in *Perceforest*, 136–41, 142; in *Remede de Fortune*, 188–89, 191, 194, 207; in *Sone de Nansay*, 128, 131; in *Tristan en Prose*, 44–51, 79, 114, 132–35, 142, 153–55, 162, 181, 286; in *Ysaÿe le Triste*, 73–77; "lay Galeren le Breton," 122–23
Laurin, Roman de, 95 n.17, 296
Lecoy, Félix, 13
letter: (prose), in *Dame a la Lycorne*, 158–59; in *Duc des Vrais Amants*, 234, 236–37, 238–39; in *Prison Amoureuse*, 214, 215, 218; in *Tristan en Prose*, 44, 45, 47, 153, 154; in *Voir Dit*, 163, 165–66, 197, 198, 202, 286; (verse), in *Castelain de Couci*, 155 n.24; in *Dame a la Lycorne*, 161; in *Guiron le Courtois*, 152 n.21; in *Meliador*, 167; in *Voir Dit*, 197; "en forme de lai," in *Tristan en Prose*, 45, 46, 153–55
liturgical songs, 282; in *Court de Paradis*, 104–5; in *Renart le Nouvel*, 106, 108
Livre Messire Ode. *See* Oton de Grandson
Lods, Jeanne, 43, 71
Ludus Anti-Claudien, 82, 114, 116–17, 296
Ludwig, Friedrich, 15
lyric insertion, 1, 3–4, 24, 25; defined, 2; functions, 19–22
lyric interlude, 127–28, 128 n.14
lyric pause, 34, 287. *See also* Interruption
lyric voice, 17, 25, 182, 187, 263, 272

Mahieu le Poirier, *Court d'Amour* (Suite), 97–99, 296; *Ju de le Capete Martinet*, 97 n.19, 296
Maillard, Jean, 16
Marchello-Nizia, Christiane, 17
Mariage des Sept Arts, 82, 114–16, 119, 295

Marie de France, *Lai de Fresne*, 121
Marthe. See *Ysaÿe le Triste*
Mathieu de Vendôme, 12, 13
Meliacin. See Girart d'Amiens
Meliador. See Froissart, Jean
memory, 11, 40, 42, 68–69, 78, 208, 216, 221
Ménard, Philippe, 42
metrical contrast, 4–5, 163, 208, 280, 284, 287
minstrel, 26, 29, 33, 44, 45, 47, 48, 62, 76, 77–78, 79, 94, 121, 131, 133, 278
motet, 54, 282–83
motet *enté*, 149, 150–51, 283
music, 5–9, 12, 48, 163, 165, 188, 298–99

narrative voice, 17, 182, 263
nature introduction, 25, 27, 28, 30, 33, 49, 51, 55, 56, 58, 265
Nevelon, Amiot, *Dit d'Amours*, 296
Nicole de Margival, *Dit de la Panthere d'Amors*, 6, 182, 183–87, 216, 225, 260, 275, 276, 285, 286, 291, 293, 296

ornatus, 12, 13
Os, J. A. van, 7
Oton de Grandson, 8, 182, 242, 276, 277; *Livre Messire Ode*, 183, 223–28, 236, 268, 271, 280, 297

Panthere d'Amors, Dit de la. See Nicole de Margival
Paradis d'Amours. See Froissart, Jean
Parfait du Paon. See Jehan de le Mote
Paris, Gaston, 16
Pastoralet, 112 n.33, 292, 297
Pastoure, Dit de la. See Christine de Pizan
pastourelle, 3, 228, 229, 231, 233, 274, 275, 283, 290
Pelerinage de l'ame. See Guillaume de Deguilleville
Peliarmenus, Roman de, 95 n.17, 296
penser, 47, 48, 50, 68–69, 78; thought, 32, 41, 48. *See also* Memory
Perceforest Roman de, 5, 77, 120, 135–41, 142, 280, 284, 285, 296; list of *lais*, 136–38
Poire, Roman de la. See Thibaut
Prison Amoureuse. See Froissart, Jean
Prison d'Amours. See Baudoin de Condé
prosi-metrum, 9

refrain (repeated), 197, 243–44, 282, 290
refrain (unrepeated), 2 n.3, 6, 8, 34, 36, 41, 54, 81–83, 85, 86, 243–45, 274, 282, 283, 287, 290, 293; in "Amors qui m'a en sa justise," 250–51; in *Aristote, Lai d'*, 125; in "Celui qu'Amors conduit et maine," 246–48; in *Chastelaine de Saint Gille*, 248–50; in *Confrere d'Amours*, 245–46; in *Court de Paradis*, 104–5; in *Court d'Amours*, 98–99; in *Escanor*, 89–91; in *Fauvel*, 149–51; in *Gracieuse, faitisse et sage*, 251–52; in *Gracieus temps est*, 252–54; in *Mariage des Sept Arts*, 115–16; in *Renart le Nouvel*, 106–8; in *Poire, Roman de la*, 155–58, 183; in *Pastoure, Dit de la*, 112–13; in *Prison d'Amours*, 256–60; in *Tournoi de Chauvenci*, 92–95; in *Trois dames de Paris*, 109–11; in *Violette, Roman de la*, 87–88, 170, 172; in *Voir Dit*, 178
register, 5 n.8, 21–22, 23, 89, 157, 284, 287, 288; "la bonne vie," 5, 81, 85, 89, 109, 150, 172, 252, 254, 287; "requête amoureuse," 5, 150. *See also Fin' amors*
Regret Guillaume, Li. See Jehan de le Mote
Remede de Fortune. See Guillaume de Machaut
Renart, Jean, 12–13, 18, 20, 23, 54, 61, 65, 94, 127, 275, 278, 290; *Roman de la Rose* or *Guillaume de Dole*, 4, 5, 9–14, 16, 23, 25, 26–35, 47, 53, 66, 70, 71, 78, 81, 83–87, 89, 95, 99, 100, 112, 118, 120, 123–24, 131–32, 141, 170, 171, 180, 274, 278, 279, 281, 284, 285, 287, 289, 291, 292, 295
Renart le Nouvel. See Gielée, Jacquemart
Renaut, *Galeran de Bretagne*, 77, 120–23, 131–32, 278, 279, 281, 295
Renaut de Beaujeu, 28
Renaut de Sabloeil, 32
"requête amoureuse." *See* Register
Richart de Fournival, 60; *Bestiaire d'Amours*, 295; *Commens d'Amours*, 295
Robert de Blois, *Castoiement des Dames*, 295
rondeau or rondel, 16, 54, 61, 72, 74, 76, 81, 274, 283; in *Amoureuse Prise*, 260–63; in *Aristote, Lai d'*, 124–25; in *Castelain de Couci*, 95–97; in "Celui qu'Amors conduit et maine," 246–48; in *Cleomadés*, 126–27; in *Dame a la Lycorne*, 158, 159, 174–75; in *Duc des Vrais Amants*, 234, 235, 239, 240; in *Espinette Amoureuse*, 210, 213; in *Fauvel*, 149; in *Livre Messire Ode*, 226, 227, 271; in *Ludus-Anticlaudien*, 116–17; in *Meliacin*, 173; in *Meliador*, 69–71, 100–102, 167–69; in *Panthere d'Amors*, 185–86; in *Paradis*

d'Amours, 203, 204–5; in *Dit de la Pastoure*, 233; in *Remede de Fortune*, 188, 192; in *Dit de la Rose*, 117–18; in *Tresor Amoureux*, 266–67, 271; in *Voir Dit*, 163–64, 166, 178–79, 197, 200; in *Ysaÿe le Triste*, 72, 74, 75
rondet de carole, 21, 81, 87, 274, 275, 283, 285, 290, 293; in *Guillaume de Dole*, 34, 83–85, 170, 285; in *Sone de Nansay*, 128–30
Rose, Dit de la. *See* Christine de Pizan
Rose, Roman de la. *See* Guillaume de Lorris
Rose, Roman de la or *Guillaume de Dole*. *See* Renart, Jean
Rudel, Jaufré, 21
Ruwet, Nicolas, 8

salut d'amour, 146, 152, 155, 250
Sone de Nansay. *See* Branque
Stevens, John, 7

Thibaut, *Roman de la Poire*, 152, 155–58, 168, 183, 284, 285, 287, 293, 295
Tournoi de Chauvenci. *See* Bretel, Jacques
Tournoiement d'Antechrist, 148
Tresor Amoureux, 245, 266–70, 297
Tristan, 60, 64, 72, 73, 278, 292
Tristan en Prose, 16, 25, 42–51, 78–79, 82, 114, 120, 132–35, 142, 152–55, 159, 162, 166–67, 181, 279, 284, 285, 286, 287, 292, 295; list of *lais*, 44–47
Trois Dames de Paris. *See* Watriquet de Couvin

Vidame de Chartres, 33
Vinaver, Eugène, 288
Violette, Roman de la. See Gerbert de Montreuil
virelai (or *chanson balladée*), 283; in *Castelain de Couci*, 61, 291; in *Duc des Vrais Amants*, 234, 235, 239, 240; in *Espinette Amoureuse*, 210, 213; in *Fauvel*, 148–49; in *Joli Buisson de Jonece*, 219–20, 223; in *Joli Mois de May*, 208; in *Meliador*, 69; in *Paradis d'Amours*, 203, 206; in *Prison Amoureuse*, 214, 217, 290; in *Remede de Fortune*, 188, 192; in *Voir Dit*, 201
Voir Dit, Le Livre dou. *See* Guillaume de Machaut

Watriquet de Couvin, *Trois Dames de Paris*, 103, 109–11, 112, 283, 296
Wenceslas de Luxembourg, king of Bohemia, duke of Brabant, 67–68, 71, 79, 202, 276
Wilkins, Nigel, 244
Winn, James A., 8
writing, 73, 76, 79, 165, 168, 180, 182, 197, 215–16, 217–19, 224, 234, 268

Ysaÿe le Triste, 25, 72–78, 79, 81, 278, 297

Zink, Michel, 244
Zumthor, Paul, 5, 34, 81, 143, 288

University of Pennsylvania Press
MIDDLE AGES SERIES
Edward Peters, General Editor

F. R. P. Akehurst, trans. *The* Coutumes de Beauvaisis *of Philippe de Beaumanoir*. 1992
Peter Allen. *The Art of Love: Amatory Fiction from Ovid to the* Romance of the Rose. 1992
David Anderson. *Before the Knight's Tale: Imitation of Classical Epic in Boccaccio's* Teseida. 1988
Benjamin Arnold. *Count and Bishop in Medieval Germany: A Study of Regional Power, 1100–1350.* 1991
Mark C. Bartusis. *The Late Byzantine Army: Arms and Society, 1204–1453.* 1992
J. M. W. Bean. *From Lord to Patron: Lordship in Late Medieval England.* 1990
Uta-Renate Blumenthal. *The Investiture Controversy: Church and Monarchy from the Ninth to the Twelfth Century.* 1988
Daniel Bornstein, trans. *Dino Compagni's* Chronicle *of Florence*. 1986
Maureen Boulton. *The Song in the Story: Lyric Insertions in French Narrative Fiction, 1200–1400.* 1993
Betsy Bowden. *Chaucer Aloud: The Varieties of Textual Interpretation.* 1987
James William Brodman. *Ransoming Captives in Crusader Spain: The Order of Merced on the Christian-Islamic Frontier.* 1986
Kevin Brownlee and Sylvia Huot. *Rethinking the* Romance of the Rose: *Text, Image, Reception.* 1992
Otto Brunner (Howard Kaminsky and James Van Horn Melton, eds. and trans.). Land *and Lordship: Structures of Governance in Medieval Austria.* 1992
Robert I. Burns, S.J., ed. *Emperor of Culture: Alfonso X the Learned of Castile and His Thirteenth-Century Renaissance.* 1990
David Burr. *Olivi and Franciscan Poverty: The Origins of the* Usus Pauper *Controversy.* 1989
David Burr. *Olivi's Peaceable Kingdom: A Reading of the Apocalypse Commentary.* 1993
Thomas Cable. *The English Alliterative Tradition.* 1991
Anthony K. Cassell and Victoria Kirkham, eds. and trans. *Diana's Hunt/Caccia di Diana: Boccaccio's First Fiction.* 1991
John C. Cavadini. *The Last Christology of the West: Adoptionism in Spain and Gaul, 785–820.* 1993
Brigitte Cazelles. *The Lady as Saint: A Collection of French Hagiographic Romances of the Thirteenth Century.* 1991
Karen Cherewatuk and Ulrike Wiethaus, eds. *Dear Sister: Medieval Women and the Epistolary Genre.* 1993
Anne L. Clark. *Elisabeth of Schönau: A Twelfth-Century Visionary.* 1992

Willene B. Clark and Meradith T. McMunn, eds. *Beasts and Birds of the Middle Ages: The Bestiary and Its Legacy.* 1989

Richard C. Dales. *The Scientific Achievement of the Middle Ages.* 1973

Charles T. Davis. *Dante's Italy and Other Essays.* 1984

Katherine Fischer Drew, trans. *The Burgundian Code.* 1972

Katherine Fischer Drew, trans. *The Laws of the Salian Franks.* 1991

Katherine Fischer Drew, trans. *The Lombard Laws.* 1973

Nancy Edwards. *The Archaeology of Early Medieval Ireland.* 1990

Margaret J. Ehrhart. *The Judgment of the Trojan Prince Paris in Medieval Literature.* 1987

Richard K. Emmerson and Ronald B. Herzman. *The Apocalyptic Imagination in Medieval Literature.* 1992

Theodore Evergates. *Feudal Society in Medieval France: Documents from the County of Champagne.* 1993

Felipe Fernández-Armesto. *Before Columbus: Exploration and Colonization from the Mediterranean to the Atlantic, 1229–1492.* 1987

R. D. Fulk. *A History of Old English Meter.* 1992

Patrick J. Geary. *Aristocracy in Provence: The Rhône Basin at the Dawn of the Carolingian Age.* 1985

Peter Heath. *Allegory and Philosophy in Avicenna (Ibn Sînâ), with a translation of the Book of the Prophet Muḥammad's Ascent to Heaven.* 1992

J. N. Hillgarth, ed. *Christianity and Paganism, 350–750: The Conversion of Western Europe.* 1986

Richard C. Hoffmann. *Land, Liberties, and Lordship in a Late Medieval Countryside: Agrarian Structures and Change in the Duchy of Wrocław.* 1990

Robert Hollander. *Boccaccio's Last Fiction: Il Corbaccio.* 1988

Edward B. Irving, Jr. *Rereading* Beowulf. 1989

C. Stephen Jaeger. *The Origins of Courtliness: Civilizing Trends and the Formation of Courtly Ideals, 939–1210.* 1985

William Chester Jordan. *The French Monarchy and the Jews: From Philip Augustus to the Last Capetians.* 1989

William Chester Jordan. *From Servitude to Freedom: Manumission in the Sénonais in the Thirteenth Century.* 1986

Ellen E. Kittell. *From* Ad Hoc *to Routine: A Case Study in Medieval Bureaucracy.* 1991

Alan C. Kors and Edward Peters, eds. *Witchcraft in Europe, 1100–1700: A Documentary History.* 1972

Barbara M. Kreutz. *Before the Normans: Southern Italy in the Ninth and Tenth Centuries.* 1992

E. Ann Matter. *The Voice of My Beloved: The Song of Songs in Western Medieval Christianity.* 1990

María Rosa Menocal. *The Arabic Role in Medieval Literary History.* 1987

A. J. Minnis. *Medieval Theory of Authorship.* 1988

Lawrence Nees. *A Tainted Mantle: Hercules and the Classical Tradition at the Carolingian Court.* 1991

Lynn H. Nelson, trans. *The Chronicle of San Juan de la Peña: A Fourteenth-Century Official History of the Crown of Aragon.* 1991

Charlotte A. Newman. *The Anglo-Norman Nobility in the Reign of Henry I: The Second Generation.* 1988

Joseph F. O'Callaghan. *The Cortes of Castile-León, 1188–1350.* 1989

Joseph F. O'Callaghan. *The Learned King: The Reign of Alfonso X of Castile.* 1993

William D. Paden, ed. *The Voice of the Trobairitz: Perspectives on the Women Troubadours.* 1989

Edward Peters. *The Magician, the Witch, and the Law.* 1982

Edward Peters, ed. *Christian Society and the Crusades, 1198–1229:* Sources in Translation, including The Capture of Damietta by Oliver of Paderborn. 1971

Edward Peters, ed. *The First Crusade:* The Chronicle of Fulcher of Chartres *and Other Source Materials.* 1971

Edward Peters, ed. *Heresy and Authority in Medieval Europe.* 1980

James M. Powell. *Albertanus of Brescia: The Pursuit of Happiness in the Early Thirteenth Century.* 1992

James M. Powell. *Anatomy of a Crusade, 1213–1221.* 1986

Michael Resler, trans. Erec *by Hartmann von Aue.* 1987

Pierre Riché (Michael Idomir Allen, trans.). *The Carolingians: A Family Who Forged Europe.* 1993

Pierre Riché (Jo Ann McNamara, trans.). *Daily Life in the World of Charlemagne.* 1978

Jonathan Riley-Smith. *The First Crusade and the Idea of Crusading.* 1986

Joel T. Rosenthal. *Patriarchy and Families of Privilege in Fifteenth-Century England.* 1991

Teofilo F. Ruiz. *Crisis and Continuity: Land and Town in Late Medieval Castile.* 1993

Steven D. Sargent, ed. and trans. *On the Threshold of Exact Science: Selected Writings of Anneliese Maier on Late Medieval Natural Philosophy.* 1982

Sarah Stanbury. *Seeing the* Gawain-*Poet: Description and the Act of Perception.* 1992

Thomas C. Stillinger. *The Song of Troilus: Lyric Authority in the Medieval Book.* 1992

Susan Mosher Stuard. *A State of Deference: Ragusa/Dubrovnik in the Medieval Centuries.* 1992

Susan Mosher Stuard, ed. *Women in Medieval History and Historiography.* 1987

Susan Mosher Stuard, ed. *Women in Medieval Society.* 1976

Jonathan Sumption. *The Hundred Years War: Trial by Battle.* 1992

Ronald E. Surtz. *The Guitar of God: Gender, Power, and Authority in the Visionary World of Mother Juana de la Cruz (1481–1534).* 1990

Patricia Terry, trans. *Poems of the Elder Edda.* 1990

Hugh M. Thomas. *Vassals, Heiresses, Crusaders, and Thugs: The Gentry of Angevin Yorkshire, 1154–1216.* 1993

Frank Tobin. *Meister Eckhart: Thought and Language.* 1986

Ralph V. Turner. *Men Raised from the Dust: Administrative Service and Upward Mobility in Angevin England.* 1988

Harry Turtledove, trans. *The* Chronicle *of Theophanes: An English Translation of* Anni Mundi *6095–6305 (A.D. 602–813).* 1982

Mary F. Wack. Lovesickness in the Middle Ages: The Viaticum *and Its Commentaries.* 1990

Benedicta Ward. *Miracles and the Medieval Mind: Theory, Record, and Event, 1000–1215.* 1982
Suzanne Fonay Wemple. *Women in Frankish Society: Marriage and the Cloister, 500–900.* 1981
Jan M. Ziolkowski. *Talking Animals: Medieval Latin Beast Poetry, 750–1150.* 1993

MAUREEN BARRY MCCANN BOULTON is Associate Professor of French in the Department of Romance Languages and Literatures at the University of Notre Dame.

This book has been set in Linotron Galliard. Galliard was designed for Mergenthaler in 1978 by Matthew Carter. Galliard retains many of the features of a sixteenth-century typeface cut by Robert Granjon but has some modifications that give it a more contemporary look.

Printed on acid-free paper.